T0227871

Machine-to-Machine Marketing (M3) via Anonymous Advertising Apps Anywhere Anytime (A5)

Machine-to-Machine Marketing (M3) via Anonymous Advertising Apps Anywhere Anytime (A5)

JESUS MENA

CRC Press
Taylor & Francis Group
Boca Raton London New York

CRC Press is an imprint of the
Taylor & Francis Group, an **informa** business

AN AUERBACH BOOK

CRC Press
Taylor & Francis Group
6000 Broken Sound Parkway NW, Suite 300
Boca Raton, FL 33487-2742

First issued in hardback 2017

© 2012 by Taylor & Francis Group, LLC
CRC Press is an imprint of Taylor & Francis Group, an Informa business

No claim to original U.S. Government works

ISBN 13: 978-1-138-41652-9 (hbk)
ISBN 13: 978-1-4398-8191-0 (pbk)

Library of Congress Cataloging-in-Publication Data

Mena, Jesus.
 Machine-to-machine marketing (M3) via anonymous advertising apps anywhere anytime (A5) / Jesus Mena.
  p. cm.
 "An Auerbach Book."
 Includes bibliographical references and index.
 ISBN 978-1-4398-8191-0
 1. Internet advertising. 2. Internet marketing. 3. Application software--Development.
4. Machine learning. 5. Electronic commerce. I. Title.

 HF6146.I58M46 2012
 658.8'72--dc23   2011052595

Visit the Taylor & Francis Web site at
http://www.taylorandfrancis.com

and the CRC Press Web site at
http://www.crcpress.com

To Lefty

Contents

Introduction

Today's wired and wireless environments allow for marketing to take place not so much at the consumer level as at the server-to-device level, with that device being anything from a laptop, an appliance, a phone, a TV, or a car.

In a RAND Corporation research paper written in 1960, Paul Baran envisioned the Internet and all future networks to follow. He proposed a system "where computers speak to one another," where such distributed interconnections "resemble those models often associated with neural networks." Neural networks are artificial intelligence (AI) technologies that use machine learning software designed to replicate the way humans think and remember.

Today, because of our abundant interconnections, Baran's vision has been accomplished where "computers speak to one another" and can be programmed to market servers-to-devices with the capability of making very precise pitches in microseconds to their human owners based on the strategic use of "models created with machine learning software."

Because marketing is at the device level, privacy becomes irrelevant, and profiles of individuals are no longer an issue. It is more accurate to profile machines via cookies, Wi-Fi triangulation, digital fingerprinting, and other machine-to-machine (M2M) mechanisms, since they offer far more precise ways to model digital devices and their behaviors using neural network models.

Anonymous advertising apps anywhere anytime (A5s) are the strategy, architecture, and framework by which machine-to-machine marketing (M3) can be executed. A5s can be embedded in a myriad of customer touch points with business rules developed by AI software and machine learning models to offer the right product or service to the right device via any consumer channel anywhere anytime. A5s can be created from historical data samples in order to develop dynamic device profiles based on the type of machines consumers are using.

The book is divided into four main chapters:

Chapter 1 discusses the interactive environments and how M3 can be deployed.

Chapter 2 covers the technologies and solution providers that can be used for executing M3.

Chapter 3 provides a list of techniques, strategies, technologies, and solution providers for M3.

Chapter 4 provides examples of how M3 and A5s are being implemented by other companies.

In the end, the reader will learn about the technologies, software, networks, mechanisms, techniques, and solution providers used in advertising now and will also learn about future prospects in the field. Marketers need to understand the underlying science of selling in today's interconnected real-time world.

This book is part data mining, part web, part social media, part marketing, and part mobile. The result is a juxtaposition of technologies and techniques that define what M3 and A5s are all about.

Every company, network, and resource mentioned in this book can be accessed via hundreds of links at jesusmena.com—the book's companion site.

Chapter 1

Why?

M3 and A5

The consumer is his digital device. If you buy into this, then you get what machine-to-machine marketing (M3) and anonymous advertising apps anywhere anytime (A5) are about. Marketing to machines is easier than marketing to humans: devices do not evolve or change, do not divorce, do not go on unemployment, or do not file for bankruptcy. Machines are stationary targets to M3 marketers and A5 programs.

Human attributes, such as income, marital status, and age, are really not very reliable to use in the modeling of consumer propensities in today's volatile economy and real-time digital marketplace. A more direct and technically sound approach is to monitor and model the consumer's device activities and behavioral patterns.

From the infancy of e-commerce, log server files have been capturing such nonhuman features as operating system, key words used, and referring sites from online visitors. Internet mechanisms such as cookies and beacons have expanded this to include other machine-to-machine (M2M) attributes such as time of day, browser type, and purchasing history. Today, new technology such as digital fingerprinting can expand these M2M attributes to include font, color configuration, and literally hundreds of very detailed and precise information unique to all types of digital devices to enhance M2M profiles enabling M3.

M2M started as a utility meter application. M2M uses a device, such as a sensor or meter, to capture an event, such as a traffic pattern, which is then instantly relayed through a network, which can be wireless, wired, or hybrid to an application, such as a program, that instantly translates the captured event into some type of action, such as rerouting traffic in a network. So far, M2M applications have been limited to monitoring machinery that works on production lines, such as the assembly of automobiles and letting the auto producers know when certain products need to be taken in for maintenance and for what reason. Another application is to use wireless networks to update digital billboards to display different messages based on time-of-day or day-of-the-week, such as for pricing changes for gasoline.

What M3 does is elevate the capabilities and functionality of M2M from that of a meter to that of a marketer. The rules used to issue alerts to divert network traffic for M2M applications can instead be rules about device behaviors, which can lead to improved sales and revenue. Some human features, such as gender and age, are useful for the triangulation marketing along with other M2M features. However, M3 is more concerned about where and what devices are looking for and maybe where they are located. As with M2M meter applications, it is important for M3 to monitor continuously activities in order to enable rules to be developed from historical data patterns to generate relevant and real-time offers in a seamless manner. To accomplish this, A5 must be developed and deployed.

Why M3? Because M2M data about devices' behaviors and their human owners are everywhere, ubiquitous in real time and intimately detailed, which marketers need to triangulate via behavioral analytics and A5s. The data about their devices' desires, needs, and passions are flowing continuously via the web and wireless worlds. M3 is about capturing that data in order to enable servers to deliver to devices precise offers and relevant content.

M3 is about the convergence of M2M data from websites, social networks, and mobile devices and using artificial intelligence software to model and monetize devices' behaviors—for the targeted placement of products, content, or services via multiple channels—in a personal manner the instant they take place. M3 is made possible by M2M technology that deals with the ability of both wireless and wired systems to communicate with other devices of the same ability. M2M was originally developed by wireless carriers to monitor traffic activity in order to reconfigure their network.

A5 enables the positioning of the right product or service in front of the right consumer via precise messages on the web, e-mail, texts, mobile devices, etc. The success of A5 involves strategic planning and measured improvement of predictive evolving models. The modeling of wired and wireless devices' behaviors can be accomplished by the strategic use of inductive and deductive analytical software, which is relatively cheap and free, such as WizRule, CART, or RapidMiner.

For the M3 marketers, the analysis of consumer activity starts with the use of a combination of human and device data using machine-learning algorithms that can generate the following:

1. Clusters of device behaviors
2. Extract key concepts from unstructured content
3. Develop predictive business rules to quantify and monetize device behaviors

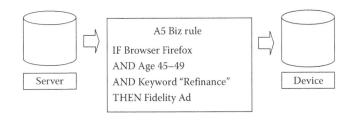

Figure 1.1   A5 "fires" a predictive rule for M3.

A5 is about an organic networked approach to advertising—framed as swarming intelligence that is a branch of artificial intelligence (AI)—which attempts to replicate via machines, networks, and software how biological species behave and react in their search for survival as in flocks of birds, packs of wolves, schools of fish, and swarms of insects. Swarm intelligence proposes that intelligence derives from interactions in a social world that is decentralized and totally self-organizational.

This is at the essence of A5 and M3 that is to offer the content, products, and services—most aligned to devices' desires, values, wants, and needs—at the microsecond they occur. Figure 1.1 shows the design and execution of an A5 predictive rule for M3; however, this simple architecture can be developed for hundreds of rules to different digital devices based on a multitude of conditional nonhuman conditions, such as location and time-of-day, along with some anonymous human attributes.

Machine learning is at the core of M3, originating from the field of AI; machine-learning algorithms can be used to analyze vast amounts of data to discover propensity to purchase behaviors. For M3, machine-learning software enables the marketer to interrogate vast and diverse datasets from the web, social, and mobile networks. Behavioral analytics is at the core of modeling, profiling, and prediction.

Machine learning is the process by which pattern recognition software can predict some event or outcome, which in the case of M3 is to discover and model devices' behaviors. The field of machine learning seeks to learn from historical activities in order to predict future behaviors (this can be anything from propensity to purchase certain products or services) to the desire to view certain specific type of content. One of the advantages to machine learning for M3 is that the server can calibrate these marketing objectives in an understandable format. The outputs of most machine-learning software are conditional predictive IF/THEN rules that are easy to understand:

IF   second visit to site
AND   font Verdana
AND   gender female
THEN   Offer Product Code 51

The success of machine learning for M3 involves the strategic planning and measured improvement of predictive evolving models and clusters. For example, the key objective for executing and leveraging behavioral analytics for M3 is to plan and design a framework from which consumers' behaviors can be captured and modeled. Similarly, this M3 strategy should be to create a continuous and systemic method of quantifying device behaviors and to continuously measure everything.

A good example of M3 and A5 comes from Groupon, the digital couponing startup that daily sends deal-of-the-day e-mails to more than 70 million subscribers around the world. But it is not the location-based coupon e-mail offers that are illustrations of the execution of M3 and A5 by Groupon. Now, it is their new offering—what the company calls Groupon Now—which uses M3 and executes A5 to advertise its discounted offerings with surgical accuracy.

Say, you sell tacos and tortas in the neighborhood around the University of Texas at El Paso (UTEP); while offering coupons by e-mail might entice some new clients, the fact is that you have long lines of clients waiting to buy your fat and juicy tortas already. This is where Groupon Now and its strategic use of M3 via A5 kick in. Let us say Tortas-R-Us does experience some slow hours during midday around midweek. Using M3 and A5 technology and techniques, Groupon Now offers are made only during the hours of 1 p.m. to 3 p.m. but only on Tuesday, Wednesday, and Thursday for Tortas-R-Us. So using a business rule such as the following, Groupon Now knows when and where to market phone devices using their mobile app:

IF   Zip Code 79902-2214
AND   Time-of-day 1:37
AND   Day Wednesday
THEN Coupon $10 for $6 at Tortas-R-Us

This is a perfect example of a server marketing to a mobile device based on its proximity to a restaurant and based on the time-of-day and day-of-the-week. At no time are human attributes, characteristics, or demographics used in the marketing of these digital coupons. Groupon Now is based entirely on nonhuman factors and it is strictly M2M. When users open up the phone app, they will be presented with two buttons by Groupon Now: "I'm hungry" and "I'm bored." Clicking either button will open up a list of time-specific daily deals based on their location. Businesses can now choose when they want these deals to be available. Local eateries have never really had a simple way to manage their perishable inventory, especially labor and food (Figure 1.2). So why waste those vital resources during slow periods when they can M3 to savings-savvy consumers with a highly targeted Groupon deal via A5?

Figure 1.2   M3 by Groupon starts by targeting a device's city.

Groupon has already filed a patent around its method for serving up deals via e-mail. This is the abstract of the Groupon patent (Figure 1.3):

> A system and methods to mutually satisfy a consumer with a discount and a vendor with a minimum number of sales by establishing a tipping point associated with an offer for a good or service. If the tipping point is met, the sale of the good or service is executed and the consumer is charged and receives an indication of the discounted sale, such as a certificate. If the tipping point is not met, the discount offer is abandoned and the consumer is not charged. Once the tipping point is established, the vendor receives a payment, even before the consumer uses the certificate. The system and methods also include a reward or loyalty program, an exchange or secondary market for the purchased deals, and a matching algorithm that matches customers to relevant goods or services.

The only human attributes used to triangulate its offers by Groupon are the devices' location by ZIP code and the age of the consumer, aside from that the company instead uses M2M data for M3 and A5 via its phone app; increasingly these are the only human attributes that M3 marketers can rely on since they are not subject to change (Figure 1.4).

Groupon has managed to build the fastest growing company of all times, and their success is based on M3 via A5. Mobile apps are the new medium for marketing via location, temporal, and behavior coordinates for triangulation at the right time to the right moving devices. A5 will increasingly become important as more and more consumers used their phones for shopping, price comparison, directions, and local discounts that are time and location sensitive. Mobile apps allow M3 marketers to target devices as they move via A5s.

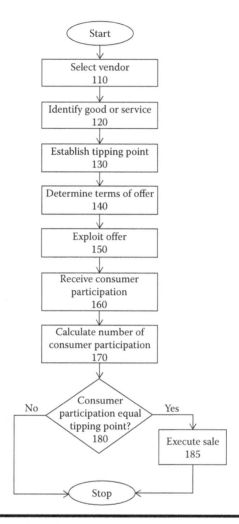

Figure 1.3 Main drawing of the Groupon patent.

Groupon Now could scale up to become an M3 advertising network, by running the deals in a lot of other third-party apps. Groupon could offer specific deals based on their dynamic, just-in-time ads based on the devices' location and time-of-day. These ads could direct people to a mobile website or a third-party app, where users could complete their purchase. Then Groupon could give some money to the app publisher, as with any lead-generated affiliate relationship, either on a cost-per-click (CPC) or cost-per-acquisition (CPA) basis. If the deals are well targeted, Groupon Now could have very high click-through rates with equally high purchase rates, via its "I am Hungry" or "I am Bored" button ad network.

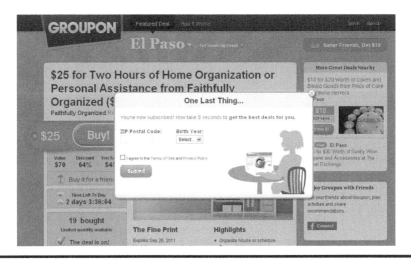

Figure 1.4   The only human attributes used are ZIP and age, and they are optional.

Mobile application development, such as the Groupon app, is the process by which software is developed for phones, for specific purposes, such as playing music (Pandora) or games (Zynga). These applications are usually downloaded by customers from app stores or from the sites of the creators of the apps. Most of the methodologies in use are based on the model-driven approach that has three different views of the application development process:

1. The app itself and its structure, in the case of Groupon getting discount deals
2. The business logic, such as location, proximity, age, gender, and time of day
3. The graphical user interface of the mobile app and its application

One of the most popular operating systems for apps is Android and it is a platform from the Open Handset Alliance, whose 34 members include Google, HTC, Motorola, Qualcomm, and T-Mobile and supported by all of these major software, hardware, and telecom companies. It uses the Linux kernel as a hardware abstraction layer (HAL). Application programming is mostly done in Java. The Android specific Java software development kit (SDK) is needed for development although any Java IDE may be used. Performance critical code can be written in C, C++, or other native code languages using the Android native development kit (NDK).

It is expected that by 2012 there will be more than 130 million Android users around the world. For the M3 marketer, it is very important to leverage the creation and deployment of these A5s, specifically for the Android phones and all Apple devices (iPhone and iPad), the two dominant players in the United States.

What, Where, and How to Monetize Device Behaviors

What: The behavior of devices, which can be on any digital channel. The M3 marketer needs to be aware and responsive to how consumer use their devices to search, share, and shop for specific services and products. The same hold true for content via the multiple-channel devices used to read and research for information.

Where: On the web, social networks, and mobile worlds where devices roam. M3 marketers need to develop strategies for knowing and anticipating how device traffic develops and how they evolve in the scheme of their advertising campaigns.

How: Via the use of AI software and web and wireless mechanism, networked strategies, and modeling techniques. The modeling of device behaviors is the key to executing M3. Coupled with the use of A5s to know how and when to M3 devices.

M3 is about advertising via any channel, web, social networks, mobile, appliances, autos, etc., at the server-to-device level anonymously and ubiquitously; it is about reacting to consumer needs and desires with precise, personal, and relevant content and offers at the microsecond that occur via A5s. The strategy for M3 is to gather and model device data to make digital marketing more personal, relevant, and comprehensive; this requires capturing, analyzing, and acting on device consumer actions via A5s, which are beneficial to both consumers and marketers. This generally involves the following steps:

1. The monetization of device behaviors via analytics for M3 and A5
2. The use of cookies, web analytics, DPI, geolocation, and ad exchanges
3. The use of social media, Twitter, WOM, Facebook, YouTube, and data harvesters
4. The use of Wi-Fi triangulation, GPS, wireless cookies, mobile websites, and apps
5. M3 via digital fingerprinting for A5 to any and all wired and wireless devices worldwide

The M3 marketer needs to map a strategy and set clear measurable objectives. The marketer must be fully aware of the available software, networks, and solution providers in order to execute their tasks and campaigns. The web and mobile environments are rapid, self-evolving marketing ecosystems in which consumers drive demand, product design, service features, and price structure. The M3 marketer needs to design and implement a framework for leveraging these streams of device behaviors, as the building blocks for the following goals:

1. *The business vision*: Increase sales, revenue, and profits, via improved customer service and content relevancy
2. *The objective milestone*: This is a quantitative metric; it measures cross and up selling ratios
3. *Goal mission*: This is a qualitative metric, measured by the improvement of the consumer experience and loyalty
4. *Tactic*: This is the executable action for meeting the vision, objective, and the mission of the M3 marketer

Machine learning for M3 is the capability to recognize patterns of device activities in order to predict when and where sales are likely to take place or what type of content to serve. For M3 to work there is a need to create a framework to capture and analyze device behaviors for pattern recognition and reactive marketing the microsecond they occur. There are two main approaches to machine learning for M3: *inductive* and *deductive* approaches.

The *inductive* approach is self-learning—involving clustering analysis and text analytics—and involves what is known in AI as "unsupervised learning." These disciplines evolved over the last couple of decades in attempts to emulate human intelligence, memory, learning, and cognition. When attempting to M2M and M3, it is important to know how machine-learning algorithms can be enlisted in the effort to market to digital devices (Figure 1.5).

To stay ahead of the competition, M3 marketers need to leverage the power of machine-learning algorithms that can analyze and model device behaviors via data mining millions of events and actions. The most common type of inductive analysis is via the use of self-organizing map (SOM) software for autonomous clustering. This type of inductive modeling simply involves the use of a clustering neural network (SOM) program to autonomously discover hidden clusters of device behaviors.

There are also techniques and algorithms for text analytics for clustering key concepts from documents, e-mails, blogs, websites, texts, social media, and other unstructured content. In this instance, text-mining software is used to extract

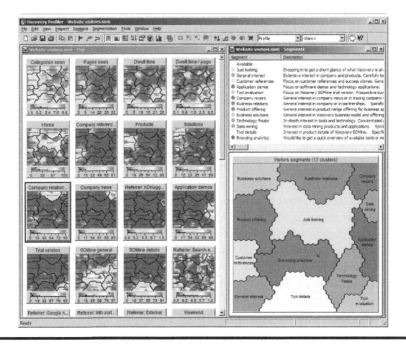

Figure 1.5   SOM clustering analysis of device website behaviors and "key words."

important concepts from millions of records residing in remote clouds, servers, and other storage devices. The M3 marketer can use this type of technology and programs to discover trends and behaviors from unstructured content, which often represents a large percentage of data stored by enterprises.

There is also a *deductive* approach to monetizing device behaviors using "supervised learning"; this involves the use of rule generators and decision trees to develop predictive rules about device behaviors and requires the "training" and creation of models to predict behaviors based on historical patterns. This is the dominant technology at the core of business intelligence and data mining. Unlike neural networks, decision trees and rule generators are easy to develop and understand, such as this rule extracted using the easy-to-use WizWhy software program:

IF OS is Android
AND Last Purchase is 60...90 days (Average = 75)
AND Gender is Female
THEN
Offer 10% Discount
Rule's Probability: 0.90
The Rule exists in 73,000 records
Significance Level: Error Probability < 0.01

The mapping of device behaviors via inductive and deductive models for M3 can be simultaneously done. Inductive analyses can discover unknown clusters of device behaviors, while deductive analyzes can further reveal ranges and values of these behaviors for predicting future events about these devices. These analyzes can take place at the server level with the ability to use A5s to market to a myriad of devices via multiple consumer channels.

Decision trees are graphical representations of device behaviors and their outcomes; they represent an ideal method by which M3 marketers can come to understand what is happening in a very simplistic manner. Decision trees can be used to segment device behaviors; they can be used to map different outcomes and can be used to predict future activities by the M3 marketer. Decision trees are highly robust and powerful software for data mining, business intelligence, and now M3 marketing. For example, in the following graphic, a decision tree is created for purposes of deciding what type of offers should be made to consumers on the basis of certain needs and day-of-the-week (Figure 1.6).

In the end, M3 is made possible by the modeling of device behaviors using clustering, text analytic, rule generating, and decision tree software to analyze and model the captured behavioral data of devices and for the creation of A5s, which are the engines of M3. In Chapter 2, we will cover in detail how and why to use each of these different varieties of programs, and in Chapter 3, checklists will also be provided on when to use these different type of software for specific M3 and A5 needs.

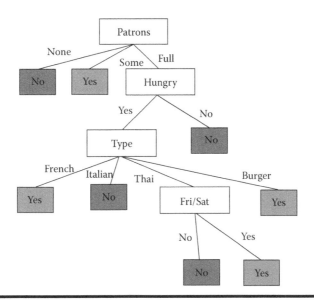

Figure 1.6   Decision tree created from historical patterns.

Building A5s

The M3 marketer needs to construct an adaptive architecture for constructing and leveraging A5s, mobile apps—designed to leverage one of the most dominant marketing designs today and in the future. Mobile application development is the process by which application software is constructed for small low-power devices, such as pads or phones. These applications are either preinstalled during their manufacture or downloaded by customers from various companies or platforms. For the M3 marketer, this commonly involves customizing specific A5s designed for selling services, products, or targeted content; as previously mentioned, the dominant devices are those of Apple and those running Google's Android operating system.

In Chapter 2, details will be provided on how to construct mobile apps based on device type and their operating system. A5s, however, are not restricted to only mobile apps; it is also possible to execute them on the web and social networks. The point is to recognize and model device behaviors as consumers search, share, and shop for products and services. Assembling the structure for executing A5s is, however, very important for M3 marketers.

Marketing via social media and mobile apps shifts companies from targeting everyone to cultivating only those that it wants via their stationary and mobile devices. Brand awareness can be accomplished in vast scales and inexpensively; it may simply require a blog or a posting at a social network to create a buzz about a brand or a new product or service; and it is a new form of micromarketing.

For example, games transform social sites such as Facebook into important hubs of interactive activities for devices, such as FarmVille, Phrases, Texas HoldEm, FrontierVille, Causes, Café World, Mafia Wars, Quiz Planet, Treasure Isle, and IHeart from gaming companies, such as Zynga, and are perfect for executing A5. Upon installation and registration, these game apps capture important attributes for segmentation marketing; they can capture age, gender, and locations for A5 via any device.

For the M3 marketer, gaming apps need to include device analytics including measuring which features are popular, which demographic group plays the longest, and which devices send the most invitations. Care must also be paid to which devices are active advocates or detractors to a brand; these metrics are vital to M3 marketers. There are hundreds of apps from which important device behaviors can be captured and modeled, such as the popular Pandora Radio station that also captures age and gender as well as important device profiles, such as whether it is a desktop, laptop, pad, or phone.

For the M3 marketer and developers, tracking these hundreds of thousands of apps can be a daunting task; however, PositionApp can be enlisted to monitor over 100,000 apps in the iTunes app store and the 10,000 new apps submitted every week to Apple. PositionApp can be used by developers to track the success of their creation and M3 marketers to measure their communications impact through sales in markets all over the world. PositionApp offers historical data covering several months with coverage of the top 300 apps by different categories around the world. PositionApp provides up-to-date country-by-country position performance stats on the top apps with historic position data, which can be browsed by country, genre, position change, and app name, free and fees paid on a daily, weekly, and monthly basis. As with Groupon, there are other retail discounters including Living Social, Tippr, Bloomspot, Scoutmob, BuyWithMe, and OpenTable all have sites and apps for targeting devices, all of which can be evaluated via PositionApp.

Another marketing firm dedicated to monitoring mobile apps is AppData which provides metrics and the tracking of apps, social platforms, social networks, and virtual goods. AppData is an independent application traffic tracking service of Inside Network, a company dedicated to providing business information and market research to the Facebook platform and social gaming ecosystem. AppData is intended for use by developers, investors, marketers, and analysts interested in tracking app traffic on the Facebook platform.

AppData publishes original research to serve developers, marketers, and analysts interested in understanding of the social gaming ecosystem. Their current research includes spending and usage patterns of the social gaming audience, tracking the U.S. virtual goods market, and exclusive data and analysis on the Facebook network (Figure 1.7).

Yet another app metric reporting firm is Appolicious that offers a directory of hundreds of Android and Apple apps, the two dominant apps in the United States. Appolicious combines social networking, journalism, and technology to assist M3

Figure 1.7   AppData Pro metrics and trends of gaming apps.

marketers discover the best of the tens of thousands of Android and Apple apps available today (Figure 1.8).

Popular mobile and web applications present new and engaging ways for brands to communicate directly with devices in increasingly targeted and contextually aware formats. There are apps in all types of categories, including books, business application, education, entertainment, health, music, news, shopping, sports, and travel, to name a few. Apple apps for their iPhone and iPad devices are clearly the dominant player in mobile marketing via A5s. The following is a partial list of companies using Apple apps for an assortment of functions and M3 marketing:

Hyundai—Uses the iPad to hold the owner's manual for its Equus model
Flipboard—Uses streaming media for converting the iPad into slick magazines
Zumobi—Builds networks of media-brand apps, such as NBC's Today show
Instapaper—Allows for "read later" piles of content for iPhone and iPad
Kony Solutions—Builds iPhone apps for banks, insurers, carmakers, and airlines
Urban Airship—Creates apps for push notification and subscriptions
Foursquare—App rewards devices for "checking in" at shops, airports, and retailers
Hipstamatic—Uses iPhone camera to sell analog prints
Dropbox—Uses cloud computing to store, sync, and share files online

Figure 1.8 Listing of Android apps on Appolicious.

Tiffen—Provides photo tools including its Steadicam

Firemint—Flight Control and Real Racing gaming apps

Foodpotting—Picture perfect dining-out app

Podtrac—Connects podcasters with advertisers

Rovio—Angry Birds game app

Square—iPhone credit card reader

IndieBound—Connects readers with independent bookstore

Appcelerator—App building tools for developers and marketers

eBay—Shopping, price comparison, and purchasing app

PointAbout—Offers its free AppMakr app building tool

Cinemek—Filmmaking tool Storyboard Composer

WordLens—Translates Spanish to English and vice versa via iPhone camera

Fidelity—Portfolio and market tracking via its app

TuneIn Radio—40,000 radio stations for the iPhone

Visible Energy—Electricity monitoring app

NewKinetix—Turns iPhone into a universal remote

Netflix—iPad movie viewer

Flurry—The Nielsen of mobile apps for thousands of companies

Glee—Karaoke app (the number one app in 21 countries)

iHandySoft—Carpenter kit app

Opertoon—Interactive books

MLB—Highest grossing game app

Google—Search app via voice command or iPhone picture

JPMorgan Chase—Photographs and deposits checks into bank account app
Dow Chemical—PaintRemedy app to try out colors
Samsung—Smooth video for iPad with its flash memory
Vito Technology—Star gazing iPad app
Simon's Cat—Piano teaching app for iPad
Sherwin-Williams—A paint color-matching app
TouchPress—Interactive textbooks for the iPad

Simply building a killer A5 is not enough for M3 marketers, who need to have a strategy to make their app a compelling program to be shared with other devices. This is where companies such as Clearspring come in via their "AddThis" button. Clearspring is one of the largest data-sharing social networks; their AddThis button allows devices and its users to alert friends and contacts to interesting information on the web and allows for the sending of an e-mail or a posting to a social site such as Facebook. More than 1.5 million websites have implemented the AddThis button, hoping the easy link helps drive online traffic.

Most important to the M3 marketer is that Clearspring is aggregating and segmenting these consumer sharing habits, which advertisers can buy to target their ads from multiple websites. The AddThis button network reaches 170 million devices or about 95% of U.S. browsers. The Clearspring's AddThis platform enables M3 marketers to distribute and track digital content such as web pages, widgets, and videos to social networks, bookmarking sites, and blogs.

Another data sharing network is ShareThis, which is also offering targeted ads based on the type of content users share and covers 88 million users in the United States. Both Clearspring and ShareThis provide true M3 marketing strategies and tools since they allow for the view of devices from multiple angles—from multiple and diverse sites—some of which are retailing sites while others cover news, music, and other types of digital entertainment. Data sharing networks, such as Twitter, can segment devices into clusters of consumer groups based on the content they are viewing as well as what media they are sharing.

Recommendation engines can also be leverage for M3 marketing by using the concept of "mob targeting," which involves the intersection of word of mouth, social media, and influences of groups of devices and their owners as the key to product placement to drive brand response. The core technology of these recommendation engines is also referred to as "collaborative filtering" and can be seen in action at Amazon and Netflix, where some devices are attracted to romance while others go for action or comedy.

Collaborative filtering is a method of making automatic predictions about the interests of a user by collecting taste or preference information from many users to make its recommendations. Amazon and Netflix use their own proprietary collaborative filtering engines; however, M3 marketers can leverage commercial recommendation engines and networks for their clients, a checklist of these engines will be provided in Chapter 3.

Search Marketing versus Social Marketing via A5s

The challenge to M3 marketers is how to deploy revenue producing A5s with the main question being whether to go search or social, or both. Google, Twitter and Facebook, and other social media companies are all competing via GPS and Wi-Fi triangulation in the marketing for a new untapped revenue stream: local businesses.

Search marketing is not "search engine marketing" also known as "search engine optimization (SEO)," which is a form of marketing on the web that seeks to promote a site by increasing its visibility in all the search engines like Google, Yahoo, and Bing—where the search results pages are prioritized through the use of paid placement, contextual advertising, or paid inclusion. "Search marketing" on the other hand is what Google and the other search engines do, which is targeting devices based on what "key words" they are searching for, so a search for a plumber will result in ads for local plumbers based on the location of that device. More and more, devices are searching for specific products by make, model, and part number, or they are copying and pasting product titles into search engines to find a retailer.

Today's crawler-based search engines have three major elements. First is the spider, also called the crawler. The spider visits a site, reads it, and then follows links to other pages within the site. This is what it means when someone refers to a site being "spidered" or "crawled." The autonomous engine spider returns to the site on a regular basis, such as every month or two, to look for changes. Everything the spider finds goes into the second part of the search engine, the index. The index, also called the catalog, is like a giant directory containing a copy of every web page that the spider finds. If a web page changes, then directory is updated with new information.

Sometimes it can take a while for new pages or changes that the spider finds to be added to the index. Thus, a web page may have been "spidered" but not yet "indexed," meaning it is not available to those searching with the search engine. Search engine software is the third part of a search engine. This is the program that sifts through the millions of pages recorded in the index to find matches to a search and rank them in order of what it believes is the most relevant to the searching devices. Because of the rankings between Google, Yahoo, and Bing (the three major engines are often very similar), competition between them often means their algorithms use the same elements, such as content, metatags, and internal and external links.

The concept behind search engine marketing is that when a device searches the web it is in a "hunt mode." This mode is unique because it indicates that the device—either stationary or mobile—is looking for information. M3 marketers should understand that in this "hunt mode," means that the searching device may very well be researching a product or service to try and satisfy an immediate or future need. This makes the search engine results some of the best sources of targeted marketing, whether that originates from organic unpaid search listings or via the strategic use of metatags or paid advertising listings, such as a directory paid inclusion or graphic search inventory.

Search marketing is unique in that it is a nonintrusive method of M3 marketing. The majority of online and offline advertising often intrudes on the audience, interrupting their activities. Search marketing is unique in that it is targeting a searching device at the exact moment they are seeking knowledge or a solution for a product or service: it is just-in-time M3 marketing.

Search marketing originates from a voluntary, device-driven search, which must be optimized to take advantage of the relevancy algorithms used by search engines like Google, Yahoo, and Bing, which use a combination of the text they index on a site, combined with other elements such as relevant links and behaviors or preferences. All of the major search engines provide maps, directions, phone numbers, advertising, and other relevant information when a device searches for a specific local product or service, such as a television repair shop combined with a specific city.

Note in Figure 1.9 how the search engine's results are composed of three elements: First, it displays those websites most relevant to the searching device, and these are prioritized by Google as being the most relevant based on over 200 elements its algorithms uses to sort and index the sites. Second, on the upper right side, a map is provided of all those sites it found. Third—and this is where the search marketing takes place—on the lower right side, paid advertisements are displayed, and this is where Google the search marketer makes millions in revenue 24/7.

Social marketing unlike search marketing relies more on the *sharing* of information between devices. Social marketing is based more on the way the owners of these devices share and recommend products and services to other devices in their

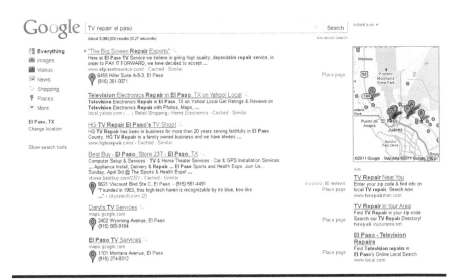

Figure 1.9 Example of search marketing as performed by Google.

group of friends. Why social marketing works is because today on the web and mobile world devices can make this communication lightning fast; it has never been faster or easier to reach so many other devices with so little effort. Back in the 1970s, Robert Cialdini, Regents' Professor Emeritus of Psychology and Marketing at Arizona State University did some groundbreaking work in the science and psychology of persuasion. He discovered six fundamental building blocks to persuasion (all of them are tightly bound up with the concept of social network marketing). They are as follows:

1. *Reciprocity*: If you do something for me, I feel obliged to do something for you in return. See this in the light of social media and interactions in a social network where one device provides information and advice to other devices for free.
2. *Authority*: We tend to obey authority figures. It is not a logical thought process we go through in our responses to this, even though we rationalize it that way. An expert is an authority on a subject, which others tend to listen.
3. *Consistency and commitment*: We tend to feel obliged to act in the way we have said we are going to act. This makes us more trustworthy to others. Our behaviors can be better predicted from our words.
4. *Liking*: We tend to be more easily influenced by people we like more than by people we do not like. We tend to like people who are like we are. Why? Because we can better predict their responses and behaviors, we tend to like to deal with people we trust and like.
5. *Social proof*: We tend to follow the crowd. If everyone is doing it, then it is probably a good idea. Often this is the reason a brand tends to become popular; emotionally, this is a very powerful motivator.
6. *Scarcity*: We want what we cannot have. Interestingly, the human trait of fighting harder not to lose something than to gain it in the first place is also prosurvival.

The success of social networks marks a dynamic shift in how people and their devices are using the web and mobile. Instead of just searching for information via search engines, social marketing is based upon the "hive" mentality where people and their devices identify themselves as part of a group with similar likes and interests that draw them together. This is easy to do on the web and wireless environments because the traditional communication barriers of physical locations no longer exist.

In terms of social marketing, there exist a couple of device types: the "connectors" and the "experts." Connectors are people with a social gift of bringing others together. They have an extraordinary knack for making friendships with lots of people across many subniches and cultures. These people are the "social glue" that makes social marketing possible. As with the common cold, connectors are those people best positioned to spread the germ throughout the population; they are like bus drivers, bank tellers, waiters, and anyone else who comes into contact with a large number of people everyday.

But connectors are not the only type of social activists for making social marketing possible, there are also the experts. Experts are information specialists who have the knowledge and social skills to start word-of-mouth (WOM) epidemics. These are the people who do all of the research necessary to solve their own problems and once they figure out that they have a good thing, they want to tell others. Expert devices provide the initial spark and message that connector devices filter through their large network of contacts (Figure 1.10).

Social marketing unlike search marketing, which relies on robots to index content and present targeted relevant ads, is human-based and is often an effort to attract attention and encourages other devices to share that endorsement via Facebook and Twitter to other devices. Social marketing usually centers on efforts to create content that attracts attention and encourages devices to share it with their social networks, which is more compelling since it is coming from a trusted, third-party source, as opposed to the brand or company itself. Social marketing if executed properly fosters brand awareness and improved customer service. Additionally, social marketing serves as a relatively inexpensive platform for organizations to implement marketing campaigns.

Social marketing benefits enterprises and individuals by providing an additional channel for customer support; it is also a means to gain customer and competitive insight, recruitment and retention of new customers, and a method of managing a brand reputation online. Key factors that ensure its success are its relevance to the

Figure 1.10 Social marketing is driven by device interactions and recommendations.

customer, the value it provides them with, and the strength of the foundation on which it is built. Social marketing tools can be used for a variety of different things such as social monitoring, aggregation, tagging, analytics, and reporting.

The device path toward a purchase of a product or a service takes many routes but most of the time it starts with a search via Google, Yahoo, or Bing, continuing with opinion posting on blogs, Twitter, and Facebook. A recent study conducted by GroupM—the world's largest advertising media company—sought to understand the relationship consumers were establishing with brands via both search marketing and social marketing. For this research study, GroupM defined "social marketing" as the destinations that create communities or networks for sharing of information in text, image, or video. These destinations range from brand-owned social media, such as a brand's blog, to earned social media, such as content about a category created by the community and fostered by the brand, to paid social media, such as sponsored and promoted areas of sites, including Facebook, YouTube, and Twitter.

The study found a strong correlation between the two channels of search marketing and social marketing. In fact, the digital device ecosystem is largely evolving around the two titans of Google and Facebook. The GroupM study suggests that the brands that listen and adapt in search marketing and social marketing cannot only capture a disproportionate amount of initial sales but also build on their device loyalty efforts. The study found that in nearly 60% of all consumer journeys that end with a purchase of a product or service, the starting point was with search. Devices use search first due to the quality and scale of information available and because search is easy to use.

By contrast, the key motivation for devices to turn to social media is to conduct additional preliminary information gathering via the referral authority exercised by respondents' "friends." While a less popular first step than search, social media clearly remains important in the process. The study found that consumers are equally likely today to use a combination of search and social media in their path to purchase as opposed to just search. Forty-eight percent of those who convert into a purchase utilize both search *and* social media versus 51% that use search alone.

It is important to note that while social media are built on human connections, this research study suggests that those connections now directly tie to the financial aspirations of businesses and thus have become more important within the context of supporting customer loyalty. The GroupM study found that only 1% of consumers will use social media *without* search to get to the purchase point. These data suggest that social media is not yet a stand-alone conduit for the consumer's decision-making process. More important than starting with search is that most consumers who convert see search as a "pricing" tool throughout the buying cycle. The study further reveals that social media are vital in the awareness (especially of new brands and products) and consideration phases, while search enables consumers to conduct product research.

Seventy-six percent of all consumer devices use either search or social media to explore and potentially buy without commitment to a brand at the outset.

This represents a definite opportunity for M3 marketers to capture that expressed intent by creating engagement in *both* channels in order to best position themselves for consideration and purchase. A clear validation from the study is that the discovery process consumers go through is lengthy, thanks in part to the multitude of available platforms and the subsequent ability to get more information. For example, in the telecommunications and consumer electronics categories, respectively, the path to purchase was 60 and 57 days, with 11 and 9 steps from start to finish. In nearly 60% of all the electronics purchases, for example, search is included in the process.

Not only do most consumers start with search, but when asked how important it is to turn to search after starting with social media or searching on company websites in their buying process, 86% of respondents cite search as being very important, significantly higher than turning to either social media or company websites. For the M3 marketer, it is clear that search marketing is critical and cannot be dismissed totally in favor of social marketing. The study also reveals that consumers, at a ratio of 2 to 1, cite quality and depth of information as reasons for using search versus social media.

For the M3 marketer, search marketing continues to make a compelling case as a valid recipient for initial investment of advertising dollars and ongoing optimization efforts via A5s. Thirty-six percent of all consumers say search helps in the decision-making process. An emerging trend is the growth of consumers searching for online deals and sales. Nearly 50% of all people surveyed indicate that they use search to look for deals and/or sales more often than pricing or store locations.

However, if search is essential for the pricing component of a buying decision, then social media is its interlinked companion in the selection process. The industry trend for social marketing has been a growing relationship between a user's social networks: their web of social connections and their ability to reference it for making choices. While this trend is important for M3 marketers, social marketing plays an increasingly complex role in the purchase path. When consumers were asked how search and social media are useful to them, respondents said social network helps in two key areas: awareness of new brands and products and eliminating brands from consideration. In the consumer product group category, social media had an even more dramatic role.

The leading companies of the social ecosystem, such as Facebook, Twitter, and YouTube, appear to have a minimal role in the purchase pathway at present. This signifies that earned social media provides a greater impact on the consumer's final purchase decision in today's social landscape. Brands with fan bases that are highly engaged may be better positioned to leverage these channel-leading properties, for example, brands with the most fans on Facebook were Coca-Cola (21.6 million), Starbucks (19 million), Oreo (16.2 million), Disney (15.6 million), and Red Bull (14.7 million).

Among the more surprising findings of the GroupM study are the types of social networks consumers use to find information. Facebook, Twitter, and YouTube are synonymous with the definition of social media. However, when it comes to aiding the purchase decision, the top-performing option for consumers is user reviews (30%), while social networking, such as Facebook (17%), and video sharing, such as YouTube (14%) and Twitter (9%), all reported to bring less value to consumers. The research also shows that the greatest motivator for social media engagement is to gather the opinions of others. This is especially true for higher-cost products.

But brands should not simply think of social as a passive tool as there are active decision-making processes occurring in the social space. A consistent finding throughout the study is that consumers are having brand perceptions shaped and altered through social engagement. One thing is true of both search and social media: both channels provide a final vote of confidence to consumers for making a sound purchase decision.

Nearly 70% of all respondents state that these social channels make them feel more confident about their purchase decisions. Once that decision to purchase is made, consumers have a high desire to stay connected with the brand. Sixty-four percent of consumers say they are likely to follow a brand via social media after a purchase and indicate aspirations for connections and content from a brand in the social space.

Seventy-four percent of all survey participants state that their desired format for future engagement is via a Facebook brand page. They also prefer to stay engaged with content in the form of videos and Tweets about—and from—a brand. Respondents emphasize that earned social media play an important role in the effort for brands to foster consumer loyalty. Respondents indicate that they

1. Feel a sense of trust with the company that produces the brands they buy
2. Feel that the company cares about them beyond a single purchase
3. Feel like an insider with the brand

Forty percent of respondents say search leads to increased usage of social media, while 46% of those surveyed say social media leads them to conduct more searches. And what stimulates the highest likelihood to move from one channel to the other? More than one quarter of all respondents say the stimulus for alternating channels is the ability to gather additional, salient information.

Consumers want accurate, timely information and they will alternate between two channels: First, search makes them feel ubiquitous and a part of their everyday life, while social is used not only to introduce a brand purchase decisions but also to alter their intentions and confirm their final purchase decision.

If brands can engage fluently in the social sphere and encourage quality content on category blogs and in video and microcommentaries about their products, then expansion of brand engagement can occur in the social sphere. Search serves as the best expression of explicit intent in advertising, and nearly 50% of consumers used search alone in the decision process. Conversely, less than 1% of all consumers use social media alone. The implicit nature of social media and the targeted advertising attempts within it show that it is more difficult to use the implicit path by itself than the explicit path represented by search.

According to Econsultancy's "State of Search Marketing Report 2011," Internet marketers are poised to make 2011 a big year for paid search. Based on the projections contained in the report, search engine marketing spend will balloon some 16% this year, hitting an estimated $19.3 billion before the close of 2011. Key findings of the study show that "the rise of the mobile internet is the trend which is regarded as having the most impact on search marketing, with more than three-quarters of companies (79%) deeming it as 'highly significant' or 'significant.'" Proving the emergent authority of social media platforms, the widespread use of Facebook, Twitter, and its social networking siblings is also factored into the projected growth.

As a result, an escalating number of companies are outsourcing search and social media. According to the study, just 44% of companies are now carrying out SEO in-house, compared to 51% last year. Only 55% are doing social media marketing in-house, compared to 62% a year ago. As expected, Google remains the dominant force in the search universe. The overwhelming majority of companies (95%) indicated that they will spend advertising dollars via search engine marketing on Google AdWords.

The use of social networks for marketing also continues to grow. The percentage of company respondents who say they use Facebook for marketing now stands at 84%, up from 73% last year. Companies and agencies are increasingly using third-party bid management technology for paid search marketing. Just under half of responding companies conducting search engine marketing rely on their own basic tools and internal personnel.

It is clear, however, that in the past 15 months, the level of engagement from consumers and interplay between these channels have evolved to a point that shows search and social media are powerful channels individually, but in combination they create a virtuous circle of knowledge and opportunity for the M3 marketer. Keep in mind that it is estimated that Facebook pulled in $1.86 billion in advertising in 2010 and that is expected to grow 118% this year to $4 billion. In the end, the message to the M3 marketer is to use *both* search marketing and social marketing since they complement each other.

Google, Facebook, and Twitter Places

Google, Facebook, and Twitter all now have new platforms they call Places. The idea of Facebook Places is to allow devices to share their physical location online with other devices of offline and online friends. This paves the way for Facebook to become a player in the growing online business of supplying local information and targeted advertising based on the location of devices and their friends' devices.

The Facebook Places follows the Google Places platform that offers up web pages dedicated to individual businesses, showing where they are located, and street level images on Google Maps along with customer reviews of services and products, be it a pub, a restaurant, or a store. Businesses can also advertise through their Google Place pages. Google sell relevant ads alongside search results, whereas Facebook will rely on the recommendations from friends to discover relevant content or available products and services. In both instances, the geographic location of a device is critical, whether it is social targeted or search targeted.

More and more people search for businesses online than anywhere else, so it is important to make sure a business listing can be easily found on Google, Google Maps, and now Google Places, which is free. Businesses that already show up on Google should still verify their listing and make sure its details are accurate and thorough. These improvements will start appearing as soon as they verify them through Google Places, with notifications included. These Google listings are an easy way to maintain an online presence even if a business does not have a website. Merchants and retailers can visit Google Places anytime to edit their information or see how many people have seen and clicked on their listing: an important metric for M3 marketing.

Local businesses can make their listing stand out with photos and videos; custom categories like their service area, including the inclusion of brands they sell and how to find parking; and coupons to encourage customers to make a first-time or repeat purchase. At the end of the sign up to Google Places, businesses are asked to verify their submission by phone or postcard. Google does this to make sure that only the right people are able to change any public data about a local business.

That business listing, also known as a Place Page, is a web page to organize all the information for every imaginable place in the world. There are Google Place Pages for businesses, points of interest, transit stations, landmarks, and cities all over the world. Once a business has verified their Google Place listing, they can enhance the Place page by adding photos, videos, coupons, and even real-time updates like weekly specials all on their Place page. Verifying their listing gives them an opportunity to share even more information about their business with Google.

Each business listing on Google represents a "cluster" of information that Google collects and organizes from a diverse group of sources, such as Yellow Pages, as well as other third-party providers and aggregators. However, the basic information that a business submits through Google Places is the information that Google trusts the most and is elevated and prioritized within the search engine. This means that it will appear instead of any basic information that Google aggregates from anywhere else. To make sure the basic information a business submits is accurate, Google will ask the merchant or retailer to verify it first by entering a PIN that will be sent to either their business address or their phone number. This is an important factor for leveraging search marketing to local businesses and M3 marketing.

Business can add other information to their listing too, such as a description of their company, as well as photos, reviews, or information about hours and parking costs. Firms such as Creative One Media are one of many approved Google Places marketing partners. They can help businesses outsource all of the marketing to leverage Google Places in order to increase their visibility (Figure 1.11).

Figure 1.11   Creative One Media can assist local businesses with Google Places.

Millions of people search Google Places everyday for local business's and services and because a user is more likely to click on a local map listing than any other web listing because it is local and trustworthy. Some statistics to keep in mind about Google, Google Map, and Google Places are that 75% of all web users look for services and products within an area close to their home or business, 65% of all Google searches contain a local reference, and 46% of all visitors that click on a listing found in a Google Map will purchase the product or service offered.

Another factor to keep in mind about Google Places is its availability for businesses in only certain countries; to check country availability, Google offers a mapping tool availability page on their Google Places site. For example, in North America, Google Places is available in Canada, Greenland, Mexico, and, of course, the United States. Google Places is available worldwide including those in most developed countries in the following geographic areas: Africa, Asia, Caribbean, Central America, Europe, Middle East, North America, Oceania, and South America.

Adding a listing to Google Places is free, and Google does not accept payment to include particular listings or sites in their search results. However, Google does offer locally targeted advertising via their AdWords program. Another requirement of Google Places is that every business listing must have a mailing address. This is the physical address where mail can be sent to a business listing with Google Places. Another restriction is that there should not be more than one listing per physical location. Even if a business covers multiple locations, they cannot have two listings.

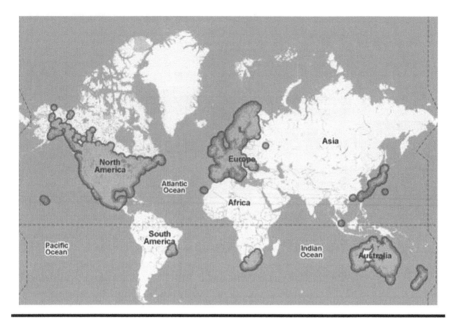

Figure 1.12   Dark sections have street views from Google Map.

Instead, they need to use the description of their business or categories to explain the different services they offer.

One of the advantages of search marketing and Google Places is its incorporation of Google Maps, which is a free service that offers a wide range of functionalities. Google Places takes advantage of Google Map by providing users several geo features for navigating toward its recommended business listing, such as their street views that cover the following sections in the planet (Figure 1.12).

Google Map also assists Google Places by providing public transit information, walking or bicycling directions as well as estimated driving costs. For example, a device can find these routes using several different kinds of roads or paths, as provided by Google Map. Biking directions are available for 150 U.S. cities; this is one of critical advantages of search marketing by Google; and it has been developing these geo data features for several years prior to the introduction of Google Places.

The cost of driving provided by Google Map is based on the distance driving between the device start point and end addresses, multiplied by the standard cost per mile that tax regulations allow businesses to deduct. This number is only an estimate and does not consider tolls, parking fees, or variations in gas mileage for different types of cars. Currently, Google Map cost of driving is available only for U.S. cities. These calculations are based on an annual study of the fixed and variable costs of operating an automobile as provided by Runzheimer International (an independent contractor), which conducts these studies for the U.S. Treasury's Internal Revenue Service (IRS).

The Facebook Places lets devices share their current location by "checking in," however, before a device can share its location with its Facebook friends. First, the social network needs to know where the device is located. To do so users need to open touch.facebook.com in a web browser or use the Facebook iPhone app on any Apple device where a tab appears under the "Inbox" called "Places." For the Apple iOS app, it will show a new icon in the middle of the home screen.

Tap *Places* and the device can see recent check-ins as well as friends' device check-ins. From here, the users can find out more details about the places their friends are checking into (map location, description, directions, comments, and other check-ins), or they can check themselves into a nearby location by pressing the *Check In* button at the top-right corner of the page (Figure 1.13).

If the device cannot find the right place to check in from, it can browse more nearby locations by pressing the right arrow button under the Places tab until it finds a location; if the device is an iPhone, it can just scroll all the way down and press *Show More Nearby Locations.*

The list of available locations comes from other people's check-ins and listings from Bing's mapping engine, so a device might have to add its location by pressing the *Add* button that will take the users to a page where they can fill in a name and description.

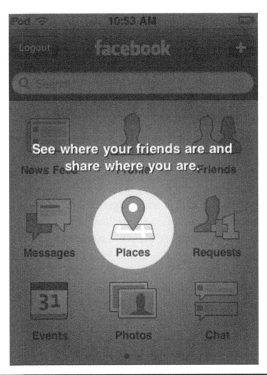

Figure 1.13　Facebook Places.

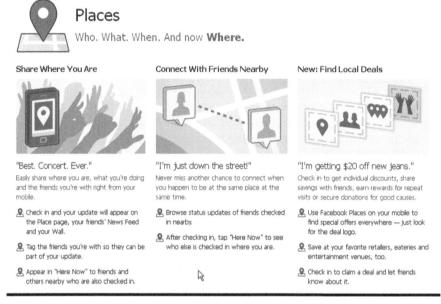

Figure 1.14 Facebook Places for sharing, connecting, and local deals.

Once the device taps the Check In button, it will be presented with a list of nearby locations where other devices have checked in. The users can tap the one they want to check into, and they can add comments on what it is doing there or add their Facebook friends (Figure 1.14).

While Places is mostly meant for mobile devices, it does not depend on GPS triangulation to find their location, and they need to check in. In addition, stationary laptop or desktop devices can also check in by going to the touch.facebook.com on their browser. While anyone can add a Facebook Place, business owners can turn the listing in Places into a proper Facebook Page, with Likes and a Wall and other social media marketing discounts, special deals, and offers. Facebook Places provides businesses with a platform for marketing and promotion; it also provides them with an opportunity to build customer loyalty.

Like current social location-based check-in services, Facebook Places lets people share where they are, see which friends are in the local area, and discover new places by following where others from their social network have checked in. The real value of services like Foursquare has been the integration with Facebook and the ability to share the check-in details with the broader social network.

Businesses can benefit from Places by going through a process to claim ownership of it, and if there is not already a Place, the business owner can create a new Place for their business. They can use Facebook Places as a tool for promoting their business, to expand their customer base, and for marketing their brand. There are several methods for leveraging Facebook Places: First, local businesses can make special offers.

That is, they can provide special discounts or promotional items for customers who show that they have checked in with Facebook Places during the current visit. The business can use signs in the store, or at the cash register, to encourage users to check in to Facebook Places to receive special time-sensitive offers.

Second, businesses can use Facebook Places to promote their business. WOM is one of the most effective forms of marketing and advertising. This is why location-based services like Foursquare or Yelp have become so popular. WOM marketing encourage customers to share their experience about a business; more importantly, it engages them to promote a business by way of offering specials, deals, or discounts for customers who post photos or reviews of that business or share Facebook Places updates from the business with their friends.

Last, Facebook Places rewards devices for customer loyalty. Getting customers is good for business, but getting loyal repeat customers is the key to a truly successful business. It gives customers a reason to keep coming back by providing a special discount every time their device check in to their Facebook Place. Similar to the "Mayor" feature in Foursquare, by declaring a Facebook Places "leader" based on the most check-ins, the business can create a special offer just for the designated Facebook Places leader and exploit the natural competitiveness of customers to drive return visits.

For a business to claim their Place, they need to search for their business name on Facebook via the normal Search bar. Then, click on their Places page; at the bottom left side of your Place, there will be a link that says "Is this your business?" Click on the link and they will be directed to a claiming flow. Facebook will then ask them to verify ownership of the business through a phone verification process and may be asked for document verification. If the claim is confirmed, the business will be able to administrate their Place on Facebook.

Of course, to realize the benefits of Facebook Places, a business should also have a Facebook page to market to its billions of users. However, there is little point in going to the effort of building a Facebook page and attracting an audience, if the business does not follow through to actively *engage* customers, which is the goal of social media. Having a Facebook page requires populating it with relevant nonintrusive content on a daily basis, such as bulletins about "what's new."

Equally important as the frequency of posting is the content of the posts. Customers want to be informed and engaged, not pitched and harassed. By claiming a Place on Facebook, a local merchant or retailer can manage their Place's address, contact information, business hours, profile picture, administration, and other settings. This is a very interactive way to encourage communication with customers' devices.

It is perfectly good to inform devices and their owners about new products and services when they are relevant, but not for using the Facebook page as a platform for traditional marketing pitches. A business can post news or stories related to their business and provide unique commentary or insight. Businesses can also use the Facebook page to provide tips, tricks, or information content.

As with other social media strategies, rather than talking at the audience, it is best to try to incite comments and feedback from the members to foster a sense of community with the customers and their devices. Facebook Places represents a huge opportunity for relevant social marketing by local businesses to promote their products and services and to take advantage of the massive audience Facebook has to offer.

It is an epic battle between search marketing and social marketing for the estimated $40 billions of small and medium businesses in local advertising for the current year. Not wanting to be left behind, the microblogging giant Twitter has also launched its own Twitter Places, which allows devices to broadcast their "tweet" and their location, including the businesses they are visiting, to all the followers of their messages.

Now, when a device Tweet with its location, they can specify an explicit Place or other point of interest. In this way, devices can provide additional information that makes their Tweets more meaningful without taking up extra characters. The opt-in Twitter's tweet with their location features allows devices to selectively add location information to their Tweets. Once a device has opted-in to the Tweets location feature, it will be able to add their location information to individual, new Tweets on Twitter.com and via other A5 devices that support this feature.

The publicly shared location information will be either the device's exact location via its self-provided coordinates (store, mall, bar, etc.) or a neighborhood or section of a city.

Tweeting via Places allows a device to add context to its updates and engage in local conversation about a businesses wherever they are. Twitter Places has integrated other location-based social networks, such as Foursquare and Gowalla. Many Foursquare and Gowalla users publish check-ins to Twitter Places. However, location is a key component of these Tweets. This means that when a device clicks on a Twitter Place, it will see standard Tweets and check-ins from Foursquare and Gowalla (Figure 1.15).

The use of Twitter's advance search by businesses can immediately limit a device's search for specific tweets within a geographic area and refine it further by searching for other specific factors such as words, people, places, dates, and attitudes (Figure 1.16).

For example, a chiropractor might search for "pain" within 15 miles of El Paso, TX, a florist might search for "anniversary" within 5 miles of Alameda, CA, and a restaurant might search for anyone within 10 miles of Normal, IL, in search of "Mexican food." The Mexican restaurant can post their lunch special, complete with a photo. And as their customer fan base grows, they can ask them for suggestions on what they would like to see on their daily special. The core of social marketing by Twitter is customer engagement.

An advanced search will bring up all the recent tweets that meet a business's criteria with the handle and avatar of the person who tweeted. From the results page, a business can follow these people or click on their profile for more information, with the probable results in harvesting new followers. Twitter has released an API that

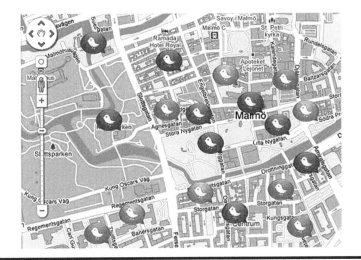

Figure 1.15 Twitter Places check-ins.

Advanced Search

Use this form to automatically construct your query. (Alternatively, you can type search operators directly into the search box.)

Find tweets based on...   [Search]

Words	All of these words	
	This exact phrase	
	Any of these words	
	None of these words	
	This hashtag	
	Written in	Any Language ▾

People	From this person	
	To this person	
	Referencing this person	

| Places | Near this place | |
| | Within this distance | 15 ▾ ⊙ miles ○ kilometers |

| Dates | Since this date | |
| | Until this date | |

Attitudes	With positive attitude :)	☐
	With negative attitude :(	☐
	Asking a question ?	☐

Other	Containing links	☐
	Include retweets	☐
	Results per page	15 ▾

[Search]

Figure 1.16 Business can search for Tweets based on multiple options.

lets developers integrate Twitter Places into their A5s. Twitter, of course, supports all the major browsers including Safari, Internet Explorer, Chrome, and Firefox.

With these location services, both Google and Facebook and now Twitter are attempting to organize and provide advertising based on the physical location of tens of millions of local businesses. Both the world's largest search engine and the largest social network want businesses to advertise online and potentially target location ads in real time to users of mobile devices right where they are. Google was the first to target local businesses based on what stationary and mobile devices were searching for.

Facebook followed by letting users "check in" via their mobile devices, which can pinpoint their location through GPS and Wi-Fi triangulation. Checking-in allows people to notify friends in their social network where they are—at a bar or a mall. Facebook not only knows who users are but also what they are interested in, and where their device is and when. Using text analytical algorithms, the social networks can readily cluster the similarities of desires and preferences of devices—who favor certain types of services and products—which Facebook and Twitter can monetize for M3 marketing purposes.

This takes A5 to a new level of sophistication and efficiency for anonymous advertising anywhere to any device. Facebook also has an ad tool called "learned targeting," which lets companies pitch ads to their friends who share common attributes. This kind of targeting is based on human preferences and desire rather than behavioral analytics. Combined with wireless technologies, this enables the M3 marketing to any type of device of any type anywhere in the world in an anonymous and yet highly effective and intimate manner.

Twitter, Facebook, Google, and Yahoo are all now incorporating this new variable of location in their A5 efforts. Facebook, however, has the advantage of knowing the likes and preferences of its users, which can be shared with small local businesses. Their "like" button allows Facebook to construct comprehensive psychographic profiles of its millions of members. Twitter has the advantage of targeting tweets via location in real time. But, clearly, the advantage is with Google who has the ability to target devices based on what they are searching for at the moment that occurs when the devices are in "search mode" and ready to buy.

M3 via GPS and Wi-Fi Triangulation

Two of the general criticisms of GPS are that the technology does not do very well in dense urban areas, and it does not get accurate enough for some A5 uses. At least two separate organizations—the Fraunhofer Institute for Integrated Circuits in Germany and Skyhook Wireless—took note of these drawbacks several years ago and began to develop new targeted Wi-Fi-based technology that can go to more places and be by far more accurate than GPS.

Back in 2005, Skyhook began to drive around the United States, Europe, and parts of Asia sniffing out and mapping Wi-Fi networks, measuring their signal strength, and comparing and building those results to their proprietary database. They continue to conduct periodic sweeps of an area in order to catalog the Wi-Fi hot spots updating their database. Their scans do not actually connect to or use any of these hot spots; they only scan them to measure relevant factors used for their database lookup and updates.

The Fraunhofer Institute says the Wi-Fi technology is strong and accurate enough to navigate department stores and hospitals, and Apple was confident enough in Skyhook's commercial offerings to build the technology into its most recent software updates for the early versions of its mobile devices, citing accuracy that typically matches or surpasses cell tower triangulation. With this kind of targeted usage in mind, this kind of triangulation technology makes A5 and M3 possible. The medium for delivery allows for tracking and targeting of mobile devices within 10 m.

Skyhook's publicly available Core Engine SDK allows developers and M3 marketers to quickly and easily target devices, enabling their applications using Skyhook's location-based system on the platform of their choice, the Core Engine supports Android (Google), Linux, Mac OS X (Apple), Symbian, Windows Mobile, and Windows 7. Skyhook was founded in 2003 to capitalize on the increasing demand for location-based services. The first location technologies (GPS and cell tower triangulation) were inadequate, leaving frustrated mobile consumers with slow and inaccurate positioning information. In response, Skyhook developed the Core Engine, a software-only location system based on Wi-Fi positioning, GPS, and cell tower triangulation.

Taking advantage of the hundreds of millions of Wi-Fi access data points throughout populated areas, Skyhook mapped their locations in order to consistently provide accurate location-based information indoors and in crowded urban areas. Their Core Engine is fast and accurate, reliable, and flexible and supports multiple devices and mobile applications. Skyhook's patented technology enables hundreds of millions of mobile applications to quickly determine a device's location within 10 m.

To quickly and reliably arrive at accurate location results, the Skyhook's Core Engine collects raw data from multiple sources including Wi-Fi access points, GPS satellites, and cell towers with their proprietary hybrid positioning algorithms. By leveraging the strengths of more than one underlying position technology, their Core Engine provides the best possible location available in any environment. A mobile device with Skyhook's Core Engine collects raw data from each of these multiple location sources. The Skyhook client then sends these data to the Skyhook Location Server and a single location estimate is returned. The client is optimized so that it communicates with the Skyhook Location Server only when the location cannot be determined locally. This behavior minimizes the user's data cost while maximizing the battery life of devices (Figure 1.17).

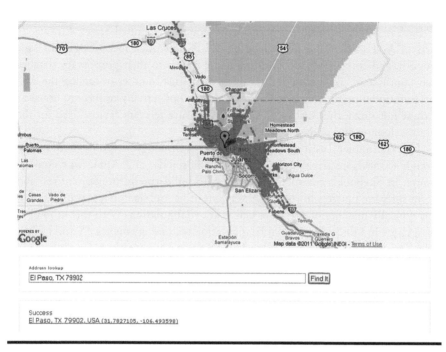

Figure 1.17   Skyhook provides an interactive view of how they locate devices.

Skyhook's Wi-Fi and cellular database is the largest and most extensive in the world. Skyhook maintains the accuracy of this database through an ongoing and continuous process of data monitoring, analysis, and collection. The three main components are as follows:

1. *Baseline data collection and establishing coverage areas*: Data collection begins with identifying target geographic areas using population analysis. Skyhook territory planners build coverage schedules starting with population centers and then moving into residential and suburban areas. Skyhook deploys a fleet of data collection vehicles to conduct a comprehensive access point survey within the target coverage areas in search of Wi-Fi hot spots. Every single passable street is included in their survey providing consistent coverage throughout the territory.

2. *Automated self-healing network*: As more users reference location for mobile devices, the Skyhook database is automatically updated and refreshed. This is what they call automated self-healing network.

3. *Periodic rescan*: Depending on the aging of the survey data and the density of user-generated updates, Skyhook periodically will rescan entire coverage areas to recalibrate the reference network, ensuring that performance remains consistent over time. Every territory added to Skyhook coverage is continuously monitored to assess the quality of the reference network and determine whether a rescan is required.

Wi-Fi positioning performs best where GPS is weakest, in urban areas and indoors. GPS provides highly accurate location results in "open sky" environments, like rural areas and on highways. But in urban areas and indoors, tall buildings and ceilings block GPS' view of satellites, resulting in serious performance deficiencies in Time To First Fix (TTFF), accuracy and availability. GPS or A-GPS alone cannot provide fast and accurate location results in all environments. Cell tower triangulation provides generalized location results with only 200–1000 m accuracy. It serves as a coverage fallback when neither GPS nor Wi-Fi is available.

Skyhook, Google, and Apple maintain a worldwide database of cell tower locations, which increases their coverage area and helps improve GPS satellite acquisition time. Up until 2010, Apple relied on databases maintained by Google and Skyhook to provide location-based services for devices running their OS versions 1.1.3–3.1; however, beginning with OS version of 3.2 for their devices, it switched to their own Apple databases to provide location-based services and for diagnostic purposes. These databases must be updated continuously to account for changes in the physical and digital landscapes.

Apple maintains their devices are not being targeted for their location. Rather, they are maintaining a database of Wi-Fi hot spots and cell towers around their current location—some of which may be located more than 100 miles away—to assist their devices rapidly and accurately calculate on their location when requested. Apple states that it is not storing device location data but a subset (cache) or the crowd-sourced Wi-Fi hot spot and cell tower database that are downloaded from Apple to their devices. The Android operating system offers more granular controls and permissions for how the devices behaves than does Apple's devices; BlackBerry devices also offer options for users to block certain types of A5s entirely.

The Apple End User Software License Agreements (SLAs) for products that provide location-based services, last updated in 2009, states the following:

> Apple and its partners and licensees may provide certain services through your iPhone that rely upon location information. To provide these services, where available, Apple and its partners and licensees may transmit, collect, maintain, process and use your location data, including the real-time geographic location of your iPhone, and location search queries. The location data collected by Apple is collected in a form that does not personally identify you and may be used by Apple and its partners and licensees to provide location-based products and services. **By using any location-based services on your iPhone, you agree and consent to Apple's and its partners' and licensees' transmission, collection, maintenance, processing and use of your location data to provide such products and services.** You may withdraw this consent at any time by not using the location-based features or by turning off the Location Service setting on your iPhone. Not using these location features will not impact the non location-based functionality

of your iPhone. When using third party applications or services on the iPhone that use or provide location data, you are subject to and should review such third party's terms and privacy policy on use of location data by such third party applications or services.

Similar provisions regarding location-based information appeared on all other Apple devices, including their iPhone 4, iPad, iPod Touch, Mac OS X, and Safari 5 SLAs. Apple revised their SLA in 2007 to update customers about the necessary exchange of information between its servers and their devices. In 2008, the SLA was updated to include the use of "pixel tags" by Apple at its website (iTunes). Pixel tags, also known as "beacons" or "bugs," are tiny graphic images used to determine what parts of a site a visitor navigates to (they are silent tracking tags used to measure the activities and behaviors of online visitors).

Apple began to provide location-based services in 2008, enabling A5s to track and allow devices to perform a wide variety of tasks, such as getting directions to a particular physical address from their current location as well as locating their friends' devices and letting them know where they are or identifying nearby restaurants or stores and other social media functions.

In 2010, Apple updated its SLA yet again to incorporate its location-based services to all of its digital devices. It updated the policy to incorporate the provision regarding new Apple services, such as MobileMe "Find My iPhone" features and their new iAd network. Most of the revisions dealt with how the company may use cookies and preserve and protect the information of children and international customers.

Important to M3 marketers and A5 developers is that the information about nearby cell towers and Wi-Fi access points are collected and sent to Apple, Google, Skyhook, and other location-based service providers when a device requests current location information and gets automatically updates to a database with known location information. To provide location-based services, Apple, Google, and Skyhook must be able to determine quickly and precisely where a device is located.

To do this, all three must maintain secured databases containing information regarding known locations of cell towers and Wi-Fi access points. They each store this information in their proprietary databases accessible only by them and yet do not reveal personal information about individuals. Information about nearby cell towers and Wi-Fi access points is collected and sent to Apple, Google, and Skyhook with GPS coordinates of devices, and if available (1) when a individual requests current location information and (2) automatically, in some cases, to update and maintain databases with known location information. In both cases, devices collect the anonymous information about cell towers and Wi-Fi access points.

All three collect information about nearby cell towers, such as the location of the tower(s), Cell IDs, and data about the strength of the signal transmitted from the towers. A Cell ID refers to the unique number assigned by a cellular provider to a cell, in this case a defined geographic area covered by a cell tower in a mobile network. Cell IDs do not provide any personal information about mobile device users located in the cell.

Apple, Google, and Skyhook also collect information about nearby Wi-Fi access points, such as their location and Media Access Control (MAC) addresses, and data about their strength and speed of the signal transmitted by the access point(s). A MAC address is a unique number assigned by a manufacturer to a network adapter or network interface card (NIC) of a device. The address provides the means by which a device is able to connect to the Internet. MAC addresses do not provide any personal information about the owner of the NIC. All three do not collect the user-assigned name of the Wi-Fi access point, also known as the Service Set Identifier (SSID), or data being transmitted over the Wi-Fi network, also known as the "payload data."

Because Apple began to provide location-based services in 2008, it handles customer requests for current location differently. The device's GPS coordinates when available are encrypted and transmitted over a secured Wi-Fi Internet connection to Apple; for devices running their OS version 3.2 or iOS4, Apple will then retrieve known locations for nearby cell towers and Wi-Fi access points from its own proprietary database and transmit the information back to the device.

However, for requests transmitted from devices running prior versions of the iPhone OS, Apple transmits—anonymously—the Cell Tower Information to Google and Wi-Fi Access Point Information to Skyhook. These providers return to Apple known locations of nearby cell towers and Wi-Fi access points, which then transmits the coordinates back to the device. The device uses the information, along with GPS coordinates, if available, to determine its actual location.

Apple automatically collects this information only if the device's location-based service capabilities are turned to "On" and the customer uses an application requiring location-based information. If both conditions are met, the device intermittently and anonymously collects Cell Tower and Wi-Fi Access Point Information from the cell towers and Wi-Fi access points that it can "see" along with the device's GPS coordinates, if available. This information is batched and then encrypted and transmitted to Apple over a Wi-Fi Internet connection every 12 h, or later if the device does not have Wi-Fi Internet access at that time.

You Are Where You Will Be

Of course, all of this triangulation of devices via location-based services is rooted on the prevalence of millions of mobile devices worldwide; it offers yet another new channel for M3 marketers and A5s to reach consumers via streaming search and social messages. The accuracy of behavioral analytics for M3 marketing can be enhanced by the merging of offline, online, and social data and its modeling via AI tools, technologies, and techniques for clustering and segmenting the behaviors of devices.

The increasing prominence of social networks as the means to communicate and share information among devices and their friends provides many ways to identify, target, and reach new growth revenues and to segment new potential customers by M3 marketers. The trick to M3 and A5 is not only to track and target device behaviors but also to model them and react to them the instant they occur in a relevant and intelligent manner. In addition, by modeling device behaviors, M3 marketers can begin to anticipate their future actions and preferences for certain products and services.

However, to accomplish this, difficult diagnostics need to be performed by Apple and Google, the two dominant players in this area. To evaluate and improve the performance of devices and their operating systems, both Apple and Google collect diagnostic information from randomly selected devices and analyze the collected information. For example, when an Apple device makes a call, Apple may determine the device's approximate location at the beginning and the end of the call to analyze whether a problem such as dropped calls is occurring on other devices in the same area. Google devices also collect location every few seconds and transmit that data to company servers at least several times an hour.

The Apple and Android devices are also equipped with GPS chips. A GPS chip attempts to determine a device's location by analyzing how long it takes for satellite signals to reach the device. Through this analysis, the GPS chip can identify the device's latitude and longitude coordinates; altitude, speed, and direction of travel; and the current date and time where the device is located. For example, Apple collects GPS Information to analyze traffic patterns and density in various areas. The collected GPS Information is batched on the device, encrypted, and transmitted to Apple over a secured Wi-Fi Internet connection every 12 h with a random identification number that is generated by the device every 24 h. The GPS Information cannot be associated with a particular customer or device.

So why are Apple and Google so interested in providing location-based services, in a word: advertising. Google purchased mobile-advertising provider AdMob in 2009 for $750 million. On 2010, Apple launched their iAd mobile advertising network for their devices running iOS4. The iAd network offers a dynamic way to incorporate and access advertising within A5s. Devices can receive advertising that relates to their interests, also known as interest-based marketing and/or their location, via location-based marketing. For example, a device that purchased a sci-fi movie on iTunes may receive an ad regarding a new movie of the same genre. While a device searching for a Mexican restaurant may receive an ad for such eateries in its proximity.

Apple collects information about the device's location (latitude and longitude coordinates) when an ad request is made, for say that Mexican restaurant. This information is transmitted securely to the Apple iAd server via a cellular network connection or Wi-Fi Internet connection. The latitude/longitude coordinates are converted immediately by the server to a five-digit zip code. Apple does not record or store the coordinates. Apple stores only the zip code. Apple then uses the zip code to select a relevant Mexican restaurant ad for that device.

Apple does not share any interest-based or location-based information from their devices, including the zip code calculated by the iAd server with advertisers. Apple retains a record of each ad sent to a particular device in a separate iAd database, accessible only by Apple, to ensure that customers do not receive overly repetitive and/or duplicate ads and for their own administrative purposes and network regulations.

If you use location-enabled products and services, such as Google Maps via a mobile device, Google will know the device's location, such as GPS Information. Google and Apple are racing to build massive databases capable of pinpointing devices' locations. These databases will allow them to tap into the $2.9 billion market for location-based services—an advertising sector expected to rise to $8.3 billion in 2014, according to research firm Gartner.

In 2008, Apple launched the App Store where devices may shop and acquire A5s offered by third-party developer for Apple devices. Currently, the App Store includes more than 200,000 third-party applications covering a wide variety of areas including news, games, music, travel, price comparison, coupons, health, fitness, education, business, sports, navigation, and social networking. Each application includes a description prepared by the developer regarding, among other things, what the application does, when it was posted, and, if applicable, what information the application may collect from the device.

Third-party application developers must register as an "Apple Developer" by paying a fee and signing the Apple Developer Agreement and the Program License Agreement (PLA).

Registered Apple Developers gain access to the Apple SDK and other technical resources necessary to develop applications for mobile devices. The current PLA contains several provisions governing the collection and use of location-based information, including the following:

- Developers may collect, use, or disclose to a third-party location-based information only with the customer's prior consent and to provide a service or function that is directly relevant to the use of the application.
- Developers must provide information to their customers regarding the use and disclosure of location-based information.
- Developers must take appropriate steps to protect customers' location-based information from unauthorized use or access.
- Developers must comply with applicable privacy and data collection laws and regulations regarding the use of transmission of location-based information.
- Applications must notify and obtain consent from each customer before location data are collected, transmitted, or otherwise used by developers.
- Applications must not disable, override, or otherwise interfere with Apple-implemented alerts, including those intended to notify the customer that location-based information is being collected, transmitted, maintained, processed, or used, or intended to obtain consent for such use.

Developers who do not agree to these provisions may not offer application on the App Store. Apple has the right to terminate the PLA if a developer fails to comply with any of these provisions. Apple reviews all applications before adding them to the App Store to ensure they run properly and do not contain malicious code. Apple, however, does not monitor applications after they are listed in the App Store, unless issues of problems arise.

The Google Android privacy policy applies to all of the products, services, and websites offered by Google Inc. The following lists all the information Google collects and how they use it:

■ *Information you provide*: When you sign up for a Google Account, we ask you for personal information. We may combine the information you submit under your account with information from other Google services or third parties in order to provide you with a better experience and to improve the quality of our services. For certain services, we may give you the opportunity to opt out of combining such information. You can use the Google Dashboard to learn more about the information associated with your Account. If you are using Google services in conjunction with your Google Apps Account, Google provides such services in conjunction with or on behalf of your domain administrator. Your administrator will have access to your account information including your e-mail. Consult your domain administrator's privacy policy for more information.

■ *Cookies*: When you visit Google, we send one or more cookies to your computer or other device. We use cookies to improve the quality of our service, including for storing user preferences, improving search results and ad selection, and tracking user trends, such as how people search. Google also uses cookies in its advertising services to help advertisers and publishers serve and manage ads across the web and on Google services.

■ *Log information*: When you access Google services via a browser, application or other client our servers automatically record certain information. These server logs may include information such as your web request, your interaction with a service, Internet Protocol address, browser type, browser language, the date and time of your request, and one or more cookies that may uniquely identify your browser or your account.

■ *User communications*: When you send e-mail or other communications to Google, we may retain those communications in order to process your inquiries, respond to your requests, and improve our services. When you send and receive SMS messages to or from one of our services that provides SMS functionality, we may collect and maintain information associated with those messages, such as the phone number, the wireless carrier associated with the phone number, the content of the message, and the date and time of the transaction. We may use your e-mail address to communicate with you about our services.

- *Affiliated Google services on other sites*: We offer some of our services on or through other websites. Personal information that you provide to those sites may be sent to Google in order to deliver the service. We process such information under this Privacy Policy.
- *Third-party applications*: Google may make available third-party applications, such as gadgets or extensions, through its services. The information collected by Google when you enable a third-party application is processed under this Privacy Policy. Information collected by the third-party application provider is governed by their privacy policies.
- *Location data*: Google offers location-enabled services, such as Google Maps and Latitude. If you use those services, Google may receive information about your actual location (such as GPS signals sent by a mobile device) or information that can be used to approximate a location (such as a cell ID).
- *Unique application number*: Certain services, such as Google Toolbar, include a unique application number that is not associated with your account or you. This number and information about your installation (e.g., operating system type and version number) may be sent to Google when you install or uninstall that service or when that service periodically contacts our servers (e.g., to request automatic updates to the software).
- *Other sites*: This Privacy Policy applies to Google services only. We do not exercise control over the sites displayed as search results, sites that include Google applications, products or services, or links from within our various services. These other sites may place their own cookies or other files on your computer, collect data, or solicit personal information from you.

Google goes on to state that it only shares personal information with other companies or individuals outside of Google in the following limited circumstances:

- We have your consent. We require opt-in consent for the sharing of any sensitive personal information.
- We provide such information to our subsidiaries, affiliated companies or other trusted businesses, or persons for the purpose of processing personal information on our behalf. We require that these parties agree to process such information based on our instructions and in compliance with this Privacy Policy and any other appropriate confidentiality and security measures.
- We have a good faith belief that access, use, preservation, or disclosure of such information is reasonably necessary to (1) satisfy any applicable law, regulation, legal process, or enforceable governmental request; (2) enforce applicable Terms of Service, including investigation of potential violations thereof; (3) detect, prevent, or otherwise address fraud, security, or technical issues; or (4) protect against harm to the rights, property, or safety of Google, its users, or the public as required or permitted by law.

The Apple iOS4 mobile operating system, found on their devices, keeps a log of user's location and saves that data to a hidden file on the device. The devices regularly record the position of the device and saving them in a hidden file. The location data are stored to a file called "consolidated.db," which includes latitude and longitude coordinates and a time stamp.

The location in the consolidated.db file is determined by cell-tower triangulation. That location-based data generally can be tied to a city or a zip code. The rise of mobile devices allows for the collection of data that are triangulated and very precise for specific locations. Apple has filled multiple patent applications that refer to this location-based technology.

A host of companies have built mobile-device applications centered on the "check-in" concept, including Foursquare and the gaming firm of Booyah both of which are based on the social targeting of local businesses via mobile devices. Eight million users turn to Foursquare to check out local restaurants or stores and share their activities with their social network, earning badges and points along the way. The users of Booyah's popular MyTown can also check in almost anywhere usually, so they can tell friends where to gather. Both location-based services support the placement of local ads.

Local businesses can attract new customers or reward their most loyal ones by offering them Foursquare "specials" in the form of coupons, prizes, or discounts, which are presented to users when they check-in to this service via their devices. Foursquare specials create extra enticement to get customers to stop by, such as a 20% discount off a meal or a free dessert, or even a reserved parking spot for their most loyal customers.

Foursquare specials can be tailored to fit the needs of specific types of businesses and merchants, whether it is a unique discount for first-time customers or rewards for their 10th visit. In addition to driving business through Foursquare specials, they can also sign up for their free "Merchant Platform," which allows businesses to access their own "Venue Stats" dashboard, allowing them to track their customer foot traffic over time.

These location-based networks let users and their friends get together when they are in the same locality. These social and location networks also let local merchants entice users with time-sensitive ads, deals, discounts, and coupons. As we have seen with the wildly successful location-based coupon networks like Groupon, Living Social, Tippr, Bloomspot, Scoutmob, and BuyWithMe, they can provide local deals to users in their specific city or zip code. M3 marketers need to leverage these services that combine social networks, mobile apps, and the location of users for A5 to local businesses.

A5 via triangulated devices is really about conversations—interactive dialogs—and not just about targeted messages. Social media create rich, relevant customer experiences that can organically grow and strategically change to fit the interests, lifestyles, needs of consumers, and their friends. Social networks cut through the message clutter to capture the attention of influencers and provides opportunities for M3 marketers to achieve their clients' goals through WOM with the help from their brand's champions.

No matter how diligently an M3 marketer works to create a brand; in the end, it is defined by the consumer's perspective. In the open channels of social networking, friends' conversations are self-propelling, free to express their ideas, concerns, and preferences. An M3 marketer's challenge is to hear what is being said about their brand via stationary and mobile devices; the marketer needs to quantify this buzz. What is being said and how often are the metrics of social media marketing by WOM. It is about measuring M2M communications, that is, what one device is saying to other devices about a merchant or a brand.

Today, M3 marketers have access to consumers' preferences, their location, and their behaviors and personality, enabling the presentation of relevant content, ads, products, and services. Leveraging the communication and influence power of social networks via A5s is an important new channel to be developed and utilized for marketing to mobile devices. The increasing prominence of social networks—7 out of the top 10 websites today are social—and hence amenable to M3 marketing via their friend's devices and via targeted influencers of brands of products and services.

Data Mining Devices

For years, the devices have been getting smarter as their internal processors and software tell them what to do on the basis of human provided parameters or rules. M2M is a protocol for devices to talk to servers. As previously mentioned, when devices "talk," they do so in a language known as "telemetry." The concept of telemetry (remote devices and sensors collecting and sending data to central servers for analysis, either by humans or by machines) is not new. But an emerging concept is taking that idea to a new level of sophistication by applying machine-learning rules coupled with networking technologies to define M2M parameters based on data mining models.

Three technologies are converging: wireless sensors, the Internet, and digital devices all are coming together to create autonomous M2M for M3 via A5s. This new concept holds great promise in promoting telemetry's use by business, government, and private individuals and it is at the core of what this book is about. M2M communications and M3 marketing using data mining technologies offer increased sensitivity and accuracy. Powerful servers and data mining software work at lightning speeds and the explosive growth of prevalent wireless networks has opened M2M communications to many sectors, including M3.

For example, in manufacturing, malfunctions in production lines can generate alerts. In cyber security, M2M can monitor patterns of traffic to signal potential attacks. In medicine, implanted devices with chips can monitor wear and tear in order to issue alerts to surgeons of possible breakdowns of hip or knee replacements.

Telemedicine offers another use of M2M, for instance, some heart patients wear special monitors that gather information about the way their heart is working. The data are sent to implanted devices that deliver a shock to correct an errant heart rhythm. In retailing, vending machines with special sensor chips can issue alerts to distributors about resupplies needed.

In the area of forensics, M2M can be used to detect potential fraudulent activity by monitoring anomaly patterns of device behaviors. On the web, cookies, beacons, geolocation, and other Internet mechanisms can be used for behavioral targeting via M2M. Last, as we have seen, GPS and Wi-Fi triangulation and mobile apps can be used to market to mobile devices via M3 and A5s. The clustering and anticipating the behaviors of devices is the key to leveraging M2M modeling, technologies, and techniques.

The momentum in marketing technology is clearly now with devices that can be carried around and the A5s that sustain them. Apple expanded this mobility with its iPad touch screen tablet, which combined a sleek device with high-resolution display, coupled with audio and video content from its iTunes store. Most importantly for the M3 marketer, the cheap sometimes silly little gaming programs, barcode scanners, and photo manipulators have turned mobile devices into great data aggregators for triangulating device behaviors, preferences, and locations via A5s.

A5s have grown from time killers into an ecosystem for keeping consumers amused, informed, and, most importantly, loyal to brands, networks, and their devices and the companies that service them. A5s, many of which are free or cheap, have spawned a new industry of developers, start-ups, and ad networks around mobile devices. Soon these A5s will go corporate as companies begin customizing them for assisting employees track sales, shipping, manufacturing, and other enterprises tasks. For the M3 marketers, these silly little location-based and interest-based A5s are a valuable source of consumer intelligence, revealing users' kicks, likes, and desires in an anonymous and ubiquitous manner.

Mobile devices are becoming powerful computers capable of experiencing streaming media, which provide exiting new opportunities for the M3 marketer, enabling them to mix and match the capabilities of the web and social media. While business users are more likely to use their mobile devices for e-mail and voice mail reporting, personal users are more likely to use their devices to play games, surf and shop on the web, take pictures, and play streaming audio and video, thus susceptible to be enticed by discounts or freebies a few feet away.

To address this consumer demand, device manufacturers are integrating advance operating systems that can manage and handle a variety of communication, information, and entertainment applications that go beyond the user experience offered by the Wireless Application Protocol (WAP); for this reason, M3 marketers need to leverage targeted multimedia application via video and mobile TV. As seen with the advent of apps, the triangulation of mobile devices for marketing is clearly the future of advertising, and in Chapter 2, we will learn about a new technology that will dynamically expand this to *all* devices: digital fingerprinting.

Marketers need to consider how to incorporate geo-targeting, profiling, time, and location variables in their propensity to purchase models. When creating their mobile websites, enterprises and M3 marketers should address presentation technologies that support multiple devices, networks, and operating systems. Consideration should also be given to incorporating temporal location-based and interest-based advertising and search and social marketing to better support and engage consumers anytime, anywhere.

For the M3 marketer, A5s will become indispensable tools for capturing important behavioral data for triangulation targeting. As we have seen, location-based services, while still in their infancy with companies like Groupon, Foursquare, Gowalla, and Loopt, as of yet attract only about 4% of U.S. consumers. But as consumer experience discounts, via coupons and other marketing offers, the market share for these location-based services will increase with an emphasis to attracting them to local businesses. The triangulation of consumers via the web, social networks, and mobile is a new form of M3 and A5s in which the consumer interacts with the ad.

Having the ability for consumers to engage with retailers and merchants encourages "situation shopping" in which they can mix and match clothes through a store-specific A5. This leads to clothing centric search features and the creation of a virtual closet, incorporating different colors and styles, where mobile shoppers can model different outfits or items via their mobile devices. Having this ability to engage shoppers via A5s in consumers' devices increases their browsing time, their loyalty, and, in the end, total sales and growth revenue.

Other retailer-specific A5s can be developed for different types of products, such as those for electronic goods shoppers, sport enthusiasts, do-it-yourself hardware consumers, auto enthusiasts, runners, gardeners, and golfers, the potential are endless. Retailers, merchants, and brands can incorporate store-specific A5s that can include scanning capabilities for price comparison abilities not only in their store but also across all retail sites on the web. Quick, short surveys can be incorporated to gather feedback from devices, enabling retailers to streamline and improve their offerings to them.

Mobile devices will soon become the future salesperson, allowing consumers to mix-and-match products by style and colors; it will allow them to barcode for price comparisons; and finally, it will enable them to purchase the product itself, so who needs store clerks when devices do it all. Already eBay, RedLaser, TheFind and Amazon's Price Check app enable consumers to perform on-the-fly barcode price comparisons while shopping in the mall; they all provide SDKs that can be incorporated by A5 marketers to enhance their own customized applications (Figure 1.18).

The tremendously popular eBay Mobile app is an example of this price comparison feature for mobile devices. Such transparent capabilities create enduring customer loyalty and ensure their engagement in the future. At that juncture, these store-specific apps are not just a one-stop destination but are in fact a *starting* point

Figure 1.18   eBay Go-Shopping A5 supports all major devices.

for search shopping, mixing-and-matching products, price comparison, and social sharing with friends via consumers' mobile devices. Furthermore, AT&T, Verizon, and T-Mobile have formed a joint venture with Discover Financial Services that will soon enable consumers to wave their devices in front of a scanner to pay for purchases at stores. A5s will soon complete the entire sale cycle—from browsing to actually purchasing all types of products and services—when devices become digital wallets.

Chapter 2

How

M3 via Machine Learning

Machine-to-machine marketing (M3) is made possible by the triangulation of web and wireless desires and preferences—modeled by machine-learning algorithms—and executed by anonymous advertising apps anywhere anytime (A5s). This can take place because data about device behaviors are everywhere, scattered across the web and wireless environments.

Machine learning is a branch of artificial intelligence; it is a discipline that allows machines to evolve predictions based on empirical digital information behaviors—from sensors, web, wireless data, or databases—or a combination of all. For example, an M3 marketer can take advantage of segmenting the key characteristics of device behaviors. Machine learning can discover the core features of device behaviors by automatically learning to recognize complex patterns and make intelligent decisions based on these data, such as what, when, where, and why certain devices have a propensity to make a purchase, while others do not.

M3 marketing is about the convergence of all of these online and mobile data from websites, social networks, and digital devices and the modeling of their behaviors via machine-learning software, enabling advertisers to monetize devices—for the targeted placement of products, content, or services via multiple channels—in a timely and personal manner. To accomplish this, M3 marketers must rely on the development and implementation of A5s—for the triangulation of historical and real-time behaviors of digital devices and their human owners. The strategy for M3 is to gather and model consumer data to make digital marketing more personal, relevant, and comprehensive.

This requires capturing, analyzing, and acting on device actions and reacting with precise counteractions, which are beneficial to their human owners. Leveraging from these behavioral analytics of devices involves the following steps:

1. Monetizing consumers via behavioral analytics for anonymous advertising anywhere to stationary and mobile devices
2. The use of cookies, web analytics, deep packet inspection (DPI), geolocation, and ad exchanges for behavioral targeting to online devices
3. The marketing via social media, Twitter, word of mouth (WOM), Facebook, and data harvesters for the social marketing to devices
4. The marketing via Wi-Fi triangulation, wireless cookies, mobile websites, and apps to mobile devices
5. Machine-learning the behaviors of any and all devices—via digital finger-printing—for anonymous advertising anywhere in the planet

M3 enables the positioning of the right product or service in front of the right device via precise messages on the web, e-mail, texts, mobile apps, etc. The success of M3 involves strategic planning and measured improvement of multiple, predictive, evolving models. As mentioned in Chapter 1, the modeling of wired and wireless device behaviors can be accomplished by the strategic use of inductive and deductive analytical software. Most important for M3 marketers is the use of decision trees and their proven class of techniques that include classification and regression trees (CART) and chi-squared automatic induction (CHAID) algorithms. Machine-learning software allows M3 marketers to perform device segmentation, classification, and prediction—these types of programs can generate graphical decision trees as well as predictive rules about classifying web and wireless device behaviors.

Decision trees are powerful behavioral analytics programs that use a tree-like graph of decisions and their possible consequences. Decision-tree programs provide a descriptive means for calculating conditional probabilities. Trained with historical data samples, these classification programs can be used to predict future device behaviors. They divide the records in a "training" data set into disjoint subsets, each of which is described by a simple rule on one or more data fields:

IF   Keyword "golf shirt"
AND   OS Android
AND   Geolocation Austin, TX
THEN   Offer GOLF Magazine app

A decision tree takes as input an objective, such as *sell a coupon*, described by a set of properties—historical device behaviors or conditions, such as *location*, *time of day*, and *operating system (OS)*—with the outputs being a binary prediction (*will buy vs. will not buy*) or a continuous value (*total expected coupon sales*). Some decision trees can also have multiple branches for the further segmentation of multiple predictions, such as what type of product or service to offer to what devices, when and where. When an M3 marketer needs to make a decision based on several consumer factors, such as their location, device being used, and total log-in time, a decision tree can help identify which factors to consider and how each factor has historically been associated with different outcomes of that decision—such as what products or services certain devices are likely to purchase based on observed behavioral patterns over time.

Modern classification decision-tree tools are highly intuitive; they have been around for a dozen years, their interfaces are easy to navigate and use, and their segmentation results (predictive rules) can readily be inspected for quick insight by M3 marketers and their clients. The value of these tools is that the graphs and rules can easily be understood and applied. For example, predicting if a device will make a purchase, a decision tree can examine multiple factors such as the number of site visits, type of payment, OS, products viewed, or the device's triangulated location.

Classification decision trees go through thousands of iterations in which independent attributes (location, time of day, etc.) representing device behaviors are measured in terms of their "information gain." For M3 marketers, they automate the identification of key device variables as they relate to sales, potential future revenue, and consumer loyalty. Almost always decision trees produce compact models to identify the most valuable attributes for predicting consumer behaviors with only a few conditional rules and are a form of "information compression" for M3 marketers.

One common advantage for M3 marketers is to use decision trees to eliminate a high number of noisy and ineffective consumer attributes for predicting say "high customer loyalty" or "likely to buy" models. To accomplish this, M3 marketers can start with hundreds of attributes from multiple data sources and through the use of decision trees; they can eliminate many of them in order to focus simply on those with the highest information gain as they pertain to predicting high loyalty or potential revenue growth from device features and behaviors (Figure 2.1).

Decision-tree building algorithms begin by trying to find the most important variable for splitting the data among the desired categories. At each succeeding level of the tree, the subsets created by the preceding split are also further split according to whatever rule works best for them. The tree continues to grow until it is no longer possible to find better ways to split up incoming records. At the start of the process, we have a training data set with a target field "total sales" also known as the dependent variable. The goal is to build a tree that will allow the M3 marketer to assign a class to the target field of new records based on the values of other fields, known as independent variables.

These classification predictive tools are both easy to use and understand as well as computationally inexpensive for predicting device behaviors. There is also

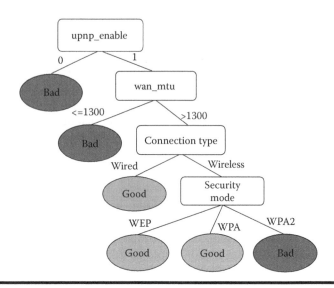

Figure 2.1 Decision tree "splitting" a data set into multiple categories.

software as a service (SaaS) from Zementis which offers an on-demand predictive analytics decision engine hosted on the Amazon Elastic Compute Cloud (EC2), based on a service-oriented architecture (SOA) and open standards for model exchange. A framework for accomplishing and leveraging these predictive models should be flexible and ongoing as conditions change. All of these software products will be identified in detail in Chapter 3 to follow about M3 checklists.

M3 marketers can also enlist both deductive and inductive "streaming analytical" software which are "event-driven" to link, monitor, and analyze device behaviors. These relatively new streaming analytical software products react to "device events" in real time. There are two main types of streaming analytical products. First, there are *deductive* streaming programs which operate by user-defined business rules and are used to monitor multiple streams of data—reacting to device events as they take place. For example, when an online form is completed, a device enters a Wi-Fi location, an e-mail is received, and/or a text is sent, triggering a marketing counteraction, such as an offer, a discount, an alert, or an invitation, based on business rules created by a marketer or an enterprise.

Secondly, there are *inductive* streaming software products which use predictive rules derived from the data itself via clustering and decision-tree algorithms. These inductive streaming products build their rules from global models involving the segmentation and analysis from multiple and distributed data clouds and networks of device behaviors. These deductive and inductive software products can work with different data formats, from different locations to make real-time predictions using multiple models from massive digital data streams.

These types of streaming analytic software products support the processes of analyzing an assortment of behaviors, location, interests, demographics, lifestyle, geo spatial, operational, etc., and other information for the personalization of offers to devices at various touch points on any channel. In this new M3 model, real-time streaming becomes a continuing and iterative process in which marketing decisions and actions are incessantly refined and perfected over time.

Everything can be measured in terms of revenue, loyalty, relevancy, satisfaction, speed, and performance. Every single metric resides in some digital format amenable to refinement and improvement. The strategic problem for the M3 marketer is mapping it into a framework of predictive models for testing and gradually perfecting them into action and measuring the revenue they generate for their marketing efforts. In the end, M3 is about delivering targeted and relevant content and offers—for customer retention and loyalty—up-selling and cross-selling and customer lifetime value calibration.

Both deductive and inductive streaming analytic systems are "event-driven" in that they respond to device interactions as they occur—reducing or eliminating the decay of data over time. Reacting at the time consumer "events" take place enables M3 marketers to make the right offer to the right device in real time with no latency, allowing them to take the opportunity to leverage behavioral analytics to a new level of customer service and relevance.

M3 marketing involves tracking and measuring all of these consumer events on the web, social networks, and mobile environments. The advantage to digital marketers is that behavioral analytics support the quantitative ability to measure success and failure on a rapid, continuous, and flexible manner in near-real time. Key indicators of revenue and loyalty flows can now be easily tracked, validated, and leveraged; ontologies can be created from structured and unstructured content for categorizing consumer groupings. Not only can device behaviors be captured instantly as events take place, but the resulting offers of products, services, or content can also be measured and adjusted for optimization.

A triangulation analytics strategy should be designed with the objective of understanding who the consumer is and what their device needs are. The strategy should strive to seek more relevant and targeted offers which are of higher value to the consumer. This can start by performing a simple segmentation analysis of profitable versus unprofitable devices—do this to discover the core features of both groups and to prioritize those predictive device attributes which are most important.

It is important that this partitioning of behaviors be based on analyses tested and measured in terms of total sales or other metrics, which the M3 marketer determines are of most valuable for sustained growth and revenue. The advantages of static and streaming behavioral analytics for M3 marketing are many; here are just a few:

■ Leverage dormant data assets into new untapped streams of sales and profitability
■ Leverage current IT investments and infrastructure "as is" for new untapped value
■ Achieve a global view of all data assets for a new level of insight and efficiency

- Tap into existing data assets despite their location, structure, or format
- Perform up-selling and cross-selling of multiple products and services
- Reduce uncertainty, predict with precision, and optimize performance
- Gain insight, find, model, and monetize device behavioral patterns
- Perform microsegmentation from large customer data sources
- Provide consumer personalization while preserving privacy
- Leverage all daily transactions into predictive profit models
- Achieve higher profits via improved consumer marketing
- Rate all customers' lifetime values from cradle to grave
- Improve efficiency at every level of operations
- Spot new growth opportunities and markets
- Increase customer satisfaction and loyalty
- Perform customer attrition management

M3 marketing and behavioral analytics enable the discovery of device preferences and needs directly from their behaviors and purchases. These cyclical feed-forward interactions can provide vital business intelligence which traditional marketing techniques cannot match in both accuracy and speed. Today, companies can subscribe or construct their own behavioral analytical systems in the support of M3 marketing—enabling them to process device events as they happen, in order to respond appropriately—much like the neighborhood merchant of yesteryears who remembered their customers' tastes and took pains to please them in order to retain them for life.

M3 marketing means focusing on device choices, which leads to actionable insight and action, consequently leading to the monetization of their behaviors. The use of modeling tools enables M3 marketers to calibrate how devices behave and how they can profit and respond with real-time relevancy. In M3, the most important issue is the location, aggregation, and use of the right data with the correlating consumer needs and preferences.

Companies do not want to offer consumers products or services they do not want or content that is not relevant to them; this is not only wasteful but also intrusive. Instead, M3 marketers using behavior models provide the right product to the right consumer at the right time and place—by modeling device behaviors—but care must be taken to protect consumers' privacy and security. Device behaviors are the most valuable assets marketers and their clients have, and they need to protect them and not share them with others.

Autonomously Clustering Device Behaviors

Clustering detection is the creation of models that find device behaviors that are similar to each other; these clumps of similarity can be discovered by the use of self-organizing software to find previously unknown patterns in data sets.

Unlike decision trees discussed in the prior section, there is no targeted variable in clustering and it is about autonomous knowledge discovery. The clustering software is simply let loose on the data with the objective of discovering some meaningful hidden structures, patterns, and behaviors.

The autonomous clustering of words from e-mails, instant messages, chats, texts, tweets, and other information from devices can be used for the creation of matrices of words along key consumer categories. This type of clustering can be done automatically by software known as *unsupervised learning*—that is, the analysis organizes by itself along key words or consumer device groups—it is a useful first step for the M3 marketer. It allows for the mapping of behaviors of devices or words to organize themselves into distinct clusters of groups without any human bias.

What distinguishes clustering from classification which we discussed in the prior section is that the analysis does not rely on predefined classes, buyers versus nonbuyers. The data sets are grouped together on the basis of self-similarity or unique features. Clustering is often performed as a prelude to some other form of data mining or modeling.

One common use for undirected knowledge discovery is market basket analysis that seeks to answer "what items sell together" or "why do some devices behave the same way?" Once the data have been broken into segments by the software, the M3 marketer can begin the process of discovering interesting device behavior patterns in various subgroups. These are some of the steps for implementing clustering analyses:

1. Identify the device behavior of most interest.
2. Compose a clustering model.
3. Evaluate the significant finding of the model.
4. Apply the model to new data.
5. Use decision tree to further discover the features of the clusters.

Undirected knowledge discovery is a good initial step to take by M3 marketers to generate ideas that can be verified by supervised learning methods. A market basket analysis can lead to questions about why certain products sell at the same time, or who is buying particular combination of products or services, and when the purchases tend to be made.

This type of undirected, unsupervised type of knowledge discovery is best performed using neural network Self-Organizing Maps (SOM) software. Viscovery SOMine, one of SOM programs, is software for explorative data mining, visual cluster analysis, statistical profiling, segmentation, and classifications. This kind of software can be used to perform "market basket analyses"—that is, to discover who buys what, when, and where—based on the behavior of devices.

As a clustering technique, market basket analysis is useful in situations where the M3 marketer wants to know what items or device behaviors occur together or in a particular sequence or pattern. The results are informative and actionable because they can lead to the organization of offers, coupons, discounts, and the offering of new products or services that, prior to the analysis, were unknown. Clustering analyses can lead to answers to such questions as *why* do products or services sell together (or *who* is buying what combinations of products or services); they can also map *what* purchases are made and *when*.

Unsupervised knowledge clustering is when one cluster is compared to another and new knowledge is discovered as to why. For example, SOM software can be used to discover clusters of e-mails, website visitors, and wireless devices enabling a marketer to discover unique features of different consumer groups. These types of clustering analyzes can involve both the autonomous grouping of device behaviors and unstructured content: words.

There is also a different variation of clustering programs, known as text mining software which can be used to sort through *unstructured content* that can be found in millions of documents, notes, e-mails, chats, web forms, voicemails, texts, news stories, regulatory filings, repair records, field representative notes, invoices, blogs, etc., that daily accumulate 24/7 in websites and servers. Text analytics generally includes such tasks as the categorization of taxonomies, the clustering of concepts, entity and information extraction (IE), sentiment analysis, and summarization, as well as the autonomous creation of ontologies.

Why is text analytics important to M3 marketers? It is because companies, networks, websites, enterprises, and social sites are increasingly accumulating a large percentage of their data in unstructured formats, which requires deep analysis of patents, blogs, reports, e-mails, surveys, documents, orders, and other text-based content which is impossible to be performed manually. Text mining refers to the process of deriving an understanding from unstructured content through the division of clustering patterns and trends.

Text mining usually involves the process of structuring the input text—usually parsing, along with the addition of some derived linguistic features and the removal of others, and subsequent insertion into a structured format such as a database—and deriving these clusters and patterns for evaluation and interpretation of their output. Text mining usually refers to some combination of relevance, novelty, and interestingness. Typical text mining tasks include the categorization and clustering of unstructured content and concept—with the final products being some sort of granular taxonomies, sentiment analysis, document summarization, and entity relation modeling.

Text analytics provides an automated solution to organizing key concepts from unstructured content, in order to discover previously unknown patterns and concepts. The information might contain hidden relationships or patterns that are buried in this unstructured content. Text analytics can use information retrieval (IR) and/or IE as well as natural language processing (NLP) techniques to organize and prioritize documents, e-mails, texts, etc., about any subject.

IR is the area of study concerned with searching for documents, for information within documents, and for metadata about documents, for searching databases and the Internet. IE is a subset of IR whose goal is to automatically extract structured information from unstructured and/or semistructured machine-readable documents. In most of the cases, this activity concerns processing human language texts by means of NLP. Recent activities in multimedia document processing like automatic annotation and concept extraction out of images, audio, or video can be seen as an example of IE.

These text analytics techniques can be used individually or combined by M3 marketers to gain new insight into unstructured content from multiple data sources, such as a social network of sites. Text analytical tools can convert unstructured content and parse it over to a structure format which is amenable to behavioral analytics via clustering and classification software. For example, all of the daily e-mails that a website accumulates on a daily basis can be organized into several piles of groupings, such as those online devices seeking information, service assistance, or those complaining about specific products or services (Figure 2.2).

Text analytics systems allow M3 marketers to narrow down the set of documents, e-mails, texts, social media, or other device-generated content—such as autonomously organizing them into multiple categories, such as "like" versus "do not like." They can automatically extract structured data from unstructured content of device behaviors. Often this involves the parsing of the unstructured content into one or more structured templates so that subsequent analyses can be performed, by decision tree and other classification types of software for constructing predictive models for M3 marketing.

Text analytics involves applying computationally intensive algorithms to large collections of unstructured content and can speed up the analysis considerably by reducing the number of documents for M3 marketers to focus on. Text mining software can convert unstructured content into a more formal format that is easier for subsequent behavioral analysis (Figure 2.3).

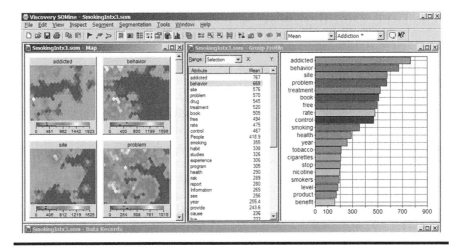

Figure 2.2   Clustering of text using an SOM neural network tool.

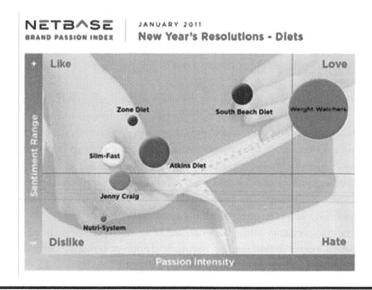

Figure 2.3 Text analytics can discover brand passions.

Aside from organizing key concepts, consumers can also be clustered by text analytics into key segments—along service and product lines. For example, device visitors to social sites can be group into those that are interested in sports, financials, music, or other topical categories. Text analytics can also discover for the M3 marketers key metrics and combine them into an intuitive visualization about brand buzz, brand sentiment, and passion intensity.

Real-Time Demographic Networks

M3 marketers often want to target their content and message about specific products and services to devices with certain demographic attributes. One possible strategy is to infer this demographic information, such as gender, age, or marital status about owners of digital devices who use the web, social media, and mobile for whom demographic information is not otherwise available. Device behaviors though largely anonymous, they nonetheless provide a certain amount of *usage information*. This usage information includes, but is not limited to, search terms entered by the web, social media, or mobile users and web pages accessed by their devices.

One approach in constructing a real-time demographic network is to collect some input data for the modeling activity via online surveys and other tracking web and wireless mechanisms. Though web and wireless users are largely anonymous, they nonetheless provide a certain amount of usage information. Usage information includes, but is not limited to, search terms entered by device users and web pages or mobile locations accessed by consumers. Once collected, some of this usage information can be used to construct predictive models. The following table contains some of the demographic variables and usage information for modeling by M3 marketers:

Variable	Value
Gender	Male, female
Age 18	True, false
Age 18–34	True, false
Age 35–54	True, false
Age 55+	True, false
Marital status	Single, married

There are also commercial real-time demographic networks, such as Acxiom Relevance-X® which can provide demographics and lifestyle consumer information in real time for association to digital devices—which M3 marketers can subscribe to—in order to enhance their relevance and sales. In this new M3 marketing paradigm, data collection, integration, and analysis are a seamless stream of activities taking place over a "reactive network" for customized targeted offers, incentives, and ads—based on what is known about web, social media, and mobile device behaviors.

A related product is Acxiom Relevance-X Social which offers consumer data intelligence for social marketing; the subscription service provides M3 marketers with a practical, data-driven, and measured approach to social marketing. Marketers get the ability to measure the effectiveness of campaigns on large-scale and individual levels. Acxiom Relevance-X Social helps marketers see the social networks of devices and how many friends or contacts they may have within online communities. It's available for individual campaigns or as an ongoing service. With Acxiom Relevance-X Social data, M3 marketers can

■ Invite device influencers in an engaging way to drive purchase behavior
■ Establish up-to-date social intelligence on their customers and devices
■ Test new products or services on multichannels to all digital devices
■ Plan media where customers and their devices are socially active
■ Interact with socially active brand advocates and their devices
■ Develop loyalty programs to reward device segments
■ Create campaigns that solicit user-generated content (UGC)
■ Identify devices that demonstrate brand enthusiasm

Acxiom works with many of the world's leading companies, including

- 12 of the top 15 credit card issuers
- 7 of the top 10 retail banks
- 8 of the top 10 telecom/media companies
- 7 of the top 10 retailers
- 11 of the top 14 automotive manufacturers
- 6 of the top 10 brokerage firms
- 3 of the top 10 pharmaceutical manufacturers
- 5 of the top 10 life/health insurance providers
- 9 of the top 10 property and casualty insurers
- 8 of the top 10 lodging companies
- 2 of the top 3 gaming companies

Geolocation Triangulation Networks

Geolocation via triangulation can assist M3 marketers in knowing where revenue producing devices are coming from, which may impact how and what ads and offers to make. Geolocation can provide meaningful location, such as a street address or zip code, rather than just a set of geographic coordinates. Specifically this involves the use of advanced radio frequency (RF) location systems utilizing, for example, time difference of arrival (TDOA)—also known as *hyperbolic positioning*, which is the process of locating an object by accurately computing the TDOA of a signal emitted from that stationary or mobile device to three or more receivers—this triangulation offers great specificity of device location to M3 marketers.

TDOA systems often utilize mapping displays or other graphical information system. In addition, Internet and mobile device geolocation can be performed by associating a geographic location with their Internet Protocol (IP) address and a media access control (MAC) address which are assigned by device manufacturers of network interface cards (NIC) that are stored in device hardware—the card's read-only memory, or some other firmware mechanism. If assigned by the manufacturer, a MAC address usually encodes the manufacturer's registered identification number and may be referred to as the *burned-in address*.

Whether a MAC address, or RF identification (RFID) which is a technology that uses communication through the use of radio waves to exchange data between a reader and an electronic tag attached to a device for the purpose of identification and tracking it. RFID hardware is an embedded device number, embedded into such software number as a universally unique identifier (UUID), exchangeable image file format (Exif) as those found in digital cameras, or a Wi-Fi connection location, or the digital device's Global Positioning System (GPS) coordinates.

However, new technologies and techniques are replacing geolocation processes that looked up an IP address on a WHOIS service and retrieving the registrant's physical address. New geolocation vendors today offer more than IP address geolocation data that they have expanded to include information such as country, region, city, postal/zip code, latitude, longitude, and time zone.

These deeper commercial data sets can determine other parameters such as domain name, a device connection speed, ISP, language, proxies, company name, and in the United States the Designated Market Area (DMA), the Metropolitan Statistical Area (MSA), and the North American Industry Classification System (NAICS) codes. Some of these geolocation service providers include Quova, Digital Envoy, GeoBytes, and MaxMind.

Quova is by far the largest geolocation service provider; their coverage is world-wide. For example, Comcast protects digitally broadcast intellectual property and customer investment by using Quova's geolocation data and services. Rooms To Go uses Quova's location data for putting users in touch with their nearest inventories. Rockyou.com is using Quova's geolocation data to locate website visitors and serve more interesting and appropriate ads. Major League Baseball is using Quova to protect local affiliates which facilitates distribution agreements.

Quova scans the Internet on an ongoing basis to determine geographic and network connection information about all assigned and allocated IP addresses on the Internet. They publish a database weekly that contains this information. Over the past decade, Quova has built a powerful and sophisticated research system for understanding and interpreting and mapping all the worldwide IP address data. Quova actively collects and analyzes data 24 h a day, 7 days a week.

Quova has data collectors all over the world that feed their proprietary database of IP address information, which is processed by both intelligent automated algorithms as well as experienced human analysts. Their analysts and algorithms work together, each indicating parts of the network the other should focus on as well as providing checks and balances that ensure quality and improve each other's output and processes.

Quova offers its GeoPoint service which provides geographic information for IP addresses including continent, country, region (United States only), time zone, state, city, postal code, longitude/latitude, and phone prefix (United States and Canada only). Quova also provides demographic identifiers for IP addresses within the United States including DMA codes (Nielsen DMAs) and network connection information, including connection type and speed.

Digital Envoy and their Digital Element service deliver *IP intelligence* and *geo-targeting* which is used by most of the world's largest ad networks and publishers for noninvasive IP intelligence for targeted advertising, content localization, geographic rights management, behavioral analytics, and local search. Geotargeting is the practice of customizing an advertisement for a product or service to a specific market based on the geographic location of potential buyers. Every country, province, state, county, or city in the world can constitute a niche market for certain products or services at certain times.

Digital Envoy collects only user's IP address—privacy-invasive techniques such as alien probes, cookies, and intrusive scripts are never used in their data collection methodology.

Feature	Country	Region	Metro Code	City	ISP	Organization	Netspeed	Domain Name
Countries	✓	✓	✓	✓				
US/CA Regions		✓	✓	✓				
Global Regions				✓				
US Area Codes				✓				
US Metro Codes			✓	✓				
Global Cities				✓				
US Zipcode*				✓				
Latitude/Longitude				✓				
ISP					✓			
Organization						✓		
Netspeed							✓	
Domain Name								✓
Site License	$50	$150	$220	$370	$15	$15	$370	$100
Monthly Fee for Updates	$12	$36	$53	$90	$3	$3	$90	$24

Figure 2.4   MaxMind geotargeting features and pricing.

Digital Element coined the phrase "IP Intelligence" to describe the more than 39 data points that they deliver to help any company with an online presence to better connect with their audience. IP Intelligence provides coverage for 99.9999% of the Internet and collects more than one million points of view daily from different online vantage points.

Other geolocation providers include GeoBytes and MaxMind, enabling M3 marketers to leverage this technology for those clients not requiring large investments for this type of geotargeting services. GeoBytes offers its GeoSelect Product Suite which provides marketers and developers with geographical customization tools needed to customize websites with various levels of geotargeting. MaxMind also offers geolocation software at very low costs (Figure 2.4).

For geotargeting mobile devices, A5 marketers and developers can insert a software development kit (SDK) from a mobile ad network, such as Greystripe Inc. This is a common practice among app makers, who use these ready-made kits to place ads and generate revenue. Greystripe uses geolocation to locate a mobile device by identifying its Internet address—that is common among websites—less so on mobile devices. Most apps use GPS satellites or maps of triangulated Wi-Fi hot spots to locate users and their devices. There are also several mobile tracking firms which the M3 marketer can leverage to create customized apps for their clients.

Deep Packet Inspection for M3

Cookies, forms, beacons, and even widgets make it possible for M3 marketers and enterprises to deliver highly relevant content to tribes of consumer segments—defined by their own device behaviors—anonymously anywhere.

All of these tracking mechanisms can be used to enhance web data streams, but a relatively new technology can make it even better: DPI, which is also known as complete packet inspection, examines the data in seven layers of packets rather than just their headers, which is commonly used to search for virus, spam, intrusions, and malicious attacks.

More importantly, DPI allows for M3 marketers to extract device behaviors at a granular level—such as what websites a device has visited, their website itinerary, information about page content, duration of visits, search engine used, mobile ID, information of IPTV viewer behavior, and patterns of channel zapping—directly from streaming Internet packets. Strangely, the enhancement of DPI for M3 marketing was made possible by a U.S. government wire tapping law known as the Communication Assistance for Law Enforcement Act (CALEA) passed in 1994.

CALEA was originally intended to preserve the ability of the FBI to conduct surveillance of Voice over IP (VoIP) communications. The core technology allowing for the decomposition of web communications for CALEA is DPI—which can be used for intrusion detection and network security—but more importantly for the M3 marketer, it also allows for the construction of very sophisticated models for mapping web device behaviors.

DPI devices and service providers have the ability to look at Layer 2 through Layer 7 of the Open Systems Interconnection (OSI) model data standard, which is an abstract description for layered communications and computer network protocol design. For example, DPI can tell if the packet is from a browser from Firefox, Google, or Microsoft; and it can identify a Skype device, an Apple app, or an Android OS. All of this vital information can be used for very specific segmentation and model creation by the M3 marketer. There are DPI service providers such as Phorm and Kindsight which recently filed a patent on what it calls "character differentiation" technology.

Phorm partners with Internet Service Providers (ISPs) to function as a recommendation engine. ISP subscribers are asked to opt-in prior to Phorm assigning them a random digital number; no IP address is captured or used. Phorm's partners include publishers, ad networks, advertisers, and agencies. Kindsight works with ISPs to detect online threats; it issues alerts and concentrates of the detection of identity theft.

As with other vendor in this M2M market sectors, many of these companies started in the fields of intrusion detection and machine-learning forensics, but their technologies and capabilities can also be used for M3. There are also DPI hardware firms like Procera and Narus which can be enlisted for M3 marketing via DPI analyses (Figure 2.5).

For example, Procera uses DPI technology to assess the impact of network services such as to plan and postpone network system upgrades, create new service tiers, enforce volume caps, and identify and resolve threats and congestions. However, this DPI technology can also be leveraged for M3 marketing for a new strategy because DPI is looking at a very precise level of device activity and

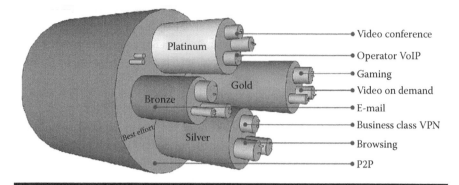

Figure 2.5 DPI can decompose device origins and behaviors at a very detailed level.

its historical behavior, all of which can be modeled for potential advertising benefits via the decomposition and modeling of device behaviors.

The common denominator for all of these DPI software and hardware providers is the need to supply the necessary network intelligence—far beyond what IP ever can do—and enforce fine-grained security policies and most importantly very precise marketing triangulation. DPI provides an awareness of what devices run (on what OS and where in a network); it can identify what application devices are running their location and type of services being used. This multidimensional intelligence enables M3 marketers to make network decisions to improve the end users' online experience and support the client's business needs.

Another DPI hardware firm, Narus, also provides dynamic network traffic intelligence and analytics software that analyzes information on IP traffic, applications, and flow data to map the digital DNA of device behaviors in real time. Through its patented analytics, Narus' software detects patterns and anomalies that can predict and identify security issues, misuse of network resources, suspicious or criminal activity, and other events that can compromise the integrity of IP networks.

Most importantly for the M3 marketer, the DPI technology can also support very precise targeting of devices. The NarusInsight system is designed to be integrated into a customer's operational environment, which strengthens security and monitoring systems—and M3 marketing—while providing traffic visibility and situational awareness across all networks.

DPI technology is a relatively new technology, where vendors such as Narus are most focused on stopping malicious traffic passing through a network—rather than enabling appropriate marketing service delivery for the millions of subscribers with relevant marketing content and product and services offerings. Another technology, deep packet capture (DPC), complements DPI. While DPI is designed to enable service providers and M3 marketers to see and act in real time, DPC solutions are designed to capture all the data passing through a network and store it for more subsequent detailed analysis via machine-learning algorithms.

DPC is the act of capturing, at full network speed, complete network packets including header and payload data crossing a network with a high traffic rate. Once captured and stored, either in short-term memory or in long-term storage, software tools can perform DPI to review network packet data, perform forensics analysis to uncover the root cause of network problems, identify security threats, and ensure data communications and network usage complies with outlined policy.

But most importantly for the M3 marketer, DPI and DPC both offer details about the actual data over a period of time and at multiple points in a network and precise device behaviors. DPC enables end-to-end capacity planning, based on the behavior of applications, devices, and network elements over a period of time. This is a diagnostic aid, enabling a network manager and M3 marketers to take more informed and targeted action based on very granular digital behaviors by devices.

Mob M3

Websites provide a gold mine of device data, everything from browsing behavior patterns to demographics, transactional histories, sources of traffic, the effectiveness of search marketing, and changes in conversion, keyword drivers, and cross-selling propensities. Metrics and adjustment to device behaviors are paramount; the key challenge is deciding.

Every enterprise has streams of transactional and behavioral device data flowing to it 24/7, but few are able to triangulate them simultaneously as events take place—enabling them to make relevant offers to their existing and new customers—at the moment they interact with them. With every event, devices are communicating with companies at their sites, their needs, and their desires. M3 marketers can leverage these events, most of which start at their website, but cascade across other operational systems within enterprises, many of which are increasingly mobile.

Advocates of brands enable marketers and enterprises to build customer loyalty by providing them a social platform by which they can communicate with their friends about what they *like* about a product or service. These existing and new friends can promote digital WOM marketing, so that if certain segments of consumers liked a product or service, they will share it with others virally and become part of the brand.

In this new type of social networking marketplace, friends represent a powerful new advertising model for interactive advertising via mobile and online *mobs*, which M3 marketers can leverage by identifying key "influencers" of products, services, and content. This type of mob marketing can lead to the discovery of new artists, music, products, services, content, and sites friends were totally unaware of; this type of M3 marketing enlists surprise, engagement, and loyalty.

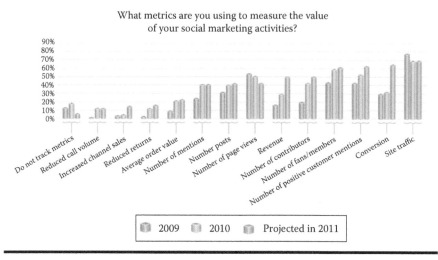

Figure 2.6 Metrics of mob marketing are difficult to execute.

Engagement marketing is a fundamental switch from broadcasting marketing messages to consumers—to that of engaging them in conversations via their digital devices—to obtain a more holistic appreciation of their preferences, reviews, survey results, interactions with their friends, recommendations, and the tracking of their influences on others. Blogs and postings in social sites make it possible for consumer influences to be quantified via their user generated content (UGC) and their recommendations to friends (Figure 2.6).

Interactions measure the most valuable of all metric for engagement marketing and UGC—in which consumers contribute content about a brand is the most valuable key performance indicator (KPI). The social UGC includes all types of digital media, such as videos, blogging, podcasting, wireless and web photos, and wikis. To capture and measure this new metric of engagement marketing, social media tools and platforms may be required, such as Bazaarvoice to track and quantify product ratings and reviews, as well as to measure the content uploaded and shared via connections on social networks.

Bazaarvoice's SaaS powers customer-generated content on more than 1000 brand websites like Best Buy, Blue Shield of California, Costco, Dell, Macy's, P&G, Panasonic, QVC, and USAA in 36 countries. The company connects organizations to their influencers through a unique network that reaches hundreds of millions of consumers around the globe, enabling authentic customer-powered marketing. Through syndication, analytics, partnerships, and consulting, Bazaarvoice conducts analysis of the impact of social media on brands from manufacturing, retail, travel, and financial services companies.

Recently, Bazaarvoice performed a surveyed of 175 chief marketing officers on their biggest challenges, plans, and expectations for social media. The survey involved both business-to-consumer companies (39%) and business-to-business companies (47%). Fourteen percent of the responding brands served both consumers and businesses, the following lists the industries covered:

- Software/hardware (21.7%)
- Finance/insurance (12.2%)
- Consumer goods (12.2%)
- Travel/hospitality (6.9%)
- Media/publishing (7.4%)
- Retail (5.8%)
- Manufacturing (5.3%)

While brands spend millions on market and consumer research, the immediacy of social media and customer feedback gives real-time and less expensive information about a brand. It also gives brands ways to interact and respond to customer input. Customer insights move beyond online conversion or even revenues; the value of these interactions multiplies exponentially. The Bazaarvoice survey found that the real value of social media lies in the processes that help real customer insights get to the most relevant departments to improve the quality of their products and services.

The engagement marketing variable of intimacy goes beyond interactions and focuses on measuring affection and sentiment a consumer has for a brand. To quantify this metric, a brand monitoring service from J.D. Power and Associates can be enlisted. This marketing intelligence company also provides engagement metrics and consumer insights into brands, markets, and trends. They can report on social brand buzz and market influencers monitoring and reporting services, which the M3 marketer can enlist as part of their WOM and social media ad campaigns.

Traditionally, the market research function of an organization has focused on validating and confirming what was already known. This application of market research is quantitative focused, providing companies with a way to measure success and failure, and research quality is defined by statistical methodologies and scientific purity. However, the increased speed at which information is disseminated in a digital world has made the patterns of the past less predictive of the future, and it is becoming increasingly important for M3 marketers to seek new research methods that measure device behaviors and communications. Social media research allows a company to study large volumes of conversation at a lower investment and with faster turnarounds. Most important, social media research is not prompted or aided, but rather is based on the unprompted, independent, autonomous, unfiltered, self-directed, and unaided conversations occurring in content created between digital devices.

The metrics of Mob M3 can take many forms starting with the web which is a major revenue channel for almost all companies of all sizes—a main source of consumer intelligence being simple server log files—which with every click devices (browsers) are communicating consumers' desires and needs. M3 marketers need to focus on what these online behaviors are demanding; for a complete listing of log tools, go to counterguide.com.

The problem with log files is that users are assigned dynamic IP addresses. One simple solution is to assign a unique ID cookie to all browsers using JavaScript (cookies are simple text files for tagging devices). The JavaScript code can be used for tracking via cookies and can instantly tag an entire site; sample code can be found in multiple websites including cookiecentral.com. In addition to JavaScript, "beacons" can also be used for tracking consumer behaviors. Beacons, also known as "bugs," and invisible GIFs can also be embedded in sites and e-mails—they are transparent images 1 × 1 pixel in size and can report on IP addresses, timestamps, and cookies set by a site or a network.

An optional method of collecting web device behaviors is via packet sniffers—which are special hardware from such firms as Clickstream Technologies and SiteSpec—they can collect absolutely everything including passwords, names, addresses, and credit card numbers since they sit between browsers and a site. M3 marketers should not dismiss or ignore the need to secure permission to use these Internet mechanisms to serve consumers.

Data Aggregation and Sharing Networks

Samples of these data sharing networks are many; the popular one is RapLeaf which harvests consumer e-mail addresses from a network of websites and some Facebook and MySpace apps and links them to a dossier of detailed consumer information from multiple categories and sources. RapLeaf can customize e-mails to devices based on gender, location, and interests to composed communications that are meaningful and relevant. The data aggregating and sharing network can recommend music, movies, articles, and associates that are interesting to profiled devices to save time; the network also offers analytics to tell its partners and network members about the loyalty of their users, and assist them to understand who is using their product and services.

RapLeaf assembles anonymous audience segments, such as "Female" and "Age 24–34," for online ad placements. They also assemble dynamic device segments based on offline demographics and online interests on their RapLeaf cookie that they placed on devices. For example, a RapLeaf cookie might look something like this:

j + ySwcJ/Al1xTGb + Z0iBLh633hmoLu3wqFcLu

This cookie might depict the device to be that of a male, age 25–30, who likes soccer. A cookie can be accessed whenever a browser is at a website that calls the cookie's host domain. That means that sites and networks that place the original cookies are the only ones that can read it and write to it. The cookie segments tell these aggregating and sharing networks what ads will most likely interest a browser—assisting marketers to offer more relevant content and companies to advertise their products more efficiently. Because their segments are based on general profile data, RapLeaf cookies enhance the user experience without identifying them personally. These are some of the RapLeaf consumer device data streams:

Consumer Categories	Device Information Captured
Donations	Consumers who made donations to different causes
Demographics	Age, gender, marital status, income, children, education
Lifestyle	Gift giver, senior, fitness enthusiast
Memberships	Gmail, Yahoo, AOL, You Tube, Comcast
Social network	LinkedIn, Twitter, shopping club member
Financials	Credit card user, trades stock, online payer
Likely to buy	Car loan, credit or retail card, online shopper
Political	Liberal or conservative, democrat or republican
Marketing	Large purchases, retired, new parent, empty nester
Interests	Hobbies, Christianity, movie stars, sports, products

RapLeaf combines this online data with offline data, such as the consumer's address, real estate property, and voting records. Next, RapLeaf sends the assembled profile to a broad array of partners and customers who use it to track consumers across the Internet—the advertising networks and exchanges that share this RapLeaf data are as follows:

Lucid Media Networks: Let advertisers and their agencies use their network to target unique demographic segments and audience capabilities. Lucid Media can reach up to 95% of the U.S. online population with one self-service interface. Lucid Media targets more than 14,000 microsegments tuned specifically for online and mobile display advertising. Lucid Media provides reports on device activities, dynamic market ad pricing, server-side cookie store, real-time assessment of ad campaigns, and the integration of third party data providers.

AppNexus: It is a real-time bidding (RTB) exchange which is expected to be a multimillion dollar business in the next 5 years for marketing to online and mobile devices. AppNexus works with 8 of the top 15 ad networks, according to comScore. AppNexus provides an ad platform and access to the major exchanges and aggregators, as well as cloud infrastructure scalable to billions of ad impressions a day.

Simpli.fi: It is a keyword-targeted display advertising service. Simpli.fi targets, bids, reports, and optimizes on keywords via its advertising network.

TARGUSinfo: It provides demographics-based data to online marketers, enterprises, call sites, and websites. The network can identify potential prospects at the point of interaction; it can pinpoint devices' precise location and verify names, addresses, e-mails, and IP addresses in real time.

Quantcast: A media measurement service for audience statistics for millions of websites and multiple channels. Quantcast can deliver look-alike *converter* segments of multiple devices for M3 marketers (Figure 2.7).

BrightRoll: It provides online video advertising services for ad campaigns. BrightRoll ad campaigns leverage contextual, demographic, geographic, and site-specific targeting methods to help advertisers reach their audiences. BrightRoll has a variety of solutions for advertisers with specific behavioral and online and mobile device targeting needs.

Rocket Fuel: It provides turnkey media and ad campaign management by combining demographic, lifestyle, purchase intent, and social data with their own suite of targeting algorithms, blended analytics, and expert analysis.

AdMeld: It assists online publishers sell their ad inventory.

AdBrite: It serves ads on 112,000 sites and is the 10th largest ad network on the Internet; its open architecture combines an array of algorithms and terabytes of data to create an online auction between advertisers and publishers. Its algorithms

Figure 2.7   Metrics of Quantcast coverage offline and online.

determine the particular combinations of ads, inventory, and devices that will generate the best return on investment (ROI) in their ad exchange.

Datran Media: Another ad network with audience metrics, behavioral analytics, and e-mail marketing services.

Invite Media: A display advertising and exchange bidding company that enables M3 marketers to automatically buy from multiple ad exchanges in real time, all through the same interface.

Rubicon Project: A digital advertising infrastructure company that automates buying and selling ads, which is comprised of four core technologies (1) SmartMatch™ Yield Algorithms, (2) Pricing Intelligence, (3) Audience and Inventory Analytics, and (4) Brand Protection.

AdExchanger: Ad exchanger optimizes placements of ads via machine-learning algorithms.

NetMining: It provides behaviorally display advertising and dynamic e-mail personalization. Their LiveMarketer is a real-time visualization proprietary profiling engine for analyzing devices at websites. It supports visualization of device profiling in real time (Figure 2.8).

InterClick: A behavioral targeted platform that combines proprietary behavioral targeting.

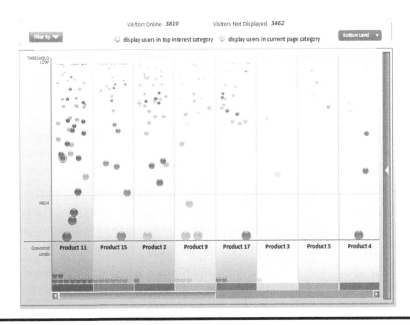

Figure 2.8 LiveMarketer displays devices' activities by product lines.

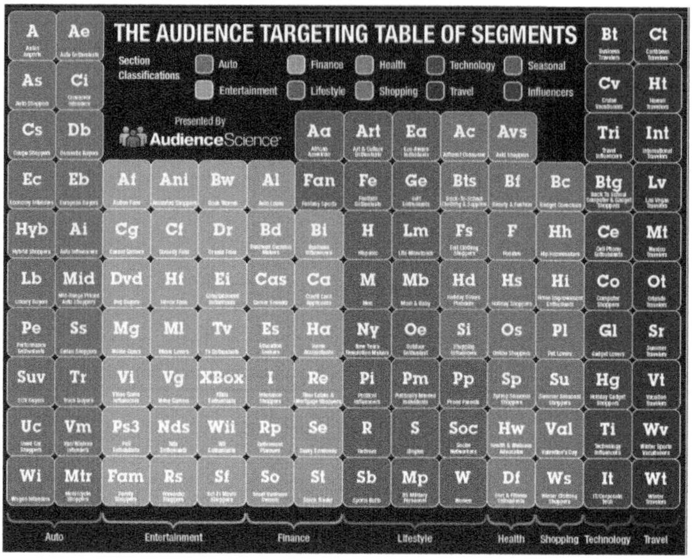

Figure 2.9   Some of device segments provided by Audience Science.

Audience Science: Ad network platform, formerly Revenue Science. Audience Science segments help M3 marketers reach highly qualified consumers based on specific interests and intent. They provide targeting data based on device behaviors, demographic, psychographic, and other attributes. They can qualify that data and aggregate it into actionable segments. They offer a broad array of standardized segments, as well as the ability to construct custom segments on the fly to satisfy any marketing objective (Figure 2.9).

PubMatic: Ad revenue optimization service reaches 95% of all U.S. Internet users and reaches 400 million unique users globally.

Turn: Company with end-to-end platform for managing digital advertising, offers a self-service interface, optimization algorithms, real-time analytics, interoperability, and scalable infrastructure.

Red Aril: It integrates client data and makes it actionable for targeted advertising. Their Red Aril Platform is designed to manage today's intense marketing and advertising environment—in support of high data volumes within a real-time environment.

DataXu: It offers a real-time ad optimization platform for advertisers—they start by assimilating client existing data—they then analyzes it, looking for patterns of device behavior that help it understand or differentiate levels of intent among target audiences.

Triggit: It integrates ads into websites using drag and drop JavaScript.

These advertising companies and third party ad exchanges work like this: the first time a site is visited, they install a cookie or beacon file, which assigns the visitor's device a unique ID number. Later, when the user visits another site affiliated with the same ad exchange, it can take note of where that device was before, and where they are now and their browsing behavior, such as what "keywords" they used in search engines.

This way, over time these data aggregation and sharing networks can build robust but anonymous advertising anywhere profiles. The information that these networks gather is anonymous, in the sense that Internet users are identified by a numbered cookie assigned to their device by these ad exchanges and ad networks, for example, they do not know the name of consumers—only their device behaviors and attributes—identified by their cookie code number.

For example, MSN plants a tracking cookie to predict a visitor's age, their ZIP Code, and gender, plus code which estimates a visitor's income, marital status, presence of children, and home ownership. The cookie is planted by *TARGUSinfo*, a network previously mentioned for MSN; Yahoo performs a similar process based on searched keywords; and, of course, Goggle has its *AdWords*, *Goggle Analytics*, and their *DoubleClick* ad network to accomplish the same tasks.

Yet another ad exchange *BlueKai* segments device behaviors into over 30,000 categories; each day the company sells 50 million pieces of information about specific browsing habits for as little as a 10th of a cent apiece. The auctions can happen dynamically and instantly, as a website is visited for anonymous advertising anywhere. However, this type of "cookie sale" may be superseded by new fingerprinting exchanges such as those of *BlueCava*—and new device identification for targeted advertising and fraud detection technology—which will be covered in detail later in this chapter.

Xplusone is another virtual ad network which can also dynamically personalized websites based on devices' characteristics and behaviors. Yet another ad network is [x + 1], Inc. which offers their Media+1—a website optimization solution that allows sites and marketers to maximize ROI—by automatically personalizing online content. This network also offers web trafficking, data tracking, reporting, and analytics services—via their Smart Tagging System—which allows the synchronization of client data into their ad platform.

M3 marketers can use some of the probability algorithms and software products discussed at the beginning of this chapter—to try to pair what they know about devices online and mobile behaviors—with data from offline sources such as household income, geography, and education, among other things. The goal is to make sophisticated predictions about device behaviors; for example, a financial company might want to segment those behaviors to make assumptions income levels.

M3 marketing at sites is about using cookies or beacons via ad exchanges and networks to customize a visitor's experience and offer relevant content to them. Data management and data marketplaces like *eXelate* allow for M3 marketing to take place in order to get a sense of that person's interests. Sites and networks do not "sell" information about their users; this would dilute the value of their consumer knowledge.

The business model of ad networks and exchanges is to sell space to marketers—and "rent access to consumer eyeballs" based on their device behaviors, demographics, and interests which they have aggregated over time.

M3 marketing is the foundation of an online advertising economy that racked up $23 billion in ad spending in 2009; however, the estimated size of that same market is projected to be over $40 billion by 2015. M3 marketing is exploding—researchers at AT&T Labs and Worcester Polytechnic Institute found that in 2010, a trend toward this type of targeting device technology will increase—exceeding 80% of the top 1000 most popular sites on the web.

Twitter Is Organic TV for M3

Twitter is not only a new social media real-time network feed, but it is also a new ad platform for targeting digital devices (Figure 2.10). Twitter is to the M3 marketer what TV was to the ad men of the fifties. But unlike 1950s TV, Twitter allows for advertisers to purchase a promoted service so that M3 marketers can calibrate the effectiveness of their client's tweets, including important feedback on how many people clicked on their links. Twitter TV provides vital metrics like reuse hashtags, and retweet of a post or marks as a favorite, or the number of devices that choose to follow a thread. Retweets are cascading tweets to other device followers on Twitter TV—it allows for an immediate method of measuring the marketing of a brand.

Twitter is organic TV; like early TV, everything in Twitter is live, and it is about a flocking audience of real-time events and communicating with other digital devices in real time. Twitter is often bundled with events taking place on TV, such as music award, late night talk, sports, news, or reality shows, and scripted

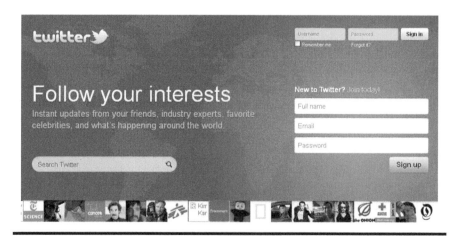

Figure 2.10 Twitter for following and targeting devices' interests.

television series are marketing via Twitter. Twitter is often the social medium by which celebrities from sports, music, movies, and TV converse with their audience.

M3 marketers can organize media events with commercial sponsors of real-time events to leverage and announce new products and services. Twitter provides not only an ad platform but also a method of determining the buzz it has created. The updated format of Twitter now supports not only the sharing of photos but also videos. Increasingly Twitter is also the new digital Nielsen—where the effectiveness of a TV ad can be tracked and measured—by the chatter and buzz it creates.

Among the applications for M3 marketing via the Twitter TV channel to digital devices are announcing specials, deals, or sales. For a retailer, this might involve broadcasts of special offers that are time sensitive, such as those commercials from Southwest Airlines about their "Ding" application which can be downloaded to devices for monitoring and issuing alerts about specials on flights. Similarly Dell has done the same type of M3 marketing, with a lot of success offering specials on various components.

Twitter TV can also be leveraged to provide live updates on events or conferences to digital devices. If an M3 marketer is participating in a large trade show or corporate event, they can use Twitter to announce last minute changes, cool events, or invitations to special meetings. Twitter TV is a great last minute M3 marketing tool for promoting blog articles, webinars, interesting news, and more. Twitter TV can also be used to post articles such as a customer success story or other PR coverage.

For the M3 marketers and their clients, there are thousands of applications for leveraging Twitter, just Google "Twitter apps" to see the most current ones. For example, *Oneforty* is an excellent online repository for Twitter apps, tools, and metrics and is a social media guide, which can be enlisted in M3 marketing campaigns. For example, Oneforty offers a Twitter service; it calls "When to Tweet" which analyzes when followers tweet and then recommends the best times for a company or marketer to tweet. It is a fairly simple and a free service that provides easy-to-understand graphs of tweet usage and traffic of devices.

A whole ecosystem of start-ups is evolving around the Twitter TV technology and platform. Some are downloadable software programs that let users send and receive messages from their devices. Twitter TV thus can be used by M3 marketers to sell local ads or to discern trends or consumer sentiments for a new form of social media analytics and a new level of real-time marketing metrics.

One of the most popular Twitter mobile app is UberTwitter for BlackBerry and iPhone users; the app can be used by M3 marketers to insert ads into users' Twitter streams. UberTwitter is now UberSocial, to reflect its broadening reach as a key social communications tool. UberSocial can be used to send and read tweets and to post rich media to Facebook. UberSocial also has a new desktop version to take full advantage of the larger screen environment to deliver a vastly richer real-time experience.

Two other popular social marketing media apps are Seesmic and Tweetdeck, which can also be leveraged by M3 marketers for broadcasting via Twitter TV. Seesmic is focused on building applications to help users build and manage their brands online. Seesmic specializes in social media monitoring, updating, and engaging at the speed of real time. Tweetdeck was recently acquired by Twitter; it also supports multiple digital devices for branding of products and services.

There is also a new company Klout that can provide Twitter metrics and behavioral analysis for M3 marketers—enabling them to identify the Twitter users who are most influential in online discussions about their brand. Klout measures the influences of devices across the social web and allows M3 marketers to track the impact of opinions, links, and recommendations of restaurants, movies, bands, or games. Klout allows M3 marketers to find influencers based on topic or hashtag.

When a device sees a pound sign, #, followed by the name of a product, service, or a brand, it is seeing what is known as a Twitter Hashtag or Tag. Hashtags offer an easy way to do a keyword search on a topic or to define a posting under that topic on Twitter. For example, if a marketer tweets about a topic related to "fingerprinting," they might want to add #fingerprinting to their tweet. Other devices searching for information on "fingerprinting" will see those tweets, along with others who are tweeting about the same subject—it is marketing via self-driven interests, a most potent and new method of advertising.

Historically lifetime value has been measured based on purchases, but with Klout marketers can understand the influencers' network value via Twitter TV. Klout allows enterprises to find out who is influential in specific industries to discover who is tweeting about brands. Klout offers an API for development of a Twitter ecosystem, with the following Twitter TV metrics:

1. *Klout Score*: Klout Score is the measurement of a device's overall online influence. The scores range from 1 to 100 with higher scores representing a wider and stronger sphere of influence.
2. *Network Influence*: Network Influence is the influence level of a device's engaged audience. Capturing the attention of influencers is no easy task, and those who are able to do so are typically creating spectacular content.
3. *Amplification Probability*: Amplification Probability is the likelihood that content will be acted upon by a device. The ability to create content that compels others to respond and high-velocity content that spreads into networks beyond their own is a key component of influence.
4. *True Reach*: True Reach is the size of a device's engaged audience. We eliminate inactive and spam accounts and only include accounts that they influence.
5. *Influential About*: The topics a device is most influential about—based not on what they talk about the most but instead on the subjects it gets the most engagement on.

Social media marketing via friends is about WOM that can be encouraged and facilitated via Twitter TV. M3 marketers and their clients can communicate with devices by making it easy for them to tell their friends. Twitter TV marketing can make certain that influential individuals know about the good qualities of a product or a service and make it easy for them to share it with other devices in a funny, cool, and relevant manner via WOM.

Blogs Are Studios for M3

Blogging broadcasting is another format for M3 marketing. A blog is sort of a "digital studio" from which a device can broadcast to the world, their views, including those of a brand. They can broadcast anything they want from that digital studio either directly or via an RSS feed reader. A blog is a place where influencers and M3 marketers can go when they want to say something to millions of other devices.

Blogs are not a live broadcasting experience either; they are, however, the equivalent of prerecorded shows that get broadcast and then remain available forever in digital archives. However, this "studio" is like a soapbox with unlimited range. A blog also has many qualities in common with traditional syndicated news, opinion pieces, or commentary content that are transmitted via traditional media, such as newspapers, magazines, television, and radio.

When set up correctly, a blog offers M3 marketers and consumers a chance to say something and interact with others who can read and respond to those comments in a social and interactive environment. The feature that makes blogs different from other methods of communications is that the content is published in a chronological fashion, with the content updated regularly, where readers have the ability to leave comments and other blog authors can interact via "trackbacks" and "pingbacks" in which the content is syndicated via RSS feeds.

So a blog is a social open medium that is interactive, self-adaptive, and independent of its creator and in the hands of those that interact with it. WOM via blogs is a genuine voice of customers, which to succeed must be natural, genuine, and honest. WOM is also about people seeking advice from each other via devices and talking about new products, services, and brands via social networks, the web, blogs, e-mails, texts, and the mobile world. WOM is acknowledging that a satisfied customer is the greatest endorsement for a brand. For the marketer, the goal is to facilitate such endorsement via social media on the web and wireless marketplaces, including "studio" blogs.

For the M3 marketer, the main task for executing WOM via blogs is to identify those influencers and evangelists; this may require behavioral analyses using clustering and segmentation software. Once these influencers are identified, the marketer must facilitate how they share their opinions about brands they like with their friends. The M3 marketer should also use classification software, such as decision tree programs, to segment and identify the key attributes and features of these early influencers to develop a model for identifying *new* influencers.

The M3 marketer must engage these influencers in an open, honest dialogue and communicate with them the value of their opinion. WOM via blogs is about emotional and passionate advertising—based on the natural desire by people to be social and share with others their passion about a brand. A secondary task for the M3 marketer is to empower these influencers with the ability to communicate with their friends and colleagues.

M3 marketers today have a novel and a new way of reaching out to consumers via online blogs. As previously mentioned, blogs are interactive broadcasting studios where marketers can post their ideas, journalize, and comment and interact with other devices sharing stories and brand benefits. A marketing strategy is to use these studio blogs as a means to promote a positive company image, defend negative blog write-ups, and spread the word about that marketer's brand.

Although blogging is no replacement to traditional media, it can create new clients or a new medium to hit a specific and narrow market not traditionally reach by broadcast and mass media. Studio blogs are an easy way of reaching a brand's target market and sustaining a dialogue with other devices in the relatively inexpensive channel, via the following steps:

1. Initiate building a community of device bloggers; it educates your present and potential customers on the merit of your products and services.
2. Use blogs as a conversional medium; they are feedback based—use them as a basis for an honest and open dialogue—offering a meaningful value proposition to tell your brand story.
3. Blogs are contributed by devices that are passionately engaged in a particular topic and desire to share their range of experience and knowledge.
4. Link to other blogs or a site as a way of networking devices to spread the word about your brand's blog.

Dialing Up iPhone and Android A5 Numbers

As previously mentioned, M3 can be performed and executed in any digital channel; increasingly, however, this involves marketing to devices that are moving. M3 marketing on the basis of frequency, device type, location, interests, recent activities, preferences, historical behavior, and keywords is critical in the triangulated modeling via inductive analytics to any type of digital devices, be they phones, pads, appliances, or cars.

Consumers demonstrate what is useful and valuable to each of them by their actions in search and social sites as well as the interactive wireless world. The role of the M3 marketer is to deliver and fulfill—if not *anticipate* their needs—on any device anywhere, at any time. Mobile marketing depends on the triangulation of a device on the move, which is transmitting by its digital unique number its desires and location.

Universally, all mobile phones have unique serial number identifiers including Apple and Android-based devices. For the marketer, these unique numbers of devices are important attributes for behavioral analysis and M3 marketing as the numbers are difficult or impossible to delete and can be triangulated via location, content sought, and social links. These unique numbers, which really represent anonymous digital devices, have behaviors which can be modeled in a very precise manner for improved customer service and revenue market growth.

Customized apps can be created by enterprises and M3 marketers with such functions as store locators, proximity coupons, and local real-time ads. The Apple Unique Device Identifier (UDID) is the most common identifier—it is stamped on all Apple mobile devices—it is a combination of 40 numbers and letters set to stay with the device forever. Stamped because of warranty issues, the UDID has also tremendous M3 marketing application potentials.

The Android ID is the second most common mobile device identifier, and it is embedded by Google on all its mobile OSs. The ID is set by Google and created when a user first boots up the device—Google does allow users to reset their ID numbers—but it also can be used for triangulated marketing of these mobile devices via interest-based or location-based behaviors.

Originally, these IMEI or "international mobile equipment identity" numbers were set up to lock down phones that had been reported stolen or lost; however, their true value is in M3 marketing. There is also the IMSI or "international mobile subscriber identity" number assigned to all devices which is use to route calls and bill users; this footprint will remain the same as long as the user owns that device. These device identifiers have important uses for M3 marketers; in addition, customized apps can be developed to market to unique Apple UDID or Android ID devices in an anonymous but highly relevant and valuable manner.

A new marketing paradigm is also evolving in which the behaviors of mobile users and their devices are beginning to take place. Targeting on the basis or frequency and recent activities based on historical behavior is critical in the modeling via inductive behavioral analytics for triangulation marketing. Consumers demonstrate what is useful and valuable to each of them by their actions in websites as well as the wireless world. Today, marketers and enterprises have access to consumers' device identity and their location—whether by Wi-Fi triangulation or GPS targeting—as well as by their online and mobile behaviors, personality, and preferences.

The wireless targeting is done by "multilateration" also known as hyperbolic positioning; this is the process of locating an object by accurately computing the TDOA of a signal emitted from a mobile device and its triangulation and synchronization by multiple receivers. A location-based service provider such as *Antenna Software* can be enlisted for customizing M3 marketing apps.

Figure 2.11 Antenna converts mobile devices into shopping carts.

The most profitable customers are return devices. These loyal devices know about products and services; it also allows retailers to know their purchasing habits. With mobility, you can take that relationship to the ultimate level by providing an interactive, personalized shopping experience to devices—wherever and whenever they are in the mood to shop.

Antenna lets mobile devices take their shopping cart with them wherever they go. They provide an intelligently designed, user-friendly mobile app that consumers can access at their convenience to securely browse and buy products right from their digital devices. With personalized alerts, coupons, discounts, deals, and other services, their "Mobile Shopping" component allows for devices to keep consumers actively engaged and more likely to make more purchases (Figure 2.11).

The Mobile Shopping app by Antenna allows devices to receive mobile coupons, point-of-sale promotions, and specials—all customized by the retailer. The A5 supports the location of retail items while shopping in the physical store of the merchant. The Antenna A5 also supports the use of the device's camera to capture product bar code for pricing, availability, and more information. The A5 can also be used to search for items, to view products and images, or to add to a shipping cart, to add to a device's wish list, and finally to check out. The Antenna A5 also can be used to find nearby stores and get directions from current location using the device's GPS.

Many of today's mobile devices typically determine location through analyzing a mix of wireless signals from GPS, cell towers, and Wi-Fi hot spots. GPS signals can be used, but they do not work well indoors or in urban areas and take several minutes to retrieve, which for M3 marketing is not the best solution. Wi-Fi signals are considered the most accurate since they work indoors, and in urban areas, they also can be retrieved quickly and are accurate to within 20–30 m. That level of precision is important to M3 marketers and the developers of their A5s, who want to be able to send time-sensitive targeted ads, offers, and coupons to consumers when they are in their mall or close to their stores.

Mobile Cookie A5s for M3

Consumers are their devices—as with the web where cookies and beacons are used to follow and identify a consumer's preferences and behaviors—the same holds true in the mobile world where wireless cookies perform the same function. A5s function as wireless cookies and are a reliable and proven method of aggregating the type of device behavioral data that is ideal for M3 marketing. For a guide to creating and utilizing wireless cookies for delivering relevant content to mobile devices, go to http://www.w3.org/TR/mobile-bp/. This site specifies the best practices for delivering web content to mobile devices. The principal objective is to improve the user experience of the web when accessed from such devices. The recommendations at this site refer to delivered content and not to the processes by which it is created, nor to the devices or user agents to which it is delivered. It is primarily directed at creators, maintainers, and operators of websites; it offers some wireless cookies requirements, delivery context, structure formats, and conformance for mobile devices.

The M3 marketer of course has the option of outsourcing the development of A5s to such companies as Ringleader Digital, which provides mobile cookie technology that allows advertisers and content owners to track mobile device users as they browse the mobile web (Figure 2.12).

The Ringleader Digital technology is called Media Stamp and is not browser based—operating on the ad server side—so it is out of the carriers' reach and not subject to their practice of gateway stripping of wireless cookies. Media Stamp can identify the device type, where it is geographically, and on which carrier network it is operating from—it does not identify the user, their phone number, or other personal data—this allows the wireless cookie to bypass privacy concerns

Figure 2.12 Ringleader Digital Device Detector for clustering and tracking.

while still enabling A5. A mobile device is inherently more personal; it is always with a consumer; and it knows where they are, how they communicate, and with whom. It is a unique combination that is unmatched by any other medium.

There have been privacy concerns with Internet tracking mechanisms, such as beacon and cookies, but the concern that they are used to target individuals is actually misplaced since they are really tracking devices, including mobile ones via wireless cookies and A5s—operating in an anonymous manner. These mechanisms allow for websites to approximate consumers' preferences and for letting companies to improve their responses to customer demands for relevancy in the content they provide, as well as the products and services they offer.

As with ad exchanges and social media, today mobile marketing mechanisms, such as A5s, can be used to target wireless ads that are uniquely relevant to consumers based on their behaviors and now their physical location. Today, the browser is mobile, and as such, A5s can be used for targeting these handheld devices. With an increasing number of mobile devices around the world, users are demanding immediate access to relevant mobile data in this new channel. Mobile users want web-based e-mail, news, weather, games, sports, and various forms of entertainment, which triangulation marketing can deliver by segmenting and classifying mobile behaviors and devices via A5s.

A retailer, for example, can use A5s to market to mobile devices to enhance customer engagement and loyalty. The mobile devices are a convenient way for customers to gather information about a retailer's products and even conduct transactions. Consumers can research prices and do comparisons shopping by scanning barcodes using their devices. The key is to provide convenient features in order to retain consumers' interest and loyalty via the mobile devices in their pockets or purses.

The challenge for M3 marketers is to integrate all channels, mobile, web, e-mail, and physical storefronts into a seamless integrated experience for consumers. Delivering local ads is a vital step for marketers, coupled with constructing the infrastructure for relevant interactions with consumers in this fast evolving mobile environment. To accomplish this, a mobile website should be deployed for optimizing mobile browsing. Mobile websites can be constructed internally by enterprises or contracted out to developers; they are important conduits to gathering mobile behaviors and locations of consumers via the strategic use of A5s.

These mobile websites are a relatively recent channel for accessing the Internet from a mobile device via a wireless network. The mobile arena, however, introduces a new layer of complexity that can be difficult for websites to accommodate since they require cross-platform functionality and diminutive displays. At a minimum, the sites should support the native Android and Apple browsers. There are many developers specializing in the creation of mobile websites for multiple devices, and a checklist will be provided of all the major ones in Chapter 3. The following table provides some of the key devices in the mobile marketplace and the components for creating customized A5s:

Device OS	Programming Language	Debuggers Available	Emulator Available	Integrated Development Environment	Cross-Platform Deployment	Installer Packaging Option	Development Tool Cost
Airplay	C, C++	Yes	Yes	Visual Studio	All	Native	License
alcheMo	Java	Eclipse	IDE	Xcode	Android, iOS	Native	License
Android	Java, C, C++	Eclipse	Yes	Eclipse	Android	apk	Free
Appcelerator	JavaScript	No	Third party	Internal SDK	iPhone	Native	Apache
Celsius	Java	Yes	Yes	NetBeans	All	Native	License
Bedrock	Java	Yes	Yes	Eclipse	All	Native	License
BlackBerry	Java	IDE	Yes	Eclipse	RIM API	alx, cod	Free
Blueprint	XML	No	No	XML	No	XML	XML
BREW	C	Visual Studio	No	Visual Studio	BREW	OTA	BREW
DragonRAD	Visual	Yes	Third party	Visual Studio	All	OTA	License
FeedHenry	JavaScript	Yes	Yes	Eclipse	All	Native	Free
iOS (Apple)	Objective C	IDE	iPhone SDK	Xcode	iPhone, iPad	Apple	License
Java ME	Java	Yes	Yes	Eclipse	All	Jad/Jar	Free

(continued)

(continued)

Device OS	Programming Language	Debuggers Available	Emulator Available	Integrated Development Environment	Cross-Platform Deployment	Installer Packaging Option	Development Tool Cost
JMANGO	JMANGO	No	No	JMANGO	All	Native	Free
Lazarus	Pascal	Yes	Yes	IDE	Windows	Native	Free
Flash	ActionScript	Yes	IDE	Eclipse	Yes	OTA	Free
Microbrowser	XHTML	Yes	IDE	Multiple	All	No	Free
MobilFlex	Visual	No	No	Web Portal	Android, iOS	No	Free
MoSync	C, C++	Yes	Yes	Eclipse	All	OTA	Free
.NET	VB.NET	Yes	IDE	Visual Studio	Windows CE	OTA	Free
OpenPlug	XML	Yes	Yes	ELIPS	All	Native	Free
Palm OS	C, C++	Yes	Yes	Eclipse	Palm OS	PRC	Free

PhoneGap	JavaScript	Yes	No	No	All	Native	License
Python	Python	Yes	Nokia	Eclipse	Nokia	Python	Free
Resco	C#	Yes	Yes	Visual Studio	All	Native	Free
Rhomobile	HTML	Yes	No	Eclipse	All	OTA	Free
Smartface	Drag&Drop	No	Yes	Designer	Android	Native	License
Symbian	C++	Yes	Yes	Multiple	All	SIS	Free
TotalCross	Java	Yes	Yes	Eclipse	All	Native	Free
webOS	C, C++	Yes	Yes	Eclipse	Palm	OTA	Free
WinDev	Wlanguage	Yes	Yes	Android DSK	Android	OTA	License
Windows	C, C++	Yes	Yes	Visual Studio	Windows CE	OTA	Free
WorkLight	JavaScript	Yes	Yes	Eclipse	All	Native	Free

Successful A5 projects typically include a focused scope with well-defined users and workflows, user requirements with supporting systems, data and interfaces, and a clear set of M3 marketing objectives that are tied to ROI goals, increased revenue growth, and improved customer service. From a resources perspective, an A5 team needs to be assembled or outsourced comprised of developers, end users, IT staff, business analysts, software engineers, test engineers, and other stakeholders.

The A5 team will require essential skills such as software development and requirements gathering. The most successful A5 projects typically rely on established business processes and workflows and business data models that are fairly mature. This includes integrating a middleware solution that allows communications via standard technologies (e.g., JMS, XML) across the client's enterprise can serve to expedite the integration of the mobile M3 marketing solution.

The A5 project scope includes the business needs—such as an increase of sales and revenue, lower operational costs, and increase customer satisfaction and device retention rates. Developing mobile applications does not require highly specialized resources, but it does involve people covering a range of disciplines, from application design to network and system integration and security. As part of the design phase, a tracing of user requirements is performed to ensure the gathered requirements are allocated and accommodated in the design of the A5 solution. The build and integration phases typically continue until all features and functionality are implemented per the project scope and requirements.

Testing an A5 application differs from conducting user acceptance testing (UAT) on traditional IT application platforms. With the mobile technology, each device OS can behave differently depending on the actual device on which it is being used and the carrier network to which the device connects. A5 deployment tests require that the use of live devices is essential; it is also recommended that a controlled introduction takes place to allow operations and administrative staff to learn how to provision users and devices in a managed A5 deployment before taking on a full rollout.

Mobile Advertising Networks for A5

M3 marketing also requires the creation of native apps (A5s) with purchasing capabilities and the integration of a device's camera for barcode scanning and the interactive viewing of product demonstrations, price comparisons, videos, and other customized features for retailers, merchants, and companies. Constructing a mobile website and A5s are essential considerations in the M3 marketing via this channel. First, considerations must be made about the expected users and what devices to support; there are really only two critical and dominant ones—Apple and Android (Google) devices.

Marketers need to consider how to incorporate geotargeting, profiling, time, and location variables in their propensity to purchase models. When creating their mobile websites and A5s, enterprises and marketers should address presentation technologies that support multiple devices, networks, and OSs. Consideration should also be given to incorporating temporal location-based and interest-based marketing to better support and engage consumers anytime, anywhere.

Having the ability for devices to engage with retailers encourages "situation shopping" in which they can mix and match clothes through a store-specific A5, for example. This leads to clothing centric search features and a virtual closet—incorporating different colors and styles—where mobile shoppers can model different outfits or items via a retailer's A5. Having this ability to engage shoppers via a retailer A5 in consumers' mobile devices increases their browsing time, their loyalty, and in the end higher sales and growth revenue.

Other retailer-specific apps can be developed for different types of products, such as those for electronic gadgets, auto enthusiasts, do-it-yourself hardware consumers, runners, gardeners, golfers, etc.; the potentials are endless. These retailers can incorporate store-specific A5s which can include scanning capabilities—for price comparison abilities not only in their store but also across all retail sites on the web. Quick, short surveys can be incorporated to gather feedback from mobile shoppers—enabling retailers to streamline and continuously improve their offerings to them.

The eBay Mobile A5 is an example of this price comparison feature. Such transparent capabilities create enduring customer loyalty and ensure their engagement in the future. At that juncture, these store-specific apps are not just a one-stop destination but are in fact a *starting point* for search shopping, price comparison, and social sharing with friends via consumers' mobile devices (Figure 2.13).

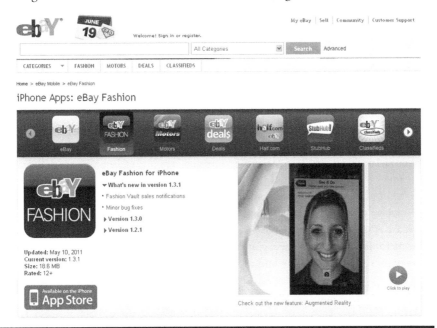

Figure 2.13   eBay iPhone Fashion A5.

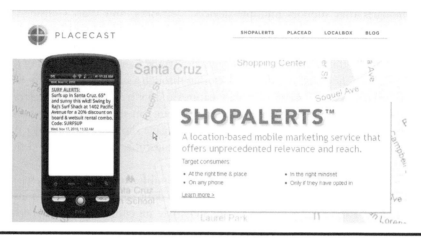

Figure 2.14   Placecast ShopAlerts A5.

Firms such as Placecast can assist retailers in detecting these shopping prospects as they enter "geo-fences" in order to deliver highly relevant messages. Placecast's ShopAlerts is an opt-in, location-based messaging service that can be customized for each mobile device based on location, time, user preferences, and behavioral modeling. Mobility shopping represents a new paradigm of marketing, real-time advertising, pricing comparison, and service competition; that is retailers will need to develop appropriate policies and strategies and they will need to quickly adapt or die in this new interactive mobile method of selling (Figure 2.14).

As more consumers weave mobile interactions into their lives, M3 marketers can gain greater insight from this interactive and highly organic channel. Mobile represents an unprecedented opportunity for enhancing customer interaction and intimacy. Mobile data can be used by retailers to develop predictive models—using decision-tree algorithms and software—for the development and deployment of business rules designed to provide customized and relevant communications, messages, offers, and recommendations.

For example, their ShopAlerts A5s use geo-fencing technology to deliver relevant text or rich-media messages to devices when they enter a predefined, virtual space around a particular location. When devices are within a determined radius, they receive a message tied to that geo-fence. In addition to location data, the Placecast A5s use day and time to make retailers and merchant messages more relevant to devices. Consumers can opt-in to receive ShopAlerts messages and can manage messaging frequency and content.

Their A5s are currently licensed and deployed by operators, digital marketing agencies, large retailers, and resellers around the world. The A5s are not tied to any single operating platform, carrier, or device, so they are highly scalable. Each message is tailored dynamically based on place, day, time, and consumer data to deliver the most relevant messages to devices; the network also provides quantitative and qualitative metrics.

These mobile advertising networks are rapidly evolving for delivering marketing messages to an array of devices, which increasingly are segmented via age, gender, and location; with time this mobile market sector will evolve, expand, and refine the data it aggregates—leading to new levels of A5 efficiency for the billions of mobile devices worldwide. As far as mobile metrics, Amethon Solutions provides reports on device activities to mobile operators, content publishers, and marketing agencies. Their intelligence captures the underlying TCP/IP traffic allowing analysis of HTTP, WAP, and other relevant web and wireless protocols. Statistics are then generated and presented via a comprehensive web-based reporting tool. The types of statistics include the following mobile advertising metrics:

- Bandwidth (total, average per visit, total per file type)
- Hits (average per visit, number of downloads, page view breakdown)
- Visits (entry page, average duration, click paths, referring search engine)
- Visitors (browser type, user agent, OS)
- Handsets (make, model, screen resolution)
- Mobile Operator (country of origin, operator name)
- Geo Location (country of origin, RDNS lookup)

These mobile attributes can be segmented via modeling tools, such as those covered in Chapter 1—for targeting devices and making modeled offers for specific

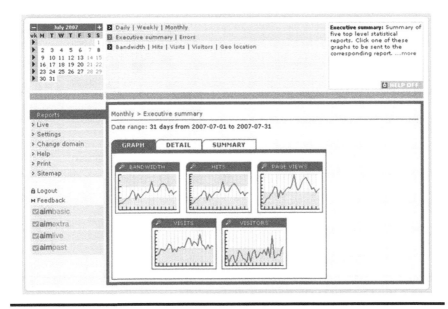

Figure 2.15   One of many device activity reports by Amethon Solutions.

products and services—via the use of decision-tree software, for extracting key device segments (Figure 2.15):

IF Average per visit 7+ minutes
AND   Number of downloads 3
AND   Android OS
AND   Search engine Yahoo
THEN Offer coupon for blouse

Amethon also provides what it calls "Content Fingerprinting" which are metrics on multimedia messaging service (MMS) which is a standard way to send messages that include multimedia content to and from mobile devices, such as videos, pictures, text pages, and ringtones. Content Fingerprinting reports on the revenue contribution and audience size of each content item or advertising campaign; they can be used by mobile operators to measure viral forwarding behavior of devices and report on total ROI of devices. This enables the M3 marketer to reward and retain devices that have the highest total value based on the MMS revenue they generate with viral interactions in their social network (Figure 2.16).

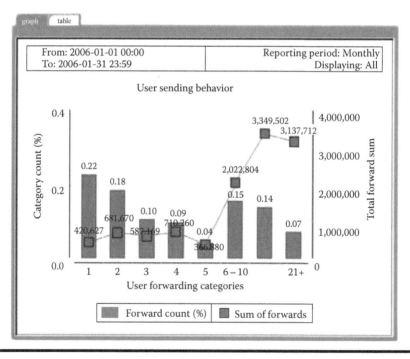

Figure 2.16   Content Fingerprinting viral report.

The M3 marketer needs to understand their consumers' decision path toward a purchase: do they seek input from peers, reviewers, retailers, or their competitors? M3 marketers need to ensure they are in a position to answer these consumer questions—all along the touch points leading to the actual sale—these are marketing priorities which need to be leveraged. Marketers need to allocate A5 resources accordingly and strategically invest in interacting with devices—before and after a purchase is made—as well as to measure their viral influence on other devices.

Several advertising networks which started as independent start-ups involved in the triangulation of mobile devices have been acquired recently—AdMob being purchased by Google (Figure 2.17).

While the Quattro Wireless ad network was acquired by Apple and is shutting down its 3-year-old operations in order to focus exclusively on supporting Apple's new iAd platform for distributing rich-media ads to its iOS devices. Jumptap is yet another advertising network for mobile devices; it offers a comprehensive set of ad formats and a full set of both display- and keyword-based inventories. The company partners with digital and media agencies, publishers, wireless carriers, and brand advertisers, to deliver an array of mobile advertising solutions.

Figure 2.17   AdMob marketplace from Google.

Jumptap has been awarded half a dozen patents in the United States; the latest one is as follows:

> The patent relates to a computer-implemented method for positioning targeted sponsored content on a mobile communication facility, the method comprising the steps of
>
> 1. Receiving data corresponding to a transaction event having occurred via the interaction of a user with the mobile communication facility, wherein the transaction event includes transmission of data representative of a first product or a first service being purchased by the user
> 2. Selecting advertising content based at least upon a relevance between a second product or a second service offered in the advertising content and the purchased first product or first service in the transaction event, wherein the relevance is further based on information relating to compatibility of the advertising content, second product, or second service with the mobile communication facility
> 3. Presenting the selected advertising content on a display of the mobile communication facility

Another firm Millennial Media also offers a full suite of mobile advertising services; its MBrand can be further integrated with Google's DoubleClick ad network and DeckTrade, another performance-based mobile advertising network. The company also designs and develops Millennial Motion, a platform that delivers media mobile campaigns.

M3 via Voice Recognition

Increasingly consumers are their device from which they can talk to them in their search for directions to places, stores, or other friends. M3 marketers need to leverage these voice, face, and device recognition technologies to facilitate interactions and increase sales and consumer loyalty. Voice recognition technologies from such firms as Vlingo, Yapme, and PhoneTag can enable consumers to converse with their devices—instructing them to perform searches for them which can be delivered with targeted content and advertisements.

Vlingo, for example, combines voice recognition technology to quickly connect with people, businesses, and activities; it can read incoming text and e-mail messages aloud. The Vlingo system allows users to say anything to their device and still be recognized properly. Accuracy is greatly improved for tasking devices and is better than humans on many tasks; any application can be speech enabled. This is accomplished through advanced adaptation techniques that learn what users are likely to say to different applications.

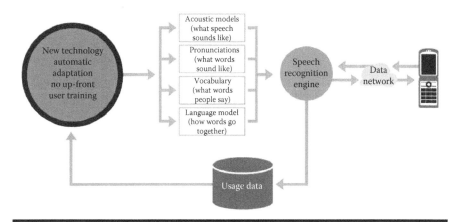

Figure 2.18   This is how Vlingo "learns" words for devices.

Central to these techniques is a technology called Hierarchical Language Models (HLMs) that allows Vlingo to scale its learning algorithms to millions of vocabulary words and millions of users. In order to achieve unprecedented accuracy at massive scales, Vlingo technology uses HLM-based speech recognition which replaces grammars and statistical language models with very large vocabulary—millions of words—these HLMs are based on well-defined statistical models to predict what words users are likely to say and how words are grouped together. For example, "let's meet at _____" is likely to be followed by something like "1 p.m." or the name of a place (Figure 2.18).

While there are no hard constraints, the Vlingo models are able to take into account what this and other users have spoken in the particular text box in the particular application, and therefore improve with usage. Unlike previous generations of statistical language models, the new HLM technology being developed by Vlingo scales to tasks requiring the modeling of millions of possible words—such as open web search, directory assistance, navigation, or other tasks—where users are likely to use any of a very large number of words.

Another voice recognition provider is Yap which can read, search, and forward voicemail. Yap performs automated speech recognition platform for "long-duration" dialogues. Long-duration dialogues are conversations and audio content ranging from 5 s to several hours. Yap specializes in accurately transcribing these dialogues for a variety of different scenarios including voicemail to text, conference call transcriptions, analysis of customer phone calls, and voice-activated mobile messaging.

These dialogues often contain valuable and time-sensitive information. Yap can convert these dialogues into text; this audio content becomes more useful and accessible. Yap Voicemail also allows for reading voice messages so that when a device receives a message, it can automatically transcribe it. The Yap Voicemail also supports the search of voicemail message via keywords. Yap's Speech Cloud™ code allows M3 marketers to quickly introduce very-high-accuracy speech

Figure 2.19 PhoneTag Conversion from voicemail to text.

recognition capabilities into their own products and services. Unlike traditional approaches to speech recognition, the Yap's Speech Cloud does not require complex software or telephony integration.

Another voice recognition provider is PhoneTag which can also convert voicemail to text and deliver it via e-mail and/or as a text message. PhoneTag works with all Major U.S. carriers and networks including AT&T, Alltel, Cincinnati Bell, Sprint, Skype, T-Mobile, Verizon, Virgin, and more. PhoneTag can be used to unify all devices whether mobile or desktop into one unlimited voicemail box. With PhoneTag, a user can read every voicemail that comes into any of their devices' phone numbers—from anywhere (Figure 2.19).

Still another voice recognition firm is TellMe which provides instruction technology, so that people can use their devices to get the information they need; it combines Internet data and a voice interface, and it allows users to simply say what they want and get it. TellMe's mantra is "Say it. Get it." Instead of fiddling with buttons and memorizing keystrokes, users can tell their devices, whether their PC, phone, car, or TV, what they want. Some of the services running on TellMe's platform include business search on 411 and information search on 1-800-555-TELL; TellMe is a Microsoft® subsidiary.

Lastly, there is Nuance, a voice recognition company, which provides solutions for multiple industries concentrating on autos. Their VSuite is a speaker-independent voice command and control framework that allows for voice-based access to a phone's core features and services. Their Nuance® Voice Control enables the use of speech to access and utilize mobile handset-based or network-dependent features, applications, services, and content. Their Vocalizer is an embedded small footprint text-to-speech engine that processes audio from static recordings and dynamically generated prompts. All of these voice recognition solution providers can be combined with location-specific services by M3 marketers to deliver targeted voice advertisements to mobile devices.

Facial Recognition

Because photos are such an important part of Facebook, they are using facial recognition technology to "tag" uploads of new photos. The facial recognition capabilities allow for the social network to match new photos from devices to other photos they have tagged in the past. Facebook can group similar photos together and, whenever possible, suggest the name of the friends in the photos.

By making tagging easier than before, the network makes devices know right away when friends post photos from their devices. Facebook will notify devices when their photos have been tagged. Facebook provides the ideal platform to develop a procedure for accurate automatic facial recognition. Facebook's Tag Suggestions feature automatically determines the identities of people in uploaded photos and suggests names the uploader can use to tag the images.

Facebook's users collectively upload millions of photos daily, and the company has long encouraged them to add digital tags identifying the people in them and is using that information to build a database of facial images. The network has a facial recognition database to identify people automatically and is using the data and software to help users identify the people in the snapshots they upload to their network.

Accurate face recognition is critical for many security applications. Current automatic face-recognition systems are defeated by natural changes in lighting and pose, which often affect face images more profoundly than changes in identity. The only system that can reliably cope with such variability is a human observer who is familiar with the faces concerned. Modeled human familiarity of face representations from naturally varying photographs increased the accuracy of face-recognition algorithm from 54% to 100%, bringing the robust performance of a familiar human to an automated system, which is what Facebook has accomplished.

Mobile Rich Media for M3 and A5

A novel approach to M3 marketing is provided by Mobile Posse; they proactively deliver information, entertainment, and promotional content to the *idle* screens of devices. Graphical and interactive messages are delivered only when the device is not already in use—ensuring that phone calls, text messaging, and mobile web browsing are not interrupted—content can include weather forecasts, sport scores, and trivia, as well as exclusive coupons and mobile discounts, offers, and deals in a nonintrusive manner.

Mobile Posse is a free service that keeps devices in the know, wherever they go! They can get weather forecasts, local gas prices, sports scores, and more—along with great savings from national and local retailers. Mobile Posse delivers informative and fun content to devices each day when they are not in use. Devices need to set their profile and preferences to specify the type of content and offers that they want to see.

Mobile Posse is a provider of mobile advertising for the active "idle screen." The firm uses its proprietary patent-pending technology; it enables M3 marketers to proactively reach consumers through the prime real estate on mobile devices. It is the first company to commercially launch graphically rich and interactive idle screen programming in North America; it delivers a unique idle screen experience for moving digital devices.

The idle screen is the main screen, or home screen, of mobile devices. It is the starting point for most activities on the mobile device, providing access to the mobile web, text messaging, phone settings, and more. The idle screen is also the most viewed screen on the mobile device; each year, the average mobile consumer will view their device's idle screen more than 1200 times. Mobile Posse's technology activates the idle screen—allowing it to deliver full-screen, graphical, and interactive messages to the home screen of the mobile device.

Requiring only creative assets, the platform allows existing campaigns to be easily ported to mobile devices. Short-form surveys are also supported, allowing advertisers and carriers to poll mobile consumers in near-real time. Messages are delivered only when the mobile device is not already in use, ensuring a superior experience for consumers, carriers, advertisers, and M3 marketers. Mobile Posse serves leading wireless carriers including Verizon Wireless, Alltel Wireless, Cricket Communications, and Revol Wireless.

Another innovative mobile marketing platform is Medialets; it combines rich-media advertising with behavioral analytics in support of Apple and Android devices. Medialets provides a platform for brands and agencies to create ads for all modern mobile devices. Their Enrich™ program enables mobile ad networks as well as ad mediators and ad servers to sell and support their cross-platform rich-media units. Advertisers can run a single set of ads without changes across a broad range of mobile devices and access a unified set of reports from which to measure marketing campaigns.

With its ability to effectively engage the growing mobile audience, mobile rich media has emerged as a must-include component of the advertising mix. Medialets provides highly engaging rich-media advertising across the broadest array of premium mobile apps and mobile devices. Medialets supports M3 marketers with high-impact rich-media ad products and services, including ad distribution delivery and deep ad campaign analytics.

As brands increasingly seek opportunities to deliver rich-media campaigns to all types of digital devices, Medialets offers the most effective way for publishers and developers to meet this demand. Medialets is not an ad network; instead, they provide publishers and developers with everything they needed to effectively sell high-value mobile A5s. Their rich-media ad platform makes it possible for M3 marketers to tap into the full value of their mobile inventory across different devices.

An innovative rich-media app known as Flipboard—which is free to download—presents a unique marketing opportunity for the iPad Apple device. The app asks users to enter their Facebook or Twitter account information and their

Figure 2.20 Flipboard rich-media digital magazine.

favorite publications. Flipboard then goes out and pulls in all the relevant links to news articles, blog items, photographs, and other streaming content through those social-networking feeds and displays it in a visually appealing—easy-to-navigate format—evocative of a traditional slick magazine (Figure 2.20).

Flipboard also supports full-screen, magazine-style advertising which M3 marketers need to know about and leverage for targeting this Apple device. Flipboard arranges stories and photos in a style that will be familiar to anyone who has ever read a magazine or a newspaper; the headlines, pull quotes, and graphics occupy the full iPad screen, giving the readers a quick take on several articles at once. It is this serendipitous quality that makes Flipboard so addictive. The app mashes up stories from all over the web in a way that feels beautifully random via rich media, and it is an A5 M3 marketers should know about.

Another rich-media player is Xtract, a company that combines social, behavioral, and mobile analytics to attract and acquire consumers. It offers what it calls Social Links, either as a licensed software product or as a hosted service for analyses of device behaviors, interactions, and demographic data from the user's subscriber network to identify the best targets for effective and personalized marketing campaigns. Xtracts' Advanced Analytics platform is capable of utilizing vast amount of versatile data. Xtract can provide some M3 marketing tools that will turn the vast amount of data into actionable information regarding future device behaviors; Xtract also offers analyses that are self-learning.

Smaato is another firm whose unique feature is the aggregation of multiple leading mobile ad networks globally. Smaato provides one single connection service for mobile advertising, capable of reaching consumers worldwide in 220 countries. Smaato also offers the widest range of mobile advertising SDKs in the mobile space for such devices as iOS (iPhone, iPad, and iAd), Android, Windows Phone 7, Symbian (Qt', WRT, and S60), Blackberry, and Bada.

There is also Nexage, an ad agency that takes a more holistic approach to strengthening mobile business by focusing on increasing monetization performance and the value of each impression and brand value. Their Nexage Rich Media Connect (RMC) is a business solution that increases the efficiency and throughput of high-yield mobile rich-media campaigns by connecting rich-media ad sources to billions of mobile website and applications.

Mobile Ad Exchanges for A5

For the M3 marketer, mobile devices are critical since they provide significant value, which can be derived from customized A5s. In the world of mobile, there is no anonymity (digital devices are always with consumers, and they are always on. A5s make possible the transmission of various user and device attributes) which an M3 marketer can use for creating predictive models of device behaviors and consumer preferences. All mobile devices reveal their phone numbers, their current location, and their device unique identification number.

Customized A5s can expand these numbers of variable to include age and gender and other location and interest attributes that allow for behavioral analytics and the clustering, classification, and prediction of consumer propensities. Personal details such as age and gender are volunteered by user when they download and register their apps; permission marketing should include a privacy notification to these new consumers. Most will not opt out since they want the free content and services apps provide, such as Pandora, the customizable radio station.

It is important to understand the insignificance of some of these data attributes captured by these A5s—which privacy advocates claim is violating consumer rights. First, an individual's name, their Social Security Number, or their device UDID is totally useless for behavioral analytics and M3 marketing. Secondly, such unique identifiers are excluded from modeling—they are too specific for behavioral analysis—instead predictive models for M3 marketing involve creating decision-tree analyses based on device characteristics and behaviors, along with network parameters combined with some human data points such as age and gender. In the end, it is about machine learning and data mining devices and their anonymous owners—that have tendencies to like certain content or products and services.

The Only RTB Mobile Ad Exchange
Where the best apps meet the best ads.

DEVELOPERS   ADVERTISERS

Figure 2.21   Mobclix mobile ad exchange.

Mobclix, a mobile ad exchange, matches dozens of ad networks with thousands of apps-seeking advertisers. The company collects phone IDs, encodes them to mask them, and assigns them to interest categories based on what apps people download and how much time they spend using an app, among other factors. By tracking a phone's location, Mobclix can calibrate the location of the device—which it then matches to demographic data from the Nielsen Company. Mobclix can place a user into more than 150 consumer segments which it offers to advertisers, from "die hard gamers" to "soccer moms"—by segmenting apps rather than individuals. Mobclix is accurate in targeting devices without identifying individuals (Figure 2.21).

Mobclix provides a supply-side platform for RTB of ad inventory. Demand-side platforms (DSPs) and RTB ad networks can bid for individual ad impressions in real time, giving advertisers and agencies dramatically better targeting and increased performance of their A5s. The RTB system gives publishers complete control over every impression so they can maximize revenue, monetize relevant audiences beyond typical strategies, and achieve improved lifts of their ad inventories up to 40%–85%.

Market researcher Gartner Inc. estimates that worldwide A5s sales this year will total $6.7 billion. Many developers offer A5s for free, hoping to profit by selling advertising inside the app itself. Users are willing to tolerate ads in A5s to get something for free. Ad sales on mobile devices is currently less than 5% of the $23 billion in annual online advertising, but spending on wireless ads is growing faster than the market overall. Many ad networks offer SDKs such as Millennial Media for capturing age, gender, income, and ethnicity, to assist advertisers, publishers, developers, and M3 marketers to provide more relevant mobile ads via customized A5s (Figure 2.22).

Google is the biggest data aggregator from A5s via its AdMob, AdSense, Analytics, and DoubleClick units; they use dozens of apps to let advertisers target device users by location, type of device, age, and other demographics. Apple operates its

Figure 2.22   Millennial Media mobile ad exchange.

iAd network for marketing on its iPhone—but dozens of other apps stream data to all Apple devices. Apple, in addition, targets its ads to mobile devices based largely on what it knows about them through its App Store and iTunes music and video store. The targeted marketing to these Apple devices can be based on the types of songs, videos, games, and apps a person has purchased over time.

Apple is waging a war for the hearts and minds of A5 developers; there are approximately 425,000 Apple apps—roughly twice as many Android—that are a big reason why consumers have purchased 200 million Apple devices. Consumers have paid more than $4.3 billion for apps sold on Apple's App Store. That includes the original purchase, plus upgrades and ads that appear with the apps. Apple makes only a few devices, so writing for the iOS software is simpler than doing so for the Android OS, which resides in many more devices. However, according to a recent survey by market research firm Evans Data, the percentage of developers writing apps for Android (43.5%) just passed the share working in iOS (39.7%).

Apple recently filed a patent application for a system for placing and pricing ads based on a person's web or search history and the content of their media library. The patent application also lists another possible way of targeting ads "via the content of a friend's media library." The patent states Apple would tap "known connections on one or more social-networking websites" or publicly available information or private databases describing purchasing decisions, brand preferences, and other data. Interestingly, Apple recently introduced a social-networking service within iTunes, called Ping, that lets users share music preferences with friends.

In announcing its iCloud hosting service, Steve Jobs stated the following: "We're going to demote the PC and Mac to just be a device. We're going to move the hub, the center of your digital life, to the cloud." By migrating and synchronizing all devices to Apple servers, Apple will be able to control and track all device behaviors and activities. iCloud is a way to keep all devices up to date—all documents, e-mails, media storage, pictures, videos, songs, movies, etc. In fact there are three major cloud services vying for control of device data and behaviors (aside from Apple's iCloud, there is also Google Music Beta and Amazon Cloud Drive); all three offer this storage service for free within space limits.

Anonymous Consumer Categories for M3

Engagement marketing uses "influence metrics" to measure a consumer's likelihood to encourage friends to consider, recommend, or purchase a brand. In an increasingly wired and mobile social web world, texts, opt-in surveys, tweets, questionnaires, chats, and instant messaging platforms provide new metrics for M3 marketers—and the clustering of anonymous consumer categories based on the behavior of their digital devices. Engagement consumer profiles can be developed from passive—to semiactive participants—to the golden nugget: the brand zealot.

Companies would do well to listen to what consumers are saying about their brands. Tracking what brand advocates are saying via their product reviews or comments in social sites is important for marketers and enterprises who may want to enlist the services of peer reviewers, such as Epinions which has product reviews on dozens of categories; here are just a few:

Cameras and photo: digital cameras, film cameras, camera lenses, etc.
Clothing and apparel: women, men, shirts and tops, sweaters, pants, outerwear, etc.
Electronics: MP3 players, GPS, cell phones, camcorders, audio, home theater, etc.
Home and garden: home furnishings, furniture, tools, cooking, heaters, etc.
Video games: game consoles, computer games, Xbox 360, PS3, Wii, DS, PSP, etc.
Gifts: jewelry, flowers, fragrances, watches, etc.
Computers: laptops, desktops, Mac laptops, Mac desktops, software, printers, etc.
Kids and family: baby care, toys, education, pets, etc.
TV and video: televisions, LCD TV, plasma TV, blu-ray players, DVD, DVR, etc.
Sports and recreation: exercise equipment, snowboard, ski, cycling, sports apparel, etc.
Media: videos and DVDs, books, music, movies, etc.
Restaurants and gourmet: restaurants, beer and liquor, wines, etc.
Travel and hotels: hotels, destinations, airlines, family travel, ski resorts, cruises, etc.
Wellness and beauty: personal care, beauty, nutrition, hair care, health, etc.
Business and technology: office supplies, websites, communications, finance, etc.
Cars and motorsports: new, used, motorcycles, RVs, tires, car stereos, etc.

Manufacturers should track social commentary to get ideas about product shortcomings and desired features consumers want. Retailers should also identify consumers who influence others' purchases, and encourage them to add new content to their viral ad campaigns. M3 marketers need to create profiles of products and services "champions" in order to target and recruit and retain more of these valuable "evangelists" with similar interests and preferences using the clustering and classification software covered in Chapter 1. A new metric is evolving in social media and that is the cost per acquired advocate (CPAA).

M3 marketers need to focus on identifying these "brand zealots" in order to attract more with similar preferences, desires, demographics, and influences. Brands that have created strong emotional and personal associations tend to have higher attraction and loyalty, in this era of social media, blogs, texts, e-mails, and other bursts of personal communications. M3 marketers should look at evangelist consumers as comarketers for their brand. Through the strategic use of engagement marketing, companies can invite consumers to become the coproducers of marketing campaigns—such as the creation of slogans, designs, widgets, videos, and other promotional viral advertisements.

The goal is to connect friends with brands by engaging them in a cooperative interaction. At the core of engagement, marketing is the realization that humans are highly social animals. Consumers have an innate need to communicate and interact which in today's interconnected 24/7 life is the grease to engagement marketing via social media. Recommendation to friends enables the creation of trust and strengthens the relationships between consumers and brands.

People embrace what they create, and marketing via friends provides them the means by which they can be part of a brand: it provides them an identity and a sense of belonging. The social networking generation shuns traditional organizations in favor instead of direct participation and influence at an organic level. Consumers possess the skills to lead, confer, and discuss via friends—enabling these "influencers" to become part of the brand itself.

Today, transparency, interactivity, engagement, collaboration, experience, and trust replace the world of mass media with that of social media. Consumers are increasingly creating messages and expressing themselves using the brands that resonate with them and their friends. They are personalizing the way they shop, interact, entertain, watch, listen, and communicate. They are creating videos and watching what others have made; they listen to podcasts and record their own; and they share photos, songs, jokes, and information via their network of friends.

Engaging consumers at an emotional level via the web or mobile can provide rich insight and customer loyalty value. The key engagement marketing drivers are surprise, emotional bonding, and above all relevancy delivered in an indirect and nonintrusive manner. Consumer engagement, however, requires a new generation of metrics for M3 marketers such as (1) involvement, (2) interaction, (3) intimacy, and (4) influence.

Involvement is the most basic of metrics and reflects the measurable aspects of a consumer's relationship with a brand. Emotional advertising has captured the imagination of marketers and enterprises that see an enormous potential to increase the recognition and loyalty of their brands. M3 marketers need to focus on the process of developing emotional connection with consumers and the development of brand bonding with them. For example, Scribd enables the sharing of reading recommendations to and from friends.

First, there were pop-up ads on AOL and then banner ads on Yahoo, followed by search ads on Google; but now there are engagement ads on Facebook. The social network encourages members to interact with the ads by leaving comments, sharing virtual gifts, or becoming fans. In doing so, consumer can begin to interact with a brand where friends become a vital component of engagement marketing via their social network. Facebook has developed a new kind of marketing model—that is vastly more powerful, intimately more personal, and engagingly social. Facebook has beaten out AOL, Yahoo, and Google and their pop-up, banner, and search ads, with new engagement ads. Engagement ads ask users to take action and become part of the brand's DNA—play a video, vote in a poll, RSVP an event, or just comment on the "like" it button—which is intended to convey a recommendation to friends.

Engagement ads provide a couple of unique methods of delivery—rather than clicking on a networked ad and being whisked away to the sponsoring website. These types of advertisements allow Facebook members to stay within the contained walls of the social site with their group of friends. Engagement ads can take the form of "comments" or "gift" formats, both of which involve the use of emotional advertising. Engagement ads allow Facebook members to increase interactions, create spontaneous social buzz, and champion brand engagements.

Comments ads are another vehicle Facebook offers its members, so they can leave recommendations on advertisements—much like wall postings or digital graffiti. Again, this type of engagement marketing is where the strategy is to allow the rabid brand evangelist to be part of the process. The whole premise of the social sites is that everything is more valuable when your friends say it is cool and you need to know about it.

Leveraging the communication and influence power of social networks for marketers and advertisers is an important new channel to be developed and utilized. The increasing prominence of social networks as the means to communicate and share information among their friends can be quantified by M3 marketers by enlisting ad agencies who focus on social media campaigns and metrics.

A new company Factual is doing just that; they are building databases from unstructured data whose primary focus is on basic information about businesses. Facebook is using Factual to populate its Places app to broadcast their locations to friends. However, more importantly, Factual is creating a web-wide ontology from this "unstructured data" as found in social media postings on the web to automatically find and sort this data into segmented categories; it then offers these segmented categories to companies that are eager to purchase it for web and mobile marketing applications.

Factual is an open data platform for application developers that leverage large-scale aggregation and community exchange. For example, the data sets have millions of U.S. and international local businesses and points of interest, as well as data sets on entertainment, health, and education. The Factual's hosted data come from our community of users, developers, and partners, and from text mining techniques and tools. The result is a rich, constantly improving, transparent data ecosystem, made up of what Factual calls "living" data.

Factual provides a suite of simple data APIs and tools for developers to build web and mobile applications. In some cases, developers who create applications with Factual data may even get paid for crowd sourced data from their users. Factual was originally Applied Semantics which used natural language for the creation of anonymous consumer categories; they also developed AdSense, the contextual advertising platform and was acquired by Google in 2003.

The Factual databases are organized along health, retail, entertainment, and other topics. This "data as a service" model is gaining competition for social sites, such as Metaweb which relies on human editors to create entity graphs of people, places, and things. The Factual system is trained on seed data, and the machine-learning stack works to validate and expand upon such data. They use a combination of algorithmic approaches which run on top of Factual's own data warehouses as well as extant third party web caches and resources provided through search engine partnerships.

Digital Fingerprinting for A5 and M3

Today, *devices* are the targets of M3 marketers, such as web cookies and wireless apps, and now a new forensic technology is evolving known as "digital finger-printing" which most importantly allows for the modeling of device behavioral data. There have been privacy concerns about cookies and other tracking mechanisms that enable the targeting of ads to individuals; but this is a misnomer. These mechanisms and techniques are actually tracking the behaviors of devices not humans.

In the 1990s, everyone was "sharing" music files via Napster, so a road manager for a famous band (INXS) figured out a way to tie an individual music download to a specific computer and thus created the "digital fingerprinting" of PCs. That patented technology now makes it possible for marketing to any and all digital devices. Thanks to rock and roll—digital devices and M3 rule—although originally developed to stop online piracy, digital fingerprinting is an ideal technology for market targeting to all types of stationary and/or mobile digital devices.

The problem is not privacy; instead, it is about relevance. The dilemma is that there is a torrent of unsolicited data bombarding consumers 24/7. There is simply too much information coming at humans; subsequently there is a need to filter and refine these streams of web and wireless data to enable the consumer to only get what they want, when they want it, and in the format they dictate. M3 marketing can make this possible by modeling the behaviors of devices and not necessarily individuals.

M3 is really about going back to the future. Years ago merchants sold their products directly to consumers; tailors, bakers, butchers, and shopkeepers all inter-acted with their customers at a very intimate level, enabling them to provide per-sonalized service and to know and learn their clients' tastes and preferences. Today, the web and mobile world replicates this intimate and congenial storefront environ-ment in a digital format.

M3 enables consumer's behaviors to drive which products and services they see. M3 marketers need to consider the platform they will use for delivering their ads and offers—perhaps based on the consumers' own media preferences, whether that be the web, social media, or mobile. Whether it is an interactive survey, a streaming video clip, or a mobile app, the consumers will drive their channel of choice, which can be uncovered through behavioral analytics. The channel itself becomes a new segmentation value in today's multichannel marketplace.

M3 marketers need to carefully consider how consumers cluster their behav-ior—across different media and devices—who buy what, where, when, and how. Marketers need to keep in mind that everything can be measured in terms of rev-enue, loyalty, relevancy, satisfaction, speed, and performance. All device behaviors today are digital in nature and thus are amenable to continuous monitoring, adjust-ment, modeling, and metrics. The M3 marketing strategy should be designed with the objective of understanding who the consumer is and what their needs are—in order to provide highly relevant offers that are of high value to them, based on their historical behaviors—to ensure their loyalty.

There is a need to recognize the fast development of mobile devices; there are 5 billion subscriptions to handsets. However, after 30 years of the PC era, there are only a billion PCs. Mobile app analytics firm Flurry issued a report recently com-paring the daily engagement of mobile devices versus web browsing on PCs. The report used data from web reporting firms comScore and Alexa; for mobile metrics it used its own analytics. The report shows that daily time spent in mobile devices surpassed web consumption (Figure 2.23).

M3 marketing is the future of advertising with more major brands turning to the web, social networks, and mobile to target their increasingly fragmented consumers, which brings us to the question on the difference between marketing and advertis-ing: well, marketing is the strategy, while advertising is the execution. Both are criti-cal, but M3 can assist by identifying the consumer devices to target, as well as what channels to pursue. The old time merchant did not need to know their customers' last names or other unique identifiers, to serve them with relevancy and superior service.

To replicate that old time merchants, M3 marketers can now rely on "device identification"—such as that provided by digital fingerprinting firms like BlueCava which strips out all personally identifiable information (PII)—so that marketers can target *machines* not people. The digital fingerprinting technology uses a new way to aggregate audiences around a universal identifier; BlueCava uses their pro-prietary token which is persistent. However, since the technology is profiling a *device*, there are no privacy concerns for M3 marketers or consumers.

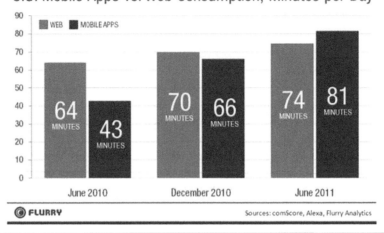

Figure 2.23   In 2011 mobile devices surpassed web browsing.

Digital fingerprinting creates a single "reputation" (profile) based on the digital device behaviors, shopping habits, and other machine-specific attributes, features, and settings. Until recently, fingerprinting was used mainly to prevent illegal copying of computer software or to thwart credit card fraud. However, BlueCava is racing to collect digital fingerprints from every type of digital device—everything from PCs to mobile phones in the world—to perform device identification for the modeling of their behaviors and targeted marketing (Figure 2.24).

So far BlueCava has identified 200 million digital devices with hopes that by the end of 2012, it will have catalogued 1 billion of the world's estimated 10 billion devices.

Figure 2.24   Machine marketing to machines.

M3 marketers should embrace digital fingerprinting since it is anonymous, very robust, and more accurate than traditional Internet mechanisms like cookies, beacons, and mobile apps. Fingerprinting involves capturing and modeling devices based on several parameters, including, but not limited to, the following settings and attributes:

Fonts: It looks to see what fonts were installed and used on a device.

Screen size: It looks to see what screen size and the color setting of the device.

Browser plug-ins: It looks and maps what optional software a device has, such as Flash.

Time stamp: It compares the time a device logs on to a server, down to the millisecond.

User agent: Like cookies, it identifies what type of OS the device is using.

User ID: It assigns a unique "token" that can be used to track all activities for that device.

BlueCava is actually a spin-off from an Australian antipiracy company Uniloc which holds U.S. patent 5,490,216; its abstract is as follows:

> A registration system allows digital data or software to run in a use mode on a platform if and only if an appropriate licensing procedure has been followed. Preferably, the system detects when part of the platform on which the digital data has been loaded has changed in part or in entirety, as compared with the platform parameters, when the software or digital data to be protected was last booted or run. The system relies on a portion of digital data or code which is integral to the digital data to be protected by the system. This integral portion is termed the code portion and may include an algorithm that generates a registration number unique to an intending licensee of the digital data based on information supplied by the licensee which characterizes the licensee. The algorithm in the code portion is duplicated at a remote location on a platform under the control of the licensor or its agents, and communication between the intending licensee and the licensor or its agent is required so that a matching registration number can be generated at the remote location for subsequent communication to the intending licensee as a permit to licensed operation of the digital data in a use mode. The code portion can be identical for all copies of the digital data. The algorithm provides a registration number which can be "unique" if the details provided by the intending licenses upon which the algorithm relies when executed upon the platform are themselves "unique."

BlueCava's device identification technology creates an electronic fingerprint based on the unique characteristics of any digital computing device. This means no two digital devices are seen as identical, as is the case with human fingerprints; digital fingerprints are unique to each machine. Being able to identify and differentiate devices represents a powerful tool that can be used for authentication, auditing, access control, licensing, and fraud detection. But most importantly, this technology can be used to achieve a new level precision and targeting for M3 marketing. BlueCava's device identification platform provides a unique combination of three characteristics essential to M3 marketing. They are (1) uniqueness, (2) tolerance, and (3) integrity:

Uniqueness: Their device fingerprinting is based on dozens of component types and attributes plus values which guarantees the uniqueness of the fingerprint.

Tolerance: Their device identification algorithms are resilient to changes in physical devices and their configuration.

Integrity: Their obfuscation, hashing, encryptions, and randomization work in unison to provide integrity to the secure device fingerprint.

They have two components: a fingerprint client and a device lookup service. The fingerprint client is responsible for generating a unique fingerprint for the device. Security code within the BlueCava client also obfuscates signs and randomizes the generated fingerprint so that it cannot be replayed or forged. The BlueCava device lookup service then accepts the encrypted and randomized fingerprints and returns a persistent device token which can be used by applications directly.

There are two kinds of fingerprint clients: physical device fingerprint clients and web fingerprint clients. Physical device fingerprint clients are installed and run on the actual device. The physical device client can be packaged within applications or can be downloaded and installed as a stand-alone. Physical device fingerprint clients are available on a variety of platforms, including Windows, Mac, Linux, iPhone, Android, BlackBerry, and many more mobile devices. The web fingerprint client, on the other hand, is run from within a browser and can be invoked automatically from a web page, with no additional download required. Both the web fingerprint client and the physical device fingerprint client produce secured fingerprints. These are passed to the device lookup service for resolution into a persistent device token.

And thus, digital fingerprinting has evolved, first and foremost for machine-learning forensic purposes designed to prevent fraud and the theft of software and content; however, the same technology can be used for M3 marketing purposes where billions of dollars will be generated over the coming years. Aside from BlueCava, there are several other firms offering fingerprinting technology including iovation, 41st Parameter, Imperium, and Auditude. All of them just like BlueCava are principally using digital fingerprinting technology for security and fraud detection but are also amenable to digital device marketing.

Iovation offers what it calls "Real IP" for identifying a user's IP address and geolocation. Location details help users of iovation's service and software pinpoint devices anywhere in the planet. The problem is that users can mask their genuine IPs, making them hard if not impossible to geotarget. That is where iovation's Real IP comes in, which bypasses proxy IP addresses and goes directly to the source—straight to the physical device—to learn the true IP and geolocation. Real IP makes it easy to triangulate the actual location of any device in the world for M3 marketing and A5 targeting.

The iovation Real IP tells the marketer where visitors to sites are coming from. Geolocation data includes country, the stated and real IP address, latitude, and longitude. Real IP verification works in real time with IP verification in milliseconds. M3 marketers can set the usage parameters and business rules, which can be developed by them or via decision-tree analyses. The iovation "ReputationManager360" exposes the behaviors and reputations of every device that interacts with a website.

41st Parameter offers what it calls "DeviceInsight" which enables websites to "converse" with all transacting devices. Through this nonobtrusive, automatically conducted conversation, a digital fingerprint for the device is created, which can be used to match devices to log-ins or transactions. DeviceInsight requires no user involvement, hardware deployment, or disruption to the user experience.

41st Parameter offers an open API of DeviceInsight which allows it to be easily integrated into existing applications—operating with any device connecting to a website—including mobile devices and game consoles via any browser connection. Web and wireless cookies are capable of profiling on the average of about 70% of all stationary or mobile devices. DeviceInsight from 41st Parameter can generate device-based proxies for virtually 100% of all devices, increasing M3 marketing without infringing on human consumer privacy.

Based on patented technology, "DeviceInsight for Marketing" generates a digital fingerprint so granular that it can serve as functionally superior replacement for cookies or Flash Local Shared Objects (LSOs). Requiring no user involvement, hardware deployment, or change to the user experience, it does not write anything to the consumer digital devices. The technology does not leave any residue in the form of a cookie, Flash LSO, or any other object—making it an effective and transparent solution for M3 marketing—even in countries with the strictest personal privacy regulations.

To further differentiate between devices, especially mobile ones which have fewer attributes available to generate a digital fingerprint, 41st Parameter's patented "Time Differential Linking (TDL)" software according to the firm increases the uniqueness of device fingerprints by up to 43.7% compared with the accuracy of fingerprinting alone. This level of differentiation allows M3 marketers to target more accurately with up to 100% longer duration than with traditional JavaScript cookies. Their technology is packaged as both a Web/HTML API and a Smartphone App SDK for Apple's iOS.

Imperium, another digital fingerprint firm, offers three products: "RelevantID" for M3 marketing and data certification, "Verity" for identity validation, and "RelevantView" for market research. As with the other fingerprinting companies,

Imperium is also involved in the dual areas of fraud detection and real-time marketing. RelevantID's digital fingerprinting technology goes beyond traditional cookie methods to create a new approach to assuring and certifying the behavioral data collected is reliable and predictive of device behaviors.

RelevantID works through a combination of watermarking and digital fingerprinting. Digital fingerprinting is the process of collecting more than 60 data points about a user's device. These data points are then processed by their proprietary algorithm to produce a unique digital fingerprint. RelevantID is Imperium's proprietary technology that is consistent with U.S. privacy and European data protection laws; marketing machine to machine is legal and highly precise and relevant to consumers and profitable to enterprises.

When a user accesses a service, RelevantID can identify the device and collects a large number of data points about its attributes and settings. The information gathered is put through deterministic algorithms to create a unique digital fingerprint of each digital device. The Imperium process is invisible to the user and does not interfere with the user experience. Once fingerprinted, a device is open to M3 marketing, for example, the fingerprinted devices can be clustered into different categories using SOM neural network software, or they can be segmented into distinct groups based on machine-learning decision-tree business rules.

Lastly, there is Auditude which focuses on video and media management, via its Connect ad platform and its ContentID indexing system. Their patented approach to content identification enables clients to identify, track, and monetize content across the web. Auditude automates identification to claim video content by applying business rules to enable ad sales, creating an entirely new revenue stream.

The Auditude system fingerprints over 100 channels of TV every second, every day, and applies the right metadata (showing name, episode, air date, etc.) to client's content no matter where it ends up. Their digital fingerprinting technology has been validated as not only among the most accurate, but at speeds that are 30–300 times faster than the rest of the industry. Auditude concentrates on fingerprinting streaming video for their clients.

Fingerprinting is the future of M3 marketing largely because it is invisible, tough to fend off, nonintrusive, more accurate than JavaScript web or wireless cookies, semipermanent; and it works with *all* types of digital devices. A typical digital device broadcasts hundreds of details about itself when it connects to a website. M3 marketers can use those details to "fingerprint" PCs, phones, tablets, automobiles, and all digital devices—in a race to meet the $23 billion U.S. online advertising industry's appetite for detailed consumer behaviors.

Each digital device has a different clock setting, different fonts, different software, and many other characteristics that make them unique. Every time a device goes online, it broadcasts hundreds of details in order to communicate with sites and their servers. Marketers can use this data to uniquely identify devices and build profiles of their owners. BlueCava and the other fingerprinting companies do not collect individual's names; they only collect the digital details of devices.

There are hundreds of attributes from all types of digital devices; the objective of these fingerprinting vendors is how to rearrange them: that is the critical task. BlueCava, iovation, Imperium, and 41st Parameter have developed software to catalog each device's individual properties. There are subtle variations among outwardly similar machines; there are literally hundreds of variables that can be configured and measured. Originally fingerprinting was a system for software registration, as was the case with Uniloc. However, BlueCava was spun off to market device identification both for fraud detection but most importantly for very specific anonymous targeted advertising.

BlueCava can embed its fingerprinting technologies in websites, downloadable games, and wireless apps. BlueCava plans to launch a "reputation exchange" that will include all the millions of fingerprints it has collected so far. The idea behind the BlueCava exchange is to let advertisers build profiles of the users of the devices that it has fingerprinted. BlueCava also plans to link the profiles of various devices—such as Apple and Android devices for instance—that also appear to be used by the same individual.

M3 marketers can develop a technique of matching fingerprints to other online and offline information, such as property records, motor-vehicle registration, income estimates, social network profiles, and other data captured from traditional Internet mechanisms, such as cookies, beacons, and e-mail addresses. This will enable a site to use a device's fingerprint, for example, to look up information about an e-mail address of that individual. The M3 marketer is at the hub of this data aggregation and modeling and must have a strategy about how to accomplish this for growth revenue and customer loyalty.

The M3 marketer needs to develop the framework to compile a profile of the assembled human information along with a detailed description of that device's behaviors. This can also include the matching and merging of mobile apps and the attributes and device behaviors capture from social and mobile websites. For example, Mobext, a mobile advertising unit of Havas SA, is already testing BlueCava's fingerprinting technology on mobile devices. Digital fingerprinting brings a new level of precision to M3 marketing; however, this not prevent the marketer from mixing and matching it with other more traditional Internet mechanisms—along with new evolving ones such as social and mobile data aggregation sources.

As previously mentioned, the M3 marketer needs to conduct a data audit which will include an assessment of the business goals and objectives, a broad analysis of the data sources for meeting those objectives—the testing of multiple models designed to optimized what data to use and how to use them and the ongoing metrics to ensure devices are being targeted in the best possible way and via what single or multiple digital channels.

M3 marketers must cut down to the core of their needs, their true objectives, and finally the goals of their marketing campaigns. There is buffet of data sources which are evolving at an explosive rate. The challenge is deciding on which ones to use and how to leverage them and in what sequence. M3 marketing is both a science and an art; it requires the knowledge of data and algorithms and most importantly how they can be configured into beautiful canvases of improved customer service and relevancy.

The process can enlist the use of clustering software to autonomously organize device behavioral data via an unsupervised method of data analysis. Undirected autonomous knowledge discovery can lead to questioning about *why* the products and services sell together, *who* is buying particular combination of products, and *when* the purchases tend to be made. An SOM neural network can be used to independently interrogate the data in order to autonomously cluster and group device behaviors. Once a clustering analysis has been performed, the M3 marketer needs to study the resulting clusters to see what they have in common and how that information might be put to optimum use (Figure 2.25).

From these self-directed data clustering analyses, structured relationships and groupings can be uncovered between digital devices—and marketed products and services using directed data knowledge discovery programs. For example, at this juncture, powerful decision-tree software such as CART can be deployed to uncover business rules from multiple data sources which can be leveraged over all types of digital channels.

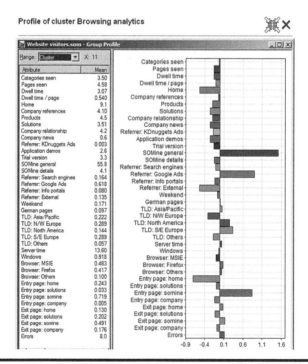

Figure 2.25   Grouping of browsing devices using SOM software.

An M3 marketer can use decision-tree software to develop predictive models using data from web aggregators, such as RapLeaf, along with information harvested by such firms as PeekYou, and wireless data aggregated by such mobile exchanges as Ringleader Digital. These predictive models can then be enhanced by merging it with digital fingerprints from BlueCava, iovation, Imperium, or 41st Parameter so that IF/THEN rules can be created to predict the behaviors of consumers via a combination of web, social network, mobile, and device data. Such predictive decision-tree rules might resemble something like the following:

IF	Female	(captured by RapLeaf from the web)
AND	Volleyball	(captured by PeekYou from a social network)
AND	iPhone	(captured by Ringleader Digital from a wireless phone)
AND	Verdana	(captured by BlueCava from a digital device)
THEN	$51–$146	(projected total sales)

As this predictive rule shows at no time is the name of the consumer used—it is totally anonymous for M3 and A5—entirely based on behaviors captured from the web, social sites, mobile A5s, and digital devices. These anonymous features can be used to predict, as this example shows, the projected total sales amount from this consumer's device. This in essence is the objective of triangular behavioral analytics for M3 marketing. The marketer needs to carefully consider performing an audit prior to the creation of these predictive models, in order to ensure the objectives for assembling the right data, from the right sources for the optimal results from these behavioral analytics.

The importance of digital fingerprinting will increase in the future as more and more devices are being manufactured with embedded processors from Intel and other microprocessor manufacturers. Intel sees digital advertising signage as a new growth market for their Atom chips. LG Electronics, for example, is using Intel Atom chips in signs that will recognize the age, gender, and other characteristics of passerby and change the advertising pitch accordingly. ARM Holdings is also marketing smart chips to Texas Instruments, Qualcomm, and Marvell who are embedding them in a diverse group of digital devices—starting with phones—but rapidly expanding to tablets, appliances, and automobiles.

A new technology known as *haptics* will add tactile dimensions to digital devices so that consumers will be able to feel the textures of products they are shopping for before they purchase them. Haptics software and digital screen start-ups like Pacinian, Senseng, and Tactus Technology are racing to add tactile sensations to gadgets, and add a new level of consumer interaction and shopper engagement and the promise to fill the basic human desire to *feel* things. M3 marketing will complete the shopping experience. Not only will A5s locate that pair of corduroy pants a consumer was looking for but it will also be able to do price comparisons and do different configurations of colors and styles. They will also be able to sense them prior to purchasing them all from their digital device.

Already millions of Nokia, Samsung, and LG devices have been preloaded with haptics software made by Immersion for gaming apps, but the true money is on M3 marketing. Touch screens and surfaces are quickly emerging as the preferred interface for new digital devices. Pacinian has developed an interface for creating the sensation of pushing a button with no mechanical parts. Senseng coated screens can produce feelings like vibrations, clicks, and textures. Tactus Technology has patents on interactive pop-up screens, allowing consumers to feel the edges of letters, numbers, symbols, knobs, guitar strings, and most importantly the textures of products that can pop up on their devices upon the request of their human owners.

Now, As to how to get it done, the next chapter will provide some checklists the M3 marketer needs to carefully go over in order to launch and implement their campaigns and projects.

Chapter 3

Checklists

Why M3 Checklists?

In this chapter, extensive checklists of processes, sources, software, networks, and solution providers are covered in detail to ensure machine-to-machine marketing (M3) marketers execute successful anonymous advertising apps anywhere anytime (A5) campaigns. Why checklists? Because they are a type of informational job aid used to reduce failure by compensating for potential limits of M3 marketers' memory, attention, and the discipline to focus on their A5 tasks and strategies.

There are aviation checklists to ensure that critical items are not forgotten. They are used in medicine to ensure that clinical proper and life-saving practice guidelines are followed. An example is the Surgical Safety Checklist developed for the World Health Organization by Dr. Atul Gawande. Checklists are used in the quality assurance of software engineering, to check process compliance, code standardization, and error prevention; they are used in civil litigation processes. The point is these checklists will help to ensure consistency and completeness in carrying out M3 marketing objectives.

It is highly recommended that the reader use the companion website of this book (www.jesusmena.com) to quickly access the resources covered in these checklists. In this chapter, a discussion takes place about the values and benefits of these various M3 marketing resources; this is the meat and potatoes manual section of the book and a catalog to the future of advertising equipment and digital mechanics for M3 marketers.

To succeed in M3 marketing monitoring, new developments in digital pattern recognition technologies is an absolute necessity. In this chapter, dozens of firms are identified for the reader; what is important is to chase the technology and not the companies. These checklists are only as current as today; new firms and resources will evolve and recognize the rapidly changing nature of M3 and A5.

As previously mentioned, one of the first and most critical tasks to M3 marketing is the discovery of device groupings and clusters via unsupervised knowledge analyzes using self-organizing map (SOM) neural networks. The objective being to perform autonomous clustering when one cluster is compared to another and new knowledge is discovered as to why. For example, SOM software can be used to discover clusters of e-mails, website visitors, and digital devices, enabling a marketer to discover unique features of different consumer groups.

Checklist for Clustering Words and Consumer Behaviors

■ Identify the source of words or behaviors you want to cluster, for example, an online survey, tweets, e-mails, texts, website behaviors, mobile apps, etc.
■ Build and train a cluster of words or behaviors, using clustering software that let the words and behaviors organize themselves into natural groupings.
■ Evaluate the accuracy of the clusters against new words and behaviors, taking unseen words and behaviors from the same source used to build the model, how accurate are the predictions?
■ Consider what the clusters have revealed and generate new analyzes, this usually involves using classification software for "supervised learning."

Text mining software can also be used to sort through unstructured content that can be found in millions of documents, notes, e-mails, texts, chats, web forms, voicemails, news stories, regulatory filings, repair records, field representative notes, invoices, blogs, etc., generated by digital devices 24/7. Text analytics generally includes such tasks as the categorization of taxonomies, the clustering of concepts, entity and information extraction, sentiment analysis and summarization, as well as the autonomous creation of ontologies.

This type of undirected unsupervised type of knowledge discovery, as previously mentioned, is best performed with neural network SOM programs. SOM software has been used for market basket analyzes to discover who buys what, when, and where. This is an important first task in M3 marketing. This type of autonomous data mining analysis is driven by the data, not the marketer.

Checklist of Clustering Software

■ *BayesiaLab*: Bayesian classification algorithms to automatically cluster digital device behavioral variables into distinct consumer groups (Figure 3.1).
A Bayesian network is a graphic probabilistic model through which one can acquire, capitalize on, and exploit knowledge. Particularly suited to taking

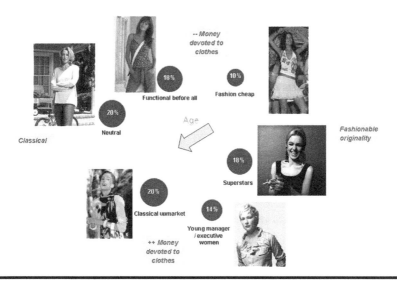

Figure 3.1   Type of typology clustering performed by BayesiaLab.

uncertainty into consideration, they can as easily be described manually by experts in the field as they can be generated automatically through learning. A Bayesian network or belief network is a probabilistic graphical model that represents a set of random variables and their conditional dependencies. For example, a Bayesian network could represent the probabilistic relationships between certain digital devices and consumer preferences. Given these preferences, a network can be used to compute the probabilities of the presence of various devices (Figure 3.2).

A Bayesian network is used to analyze data in order to diagnose clusters and the resulting probability distribution on the effects. A Bayesian network is a graphical model that encodes probabilistic relationships among variables of interest. When used in conjunction with statistical techniques, the graphical model has several advantages for data analysis and the discovery of hidden relationships for the M3 marketer.

There are several advantages to the use of Bayesian network software. First, because the model encodes dependencies among all variables, it readily handles situations where some data entries are missing. Second, a Bayesian network can be used to learn causal relationships and hence can be used to gain understanding about a problem domain and to predict the consequences of intervention. Last, because the model has both a causal and probabilistic semantics, it is an ideal representation for combining prior knowledge in large data sets for the M3 marketer.

With BayesiaLab, M3 marketers can develop various scenarios by changing the key factors of the problem addressed. The software is extensive and no cause is overlooked and all possibilities are considered. BayesiaLab is an ideal tool for

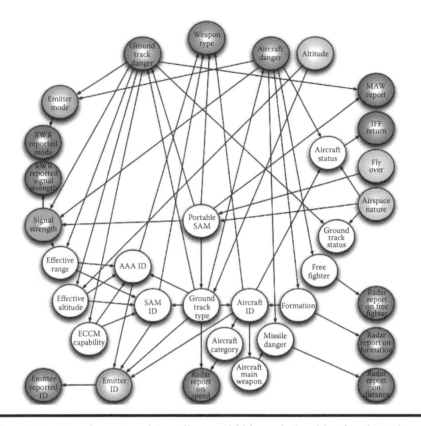

Figure 3.2 Bayesian network can discover hidden relationships for clustering.

analyzing the uses and attitudes of a group of customers, satisfaction questionnaire analysis, brand image analysis, segmentation, clusters, and groupings of customers or products, assessment of appetence scores in relation to new products, and multiple digital devices. The Bayesia Market Simulator (BMS) is a program through which can be compared the influence of a set of competing offers in relation to a defined population of devices and consumer behaviors and groupings.

Viscovery can be used for cluster analysis with metrics of defined segments. Viscovery is the best SOM clustering technology company in the world and is one of the most powerful unsupervised programs for knowledge discovery. Device behavior is constantly changing, often in subtle ways that are not immediately apparent. To react with the right action at the right time, this behavioral data needs to be segmented accurately to ensure an effective response in real time and to increase revenues (Figure 3.3).

SOM software, like that from Viscovery, can be used by M3 marketers to target group specification and campaign design based on digital device behaviors. It can be used for customer segmentation and scoring, churn

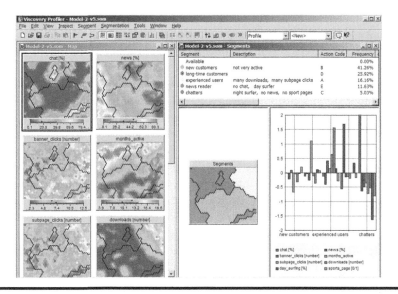

Figure 3.3   Device behavior clusters discovered by Viscovery SOMine.

prevention, device key-performance indicator analysis, user device profiling, real-time A5, and the integration of empirical data. The M3 marketer can download a free evaluation of the software.

■ *PolyAnalyst*: From Megaputer, PolyAnalyst offers clustering analysis based on a localization of anomalies (LA) algorithm.

This is a Russian-based company operating out of the corn fields of Indiana. They offer more data mining algorithms in their software than practically anyone else in the industry, including SPSS (now IBM) or SAS the behemoths of data analytics. The analytical algorithms they offer include the following:

Predictive neural networks	R-forests
Classification neural networks	Association rule learning
Rule induction	Temporal association learning
Linear regression	Anomaly detection
Logistic regression	Support vector machines
Case-based reasoning	Naive-Bayes classification
Bayesian networks	Expectation maximization clustering
CHAID	Correlation analysis
Decision trees	Instance-based reasoning

Megaputer has a dynamic software product. It calls this X-SellAnalyst, which empowers websites to recommend new products in real time to devices and customers. Every site interaction is an opportunity to sell more and it is less costly to sell to existing customers rather than acquiring new customers. X-SellAnalyst offers products or services that fit the needs of individual visitors to build customer loyalty. In today's environment, sophisticated customers expect personal and highly relevant information. This includes new customers; X-SellAnalyst allows sites to maximize every device interaction.

In the current competitive world where customers have a high propensity to switch, it is imperative that retailers try to maintain visitors' interest with relevant and useful information. X-SellAnalyst trains itself on available transactional data and develops and stores a recommendation filter that can be used for quickly calculating the most attractive cross-sell opportunities. Once trained, X-SellAnalyst can serve as an intelligent adviser recommending not only the products—which have the best chance to be purchased—but also those with a higher margin and volume products that are likely to be purchased (Figure 3.4).

X-SellAnalyst attempts to maximize a site's overall potential profit when recommending additional products to customers. X-SellAnalyst is extremely scalable: it can train quickly on data involving dozens of thousands of products and millions of customers and transactions. X-SellAnalyst can be easily incorporated in any external system: it is packaged as a component object model (COM) module. One of the features of X-SellAnalyst is its amazing scalability. The calculation time for 100,000 products has a recommendation time that is a fraction of a second.

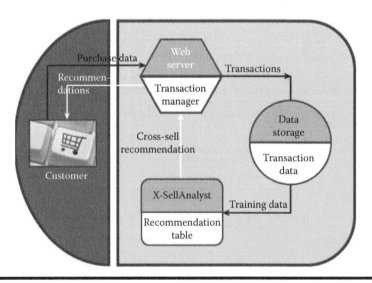

Figure 3.4   X-SellAnalyst makes recommendation from streams of data.

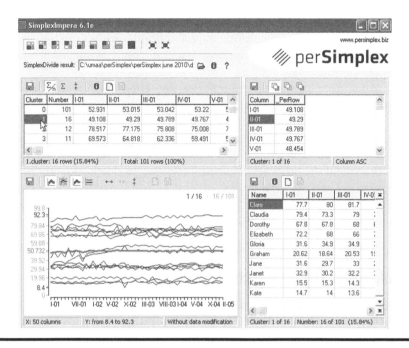

Figure 3.5   Clusters discovered via perSimplex.

■ *perSimplex*: Clustering software based on fuzzy logic, free download available. perSimplex helps to find hidden connections in device data. It is a software based on natural shape analysis: fuzzy logic. The software is able to process interaction and behavioral data via visualization designed to influence M3 marketer's decisions. They do this by generating curve shape to clarify hidden relations within device activities (Figure 3.5).

   perSimplex selects the relevant pieces of information from huge volumes of data sources and creates clustering analyzes based on natural shape of data curves using fuzzy logic technology. Fuzzy logic is a form of reasoning that approximates behaviors rather than fixed logic or exact shapes. perSimplex is fast and simple with the ability to identify natural data clusters and data abnormalities. perSimplex can identify adequate clusters and has the ability to distinguish the level of similarity and to identify the abnormalities of input data via its proprietary nonhierarchical cluster algorithm for linear computing complexity.

■ *Visipoint*: SOM for autonomous clustering and visualization.
Visipoint clustering software is primarily designed for informatics, that is, software designed to expedite the discovery process of new bioactive molecules, processes, and techniques in the fields of pharmaceutical, cosmetic, food, and the chemical industry. However, the accuracy of the clustering

software can also be leveraged by M3 marketers. The accuracy of this type of technology can not only provide improved health care but can also be leveraged to assist marketers for the autonomous discovery of important segments of device behaviors.

Aside from organizing key concepts, clustering software can be used to self-organize device behaviors. Devices can also be clustered by text analytics software into key segments along service and product lines. For example, visitors to social sites can be grouped into those that are interested in sports, financials, music, or other major topical categories. The following checklist is of some of the major text analytical software products. They are relatively easy to use and can yield important results for M3 marketers by performing data analyses of unstructured content for consumer sentiment categorization, social, web, and mobile intelligence gathering.

Checklist of Text Analytical Software

1. *ActivePoint*: Software for interactive search and product suggestion.
   ActivePoint's patented TX5™ system is a contextual dialogue-oriented natural language system that is combined with engines that utilize rule-based reasoning and algorithms. The TX5 systems are able to automate virtually all multiple marketing channels. The software's uniqueness is that it has the ability not only to find products but also to educate, convince, suggest relevant products, answer consumer questions, compare products, handle objections, and offer alternatives. It can ultimately encourage consumer devices to make purchases, mimicking all of the functions of a live sales assistant.

   The TX5 system is a server-side application designed with a flexible, object-oriented architecture for seamless integration with an enterprise's existing databases, web servers, and other mobile applications. The system can also take advantage of repetitive questions by learning them and improving on its ability to provide answers. The TX5 system is built from multiple intelligent engines, with each engine having a defined task. The engines enable the system to compare, suggest, convince, negotiate, offer, answer simple or complex natural language queries, and, most importantly, perform a flexible dialogue, adapted in real time according to the user's needs. The ActivePoint patent for its *Virtual Sales Rep* was approved in the United States; altogether three patents were approved, with another one pending in Europe (Figure 3.6).

   The TX5 System Series incorporates dual functionalities with its natural language engine: first, with sentence contextual understanding, it helps devices find the product or service information they are looking for; second, its guidance engine can help and direct devices toward appropriate solutions using natural language interactions.

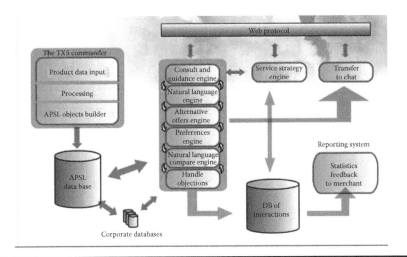

Figure 3.6   TX5™ natural language technology chart.

2. *Aiaioo Labs*: Text categorization and sentiment analysis software.

Online, social network, and mobile reviews of products or services often express positive or negative sentiments that are valuable to collect and summarize. This task requires the classification of an utterance about products or services into positive, neutral, or negative utterance. This task is known as *sentiment classification*. (This is what their software can do.) Aiaioo Labs is a small research company based in Bangalore. Their text analytical software can look at the word devices use in their searches to assign them into categorical clusters such as the following:

a.   Crime
b.   Politics
c.   Business and Finance
d.   Sports
e.   Entertainment
f.   Lifestyle
g.   Environment
h.   Education

The technology they used is Naive Bayesian classifier based (using a multinomial distribution and Laplacian smoothing); it executes very fast. The software's precision and recall figures are both fairly high—around 90%—with incremental improvement as the software collects more samples; the more data you give it, the better it categorizes.

3. *Attensity*: It can extract "who," "what," "where," "when," and "why" and their relations.

M3 marketers recognize that customer conversations with and about a brand or a company are multiplying as consumers use mobile devices and social

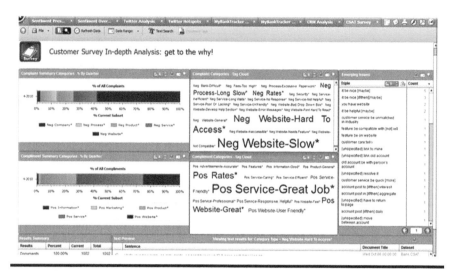

Figure 3.7   Negative and positive comments extracted by Attensity.

networking to share opinions and recommend products and services. Buried in the millions of reviews, comments, e-mails, surveys, and tweets generated every day is a wealth of customer intelligence that can be mined and used to improve the consumer's device experience (Figure 3.7).

Attensity provides a suite of integrated applications that allow M3 marketers to extract, analyze, quantify, and act on customer conversations from unstructured content, no matter where they take place: internally in e-mails and customer surveys or externally on blogs, tweets, review sites, or social media networks. The Attensity suite consists of three components: (1) Attensity Analyze, (2) Analyze for Social Media, and (3) Attensity Respond.

Attensity Analyze lets the M3 marketer measure and understand customer conversations stored in internal sources, such as contact center notes, surveys, and incoming e-mails, and how they relate those conversations to an enterprise's internal data sources, such as sales figures, inventory numbers, customer service records, and more. The component provides reports, dashboards, and alerts to keep the M3 marketer up to date on the latest trends, issues, and customer sentiments. Attensity Analyze includes sophisticated analytics that makes it possible for M3 marketers to extract unprecedented business insights from customer conversations, including

a. Customer device behavior profiling
b. Detailed consumer sentiment analysis
c. Root cause of issues about product and services
d. Hotspotting: alerts about emerging issues
e. Predictive device behavioral analytics

With its turnkey reporting wizard and analysis tools, Attensity Analyze offers a drag-and-drop approach and out-of-the-box widgets that allow the M3 marketer to quickly and easily build ad hoc reports around key themes, such as customer sentiment, product and service issues, consumer intent to churn, and emerging trends. In addition, a comprehensive set of out-of-the-box reports and dashboards helps M3 marketers to start gaining insights in a matter of minutes.

Analyze for Social Media continuously monitors and analyzes customer conversations across external media, including review sites, blogs, forums, Twitter, Facebook, YouTube videos, mainstream news sites, and mobile A5s. A wide variety of out-of-the-box reports help the M3 marketer track and analyze ongoing relevant conversations about their client's brands, products, services, and competitors. The component can also identify influential opinion leaders and sources and understand sentiment and issues, along with industry trends.

It is software as a service (SaaS) solution that lets the M3 marketer monitor and analyze millions of online sources for customer intelligence. It works seamlessly with Attensity Analyze allowing the marketer to analyze social media and other customer conversation channels side by side. Analyze for Social Media continuously monitors and analyzes social media conversations and delivers a wide variety of out-of-the-box web-based reports that help the M3 marketer to track and analyze ongoing relevant conversations about their brands.

Attensity Respond is a component for multichannel monitoring that lets M3 marketers proactively respond to customer conversations when and where those conversations take place and whether those conversations are direct, via their e-mail channels, or indirect, via forum posts or tweets. Attensity Respond handles all incoming e-mails, contact form submissions, comments in customer forums, letters, short message service (SMS) messages, tweets, and other types of customer communications. It then categorizes, routes, and queues them using Attensity's text mining pattern recognition technology.

Attensity Respond allows those messages to be tracked as trouble tickets and generates a suggested response that can be automatically sent to the customer or routed to a contact center agent for servicing by the appropriate person or team. Their Attensity Respond for Social Media is specifically designed to help enterprise social media teams more effectively listen and respond to customers communicating via mobile as well as tweets, Facebook posts, forums, blogs, communities, and other social media. Working in conjunction with Attensity Analyze, Attensity Respond for Social Media scans can be performed in seeking out cries for help, issue reports, compliments, and complaints.

The Attensity software suite and its components can also be used to track, manage, and control business processes by retaining all customer interaction-related history to stay compliant with both company rules and external regulations, such as FINRA, Sarbanes-Oxley, or HIPPA, and support multiple departments and business units through a multitenancy architecture. Last, the software and its components can be integrated with all the leading customer relationship management (CRM) systems such as SAP, Oracle-Siebel, salesforce.com, Kana, eGain, and Microsoft. Attensity provides hosted, integrated, and stand-alone text analytics solutions to extract facts, relationships, and consumer sentiment from unstructured data, which comprise approximately 85% of the information companies store electronically.

4. *Clarabridge*: It can perform sentimental and concept extraction.

   Clarabridge transforms text-based content into quantitative and easily consumed reports and analysis. Clarabridge integrates the broadest continuum of customer feedback, regardless of channel, from internal and external sources, in structured and unstructured format, and in any language. After collecting the feedback, Clarabridge extracts linguistic content, categorizes, and assigns sentiment scores to distinguish the "who," "what," "how," and "why" of any customer experience. Because Clarabridge makes data accessible from a variety of interfaces, the M3 marketer can receive critical voice of the customer intelligence, when and how they need it.

5. *ClearForest*: It derives meaning from websites, news feeds, blogs, tweets, e-mails, etc.

   The OneCalais algorithm uses natural language processing (NLP), text analytics, and data mining technologies to derive meaning from unstructured information, including news articles, blog posts, research reports, etc. OneCalais categorizes each piece of content using both data streams with hidden codes and social tags. The software then identifies and classifies people, places, companies, facts, and events in the unstructured content, for metadata categorization and behavioral analysis.

   ClearForest was contracted by the Federal Bureau of Investigation (FBI) for counterintelligence assistance in sorting and organizing millions of data streams of unstructured monitored intelligence. However, this same technology can be leveraged by M3 marketers for enhancing their knowledge from unstructured content for consumer and device intelligence.

6. *Crossminder* is an NLP tool for analyzing sites, other depositories, and e-mails.

   The software helps M3 marketers automate processes where languages and the meanings of documents play a central role, whether they want to transform the linguistic data into something machines can use or the marketer wants to analyze texts and retrieve the key information in a structured format. The software can identify market trends, interpret, and predict customers' behaviors from their digital messages and develop lexical terminological categories.

7. *dtSearch*: Fast indexing, searching, and retrieving software from millions of text files.

The dtSearch product line can instantly search terabytes of text across a desktop, network, web, or mobile depository. dtSearch products serve as tools for publishing, with instant text searching, large document collections for sites or mobile devices. M3 marketers can embed dtSearch's instant searching and file format in support of their own A5s. dtSearch products can directly access items in Outlook including all contacts, appointments, and messages, along with the full-text of attachments, including zipped and nested attachments, and display all retrieved items with highlighted hits.

8. *Lexalytics*: It converts unstructured text for social network monitoring.
The software can automatically extract companies and brands and understand the sentiment (tone) being directed toward each; it does this across any type of text. Lexalytics uses thematic analysis to understand the concepts present in conversations, and it uses these themes to understand the words that people are naturally using to convey their view of brands. Marketers can gain a complete understanding of everything that is being said by any brand or company on any channel. One of the most sophisticated areas of text analytics is the ability to ascertain the tone being directed toward a concept, entity, company, or brand. Mechanically processing sentiment across thousands of concepts and entities leads to a much greater understanding of the semantic map of potential bias.

9. *Leximancer*: Concept maps for customer and web intelligence monitoring.
Leximancer support numerous data-file sources. It also provides web-crawling capabilities of online social media. Their software is presented as a visually "Concept Map," depicting the salient concepts and their relationships, which can be readily interrogated at either the theme, concept, or thesaurus level, with drill-down capability to the supporting text. Its Insight Dashboard is designed to get immediate views into the data and solution characteristics. Leximancer's latest technology is its *Sentiment Lens*—an extension of its "thesaurus-learning" methodology that greatly enhances the accuracy of sentiment detection by "conceptualizing" sentiment seed words, to better identify their true meaning, removing "rogue" or ambiguous sentiment usage, and identifying any newly emergent sentiment terms (Figure 3.8). Sentiment is becoming a paramount concern for M3 marketers especially in today's burgeoning blogging and interconnected social media world to answer what consumer devices are saying about brands and why they are promoters, detractors, or simply passive.

10. *Nstein*: Semantic site for website content management.
Nstein's text mining engine (TME) helps extract the value from content and maximize it, all while reducing content-related costs. Nstein's technology automatically ingests and analyzes unstructured data, identifying context, meaning, people, categories, entities, and even sentiment and returning standardized, interconnected, structured data that can be viewed on a macro- or micro-level. With its patented algorithm, Nstein creates a "semantic fingerprint" for every asset for easy identification and association. Nstein identifies nuance and meaning in content, making it ready for M3 marketers.

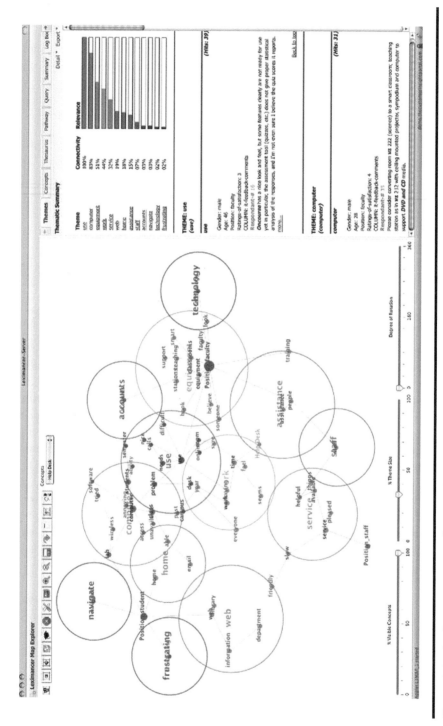

Figure 3.8 Leximancer map explorer analysis of words from a website.

11. *Recommind*: It automatically tags e-mail and uses probabilistic latent semantic algorithm.

    Their Decisiv E-mail Management tool solves enterprise e-mail issues by automating the categorization and filing of e-mail-based information, storing e-mail efficiently, and providing robust user centricity to enable users to quickly locate and retrieve e-mails out of the system. Recommind is powered by its context optimized relevancy engine (CORE) platform, a fully integrated set of technologies, which deliver the most accurate information, irrespective of language, information type or volume, and keyword for the M3 marketer. Recommind uses its proprietary machine-learning techniques including its Probabilistic Latent Semantic Analysis (PLSA) algorithms. They are the result of the latest developments in machine learning for concept search and categorization.

12. *Wordstat*: For automatic tagging and classification of unstructured content.

    WordStat provides text mining for the M3 marketer via its Simstat, a statistical data analysis tool and QDA Miner, a qualitative data analysis component for analyzing text and relating its content to structured information including numerical and categorical data.

    There is also a machine-learning software for consumer device segmentation, classification, and prediction. These types of programs can generate graphical decision trees as well as predictive rules about web and mobile behaviors for the M3 marketer. The following checklist contains some of the most powerful and effective deductive classification software tools.

    When an M3 marketer needs to make a decision based on several behavioral factors, such as location, device being used, and total log-in time, a decision tree can help identify which factors to consider and how each factor has historically been associated with different outcomes—such as what products or services a device is likely to purchase—based on captured consumer behavioral patterns over time. Almost always these classification programs produce highly compact models. They can identify only the most valuable attributes for predicting device behaviors with only a few conditional rules. This type of classification analysis is a form of "information compression" for M3 marketers.

Checklist of Classification Software

- *AC2*: A graphical tool for building decision trees.
  AC2 is a software for data mining by decision tree. It is a powerful and inviting tool that allows the creation of segmentation models; includes interactive decision trees; generates reports and the construction of cross tables, utilitarian, and dynamic; measures dependencies of all variables; regroups similar individuals in classes; compares numerous data sets; and makes forecasts by the attribution of scores to populations.

■ *Angoss KnowledgeSEEKER*™: Multiple-branch trees for segmentation.
This is one of the most powerful and robust classification software in the marketplace. It generates multiple-branch decision trees (rare), code, and predictive rules and can assist the M3 marketer in device segmentation. Device segmentation is the first step in formulating effective strategies to address M3 marketing goals. This requires the analysis of device history in order to define and describe profitable device segments according to their buying and transactional behavior. These types of analyses can lead to M3 marketing strategies for cross-sell, up-sell, and consumer retention. This software can calculate the predicted return on investment (ROI) for multiple M3 marketing strategies. It can also identify the specific products or services consumers' devices are most likely to be interested in for their next purchase for up and cross-selling. One unique feature of this software is that it can work with discrete (categorical) and continuous (numerical) independent and dependent variables. It uses four algorithms based on improved variants of CHAID and CART algorithms. The software has an advanced algorithm control and user preferences to fine-tune tree growth and can generate code in structured English, generic code, SAS, SPSS, SQL, Java, PMML, and XML.

■ *C5.0*: It constructs classifiers in the form of decision trees and predictive rules. C5.0 uses an "information gain" algorithm and has been designed to analyze numeric, time, date, or nominal fields. To maximize interpretability, C5.0 classifiers are expressed as decision trees or sets of if-then rules ready for use by M3 marketers. The software is virtually free from its creator Dr. Ross Quinlan who has spent more than 30 years in data mining and machine learning and is the author of the ID3, C4.5, FOIL, and C5.0 algorithms.

■ *CART*: It creates compact decision tree for predictive modeling of device behaviors.
It is available from Salford Systems. The Classification And Regression Trees CART® algorithm is a robust, easy-to-use decision tree software that automatically sifts large, complex databases, searching for and isolating significant patterns and relationships. This discovered knowledge is then used to generate reliable, easy-to-grasp predictive models for applications such as finding best prospects and customers via the targeting of M3 marketing models of digital devices (Figure 3.9).

CART can quickly reveal important data relationships and is based on the landmark mathematical theory introduced in 1984 by four world-renowned statisticians at Stanford University and the University of California at Berkeley. CART supports high-speed deployment, allowing M3 marketing models to predict and score in real time on a massive scale.

■ *DTREG*: It can generate classification and regression decision trees.
This software supports the creation of decision tree forest, which is an ensemble of decision trees, whose predictions are combined to make the overall

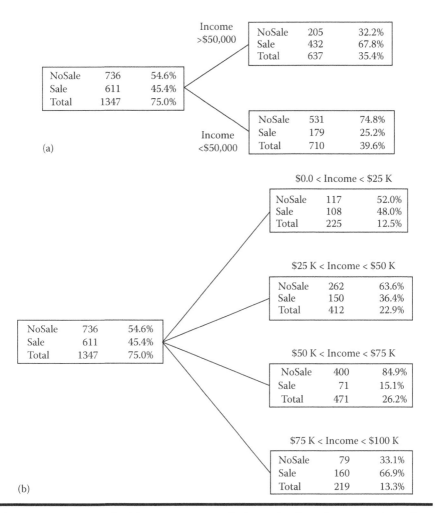

Figure 3.9 A CART decision tree can predicting sales, here it segmenting a data set by two income levels (a) and (b).

prediction for the forest. A decision tree forest grows a number of independent trees in parallel. Their models often have a degree of accuracy that cannot be obtained using a large, single-tree model. Decision tree forest models are among the most accurate models yet invented.

■ *PolyAnalyst*: It includes an information gain decision tree and other algorithms.

From Megaputer this software supports all the key steps of data preprocessing and modeling and results delivering. PolyAnalyst enables you to solve tasks of predicting, classifying, clustering, affinity grouping, link analysis, multidimensional analysis, and interactive graphical reporting of digital device behaviors.

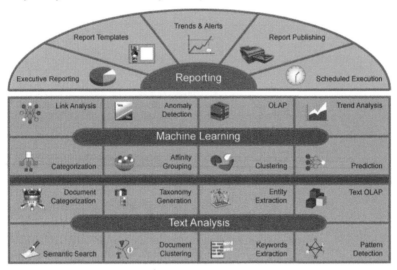

PolyAnalyst™ 6 : Data Analysis Capabilities

Figure 3.10   PolyAnalyst supports prediction via decision trees and much more.

It provides a variety of machine-learning algorithms for modeling, such as Regression, Neural Network, Decision Tree, Bayesian Network, CHAID, Support Vector Machine, and Random Forest (Figure 3.10).

■ *XpertRule Miner*: It offers graphical decision trees with embed ActiveX components.

The XpertRule technology features a graphical environment for developing rules; the software supports the development of applications in Java, VB, and .net programming. Predictive rules are deployed as automated advisors available as licensed software for on-premise hosting or as on-demand hosted SaaS.

Checklist of Streaming Analytical Software for M3

M3 marketers will also want to enlist both deductive and inductive "streaming analytical" software, which are event driven to link, monitor, and analyze digital device behaviors. These new streaming analytical software products react to "device consumer events" in real time. There are two main types of streaming analytical products. First, there are deductive streaming programs that are operated by user-defined business rules and are used to monitor multiple streams of data, reacting to consumer events as they take place.

Second, there are also inductive streaming software products that use predictive rules derived from the data itself via decision tree algorithms. These inductive streaming products build their rules from global models involving the segmentation and analysis from multiple and distributed data clouds and networks. These deductive and inductive software products can work with different data formats, from different locations to make real-time predictions using multiple models from massive digital data streams.

1. *Progress*: It enables adjustments to changing device interactions as they occur. Device events flowing in and out of a site or an enterprise can be subtle such as an order being processed or a question by a new device. The ability to respond in real time to these consumer events can provide a competitive advantage to the M3 marketer. The speed of advertising and the ever-changing marketing conditions means that traditional methods of handling behavioral data do not go far enough. The past tense nature of existing marketing solutions to *human* consumers often results too little targeting intelligence delivered to their devices. That is why real-time processing is so important. It requires response to "events" as they happen. The capturing and analysis of device events for modeling is paramount for the M3 marketer, who must respond accordingly and accurately via the right channel with the right sense of relevancy and customer care (Figure 3.11).

   The Progress® Apama® Event Processing Platform can provide the ability to monitor the activity of digital devices via its dashboard providing up-to-the-second visualization of key performance indicators (KPIs). The streaming analytical software gives M3 marketers the ability to see operational activity in real time, generating offers of products and services when conditions warrant them. The processing platform monitors rapidly moving event streams, detects and analyzes important patterns, and acts, in sub-millisecond time.

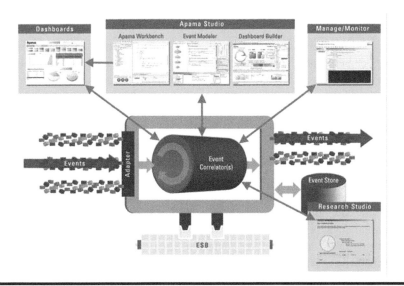

Figure 3.11   Progress event processing components.

With this type of streaming software marketing, events can be correlated and analyzed across multiple data streams in real time, providing new levels of decision making that dramatically improves marketing precision.

Complex Event Processing (CEP) is a new architectural approach that enables M3 marketers to respond more quickly to continuously changing device behaviors. CEP allows marketers to monitor, analyze, and act on data streams, often within milliseconds. As organizations, products, people, and their supporting technology systems become more connected, the speed at which data flow increases tremendously. CEP technology allows organizations and marketers to respond to these data streams more effectively.

Progress Software also provides solutions for algorithmic trading, database replication, enterprise messaging, integrated trouble management, real-time visibility, business process management, and other real-time data scenarios via the following software components:

a. *Apama Event Modeler*: This unique graphical environment enables marketers to compose, deploy, manage, and evolve event processing scenarios in days or hours instead of weeks or months. Logic flows are rendered graphically and users can create highly sophisticated scenarios that correlate events across multiple data streams.

b. *Apama Dashboard Studio*: Allows marketers to create sophisticated, graphical BAM dashboards that intuitively monitor event processing execution.

c. *Apama Research Studio and Event Store*: Gives marketers the tools to test new event processing applications and audit the operation of those already deployed.

2. *Sybase Platform*: It supports "event-driven" analytics from user-defined rules. It is a highly competitive marketplace. The M3 marketer and their offers of products and services need to be event driven. Delayed response to changing conditions can mean missed opportunities from streams of incoming data device behaviors. Sybase Aleri Streaming Platform enables rapid application development and deployment of real-time marketing applications that derive insight from streaming event data, empowering instant responses to changing conditions. The Aleri Streaming Platform consists of a high-performance CEP engine, the Sybase Aleri Studio, for rapid application development, and a range of integration tools including adapters and APIs. The streaming analytic software can process multiple streams of event data in real time. It can apply custom business logic to normalize, filter, correlate, and aggregate events; generate a stream of actionable information from one or more streams of raw data; and initiate automatic responses to changing conditions based on digital device events or combinations of events.

3. *StreamBase*: It does CEP for analysis of streaming data.
StreamBase is another CEP platform enabling the rapid development, deployment, and modification of applications that analyze and act on

large amounts of real-time streaming data. CEP is a technology for low-latency filtering, correlating, aggregating, and computing on real-world event data. The StreamBase Event Processing Platform is a software for rapidly building systems that analyze and act on real-time streaming data for building real-time marketing systems. StreamBase's CEP software is distinguished by bringing together three significant capabilities in one integrated platform: rapid development via the industry's first and only graphical event-flow language, extreme performance with a low-latency high-throughput event server, and the broadest connectivity to real-time and historical data.

4. *InferX*: Rules can be constructed from multiple distributed data sources. Distributed digital marketing analytics over multiple, disparate, and remote databases requires the use of software agent to access, analyze, and perform predictive analyses in real time on these data sources, simultaneously and in real time. This software can work on multiple formats during the same analysis and it involves a number of independent Modeling Agents (MA) operating within a network-based environment. Each MA operates on its own local database and is responsible for analyzing the data contained by the data set. Distributed data analytics is achieved through a synchronized collaboration of MAs facilitated by a Collaboration Server (CS) environment. This process results in a set of global rules generated by the partial contribution of each MA and assembled through a CS communication mechanism. Collective decision making is similarly achieved through the collaboration of Decision Agents, operating independently on their own data.

A5 Checklist

M3 marketing means focusing on consumer device choices, which leads to actionable insight and action, consequently leading to the monetization of web, social, and mobile device behaviors. The use of these clustering, text, classification, and streaming software tools enables M3 marketers to calibrate how devices behave and how brands can profit and respond with real-time relevancy. In A5, the most important issue is the location, aggregation, and use of the right data with the correlating consumer needs and preferences.

Marketers do not want to offer consumers devices products or services they do not want or content that is not relevant to them; this is not only wasteful but intrusive. Instead, A5s should be constructed and used based on historical behavior models in order to provide the right product to the right consumer at the right time and place, but care must be taken to protect consumers' privacy and security. Device behaviors are the most valuable assets M3 marketers and their clients have. They need to protect them and not to share them with others. The following checklist provides some best practices on A5s:

- Design the A5s to make the consumer experience so unique that it will ensure their loyalty for life: A5s should "anticipate" the devices' preferences, desires, and activities. In order to accomplish this, the clustering and modeling of device behaviors must be continuously refined by the M3 marketer. The marketer must consider the preferred method of shopping by devices, and how and what channel they like to use—web, social, or mobile.

- Ensure an enterprise's IT systems and the behaviors they capture for device analyzes are aligned with the business goals of the company and its marketing efforts. For example, if a marketing campaign is being planned via A5s for mobile devices, the IT department must be prepared to construct or contract for the creation of a mobile website. The marketer must also be prepared to determine what mobile devices to target, whether Android, Apple, or others.

- Incrementally measure the results of the unsupervised and supervised models to optimize their performance: The M3 marketer must understand that this is an ongoing process and not a one-time project. If streaming analytical software is being used, the M3 marketer must monitor the results of the inductive or deductive rules to ensure optimum performance, yield, sales, revenue, and relevancy.

- The M3 marketer must recognize that analytical systems need to be flexible and adaptive to change within a rapidly evolving business environment, model often and if possible continuously; the marketer should measure *everything*. Listen to what consumer devices are saying about a brand or a company. As previously mentioned, there is an assortment of firms and techniques that can be enlisted to accomplish this.

- Leverage existing IT legacy systems with external analytic services, such as psychographics networks, ad exchanges, recommendation engines, social media, and mobile apps. The M3 marketer needs to conduct a comprehensive data audit of the internal and external data sources in order to create a framework for strategically developing a marketing campaign to ensure customer devices are being served with relevant information about products and services.

- Protect consumer privacy and respect their desire, state, and share clearly why analytics and modeling is being performed: to ensure consumer relevancy and improve customer service. The M3 marketer needs to ensure anonymous techniques and technologies are properly being used, such as digital fingerprinting that targets digital devices rather than human consumers.

- Recognize that every company is unique, so its analytical strategy, components, architecture, and design will be driven by its industry and marketplace, as well as the type of product or service it offers to consumer devices. The responsibility for ensuring the alignment of these factors rests with the

M3 marketer and how the A5s are developed and deployed. Consideration should be given to the ownership of the marketing strategy and efforts and how much will be outsourced and retained internally.

M3 Privacy Notification Checklist

A privacy notification policy is a legal document that discloses some or all of the ways an enterprise and marketers gathers, uses, discloses, and manages a customer's data. The exact contents of a privacy policy will depend upon the applicable law and may need to address the requirements of multiple countries or jurisdictions. While there is no universal guidance for the content of specific privacy policies, it is critical that M3 marketers ensure such privacy policies and notifications are developed and prominently displayed to consumer devices.

The privacy notification policy statement should include compliance with various state and federal privacy laws and third-party initiatives, including the Federal Trade Commission Fair Information Practices, the California Online Privacy Protection Act, the Children's Online Privacy Protection Act (COPPA), Trust Guard Privacy guidelines, the CAN-SPAM Act, and the Google Adsense and Adwords Privacy Policy requirements. A good template for developing an M3 privacy notification policy is the five following Google privacy principles:

1. Use information to provide our users with valuable products and services.
2. Develop products that reflect strong privacy standards and practices.
3. Make the collection of personal information transparent.
4. Give users meaningful choices to protect their privacy.
5. Be a responsible steward of the information we hold.

- Provide an option for consumers to opt-out from Internet and mobile mechanisms used to track and target their digital devices. Explain why these mechanisms are being used for enhancing the relevancy and customer service to digital devices. If anonymous techniques and technologies are being used, such as device fingerprinting, let consumer know, so that they can make their choice over privacy and relevancy. Explain the technologies being used to ensure anonymity of consumers and the focus of marketing to their devices.
- List what information is being captured by cookies, beacons, digital fingerprinting, and other mechanisms. Total transparency should be the policy to follow by M3 marketers. Explain what data are being collected and for what purpose. Educate consumers on the benefits of these information collection techniques. Openness is a good general policy for M3 marketers; when a myriad pitfalls and unexpected dangers may loom, total transparency is their best insurance, policy, and overall defense.

- State the purpose of setting first- or third-party cookies from ad networks. Marketers should limit the use of third-party cookies as they dilute proprietary consumer knowledge, which is possibly the most valuable asset companies have. M3 marketing involves capturing customer events and actions over time and modeling these stored interactions to determine typical behavior and deviations from those device actions and the predictions of future revenue growth and consumer relevancy.

Checklist of M3 Marketing Terminology, Techniques, and Technologies

There is an assortment of descriptions M3 marketers need to be aware of. They involve networks, sites, processes, techniques, technologies, and methods by which marketing can take place in today's digital environment. This M3 marketing checklist is about what these entities, companies, services, networks, mechanisms, and strategies are all about.

- *Ad exchange*: A marketplace where M3 marketers can bid to place ads in websites. Ad exchanges are technology platforms that facilitate the bid buying and selling of online media advertising inventory from multiple ad networks. The approach is technology driven as opposed to the historical approach of negotiating price on media inventory. Ad exchanges can be useful to both buyers (advertisers and agencies) and sellers (online publishers) because of the efficiencies they provide. The major ad exchanges include AdECN, owned by Microsoft; Right Media, owned by Yahoo!; ContextWeb's Exchange, the leading independent exchange; DoubleClick Ad Exchange, a Google subsidiary; and Zinc Exchange.
- *Ad network*: A company that sells ads on behalf of website publishers and clients. An ad network connects advertisers to websites that want to host advertisements. The key function of an ad network is aggregation of ad space supply from publishers and matching it with advertiser demand. Ad networks provide a way for media buyers to coordinate ad campaigns across dozens, hundreds, or even thousands of sites in an efficient manner. The campaigns often involve running ads over a category or an entire network. Site-specific buys are not a major emphasis when dealing with advertising networks. Ad networks vary in size and focus: large ones may require premium brands and millions of impressions per month, and small ones may accept unbranded sites with thousands of impressions per month. One of the key issues for publishers is exclusive versus nonexclusive representation. Exclusive representation generally brings a higher percentage of revenue sharing, but sometimes results in a smaller percentage of advertising inventories being sold. In nonexclusive

arrangements, publishers may use secondary advertising options to fill the space left unsold by the primary ad network.

■ *Aggregated information*: Data combined from many sites, but it cannot identify anyone. Aggregated information refers to a website or computer software that aggregates a specific type of information from multiple online sources. This information may be aggregated based on the interests or location of digital devices. It may also involve information aggregated internally from such mechanisms as cookies along with external information shared via ad exchanges and networks. Aggregated information can be used to create anonymous consumer profiles based on the features and behaviors of their digital devices, such as that from digital fingerprinting.

■ *Anonymous information*: Features about web visitors that do not identify them personally. M3 marketing is about using anonymous information about consumers and is focused on the aggregation and modeling of their digital device features and behaviors.

■ *Beacons*: Also known as "bugs" or "pixels." They can track users' location and activities. Also called a *clear GIF*. They are commonly used in combination with cookies. A beacon is an often transparent graphic image, usually no larger than a one by one pixel, which is placed on a website or in an e-mail that is used to monitor the behavior of users visiting a site or sending an e-mail. When the HTML code for the beacon points to a site to retrieve the image, it can pass along information such as the IP address of the device that retrieved the image; it can report on the time the beacon was viewed and for how long, along with the features of the digital device that retrieved the image and the previously set cookie values. Beacons are typically used by a third party to monitor the activity of a site. A beacon can be detected by viewing the source code of a web page and looking for any image tags that load from a different server than the rest of the site.

■ *Behavioral targeting*: Information about where visitors go and what they search for online. Behavioral targeting is a technique used by online publishers and advertisers to increase the effectiveness of their campaigns. Behavioral targeting uses information collected on an individual's web-browsing behavior, such as the pages they have visited or the searches they have made, to select which advertisements to display to that individual. Marketers believe that this helps them deliver their online advertisements to the users who are most likely to be interested. Behavioral marketing can be used on its own or in conjunction with other forms of targeting based on factors like geography, demographics, the surrounding content, or the features and behaviors of digital devices. Behavioral targeting allows site owners or ad networks to display content more relevant to the interests of the individual viewing the page. The idea is that properly targeted ads will fetch more consumer interest, as such the seller may ask for a premium for these targeted ads over random ads based on the context of a site.

■ *Cookie*: A text file put on devices by sites to remember preferences or to track online visitors across a single or multiple websites. A cookie, also known as an HTTP cookie, web cookie, or browser cookie, is used for an origin website to send state information to a user's browser and for the browser to return the state information to the original site that placed the cookie. Cookies were originally created by Netscape in support of shopping carts. The state information can be used for authentication and identification of a user session, user's preferences, shopping cart contents, or anything else that can be accomplished through storing text data. Cookies are not software. They cannot be programmed, cannot carry viruses, and cannot install malware on the host computer.

■ *Data exchange*: A marketplace where advertisers bid for access to data about users. A data exchange allows website owners to sell data on their users to potential advertisers. So, rather than buying a single banner ad at the top of the page for all to see, data exchanges allow advertisers to target specific portions of the site's audience based on their interests, behaviors, and preferences. Content providers would have the details on their users and they would sell that to the ad companies who could tailor ads. These marketplaces bring together the relevant players in advertising and audience data to make it easier for media companies and advertisers to target relevant groups. Data exchanges are evolving as a venue for media companies to buy, sell, and share audience data. Media companies can use audience data exchanges in two ways: They can purchase audience data to improve their advertising revenue streams with better ad targeting and they can also sell audience data to marketers, creating a new revenue stream.

■ *First-party cookie*: A cookie installed on computers by a single website to ID preferences. A cookie is a text string that is included with Hypertext Transfer Protocol (HTTP) requests and responses. First-party cookies are used to maintain state information as devices navigate different pages on the website that originally planted it and return to the site at a later time. One of the primary purposes of cookies is to provide a convenience feature that the device can use to save time. The purpose of a cookie is to tell the web server that a specific device has returned to a specific web page. First-party cookies can only be read by the website that originally placed it on the device. A third-party cookie is issued by a site other than the one a device is currently surfing; they are normally set by ad networks.

■ *Flash cookie*: A cookie put on computers by Adobe's Flash software to display video or ads. Local Shared Objects (LSO), commonly called flash cookies due to their similarities with HTTP cookies, are pieces of data that websites which use Adobe Flash may store on a user's computer. LSOs are used by all versions of Adobe Flash Player. Flash cookies are not shown in the list of cookies that can be seen when on a web browser. Normal HTTP cookies cannot save more than 4 kB of data while Flash cookies can save up to 100 kB.

- *Internet Protocol (IP) address*: A unique number assigned to a device connected to the web. An IP address is a numerical label assigned to each digital device participating in a computer network that uses the IP for communication. An IP address serves two principal functions: host or network interface identification and location addressing. IP addresses are binary numbers, but they are usually stored in text files and displayed in human-readable notations, such as 172.16.254.1 for the 32 bit number version and 2001:db8:0:1234:0:567:8:1 for the 128 bit number version since the mid-2000s.
- *Off-line data*: Information from sources other than the web. This can be demographics or lifestyle information.
- *Personally identifiable information (PII)*: Data identifying visitors uniquely, such as their name. PII, as used in information security, refers to information that can be used to uniquely identify, contact, or locate a single person or can be used with other sources to uniquely identify a single individual. The abbreviation PII is widely accepted, but the phrase it abbreviates has four common variants based on personal, personally, identifiable, and identifying. Not all are equivalent, and for legal purposes, the effective definitions vary depending on the jurisdiction and the purposes for which the term is being used.
- *Third-party cookie*: A cookie or beacon installed by an ad network or exchange. Third-party cookies are sent to the advertiser when loading their ads or visiting their website. The advertiser can then use these cookies to build up a browsing history of the user across all the websites this advertiser has footprints on via its ad networks. Also known as tracking cookies, these kinds of cookies are typically sent to devices by marketing companies. Third-party cookies can create a long history of a device's web browsing activities. These kinds of cookies allow M3 marketers to track a device's movements across many different websites.

Checklist of Web A5s Software and Services

Increasingly reporting and analyzing the behaviors of devices at websites is crucial to M3 marketers. A5s are not just a tool for measuring website traffic but they can be used as a tool for business and M3 market research. Web analytics applications can also help enterprises measure the results of traditional print advertising campaigns. A5s help to estimate how traffic to a site changes after the launch of a new advertising campaign. Web analytics provides information about the number of visitors to a website and the number of page views. They help gauge traffic and popularity trends, which is useful for M3 marketing. The following comparison table is that of web analytics software released under an open source license.

Name	Platform	Supported Databases	Tracking Method
Analog	C	Logfile-based	
AWStats	Perl	Logfile-based	
CrawlTrack	PHP	MySQL	php pagetag
GoAccess	C	Logfile-based	
LogReport	Perl	Logfile-based	
Open Web Analytics	PHP	MySQL	javascript/php pagetag
Piwik	PHP	MySQL	javascript or php pagetag
Visitors	C	Logfile-based	
W3Perl	Perl	Logfile-based	
Webalizer	C	Logfile-based	

The following is a checklist of the most popular commercial web analytical software products and services.

- *AlterWind*: Log analyzer with search engine optimization (SEO) and website promotion.

  This software has its own unique analysis code of the URL for each search engine, taking into consideration the specialties of each search engine. This will help the M3 marketer gather valid information, more clearly understand the interests of website devices and visitors, and receive additional data for website SEO. AlterWind Log Analyzer Professional database contains more than 430 search engines and catalogs from over 120 countries (Figure 3.12).
- *Google Analytics*: Free log and ecommerce analyzer.

  Google Analytics is a web analytics solution that gives M3 marketers rich insights into website traffic and marketing effectiveness. The service can track web-enabled phones, mobile websites, and mobile apps, as well as sales and conversions. It can measure site engagement goals against threshold levels defined by the M3 marketer. The analytic service can trace transactions to campaigns and keywords, get loyalty and latency metrics, and identify revenue sources. It can measure the success of display, search, new media, and off-line advertising efforts. Compare a site usage metrics with industry averages and track Flash, video, and social networking sites and applications. An M3 marketer can uncover trends, patterns, and key comparisons with funnel visualization and motion charts; this analytical tool complements a suite

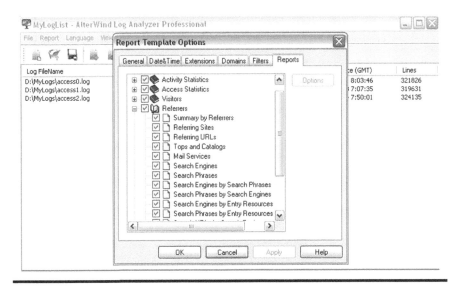

Figure 3.12 AlterWind report by several server activities.

of Google of related products, such as AdNet and DoubleClick networks. Google+ offers a whole new source of device information in the social media and mobile space.

■ *Nihuo*: Shows "who, what, when, where, and how" via a log analyzer.
Nihuo Web Log Analyzer is a fast and powerful web access log analyzer for small and medium size websites. It can tell M3 marketers where website visitors come from, which pages are most popular, and which search engine phrases brought visitors to the site. Nihuo Web Log Analyzer can analyze logs generated by Apache, IIS, Ngnix, and lighttpd web servers. It can even read GZIP, BZIP, ZIP, and ZIP64 compressed log files, so M3 marketers do not need to unpack them. Nihuo Web Log Analyzer is highly configurable; it enables the marketer to create their own custom reports or tailor standard reports to meet their client's specific needs.

■ *SAS*: Web analytics and reports, from the world's largest statistical company.
SAS Web Analytics automatically turns raw web data into valuable business information. Through the use of advanced analytics, the solution lets the M3 marketer monitor KPIs and understand the factors that influence each business metric. KPIs display for quick identification of areas performing above or below expectations, along with trending graphs that show both current and past performance of the KPIs. Forecast graph shows trend and projection with upper and lower confidence levels (Figure 3.13).

■ *Unica* (now IBM): It offers web analytics and interactive marketing.
Unica NetInsight allows M3 marketers to have a dramatically simple approach to collecting visitor data and unparalleled reporting flexibility.

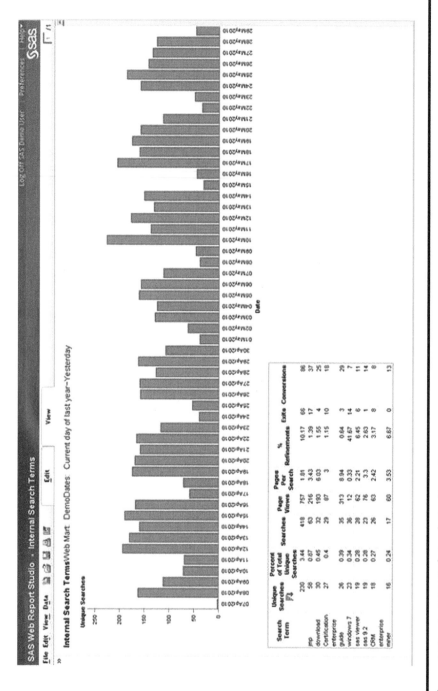

Figure 3.13 An SAS Web Analytics Report.

Figure 3.14   WebTrends multiple analytics.

Unica NetInsight is a new type of web analytics product designed to meet the full range of online analysis requirements with minimal complexity, little up-front cost, and no technical infrastructure investment. Unica Interactive Marketing also allows M3 marketers to quickly analyze visitor and customer behavior, and design and deliver e-mail and web content that is more personal, relevant, and effective. The software unifies best-of-breed web analytics, e-mail marketing, and web personalization, without burdening IT or requiring complex multivendor integration.

■ *WebTrends*: Web, mobile, and social network analytic suite.

It can measure anything happening on a website and can import data from Facebook and Twitter. It can compare apps and mobile sites on all mobile platforms, such as iTunes App Store downloads and revenue. It provides the racking for pages and enhanced measurement for apps. It can measure Facebook data stored for long-term trending. This software can monitor millions of blogs, tweets, video-sharing sites, Facebook, and other social media venues in real time to find conversations pertinent to brands (Figure 3.14).

■ *SeeVolution*: A heat map web analytic firm.

Click heatmaps are used to analyze how people click in a website. They radiate the section of a website that is most hot (active). This information is important because it allows the M3 marketer to see where the most important areas of their site are. They can use this marketing knowledge to find a better place for their ads and improve the usability of their pages. There are also services such as *Clickdensity* and *CrazyEgg* that provide hosted heatmaps solutions (Figures 3.15 and 3.16).

Heatmaps can discover what devices are clicking on what parts of a site. They can show which objects visitors are clicking on. These objects can

Figure 3.15 A Clickdensity menu for creating a heatmap.

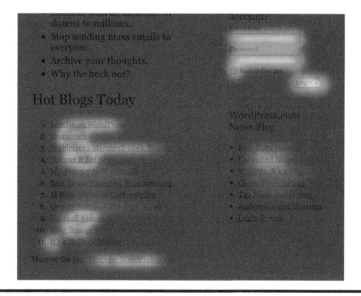

Figure 3.16 CrazyEgg heatmap of a website.

include links, images, flash, and buttons. For example, heatmaps can show how far down the page devices are scrolling. The M3 marketer can scroll heatmaps account for screen resolutions and different monitor sizes. They display clicks movements as they are happening. The software can aggregate all mouse movements from visitors and displays hot and cold areas of a website.

The SeeVolution heatmap technology gives site overlays that span the entirety of their tracked pages and illustrate areas of high and low user activity—generated by the monitoring of thousands of visitor clicks, scrolls, and mouse movements. Heatmaps break down the user interaction within a web page and provide a narrative on how individual visitor sessions are taking place. SeeVolution offers four types of heatmaps: (1) Click Heatmap, which shows which objects visitors are clicking on, like links, images, flash, and buttons; (2) Scroll Heatmap, which demonstrates how far down the page people are scrolling; (3) Live Click Heatmap, which displays clicks as they are happening; and (4) Mouse Movement Heatmap, which aggregates all mouse movements from visitors and displays hot and cold areas at a website.

The SeeVolution heatmap technology is generated by monitoring thousands of visitor clicks, scrolls, and mouse movements. Heatmaps play a crucial role in understanding how a site's usability can be enhanced. If the Click Heatmap indicates that a high volume of users are clicking in areas where there are not any links, an M3 marketer can restructure the site to ensure that hotspots are connected to links that are directing customers toward a desired section or action. Heatmaps allow the marketer to organize and optimize the design of a site and its pages for maximizing device interactions and the elimination of those areas that indicate user frustration.

■ *ClickTale*: Provides heatmaps to break down device's interactions and behaviors. This web analytic software also uses heatmaps to see absolutely everything visitors do on a site. It records full browsing sessions to discover exactly how devices use a site. The heatmaps capture every mouse move, click, scroll, and keystroke, by using a tiny piece of JavaScript copied into a website. The whole process is completely transparent to the end user and has no noticeable effect on site performance. The software allows the M3 marketer to see everywhere visitors click—anywhere on the page—whether it is links, images, text, or dead space. The heatmaps can find the obstructions in conversion sales funnels by seeing what advertisements, images, and links are not getting enough clicks, and what "call to action" buttons are being ignored.

The marketer can discover what devices are clicking on, such as "Special Offers" banners, buttons, or icons. By aggregating the mouse movements of thousands of visitors on a webpage, the heatmaps create a comprehensive, visual representation of what devices are looking at and focusing on within a website. The software supports marketing campaigns and their testing processes, that is, completely transparent and anonymous, while most visitors are not even aware they are being tracked and recorded. Heatmaps support the optimization of a site's conversion rates by visualizing where customers convert and where they leave the conversion process. In addition, any e-mail campaign, survey, or newsletter can be tagged with accurate and in-depth data such as demographic or psychographic information, in order to discover exactly which communication generates the most conversions and sales.

Ad Network M3 Checklist

There are dozens of ad networks that focus on specific market sectors or consumer interests for the placement of their ads. There are also contextual ad networks to choose from, some of which are very narrow in their scope. In any event, whether targeted, first or second tier and now mobile, ad networks are another conduit M3 marketers who can leverage and execute as part of their overall strategy in assisting their clients. The following is a checklist of different pricing models of ad networks, such as cost per thousand views (CPM), cost per acquisition (CPA), and cost per click (CPC). Primarily CPM-based ad networks are as follows:

1. *24/7 RealMedia*: The digital landscape is overrun by widgets, applications, networks, and exchanges. Advertisers are finding it difficult to utilize all the options available in the most effective manner. Publishers are struggling to maintain the quality control and channel management they require. This network's m.e.n.u. platform delivers the outcomes advertisers seek, and the yield and control publishers' demand. Advertisers can select their partners, audiences, and delivery options and focus only on their brand outcomes. Publishers control when, where, and with whom they will interact via the m.e.n.u. platform, which connects marketers with the appropriate technology and data partners that create scalable and replicable campaigns.

2. *Advertising and search network (ASN)*: ASN assists M3 marketers in converting traffic at a lower price. Their integrated system can deliver large volumes of quality traffic via sophisticated advertorial, e-mail, and banner advertising. ASN has become one of the largest and best-performing ad channel; the platform makes it easy to set up, test, and manage marketing campaigns. Advertisers can set daily caps on their spending while they assess their traffic quality and benefit from easy cancellation terms. Clients also have access to real-time campaign reporting.

3. *Ad World Network*: This network provides an extensive directory to online advertising, ad management software, brand marketing, contextual advertising, direct marketing, pay per click, and creative advertising providers.

4. *AdAgency1*: Web advertising networks such as AdAgency1 simplify the acts of buying and selling for both the advertisers and the publishers. AdAgency1 acts as a broker to unite the web advertisers, the buyers of ads, and the web publishers, the sellers of ads. AdAgency1 acquires and aggregates advertising inventory from websites, typically each page view or impression; it offers at least one ad placement opportunity and sells them to online advertisers on their behalf.

5. *Addynamix*: Ybrant Digital offers Digital Marketing solutions to businesses, agencies, and online publishers worldwide. It connects marketers with their audience across any form of digital media, using its local presence to deliver appropriate messages to the right audience, through the most relevant digital channels.

6. *AdOrigin*: This network offers a comprehensive program of advertising solutions designed to furnish clients with state-of-the-art advertising concepts that extend beyond traditional banner advertising.

7. *AdPepper*: Semantic targeting covers all common campaign formats in over 3000 categories to precisely match the right websites. This network ensures campaigns are placed on pages that are contextually relevant to them, whatever the format and medium. The ad server analyses the content, determines the semantic context and its key topics, and places the targeted advertising in the desired surroundings.

8. *Adtegrity*: A broad spectrum ad network that delivers over 200 million impressions daily to thousands of website publishers.

9. *Bannerconnect*: This network specialized in offering its advertisers and publishers a unique blend of marketing solutions. It offers a complete range of advertising services.

10. *BannerSpace*: This network offers its AreaPoint™ and AreaDirect™ services to make geographic and local targeting of ads via its network.

11. *BURST! Media*: Through its media divisions Burst Media, Burst Direct, and Giant Realm, this network also markets, its ad management platform, adConductor™, to empower content websites, online ad networks, and web portals to manage the complete process of ad sales and service.

12. *Casale Media*: This network uses the Nielsen PRIZM Digital psychographics to focus video ads on the strongest household and demographic segments for each brand. This network combines audience targeting with site-level filters for the best possible ad placements.

13. *Claxon Media*: This network delivers results to both web publishers and web advertisers alike.

14. *Click Agents* (now *ValueClick Media*): This network reaches over 593 million unique monthly visitors worldwide and over 172 million in the United States. They market to 80.5% of the U.S. Internet audience across more than 8500 sites. The network serves more than 31 billion ads every month to users in 275 countries and they manage over 750 million anonymous consumer profiles and have access to over 2.5 million proprietary and third-party behavioral attributes for ad targeting.

15. *CPX Interactive*: This network delivers more than 30 billion impressions to more than 200 million unique users in more than 60 countries every month.

16. *Federated Media*: This network uses proprietary processes and tools to identify and connect conversations across the web and provides streamlined ways for M3 marketers to add value with deep engagement within these conversations.

17. *Gorilla Nation Media*: Their platforms holistically interact and connect with users within premium entertainment and lifestyle communities. They have publisher relationships, proprietary technologies, marketing research team, and a creative studio.

18. *InterClick*: A self-service audience recommendation and planning platform.

19. *Quake Marketing*: A medium-sized ad boutique network.

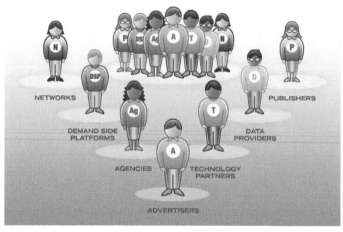

Figure 3.17   Right Media exchange works with multiple advertisers.

20. *QuinStreet*: This network offers vertical marketing and media analytics.
21. *Revenue.net*: Traffic sourced from 2.5 million owned or managed domains on the Oversee.net network, serves 233 million unique searches performed per month, 30 million clicks generated per month across major online verticals, with 94 verticals covered including Travel, Shopping, and Finance.
22. *Right Media*: Right Media assist all types of digital advertisers (Figure 3.17).
23. *The Robert Sherman Company*: It does targeting of the 20 most critical consumer and business categories; all campaigns are reoptimized every minute to ensure maximum ROI.
24. *TMP*: This is a recruitment advertising agency network.
25. *Tribal Fusion*: This is a technology-enabled media services company that delivers innovative services to today's digital advertisers and publishers.
26. *Valuead.com*: This network generates leads; builds brands; and performs campaign planning, seven-layer deep custom reports, quality geotargeting, and on-the-fly optimization works with 35 vertical markets.
27. *Yes Advertising*: Variety of offers selection with high payout, high conversions offers. They test ads first, 24/7 system access, and dedicated service with no setup fees.
28. *HyperBidder*: An advertising marketplace for advertisers and publishers to buy and sell in a trusted environment. Both buyers and sellers use their bidding process to optimize their advertising spending and/or sell their advertising space. Their secure and reliable system delivers advertisements, monitors performance, and distributes payment on a real-time basis after impressions and click-thru are measured and verified.

These are the primarily CPA-based ad networks:

1. *Advertising.com*: This network offers its Sponsored Listings Network for targeting text ads by website, web section, or web page. This network is part of AOL Video; this platform also offers video ads with trafficking for measurement via this video service.
2. *Amazon.com*: Amazon has a network of affiliates—they place ads for Amazon products with links to their site—Amazon offers them a 15% commission on all purchases.
3. *Axill*: A multimodel media company. It deals with CPM, CPC, and CPA ads. *ClickBank*: A secure online retail outlet for more than 50,000 digital products and 100,000 active affiliate marketers with over 35,000 digital transactions a day. This network serves more than 200 countries.
4. *ClickBooth*: This network supports CPA and CPC billing. They get 5,000,000,000+ impressions, 10,000,000+ leads, and 1,000,000+ actions and sales generated every month.
5. *ClickXChange*: This network provides both the software and the human expertise to develop the most effective ad campaigns for products or services. Their platform can get the M3 marketer started by setting the margins and determining the goals of their ad campaign. Their team can assist marketers to ensure they are competitive in their market. They can match them with the right publishers who will get the most reach and return for their budgeted dollars with real-time tracking.
6. *Commission Junction*: They facilitate and support equitable, lucrative relationships between advertisers and publishers. They can align incentives, provide accountability, and drive innovation in the performance marketing space.
7. *CoverClicks*: Performance-based offer marketplace for M3 marketers, featuring exclusive campaigns, rapid on-time payments, and real-time reporting to maximize advertisers' media inventory.
8. *DrivePM* (now a part of the Microsoft Media Network): It brings together everything an M3 marketer wants in an ad network: broad reach, premium publishers, and a diverse portfolio of performance and targeting options.
9. *Linkshare*: This is a provider of full-service online marketing solutions specializing in the areas of Affiliate Marketing, Search Marketing, and Lead Generation.
10. *Epic Direct*: A division of the Epic Media Group. This performance-based ad network focused primarily on customer acquisition and pay-for-performance online advertising campaigns, and it has over 45,000 publishers.
11. *Maxbounty*: This network supports pay per click search, social network, contextual, e-mail marketing, or co-registration.
12. *ProfitCenter*: This network offers M3 marketers a range of customizable services and turnkey technologies designed to increase sales while reducing marketing costs.

13. *ShareASale*: This network offers customer acquisition tools for the M3 marketer, who can decide the commission structure to pay and only pay when results come in.

14. *WebSponsors*: This network offers a response-based network to drive registrations, sweepstakes, and online sales. It utilizes a variety of preapproved direct response mediums. Network publishers can guide targeted consumers to an advertiser's website or a branded lead capture form hosted by this network.

These are primarily CPC ad networks:

1. *AdBright*: The largest independent ad exchange, offering an entirely transparent marketplace—direct access to superior campaign data and analytics and ultimately, greater control over what matters most—results.

2. *AdForce*: With rising prices on the pay per click listings of most search engines and the variety of terms, M3 marketers often find it difficult to know whether their marketing campaigns are profitable. This network offers the expertise and technical skills to help the M3 marketer run their pay per click advertising campaigns in the most effective way possible.

3. *AdHearUs*: Based on a revolutionary, placement-by-performance model, this network enables M3 marketers to reach more customers and sales via the pay per click model.

4. *AdKnowledge*: Using their BidSystem platform, they match ads to the most relevant users to deliver the highest ROI. Ads are dynamically generated and placed within category-specific channels and delivered to those users who are most likely to respond.

5. *AdSonar*: This is Advertising.com's premium sponsored listing network for targeting text ads by site, section, or page on the web's most popular sites.

6. *BClick*: This is a result-based ad network. They provide targeted controlled network of host sites, which will feature ads on a fix pay amount per unique visitor.

7. *Bidvertiser*: The placement of ads by M3 marketers on this network is simple:
   a. They can browse the network's categorized directory of websites.
   b. They can select the appropriate channels for their market.
   c. They can choose their desired keywords.
   d. They can set their desired geographic targeting.
   e. They can set their amount of their pay per click bids.
   f. They can have their ads are up and running.

8. *CBprosense*: Plugging CBprosense into a site is fast. Simply copy their generic HTML code, place the ad code on the site, and upload them online. Their spider will immediately visit the site and index its content. The system will then start to deliver a real-time feed of highly targeted products, closely matching the content of the site.

9. *Chitika*: These are the targets and connects devices looking for products and services across their network of over 100,000 websites. They can display search targeted, mobile and local ads that are suited to multiple audience's interests.

10. *Clicksor*: Their contextual targeting can automatically match ads to the most relevant websites in their Content Network. M3 marketers can set and adjust their daily budget anytime with no minimum spending requirement: Payment options include PayPal, credit card, and wire transfer. Their local advertising allows marketers to target the cities or countries that they want to direct their ads to.

11. *Google AdSense*: This network offers a contextual advertising solution to web publishers. It delivers text-based Google AdWords ads that are relevant to site content pages.

12. *IndustryBrains*: These are the targets pay-per-click or display ads to a specific category or premium branded websites. It leverages content to generate revenue from contextually targeted ads that are consistent with brands.

13. *Mirago*: This is a targeted advertising that only charges when a device clicks on a site.

14. *MivaNixxie*: This network enables sites to boost online income with precisely targeted ads from leading providers such as Yahoo!

15. *Textads.Biz*: This network increases traffic. Marketers can have ads up and running in minutes, low cost. They can reach niche audiences via their directory. M3 marketers can tweak their ad while they are up and running with real-time tracking.

16. *Text Link Ads*: This network improves natural search engine rankings from their publisher base to generate targeted traffic and improve natural search engine rankings.

17. *TTZ Media*: M3 marketer can use this network via pay per click earnings. They provide a very intuitive ad code generation system as well as a tracking system. Their ad banners are one of the most flexible on the web.

18. *Vibrant Media*: Their technology identifies the "core words of interest" within a site to minimize wasted impressions and deliver an ad that relates directly to a device's interest.

19. *Yahoo! Publisher Network*: This network offers a wide range of products and a breadth of expertise. It offers publishers and marketers customized solutions for the monetization of their websites. This network is built on sponsored search, and they offer new revenue sources to a growing list of portals and content providers.

"Non-Standard" ad networks that offer pop-ups, expendables, pay per post, etc., are as follows:

■ *Opt-Media*: This network can reach over 2 million devices a day via e-mail lists, banners, or full page ads throughout their "Mail to a Friend" network.

■ *PayPopUp*: Their pop-up layer ads can effectively attract audiences' attentions and still be unobtrusive.

- *PointRoll*: This network provides banner ads, in-banner videos, rich media, and numerous technologies that enable M3 marketers to create, deliver, and measure display ads with rich and full featured content without disrupting the user experience.
- *PayPerPost*: An online marketplace that connects the marketer to bloggers in order to create sponsored conversations through blog posts. The system allows the marketer to compensate bloggers with cash in exchange for promoting their product, service, or site.
- *ReviewMe*: A buzz and blog ad network.

These are demographic-specific ad networks:

- *Batanga*: This network delivers to over 15 million online U.S. Hispanics on premier Spanish-language websites.
- *BlogAds*: A blogs network.
- *CrispAds*: Blog, e-mail, and lead generating network.
- *HerAgency*: They specialize in creating customized ad packages that are highly integrated within premier female-focused sites.
- *Pheedo*: RSS streaming banner network.

These are non-U.S. primarily CPM-based ad networks:

- *ClickHype*: A performance-driven agency.

These are non-U.S. primarily CPC ad networks:

- *PeakClick*: Austrian network that pays in Euros.

These are non-U.S. primarily CPA/CPL ad networks:

- *TradeDoubler*: It is based in Sweden. They cover 18 markets across Europe.
- *Commission Monster*: Australia's leading affiliate network.
- *Sedo*: A German affiliate marketing network.

Despite the rich variety and number of ad networks, only 16% of U.S. web users click on display ads, according to a study performed last year by the research firm *comScore*, which is a drop from 32% in 2009. To remedy this problem of banner blindness, new techniques are being developed to make ads more interactive including blogs, videos, and interactive features.

M3 Marketers Web Checklist

Every enterprise has streams of transactional and behavioral device data flowing to it 24/7, but few are able to triangulate them simultaneously as events take place, enabling them to make relevant offers to their existing and new customers at the moment they interact with them. With every consumer event, devices are communicating with companies and marketer their needs and desires. M3 marketers can leverage these digital device events, most of which start at websites that cascade across other operational systems within enterprises. The following is a short list of critical items an M3 marketer needs to consider as part of executing a comprehensive web A5 analytical strategy:

1. *Log analyzer*: This is the simplest kind of web analytics software that parses a log file from a web server and based on the values contained in the log files, which can yield important indicators such as about whom, when, and how a web server is visited. Usually, reports are generated from the log files immediately, but the log files can alternatively be parsed to a database and reports generated on demand using open source and commercial programs. Some of the common data features captured by log analyzers are as follows:
    a. Authenticated users and last authenticated visits
    b. Number of visits and number of unique visitors
    c. Domains/countries of host's visitors
    d. Most viewed, entry, and exit pages
    e. Visits duration and last visits
    f. Days of week and rush hours
    g. Number of total pages viewed
    h. Conversion tracking
    i. Device on the site
    j. Key phrases used
    k. Page navigation
    l. Keywords used
    m. Browsers used
    n. HTTP referrer
    o. Search engines
    p. HTTP errors
    q. Visit time
    r. Hosts' list
    s. Files' type
    t. OS used
    u. Robots
2. *IP geolocation*: To help servers to identify the visitor's geographical location, that is, country, region, city, latitude, longitude, ZIP code, time zone, connection speed, ISP and domain name, IDD country code, area code, weather

station code and name, and mobile carrier information. There are a number of free and paid subscription geolocation databases, ranging from country level to state or city, including ZIP code level, each with varying claims of accuracy, generally higher at the country level. These databases typically contain IP address data that may be used in firewalls, ad servers, mail routing systems, websites, and other automated systems where geolocation may be useful. An alternative to hosting and querying a database is to obtain the country code for a given IP address through a domain name service block list (DNSBL) style lookup from a remote server.

3. *E-mail marketing*: A means of communicating to a device. Every e-mail sent to a potential or current customer can be considered e-mail marketing, such as sending e-mail messages with the purpose of enhancing a relationship to encourage customer loyalty and repeat business and sending e-mail messages with the purpose of acquiring new customers or convincing current customers to purchase something immediately after a purchase.

4. *Digital fingerprinting*: Coded string of binary digits—generated by a mathematical algorithm that uniquely identifies a data file. Digital fingerprinting is used in detecting the tampering of electronically transmitted messages or more importantly to the M3 marketer it can be used to track and identify digital devices for advertising purposes. Digital fingerprinting is just like an analog fingerprint of a person. It cannot be reconstructed from any other digital fingerprint. It is because two files that differ even by a single character will have completely different digital fingerprints, which for the M3 marketer means a more precise level of behavioral targeting.

5. *Social media marketing*: This is the multifaceted, orchestrated marketing strategy to communicate and coordinate promotional elements and is the center of efforts to create content that attracts attention and encourages readers to share it with other digital devices. A social media message spreads from user to user and resonates because it is coming from a trusted, third-party source, as opposed to from a brand or a company itself. Social media has become a platform that is a relatively inexpensive methodology for M3 marketers to implement with strategically higher value.

6. *Search engine optimization*: This is the process of improving the visibility of a site in Google, Yahoo!, or Bing. SEM techniques and strategies include paid listings, but it most likely involves the optimization of the popularity and prominence of a site by the use of keywords for the autonomous indexing of search engine spiders. SEO is a method of getting a website to rank higher in search engines, such as the BIG 3.

7. *Model web device behaviors*: This is the study and modeling of when, why, how, and where people do or do not buy a product or a service. It blends elements from psychology, sociology, social anthropology, and economics. For the M3 marketer, it is an effort to understand the buyer decision-making process, both individually and in clusters and groups of devices. It studies characteristics of

digital devices behavior variables in an attempt to understand people's wants, desires, and preferences. It also tries to assess influences on the consumer from groups such as friends, reference groups, and social media. Device behavior models are based on consumer buying patterns with the customer playing the three distinct roles of user, payer, and buyer. Relationship marketing is an influential asset for device behavior analysis as it has a keen interest in the rediscovery of the true meaning of marketing through the reaffirmation of the importance of the customer or buyer. A greater importance is also placed on consumer retention, CRM, personalization, customization, and one-to-one marketing.

8. *Cookies, JavaScript, Beacons, and Apps Creation*: The strategic use of these Internet and wireless mechanisms is vitally critical to M3 marketers. They represent the components for ensuring the capturing and modeling of device behaviors for predicting consumer preferences, desires, and needs. The web is a rapid, self-evolving marketing ecosystem in which consumers drive demand, product design, service features, and price structure. The M3 marketer needs to design and implement a framework for leveraging these streams of device behaviors at websites and mobile devices via the strategic use of these marketing mechanisms.

Checklist of Social Metric Consultancies for M3

Engagement device marketing uses influence metrics to measure a consumer's likelihood to encourage friends to consider, recommend, or purchase a brand. In an increasingly wired and wireless social web world, texts, opt-in surveys, tweets, questionnaires, chats, and instant messaging platforms provide new metrics for marketers and enterprises. Engagement consumer profiles can be developed from passive to semi-active participants, to the golden nugget: the brand champion. The following boutiques can assist M3 marketers on leveraging these new social interactions and metrics.

- *TNS Global*: This market research company provides customized reports organized around their clients' specific industry sector. This market research firm is based in London; it, however, operates in over 80 countries with a powerful global network. In each country, they combine the benefits of industry specialization and research expertise to deliver marketing insights. TNS is a provider of customized reports to manufacturers and brand owners, retailers and outlets, and advertising and media agencies. Their technology team consists of over 500 researchers across 60+ countries offering their clients a range of global market research services and market research analysis solutions. TNS helps clients define brand strategy by identifying category dynamics, brand positioning, and consumer needs to make their brand stand out from the competition.

  TNS provides world-class research and insights to help their clients align their marketing activities and bring strategy to their brand. TNS tracks performance against the brand's strategic goals to help their clients optimize their in-market performance. They leverage technological advancements and social developments to achieve a deeper knowledge of devices' behaviors. Drawing upon new data access opportunities, they measure what people actually do, say, and see on the web and wireless worlds. They combine data and research techniques to deliver faster, more accurate, and powerful insights, in a cost-effective way to their clients (Figure 3.18).

■ *MotiveQuest*: They can monitor and report on "brand buzz" to understand customer motivations. They concentrate on understanding prospects and customers so that clients can grow their market share. They call their social research approach *online anthropology*. With their MotiveQuest Framework, clients can discover what motivates groups of devices and what they can do to turn them into brand and company advocates.

Central to their philosophy is the belief that all device behaviors are driven by primal human motivations. The key to improving consumer relationships is lassoing the right customer passions. The firm has found that online attitudes are highly correlated with off-line sales. Most researchers focus on "what," and MotiveQuest focuses on "why." Finding the reasons why something is said enables clients to change that online conversation to change chatter into advocacy. MotiveQuest helps their clients understand their customers better, work out how to communicate with their customers effectively, and measure the results of their efforts.

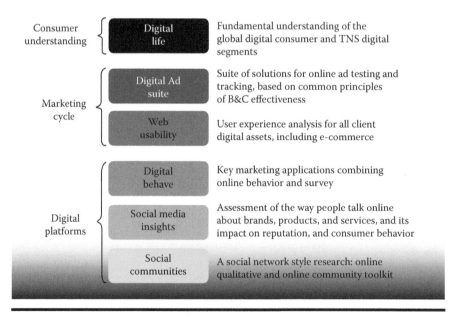

Figure 3.18 TNS focuses on a number of areas important to M3 marketers.

They see social market research as an effective alternative to traditional market research alternatives like segmentation studies, ethnography, focus groups, and quantitative studies. The company helps clients understand consumer trends and motivation segmentation and identify innovation opportunities. They also assist their clients communicate brand positioning and formulate a strategy and tactics. Finally, they assist clients in measuring brand advocacy, campaign impact, and econometrics.

▪ *Attensity*: This is a consultancy specializing in the analysis and reporting on social messages by the use of advanced text mining algorithms. In today's hyperconnected world, social media and online customer interactions are changing the way companies do business from the outside in. Leading brands recognize that their customers are both passionate and vocal about their products and services, and they are sharing their experiences in conversations every day. These conversations take place both directly with the company through e-mails, phone calls, and surveys, and indirectly online as customers share their opinions on review sites, blogs, and social media about their experiences or solicit recommendations from friends on social networks.

In the past, the company could deal with it in its own timeframe, directly and one on one with the customer. Response times could be anywhere from minutes to days, depending on the question or issue. Today, driven by the widespread adoption of mobile devices and social media, customer conversations are multiplying, they are often shared publicly, and they can quickly go viral. Buried in these millions of off-line and online conversations is a wealth of customer intelligence that can provide critical insights into key business drivers. Until recently, however, businesses were largely limited to analyzing only structured data contained within their business systems: things like customer names, contact information, device data, etc. Now, recent advances in text analytics have made it possible for companies to analyze unstructured text from these customer conversations, captured in call center notes, e-mails, surveys, and even in online sources such as blogs, review sites, and social media.

M3 marketers recognize that customer conversations with and about their clients are multiplying as consumers use mobile devices and social networking to share opinions, recommend products and services, and express sentiment about their favorite, and not so favorite, brands. Buried in the millions of reviews, comments, e-mails, surveys, and tweets generated every day is a wealth of customer intelligence that can be mined and used to improve the customer experience with their brand. Attensity can provide the text mining technology to capture these unstructured digital conversations taking place via the web and now the mobile worlds.

▪ *Cymfony*: They can evaluate what is being said about brands in social media. Their Maestro platform gives clients real-time access to a comprehensive, custom-built archive of traditional and social media, filtered and classified to be relevant to a company's brand and business goals. The consultancy uses at its core an information extraction engine that combines information retrieval via NLP with an intuitive user interface. While many social media monitoring tools use keyword-based search, Cymfony's technology uses a more sophisticated form of information extraction based on detailed grammatical analysis of text. This grammar-based approach eliminates irrelevant content and is far more intelligent than keyword searching.

Their natural language engine can dissect articles, paragraphs, and sentences to determine who and what is being talked about, whether something or someone is a key focus or a passing reference, and how the various entities mentioned—companies, brands, people, and events—and how they relate to one another. This firm can develop a conceptual framework to analyze, summarize, highlight key findings, and make recommendations for market landscape analysis and audience profiling for understanding the types of sites where influential and relevant discussion are occurring and the identification of marketing opportunities. This social metric consultancy can answer such questions as, what is the consumer experience with via various touch points and what can be discovered with respect to the attitudes and behaviors of various device profiles? This consultancy offers specialized solutions that are available for the following industries: consumer products, financial services, media, pharmaceuticals, retail, technology, travel, and hospitality.

- *Kantar Media*: A multimedia global metrics consultancy. They explore all media 24/7 all over the world: radio, TV, Internet, social media, and outdoor. They continuously track all types of emerging communication channels. Their media researchers provide clients with quick and exhaustive analyzes. They assist them in creating efficient communication strategies and multimedia marketing campaigns. They provide real-time digital intelligence to achieve client sales, profit, and market share goals. They also offer access to a large pool of device behavior data—drawn from many sources—constructed and organized with their proprietary and rigorous market research methodologies. Their analytical experts deliver actionable insights and recommendations to leading brands in many markets: automotive, financial services, media, mobile, online, retail, telecom, and travel. The consultancy assists brands improve their marketing effectiveness.

M3 marketers need to create profiles of product and services "champions" in order to target and recruit and retain more of these valuable "evangelists" with similar interests and preferences using clustering and classification software. A new metric is evolving in social media, which these consultancies can assist M3 marketers and that is the cost per acquired advocate (CPAA). Marketers and enterprises need to focus on identifying these "brand zealots" in order to attract more with similar preferences, desires, demographics, and influences. Brands that have created strong emotional and personal associations tend to have higher attraction and loyalty, in this era of social media, blogs, texts, e-mails, and other bursts of brands. M3 marketers need to look at evangelist consumers as comarketers for their brand. Through the strategic use of engagement marketing, companies can invite consumers to become the coproducers of marketing campaigns, such as the creation of slogans, designs, widgets, videos, and other types of viral communications.

Social Marketing Agencies' Checklist for M3

In the world of social media marketing, Facebook and Twitter dominate, but advertising on YouTube, LinkedIn, and Foursquare is expected to increase in the coming year, according to research conducted at the May 2011 Pivot Conference. Of the marketers surveyed, two-thirds were already participating in social media advertising, and 18% of those marketers planned to initiate social marketing campaigns in the next year. Success rates were nearly split down the middle, with 54% of those running ads reporting that they were satisfied with their social advertising activities. Among survey respondents, 93% have deployed campaigns on Facebook, while 78% of respondents have advertised on Twitter. The survey points toward an increase in advertising spending on YouTube, LinkedIn, and Foursquare. At least 20% of those marketing respondents plan on deploying programs on those platforms in the next year.

Leveraging the communication and influence power of social networks for marketers and advertisers is an important new channel to be developed and utilized. The increasing prominence of social networks as the means to communicate and share information among their friends can be quantified by M3 marketers by enlisting some of the following marketing ad agencies who focus on social media campaigns and metrics.

- *Getfoundnow*: They provide SEO, social marketing strategies, and blogging services. Their "Get Found Now Managed Content Syndication Service" can propel their client's website to the top of the search engines for their chosen key word search terms. They also produce and edit content for RSS syndication and a social marketing strategy for their clients.
- *Jivox*: They enable advertisers and publishers to deliver interactive video spots. This agency is a technology driven interactive video advertising delivery platform. Jivox enables brand advertisers to use the powerful medium of the Internet and the wireless channels to reach audiences via interactive video ad units yielding maximum engagement. This agency is used by top global brands like Microsoft, Yahoo!, Nokia, HP, Google, General Motors, etc.

  This agency can deliver highly interactive video ads for maximum engagement and social sharing, providing significant uplift in campaign performance.

They can plan and execute interactive video ad campaigns on any distribution outlet of a client's choice. They can deliver video ads across multiple platforms, via all types of digital devices, and virally over social networks and video sharing sites. Finally, they can track, analyze, and report on video ad performance in real time, including interactions, engagement, and other key brand metrics

Jivox is a complete platform for interactive video advertising from creative customization to campaign execution and analytics. The agency's technology enables brand advertisers, digital agencies, and publishers to deliver highly engaging video ads powered by interactive and social sharing widgets. This agency can provide metrics of interactive video advertising online and to popular HTML5-compatible Apple and Android devices. Their license and platform can deliver video ads online to all types of digital devices and manage all aspects of ad operations through an easy-to-use web-based interface. The agency provides campaign performance tracking, brand awareness, and purchase intent analytics for advertisers via its proprietary real-time analytics platform. The end result is a better-informed, more-engaged customer, improved ad performance, and ultimately higher ROI on video ad campaigns.

Jivox ads are automatically preinstrumented with analytic tags that report back to their platform several hundred million events per campaign relating to user interaction with their video ads. The agency collects user engagement data in real-time from its video ads and uses sophisticated, patent-pending algorithms to determine user intent, and what stages of the purchase funnel they are likely to be in: awareness, consideration, engagement, or intent to purchase. Connecting advertising with purchase intent in real-time eliminates the limitations of current approaches and raises the bar for online video advertising measurement and performance. Rich interactivity features enable viewers to engage with brands, right on the spot.

The agency provides real-time dashboard of ad engagement events, including social analytics such as sharing, liking, following, and tweeting, selection of each custom interactive feature, and viral sharing of video. The agency also provides in-flight campaign analytics that enables optimization of interactive widgets, ad placements, or creative to heighten brand engagement and ad ROI. Compared with noninteractive video ads, interaction rates are usually five times higher. Finally, they provide real-time analytics of user engagement that enables more effective A/B and multivariate advertising testing of creative, targeting, interactive elements, etc., to understand and optimize campaign performance. The end result is a better-informed, more engaged customer, improved ad performance, and ultimately higher ROI on video ad campaigns.

◾ *ContextOptional*: It builds brands in social media, including Facebook and Twitter. This social marketing agency takes advantage of the recent transformation from the "Me" generation to the new "We" generation. The agency is acutely aware of the socially conscious and digitally connected consumer all of whom want to make a difference and their conversations about brands and companies. Social networks enable an unprecedented and seemingly boundless level of advocacy and awareness. It is impossible to accurately predict participation, but people are passionate about products and services in social settings, and Facebook and Twitter are two social networks. They represent one of the most effective ways to go viral. The challenge is first getting the word out. ContextOptional integrates Facebook campaigns across traditional marketing and advertising initiatives to attract participants and champions.

Once engaged, ContextOptional delivers feature-rich, compelling experiences to encourage viral sharing. ContextOptional's campaigns have historically achieved 300% word-of-mouth (WOM) lift. Once a campaign is completed, this agency also provides an opportunity to continue to engage with the community to reinforce brand messaging. Their Social Marketing Suite makes it easy to launch highly engaging applications, monitor and moderate social network conversations, and analyze the results for long-term impact.

■ *33Across*: It uses social graph data to dramatically improve online marketing. They are one of the leading social targeting platforms. They have developed a technology called SocialDNA™ that uses social graph data to improve online marketing. The company is led by a team of executives with backgrounds in advertising, social network analysis, and machine learning. They develop scalable, custom, ad programs that harness the social connections around brands.

They offer a broad selection of rich media capabilities, including in-banner videos, preroll video, dynamic creative optimization, as well as standard interactive advertising bureau (IAB) ad units. Their SocialDNA Platform is used to gain insights into the underlying social networks, which surround a marketer's brand. At its core, their technology helps M3 marketers identify high-potential prospects that are socially connected to existing customers and brand loyalists. The agency builds customized social networks of consumers who are connected to a marketer's most valuable customers and prospects. 33Across is an active member of the Network Advertising Initiative (NAI), the IAB, and the Social Media Advertising Consortium (SMAC). 33Across does not capture any personally identifiable information.

■ *PandemicLabs*: This agency specializes in viral and social media marketing and can assist clients in creating, executing, and tracking campaigns where brands and consumers actively engage in two-way communication. This agency can develop social profiles and pages on Facebook, Twitter, or YouTube channels. They assist clients in building blogs and microsites in any digital strategy. Pandemic Labs works with clients to create a media list of influential writers, bloggers, podcasters, videographers, and other content producers for influencer targeting. Pandemic Labs' brand tracking engine, Indigo, tracks consumer sentiment of not only a client's brand but also competing brands to gain insight and custom influencer metrics.

■ *KickApps*: It allows for users to build their own community. Their KickApps App Studio is a web-based development environment that allows marketers to quickly and easily assemble dynamic, interactive, tractable Flash and widgets that can easily be shared around the social web. Clients can build custom video players, photo galleries, audio players, Facebook fan page tabs, and more; in a fraction of the time, it would typically take to code those experiences by hand. Clients can easily promote custom RSS feeds from their site, blog, or social profiles on Twitter, Flickr, or YouTube via monetized widgets that can easily be embedded on any site or social network.

The KickApps platform supports the creation of social networks for clients, with unique and customized user profiles for every person on their site, and allows them to track the relationships and interactions between them. It allows clients to gather feedback from devices and interact with every piece of content on their site, with customizable comments and ratings. The platform gives site administrators or users the ability to quickly gather feedback from the crowd, with a configurable polling app. Their platform supports an expanding array of social features that can be enabled with a single click: user profiles, forums, comments and ratings, and user-generated video and photos.

■ *Mindset-Media*: Uses psychographics to target consumers and their devices. This agency offers marketers measure consumer psychographics. Each Mindset Profile shows exactly how a specific group of consumers differs on 21 elements of personality known to drive buyer behavior and brand choice (Figure 3.19).

Marketing via social media shifts companies from targeting everyone to cultivating only the customers they want. Brand awareness can be accomplished in vast scales

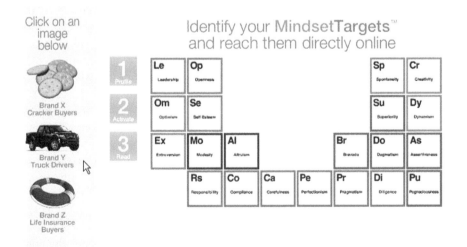

Figure 3.19 Psychographic map offered by Mindset.

and inexpensively; it may simply require a blog or a posting at a social network to create a buzz about a brand or a new product or service. It is a new form of micro-marketing. We next move to another technology that M3 marketers need to leverage or, at the very least, know about and that involves *collaborative filtering*, which is the association of one preference against another. In other way, it is software and networks which say "if you like this chance you will also like this." Amazon does this like no one else.

Recommendation Engines' Checklist for M3

Recommendation engines can also be leverage for M3 marketing by using the concept of "mob targeting," which involves the intersection of WOM, social media, and influences of groups of consumers as the key to product placement to drive brand response. The core technology of these recommendation engines is also referred to as "collaborative filtering" and can be seen in action at Netflix. Collaborative filtering is the process of filtering for information or patterns using techniques involving collaboration among multiple agents, viewpoints, data sources, etc. Collaborative filtering is a method of making automatic predictions about the interests of a user by collecting taste or preference information from many users to make its recommendations.

The underlying assumption of this marketing approach is that those who agreed in the past tend to agree again in the future. Collaborative filtering systems can be reduced to two main processes: first, look for users who share the same rating patterns with the active user, the user device whom the prediction is for. Second, use the ratings from those like-minded users found in step one to calculate a prediction for the active user device. This falls under the category of user-based collaborative filtering via the use of a nearest neighbor algorithm. Amazon and Netflix use their own proprietary collaborative filtering engines; however, M3 marketers can leverage commercial recommendation engines and networks for their clients from the following firms:

- *ATG*: This is acquired by ORACLE. They provide a complete commerce suite that incorporates a recommendation engine. The engine focuses on treating consumer devices uniquely. It takes into account what they know about the shopper or buyer to serve them more intelligently. To do this, the engine creates dynamic sites and applications to deliver targeted content—whether a promotion, a recommendation, or product information—based on the consumer's profile and shopping context. This type of personalization filters out the noise for consumers, helping them avoid information overload.

  This recommendation engine provides an e-commerce platform and optimization solutions, enabling marketers to tailor the buying experience and present relevant recommendations to devices, marketing promotions, and product information that increase sales and customer satisfaction. The ATG Adaptive Scenario Engine, segmentation and content targeting software, provides the personalization technology and core functionality needed to deliver an engaging customer experience at every stage of the buying process. With this personalization engine, M3 marketers can develop and manage robust, adaptable, scalable, and personalized e-commerce software applications across all digital channels through the complete customer life cycle.

▪ *Aggregateknowledge*: It offers data management and an ad optimization platform. This engine enables marketers control over their advertising campaigns with device segmentation, data management, real-time decision, and optimization. The engine can dynamically assemble and serve the most relevant message for each user device.

Their AK Platform provides audience management infrastructure to collect and distribute data; configure audiences and custom attribution; and track, analyze, and measure marketing campaigns. It serves ads across any connected digital channel. The platform ingests and normalizes both, first- and third-party data (website data, conversions, ad serving, and click stream data), in any format, via any transfer protocol, from any data source (Figure 3.20).

AK Ad Server is able to track and deliver dynamic or static ads. It supports all the usual features such as frequency capping, day parting, and multiple ad formats. The AK data collection component relies on the universal ad tagging technology and external feeds to ingest and normalize heterogeneous data from websites, ad servers, client systems, and third-party data networks. The AK Platform Engine implements high-performance collaborative

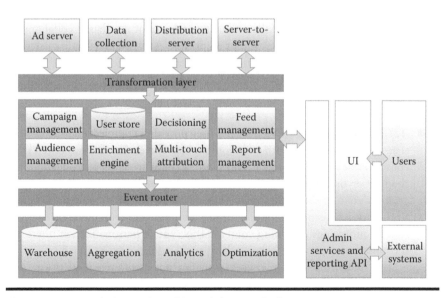

Figure 3.20 Analytics and tracking of the AK Platform.

filtering algorithms to identify the best creative assets to display for a given unique user based on their cluster and their click stream data from the advertiser's website.

■ *ChoiceStream*: It personalizes its recommendations via their CRUNCH recommendation engine network. It mixes data plus intelligence. The ChoiceStream's rich, proprietary database of consumer activities mixes behavioral data from ChoiceStream's select group of partners to predict what types of individuals will respond to an advertiser's brand campaign, and because people are dynamic, the engine is dynamic. CRUNCH calculates an advertiser's ideal audience in real time and automatically adjusts the marketing buy minute-by-minute throughout the campaign.

This engine lets devices know that they are in the right place, in their first critical seconds on a website. The engine supports intelligent shopping cart and order confirmation for cross-sell, up-sell, and next-sell based on a device actual shopping behavior. ChoiceStream supports customized e-mail marketing via their engine to reengage customers with the offers they are most likely to value. This engine sets out to help devices discover the brands that would make their lives better and to help brands be discovered by the audiences that would truly value them. It works like high-tech consumer matchmaking.

■ *Avail*: It offers consumer recommendations via its behavioral recommendation engine providing an online merchandising solution that lets retailers automatically recommend the most relevant products to each visitor, creating a truly personal shopping experience. It works at every step in the buying cycle and in every channel, attracting shoppers, helping them find what they came looking for, and stimulating them to buy more. Avail relies on a unique personalization and its proprietary product recommendation engine, developed in 2000.

Avail's technology platform combines sophisticated algorithmic and online merchandising research to analyze the behavior of every website visitor: What ads they click, what search phrases they use, and what products they view and buy. It uses that "collective intelligence" to predict what each visitor might be attracted by and presents that to them. It lets devices to help each other to buy more. Avail's recommendation engine automatically correlates search terms used and ads clicked with purchases made by others.

These recommendation software products and networks can bring social consumerism to marketers and their clients by enabling consumer devices to interact easily, allowing them to give each other tips about products and services. It also allows them to influence, recommend, and socialize, exchanging communications about content or sites they have discovered. Social networking and collaborative recommendation engines and networks have added a whole new element of communication. They introduce personal reputation systems and rankings on a global scale, where influential consumers can become new marketing champions, especially in the area of social media, retailing, and entertainment.

Data Harvesters' Checklist for A5

There are also data harvester firms also known as "data scraper" or "listening services." These companies monitor in real time thousands of news sources, blogs, and websites to discover what people are saying about products, companies, services, or topics selected by clients or marketers. These listening services help marketers and enterprises understand the likes and dislikes of online customers. They also provide social media monitoring. For example, Nielsen's Buzz Metrics offers a service it calls "ThreatTracker," which alerts a company if its brand is being discussed in a negative light. The following is a listing of some of these harvesting providers and listening services.

- *Nielsen's Buzz Metrics*: Consumer-generated media (CGM) is today's fastest growing media segment. Every day, millions of consumers go online to express opinions, share ideas, and create new media for mass consumption. In this era of consumer control, M3 marketers must work harder than ever to manage perceptions and reputations, and they require dynamic, customizable, and robust market intelligence to ensure swift response to online opportunities and threats. Their *My BuzzMetrics* service is a fully customizable dashboard that allows brand managers to easily monitor and analyze what is being said online about their brand or organization from a wide range of CGM sources. The service is accessible via a browser to provide real-time analysis and segmentation capabilities, at-a-glance-metrics, and a range of report and delivery options to support brand, marketing, and product managers who must comprehensively analyze their marketing campaigns and overall brand strength and deliver quantifiable results to clients.
- *Dow Jones*: They monitor how corporate clients are covered in news articles, blogs, and websites. They provide comprehensive information on more than 18 million companies. They can search key industries to find more than 36 million executive profile biographies and news from more than 28,000 top business sources to locate financial statements and regulatory filings.
- *InfiniGraph*: Listening service assists companies on what consumers are saying about them. InfiniGraph enable brands a smarter, faster, and more intelligent way to source content "curation" that is highly relevant to them. Using their "Real Time Social Intelligence," they can increase clicks, engagement, and reach, maximizing their social investment. M3 marketers can search on a brand name that has a Facebook or Twitter site. They can access "Trending Content," that is, what content is getting the most action over time, and "Affinity Content," which reports on what content is getting the most interaction around their brand. Marketers can start to increase engagements—via Facebook Connect to access trending affinities. Last, this harvester can identify "influencers," that is, which people have the most reach and relevance to their brand (Figure 3.21).

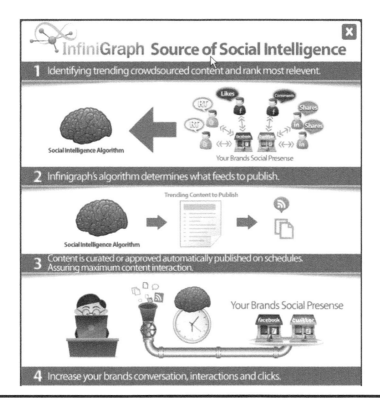

Figure 3.21   Data harvester monitoring what is being said about brands.

InfiniGraph is designed to simplify identification of social keywords as they trend based on collective social interaction linked to proprietary social brand groupings to inform Facebook ad buying and social media optimization (SMO) or social SEO. This harvester can improve the process of identifying key influencers for engagement and activation. Their platform can generate one-click content recommendations for broadcast with real-time tracking. InfiniGraph can derive relevant conversation content from crowd sourced social interaction within product verticals to help increase brand-to-consumer engagement and conversion events.

■ *NM Incite*: They provide social-media monitoring, online-brand metrics, and real-time market intelligence. NM Incite assists M3 marketers with "social media intelligence" that provides them high-quality metrics, insights, and advice. This harvester leverages the strengths of two world-class brands: Nielsen, the data provider, and McKinsey, the strategic advisors. They work side by side with their clients integrating industry and functional expertise to develop innovative social media strategies and solutions that make a mea-surable business impact. NM Incite helps marketers harness the potential of social media intelligence to drive superior business performance.

Consumers are increasingly going about their lives in a digital environment via their devices. They use blogs, social networks, and other social media to evaluate products, make purchasing decisions, share opinions, and connect with friends. Traffic to social networks is skyrocketing and more and more consumers rely on WOM and peer recommendations when evaluating a product or making a purchase decision. This harvester firm assists marketers to capitalize on the insights available as a result of consumer-generated activity via social media as an integral source of consumer knowledge. NM Incite assists M3 marketers with the capabilities to better understand, value, and take advantage of these rich consumer insights. It provides social media monitoring tools and listening processes to improve product development, engagement marketing, and customer service operations.

■ *SocialFlow*: This harvester monitors Twitter and other social media networks and sites and helps publishers, brand marketers, and online retailers increase click-throughs, ReTweets, Mentions, sharing, and organic follower growth, on Twitter, Facebook, and Google+. Their software "listens" to what devices are interested in and talking about in real time. They monitor Tweets and posts in real time and release the message that is most likely to earn the most attention. SocialFlow is used by media companies, brand marketers, and online retailers to drive traffic to their websites and grow their audiences in social channels. They are SaaS application, which requires no integration or development by M3 marketers. Their dashboard provides an at-a-glance view of client's social accounts and their performance and audience KPIs, including Clicks, Tweet, ReTweets, Mentions, and Followers growth. Their real-time dashboard is designed to help inform improved marketing and editorial efforts on the social web.

These data harvesters and listening services can provide the M3 marketer answer as to what, when, and where the buzz is most likely to take off. For example, they can monitor what is being shared and said via Facebook and Twitter, that is, marketing by the minute. The challenge to the M3 marketer is utilizing these data from these harvesters using text analytic software for organizing the unstructured bits of data strew across these social sites and networks to generate WOM buzz and velocity.

WOM Techniques and Companies' Checklist for M3

Social media marketing via friends is about WOM communications that can be encouraged and facilitated. M3 marketers and their clients can communicate with their consumer's devices and potential new customers by making it easy for them to tell their friends. WOM marketing can make certain that influential individuals know about the good qualities of a product or a service and make it easy for them to share it with their friends in a funny, cool, and relevant manner.

■ *Community Marketing*: This is niche communities likely to share interests about a brand. Community marketing is a strategy to engage an audience in an active, nonintrusive prospect and customer conversation. Whereas marketing communication strategies such as advertising, promotion, PR, and sales all focus on attaining customers. Community Marketing focuses on the needs of existing customers. This accomplishes four things for M3 marketers: (1) it connects existing customers with prospects, (2) it connects prospects with each other, (3) it connects a company with customers and prospects to solidify loyalty, and finally (4) it connects customers with customers to improve product adoption and satisfaction. There are two types of community marketing the M3 marketer needs to be aware of: *organic,* which is created by users with no company intervention, and *sponsored*, which is fostered and hosted by a company. The M3 marketer should strive for the organic type of WOM. Continuing success in community marketing strategies has been found in engaging and cultivating the natural communities by M3 marketers that form around their brand and product or service.

■ *Viral Marketing*: Creating messages designed to be passed along in an exponential fashion. Viral marketing refers to M3 marketing techniques that use preexisting social networks to produce increases in brand awareness or to achieve other marketing objectives, such as new product announcements, through self-replicating viral processes, analogous to the spread of biological or machine viruses. Its delivery is via WOM on the web or mobile networks. Viral marketing may take the form of video clips on You Tube, interactive Flash games, Tweets, Facebook postings, or text messages. The goal of the M3 marketer interested in creating successful viral marketing programs is to create viral messages that appeal to individuals with high social networking potential (SNP) and that have a high probability of being presented and spread by digital devices with others in burst of conversations in a short period of time.

■ *Influencer Marketing*: The concept is to identify key opinion leaders who are likely to influence the opinions of others. These key influencers do not buy, are not obvious, and usually start off neutral; that is why their potential to affect sales is so great. Influencer marketing is a form of WOM marketing that has emerged from a variety of recent practices and studies, in which the focus is placed on specific key individuals or types of class of individuals, rather than the target market as a whole. For the M3 marketer, the key focus is to identify the features or characteristics of these individuals that have influence over potential buyers and to target these influencers in order to find others with similar distinctiveness. Influencers are customers or potential buyers, or they may be third parties. These third parties exist either in the supply chain, such as retailers, manufacturers, etc., or they may be so-called value-added influencers, such as journalists, academics, industry analysts, professional advisers, etc., ideally, however, for the M3 marketers is to identify and to leverage first party influencers.

■ *Grassroots Marketing*: Organizing and motivating devices to engage in local outreach. It is getting consumers and influencers in your key markets to care so much about what you are doing so that they become your cheerleaders and most vocal supporters. To make it work, it should be a feel-good campaign that motivates people and brings out their passion. Grassroots is about permeating a community and building relationships locally on many levels, so the buzz grows. One of the best ways to get people excited about products and services are having them taste, feel, or use it for free.

■ *Evangelist Marketing*: It cultivates advocates, encouraged to spread the buzz on a brand. The six basic tenets of creating customer evangelists are as follows: (1) continuously gather customer feedback; (2) make it a point to share knowledge freely; (3) build the buzz via WOM; (4) create community, and encourage devices to meet and share; (5) make bite-size chunks offerings to get devices to try out offers; and (6) create a cause that focuses on making your brand and the world better.

■ *Cause Marketing*: Supporting a social cause for people who strongly believe in an issue. Cause marketing refers to a type of marketing involving the cooperative efforts of a "for-profit" business and a nonprofit organization for mutual benefit. The term is sometimes used more broadly and generally to refer to any type of marketing effort for social and other charitable causes, including in-house marketing efforts by nonprofit organizations. Cause marketing is a marketing relationship not necessarily based on a donation but more importantly on support of a brand for the good.

■ *Referral Marketing*: It is a method of promoting products or services to new devices through referrals, usually WOM. Such referrals often happen spontaneously, but M3 marketers can influence this through appropriate strategies. Referral marketing is a structured and systematic process to maximize WOM potential. Referral marketing does this by encouraging, informing, promoting, and rewarding customers and contacts to think and talk as much as possible about their brand, product, and service and the value and benefits they provide to devices and their owners. Referral marketing takes WOM from the spontaneous situation to one where maximum referrals are generated.

■ *Buzz Marketing*: It uses entertainment or news spots to get people to talk about a brand. It is about using WOM to increase interactions of devices about product or service, which serves to amplify the original marketing message. It is a vague but positive association, excitement, or anticipation about a product or service—positive "buzz marketing" is often a goal of viral marketing, public relations, and of advertising on the web and mobile channels. The term refers to both the execution of the marketing technique and the resulting goodwill that is created.

■ *Product Seeding*: It provides targeted information or samples to influential individuals. Product seeding is quite similar to celebrity endorsements and evangelist marketing and is a grassroots way of planting a product so that it can be seen by important or influential people. An example of product seeding would be getting a celebrity to wear a certain hat or to hold a particular drink when being photographed or interviewed. Product seeding also can be done in smaller ways online, such as visiting forums and advocating for a particular product by someone who has a good reputation there.

WOM is the genuine voice of customers, which to succeed must be natural, genuine, and honest. WOM is also about people seeking advice from each other and talking about new products, services, and brands via social networks, the web, blogs, e-mails, texts, and the mobile world. WOM is acknowledging that a satisfied customer is the greatest endorsement for a brand. For the M3 marketer, the goal is to facilitate such endorsement via social media on the web and wireless marketplaces. Exclusivity and scarcity invite curiosity from influencers for new product announcements—the bait of limited prerelease edition products—combine with WOM is an excellent method to disseminate brand awareness. The following firms provide some vital services enabling marketers to execute WOM campaigns effectively and professionally.

1. *Hyperdrive Interactive*: They attract, engage, and motivate digital devices on a one-to-one basis. This WOM agency focuses on practical marketing communications that engage customer devices. They strive to understand and address the unique interests and needs of real customers. They analyze their clients most valuable customers—who are they, how do they act, what do they buy, and when. They harness the power of WOM to create brand advocates; focus to acquire, retain, and grow highly engaged brand fans; and provide the metrics for measuring the revenue growth and impact of WOM campaigns.

2. *Brains on Fire*: They help M3 marketers build movements using WOM and identity development. They create fans rather than customers because fans embody loyalty and they have a vested interest. They defend brands passionately. A true fan loves a team, a brand, or a band whether they win or lose. Fans don't just join a movement. They help grow it. Fans have a sense of ownership and shared identity because a client's success is a fan's success and it is a two-way street. Their WOM approach and key question is not "what can we sell this person?" It is "what can we do to keep this person and make them even happier?"

3. *Likeable Media*: They provide social media, WOM, community engagement, and Facebook strategies. They are a full-service social media leveraging and WOM firm. They assist M3 marketers in building social media campaigns into effective communication plans, along with the tools to help their clients. They search the social web for mentions of a client's brand on a daily basis and assure that positive mentions are amplified and negative mentions are responded to and fixed.

4. *360 Digital Influence (Ogilvy) PR*: A digital, social media, online, marketing, and WOM agency. The new reality for brands is people are consuming and creating more content in more ways than ever before and this worldwide agency can assist M3 marketers in the execution of their WOM campaigns.

5. *BzzAgent*: It connects consumers and brands to activate their WOM network across all digital channels. They are a WOM network powered by over 800,000 devices. BzzAgent creates measurable business results for M3 marketers through an advocate network, an engagement platform, and analytics.

6. *Keller Fay Group*: A research and consulting company dedicated to WOM marketing. They measure and deliver insight based on all channels of WOM both online and off-line and all the consumer touch points that drive the conversations that drive brands. The WOM dynamic metrics collected at the brand level includes the following:

   a. *Polarity*: Positive, negative, mixed, neutral opinions
   b. *Recommending*: Buy, consider, avoid
   c. *Content*: What was said?
   d. *Credibility and intended actions*
   e. *Influences*: Customer experience, media/marketing
   f. *Sender versus receivers*

7. *Gaspedal*: They provide training and presentation on implementing WOM and social media strategies to companies of all sizes.

8. *Zocalo Group*: They create WOM strategies and campaigns for global brand marketers. Zócalo Group is a full-service WOM and social media marketing company, seamlessly integrating them in PR, experiential marketing, optimization, and influencer marketing. They enlist, encourage, and empower the right people in the right way and in the right places to talk about and recommend client's brand and consumer engagement strategies for global marketers.

9. *Nielsen*: They provide clients an understanding of what consumer devices watch and buy. Their solutions focus on the intensity and immediacy of social media as a source of consumer feedback, trends, and information. The fastest growing media are being shaped by the consumers themselves. The opinions they express in social media are highly trusted, widely shared, and can have significant short- and long-term impact on a client's brand.

10. *Leverage Software*: They use collaboration to create enterprise social networks inside companies.

11. *Fanscape*: A social media marketing agency that fosters WOM marketing. They engage consumers and inspire WOM communication through their fan and influencer outreach network, their site and blog integrations, digital content distribution, and social network loyalty and engagement services.

12. *BrickFish*: They are a social media campaign platform that allows brands to engage with their consumers through multiple campaign modules that can be simultaneously embedded on a brand's Facebook page, a brand's

website(s), microsites, mobile websites, and across the social web via consumers. They track and encourage consumers to opt into a client's brand via "like" on Facebook and "follow" on Twitter. Once a social media campaign is created, the Brickfish platform tracks all active engagements or consumer interactions and displays the results via their viral mapping technologies. The Brickfish campaign platform empowers consumer devices to share, compete in, and influence a brand's campaigns by interacting with their peers in their social graph.

13. *TREMOR*: This is a WOM marketing organization developed by Procter & Gamble. TREMOR is an agency that focuses on creating consumer advocacy as the driving force behind effective, measurable WOM campaigns. A TREMOR campaign creates consumer-to-consumer conversations on a national scale that deliver measurable results using quantitative and qualitative measures of effectiveness. TREMOR is a complete end-to-end marketing solution that includes intensive consumer research, message development, and campaign execution. With TREMOR, an effective, targeted message about a client's brand can be amplified through waves of consumer advocacy.

14. *Porter Novelli*: A public relations firm that is part of Omnicom Group. The agency transforms the opinions, beliefs, and behaviors of their clients. They make this happen through a consistent and systematic approach that pairs a deep, data-driven understanding of what makes people think and act the way they do with sophisticated metrics that enable them to identify, monitor, manage, and engage the most influential audiences.

15. *Room 214*: This is a social media, WOM, and search marketing agency. They serve organizations desiring to go deep with social media. They help clients engage their customers, humanize their brand, and build upon what works. Among the agency's offerings are social media monitoring, influencer identification, social intelligence, and viral tracking. They assist their clients with Facebook applications, marketing dashboards, social network software, and mobile applications.

16. *Converseon*: A social media consultancy. They utilize an industry-leading framework to help clients bolster their social media engagement strategies and establish their own meaningful social purpose to position their brand at the forefront of their industry. This agency uses their own proprietary software, their Conversation Miner, for optimizing a brand's SEO strategy, executing social media activation campaigns, buying the right media placements, and implementing new creative ads and the metrics for measuring their success.

17. *Odcast*: A viral marketing agency. They provide end-to-end applications for creating social and participation media campaigns to engage with client's target audiences.

18. *Mr. Youth*: A WOM, social interactive, and experiential marketing agency.

WOM marketing empowers people to share their likes or dislikes about products, services, and companies; but, most importantly, for the M3 marketer, it is about harnessing the voice of people for the good of the brand. To execute WOM over multiple channels includes the development of mobile websites for allowing conversation to take place via wireless digital devices via A5s. The following checklist identifies some software developer firms that specialize on creating mobile websites for M3 marketers.

Checklist of Mobile Website Developers for A5s

Mobile websites are a relatively recent channel for accessing the web from mobile devices via wireless networks. The mobile arena, however, introduces a new layer of complexity that can be difficult for websites to accommodate since they require cross-platform functionality and diminutive displays. At a minimum, the sites should support the native Android and Apple browsers. There are many developers specializing in the creation of mobile websites for multiple devices, and the following list contains some of the best developers in the industry.

- *Blue Corona*: They offer mobile websites, marketing analytics, and mobile metrics. Blue Corona can construct a mobile website optimized specifically for mobile devices in just 5 days for $500 with key mobile website features, such as prominent company logo and contact information—click to call functionality and direction via Google Maps—service overviews and coupon options. They also provide metrics via Google Analytics in order to know what percentage of website visitors come from mobile devices. Before constructing a mobile website, M3 marketers need to consider the circumstances in which someone on a mobile device would be on their client's site in the first place. For example, if the client is a plumbing, heating and air-conditioning, or roofing company, someone might visit the mobile website on their mobile device because they are in an emergency situation (Figure 3.22).

  Mobile websites need to ensure contact information, such as their phone number is prominently placed on every page of the site. It should be a click-to-call phone number. In addition, it is not a good idea to overload the mobile website with the same content of the main website. Images and pictures on mobile website should also be minimized.

- *Phonify*: They construct mobile websites geared for shoppers on the go. Mobile devices are always moving and want to compare prices and to find the nearest store location instantly.

  On the left side of Figure 3.23 is the original website viewed on the iPhone. Because it is mainly Flash based, which Apple does not support, the site is almost completely unusable to mobile digital devices. This mobile website developer converted the site by giving it a simple menu—without Flash—and embedding a Google Map for quickly locating a store.

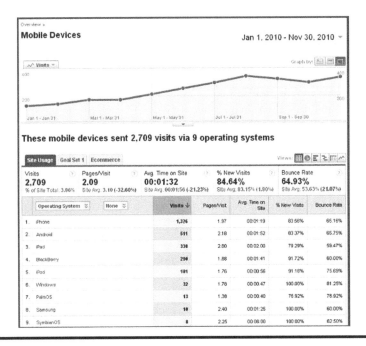

Figure 3.22 Google Analytics as integrated by Blue Corona.

Figure 3.23 Before and after a mobile website is "Phonified."

They design mobile sites by simply adding a small block of Javascript on a client's main website to automatically redirect traffic from mobile devices. Phonify provides, at no cost, up to seven static pages which they host on their servers with a custom iPhone icon with click-to-call or click-to-e-mail, plus a link to Google Maps.

■ *Mozeo*: They provide mobile website construction, text messaging, and advertising services. They provide all the services to assist marketers in creating client mobile websites. M3 marketers have full control of the style, look and feel, and the content of their mobile market-friendly website. This developer uses their mobile websites to complement marketer campaigns with mini-sites or to create their own mobile website with rich media optimized for the mobile devices. They provide their clients the ability to get more information by using their mobile devices to snap a photo of marketer's QR code.

They can connect with marketer's audience based on the real-world geographic location of their mobile devices by adding geolocation to any mobile marketing campaign. They can create a shopping catalog and add the products or services marketers want to sell. Devices will be sent to a mobile website with their shopping cart and items. Devices can browse and purchase when ready. Their mobile shopping catalog can have full credit card capabilities so that devices can buy on the go. As mobile devices get better at supporting rich multimedia, Mozeo gives clients the ability to take advantage of these features in a completely integrated environment.

■ *mobiSiteGalore*: Users can create free mobile sites in minutes; hosting is available. mobiSiteGalore claims that it takes an average time of 54 min to create a mobile site designed to be viewed on any mobile device. The WAP websites built with their mobiSiteGalore wap site builder are guaranteed to work on any mobile device. The websites created using mobiSiteGalore work on the iPhone, Android, Blackberry, and even in low-end digital devices. This developer claims that no technical knowledge, programming skill, or web design experience is required to build a mobile website with their WAP builder. There is no software to download or install and no plug-ins are required either.

A fully integrated HTML rich text editor helps the marketer create rich XHTML content with text and images in a WYSIWYG—what you see is what you get—mode with absolutely no need for prior knowledge or experience in HTML or XHTML. With mobiSiteGalore, marketers can choose from a range of attractive readymade design templates with customize colors, fonts, and layouts. Mobile websites built with mobiSiteGalore are compliant with W3C.org's Mobile Web Best Practices and the W3C mobileOK Basic Tests.

■ *Mobile Web Up*: They provide mobile-friendly sites optimized for hand-held devices. They offer free evaluations. This developer can create mobile website, designs, hosting, marketing, and advertising.

■ *Mobify*: They provide a mobile website studio. They also support mobile ads and apps design and construction. Mobify uses HTML5, CSS, and powerful JavaScript to fully integrate with existing desktop websites to make the mobile experience amazing for the end user device. With mobile browsing set to outpace desktop browsing by 2015, having a mobile site is a necessity for any enterprise and M3 marketers. Mobify mobile websites takes advantage of touch-based navigation and widgets like tactile image carrousels. This enables users to tap and swipe their way through say a store with a finger-friendly interface and elements that resize based on device specifications and capabilities.

When browsing a desktop site on a mobile device, images and text are too large, resulting in lots of panning, zooming, and lagging of content, leading to a frustrating user experience and high bounce rates. Their Mobify Enterprise lowers bounce rates and increases conversion rates by vastly improving mobile checkout flow, a rich user interface, and increase performance and revenue growth.

■ *Usablenet*: The Usablenet platform requires no client IT resources—no systems integration, no web development. All mobile devices and all types of output are supported. There is no aspect of their mobile sites that they cannot transform. The mobile device is no longer all that is mobile—the consumer is mobile—with online brands being highly dynamic. Their development platform is crafted and refined to support their clients' objectives and all types of mobile devices.

■ *Digby*: Their Mobile Commerce Software Platform enables mobile website with rich A5s for iPhone, iPod touch, BlackBerry, and Android Devices. They make remote storefronts available to all types of digital devices anytime, anywhere. They make every device a virtual sales representative, with access to product information, reviews, and promotions, which complement a retailer's catalog with up-to-date product information, videos, and reviews. Mobile represents a fundamental shift in the way consumers are discovering, buying, and interacting with retailers when mobile or when in their store. With more than 100 million digital devices activated in the United States today and with more than 4 billion worldwide, the opportunity for mobile engagement between retailers and consumers is significant.

Due to this shift to mobile, this developer believes that consumers and their always-on, always-connected, location aware devices represent a strategic new channel that retailers must recognize—as fundamentally different than their other channels—but one that can unify them all. Digby believes that retailers should take a strategic approach to deliver a unique mobile commerce experience, as well as an engaging in-store mobile experience within a retail branded and optimized mobile website, and rich A5s for iPhone, Android, and BlackBerry devices.

Mobile marketing also requires the creation of native apps (A5s) with purchasing capabilities and the integration of a device's camera for barcode scanning and the interactive viewing of product demonstrations, price comparisons, and videos. Constructing a mobile website and A5s is an essential consideration in the marketing via this channel. First, considerations must be made about the expected users and what devices to support. There are really only two critical and dominant ones—Apple and Android.

Checklist for Constructing A5s

■ What functionality to include—it should excite devices.
■ Let users browse, search, compare, and transact via the A5.
■ Make the experience match that of the website; list the entire catalog.
■ Which platform to support—Apple or Android—which one to support first.
■ Who will build it—most likely outsource to an app developer with experience.
■ Measure everything: downloads, starts, average usage time, order value, location, etc.

In the end, M3 marketers will probably want to go through a request for proposal (RFP) process with several app developer vendors, such as the following companies.

Checklist of A5 Developers

■ *Elance*: This is an apps developer exchange with over 300,000 freelancers. M3 marketers can post jobs for bids to have custom developed A5s. A recent search for "mobile app professionals" found over 10,000 available contractors.
■ *My First Mobile App*: They are developers of A5s for all mobile devices. They offer a full-spectrum, end-to-end services across diverse categories, such as business, utilities, entertainment, and gaming among various others. They offer custom mobile application development on mobile operating platforms including Apple's iOS, Google's Android, Windows Mobile and Phone, BlackBerry OS, and Symbian OS.
■ *Zco*: Mobile app development service extends to all major mobile platforms. They are another developer for hire; clients have a concept in mind for their apps; they hire Zco to build it. They offer mobile A5 development, including multiplatform and backend system integration capabilities, marketing packages, and affordable prices.
■ *Mutual Mobile*: This is the largest mobile A5 development company in the United States. They assist clients in taking full advantage of modern device mobility. They provide expertise and the ability to execute the design, engineering, and project management resources they have experienced with Android and Apple devices.
■ *Bianor*: They provide free analysis and rapid development and specialize in complete mobile solutions ranging from telecom-grade back-end services to A5 development.
■ *xCubeLabs*: Experienced, low cost, fast results, and free quotes. Their specialization includes developing A5s across multiple verticals. Strong technical competency, well-defined methodology, and a team of expert engineers and designers.
■ *Best Fit Mobile*: They support all major mobile platforms. They design, develop, and optimize mobile solutions for companies who want to engage their customers.

Both Apple and Android A5s capture different type of data, for example, Android apps that capture age and gender are limited to Pandora and MySpace Mobile; however, the following Android apps do capture location: Alchemy, Barcode Scanner, Beautiful Widgets, Calorie Counter, Cardio Trainer, CBS News, Foursquare, Fox News, Groupon, Movies by Flixster, Pandora, Paper Toss, Shazam, The Coupon App, Toss It, Tweet Caster, U.S. Yellow Pages Search, Weather & Toggle Widget, The Weather Channel, and WeatherBug.

Apple captures age and gender on Grindr, Pandora, and TextPlus 4. The Apple apps that capture location are Angry Birds, Aurora Feint It, Best Alarm Clock, Bible App, CBS News, Dictionary.com, Foursquare, Fox News, Google Maps, Grindr, MyFitnesPal, NYTimes, Ninjump, Pandora, Paper Toss, Pimple Popper, Pumpkin Maker, Shazam, Talking Tom Cat, TextPlus 4, The Moron Test, Tips & Tricks iPhone Secrets, TweedDeck, The Weather Channel, and Yelp.

A5s developers can insert a software development kit (SDK) from an advertising network, such as Greystripe, Inc. It is common practice among A5 developers, who use these ready-made kits to place ads and generate revenue by targeting devices based on their interests and/or their location. There are several mobile marketing and tracking firms, which the M3 marketer can leverage to execute these features for their clients.

Checklist of A5 Marketing Companies

- *Mobile Defense*: Originally developed to track lost or stolen digital devices, the firm is now marketing to them. They were the first security solution for Google Android devices; however, tracking for forensics is not far removed from M3 and A5. They provide military software to M3 marketers.
- *Glympse*: It offers software that allows GPS-enabled mobile devices to be tracked (Figure 3.24).
- *MobiWee*: It runs on Windows, Android, Apple, and BlackBerry mobile devices. The software offers one-click remote access and transfers files from any stationary to a mobile device and back—for contact backup, restore, merge, and transfer access.
- *iLocalis*: Their software can track mobile Apple devices via the web. iLocalis supports location tracking, remote iPhone control, and SMS commands and alert zones.
- *Navizon*: It offers an SDK for A5 purposes. Navizon can provide the location—latitude and longitude—of mobile devices based on the triangulation of Wi-Fi or cellular signals. Their Client-Side SDK is a library that marketers can include in their own client applications. The Navizon Positioning System can collect the wireless information surrounding the user device and turn that information into a geographic location, which is then relayed to the client's application to use any way they see fit.

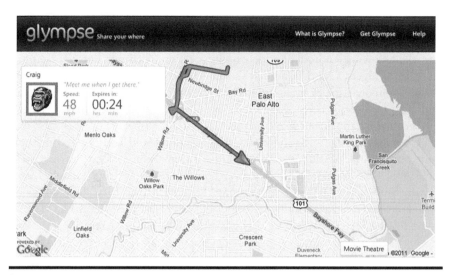

Figure 3.24 Glympse in action—tracking a device in real time.

M3 marketing is the future of advertising with more major brands turning to the web, social networks, and mobile to target their increasingly fragmented consumers. The following checklist details some major issues they need to focus on in a continuously evolving manner that is both engaging and organic between marketers and digital devices.

M3 Marketer's Checklist

- Identify areas of opportunity and take action.
- Validate the accuracy of the data continuously.
- Set team goals and incentives; make it a nonstop process.
- Focus on actionable consumer data: website, mobile, transactional, A5s.
- Set success metrics; continuously measure KPI.
- Monetize all models; measure ROI, sales, conversions, profitability, revenue, and WOM.

New digital ad agencies have recently sprung up that can deliver automated ad-buying and self-evolving M3 marketing campaigns and A5 platforms.

Checklist of Digital M3 and A5 Agencies

- *DataXu*: It provides media management platform for ad campaigns across all channels. The agency starts by assimilating the client's existing data. Then it analyzes it, looking for patterns of behavior that help it understand or differentiate levels of intent among their target audience. These insights are refined

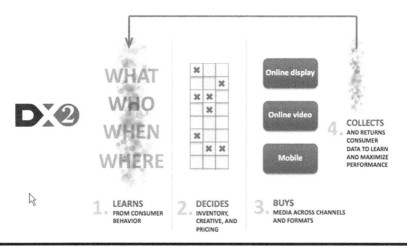

Figure 3.25   DX2 four-step process.

to zero in on new potential devices. Their DX2 system continually pushes these insights into a bidding system, which dynamically makes thousands of decisions based on more than 100 creative, consumer, and contextual parameters. Based on the client's specific goals, it determines the precise value of each in market impression and bids accordingly (Figure 3.25).

■ *BBDO*: It offers marketers insight into the everyday routines of people across the globe. BBDO is a worldwide advertising agency network, with its headquarters in New York. The agency began in 1891 with George Batten's Batten Company. Later in 1928, through a merger of BDO (Barton, Durstine & Osborn) and Batten Co., the agency became BBDO. It is the atypical New York ad agency.

■ *Razorfish*: A large interactive agency offering digital advertising helping companies build their brand through strategy planning, interactive design, social influence marketing, search and e-mail marketing, analytics, technology architecture, and development.

■ *GeniusRocket*: An agency that connects creative talent to marketers, publishers, companies, and their brand managers. This agency has over 200 production companies, 100 animation teams, 50 copywriters, and 50 creative directors.

■ *Lotame*: This agency provides social media ad campaigns via their Crowd Control Technology. Crowd Control seamlessly targets consumer devices across multiple media outlets. Their affinity reports identify related audience attributes that are not initially considered. The agency seeks target segments with the highest likelihood to perform desired behaviors such as interacting, clicking, and viewing a video to completion. They perform ad planning and campaign delivery most align with target audience interests and habits.

■ *MediaMath*: They provide digital media services via its demand side platform (DSP). This agency uses data to understand consumer behavior and identify opportunities. They translate those insights into integrated marketing strategies across channels, with clear and measurable goals. They use advanced analytics to identify the media and audiences that will best reach those goals and quantify the value of each. They analyze results and optimize to deliver more of what is working. They use technology and data to turn ideas into results.

■ *Big Spaceship*: This digital creative agency specializes in web design, strategy, marketing, and branding. They are designers who work with brands to solve their business problems. Their clients include 20th Century Fox, A&E, ABC, Adobe, Coca-Cola, General Electric, Glaceau, Google, Gucci, HBO, Linden Lab, Microsoft, MoMA, NBC Universal, Nike, OfficeMax, Royal Caribbean, Sony Pictures, Target, Victoria's Secret, and Wrigley.

■ *Profero*: A U.K.-based interactive agency focusing solely on online marketing. They provide media, technology, and creative services.

■ *x + 1*: This agency provides audience targeting at websites and digital media (Figure 3.26).

x + 1 works with brands, agencies, and media companies to determine the most valuable customer attributes. Those characteristics that indicate who is most likely to respond favorably and then interact with those people when and where they are online. Their Predictive Optimization Engine makes it possible to enable an automated, real-time decision making, and personalization, ensuring that the right ad or message is delivered to the right person at the right time. Their clients include leading digital marketers and agencies in financial services, telecommunications, online services, travel, and other industries.

Figure 3.26 *x + 1* **audience marketing report.**

Figure 3.27   Digitas agency storefront.

- *Victors & Spoils*: A creative digital ad agency built on crowd sourcing principles. Current clients include DISH Network.
- *Buildabrand*: This agency offers an online instant branding system that allows entrepreneurs, businesses, and individuals to create, manage, and apply instant and personalized branding to their business.
- *The Factory*: A digital design and marketing agency. Among the services they provide are brand development and strategy, corporate logo design, marketing strategies, graphic design, website development, SEO, social media marketing, and online reputation management.
- *Digitas*: An integrated brand agency (Figure 3.27).

A recent Gallup poll found that nearly half of all young and affluent devices said they do not mind behavioral targeting as long as they have their permission. Finally, the following checklist is provided to ensure that the M3 marketer does not miss anything.

Final M3 Marketer Checklist

Q. What behavioral analytical software to use?

- *Viscovery*: SOM for cluster analysis and segmentation with measures to defined segments. They offer complete enterprise software to create, apply, automate, and integrate predictive models. They offer a data mining system for visual cluster analysis and classification based on SOM.

■ *Attensity*: Ability to extract "who," "what," "where," "when," and "why" from text. Attensity also offers customer experience solutions powered by semantic technologies that allow organizations to listen, analyze, relate, and act on multichannel customer conversations.

■ *BayesiaLab*: Bayesian classification algorithms to automatically cluster device behaviors. Bayesian Belief Networks can provide the marketer with driver analysis, scoring, customer, and product segmentation.

■ *Angoss KnowledgeSEEKER*: Decision trees for predicting consumer device behaviors. KnowledgeSEEKER is business intelligence software product with data mining and predictive analytics capabilities including data profiling, advanced data visualization, decision tree, and strategy design functionality.

Q. What web log analytics tool to use?

■ *WebTrends*: They provide web analytics and other server log reports. They help marketers turn their website, blogs, online campaigns, and enterprise systems data into a business opportunity.

■ *ClickTracks*: It provides visual analysis of website device behaviors based on the uses of server log files. ClickTracks features analytics, ROI tracking, revenue conversion, and marketing campaign performance, all merged into a multiuser web analytics package (Figure 3.28).

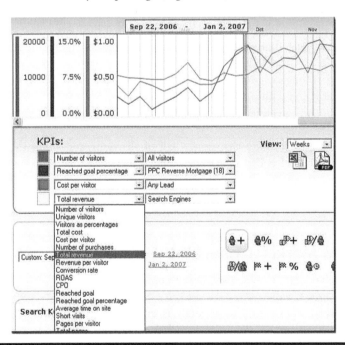

Figure 3.28   ClickTracks log analyzer report.

- *IBM Coremetrics*: This is an application service provider (ASP) service for reporting device browsing and purchasing behavior. Coremetrics encompasses online analytics with integrated marketing optimization applications—search engine bid management, e-mail targeting, ad impression attribution, cross-sell recommendations, and social media ROI.
- *SiteSpect*: They provide multivariate testing for increasing conversion rates on website landing pages. SiteSpect provides nonintrusive web optimization solution, enabling M3 marketers to perform rapid A/B testing, targeting and personalization, mobile content, and web performance optimization.
- *Google Analytics*: This is a free service that generates statistics about visitors to a website. The service assist marketers in business intelligence, CRM, campaign and content management, data collection, e-commerce, e-mail marketing, phone call tracking, search optimization, and social media analytics.

Q. What WOM marketing engine to use?

- *Blogsvertise*: This is a pay blogging promotion service. Marketers can greatly enhance their advertising efforts, drive traffic to their website, and build links using this cost-effective blog advertising platform.
- *Buzz*: This is a WOM marketing firm for creating social buzz. They are a new offering from AT&T Interactive focused on helping businesses connect with their customers through social media.
- *Zuberance*: It enables devices to recommend brands to friends via social recommendations on Facebook, Twitter, and LinkedIn. They provide social applications for marketers to systematically identify brand advocates to drive social recommendations and track results.
- *ClearSaleing*: They offer online advertising and marketing services. Their platform helps marketers measure the success and improve the performance of any campaign, including pay-per-click, organic, social media, e-mail marketing, and shopping comparison engines.

Q. What mob marketing recommendation software or network to use?

- *Criteo*: They find devices after they leave a website. They provide a personalized retargeting solution that combines retargeted banners with a PPC business model.
- *ORACLE ATG*: They provide software used by websites to personalize information to devices. They help businesses grow revenue, strengthen customer loyalty, improve brand value, achieve better operating results, and increase business agility across all commerce environments.
- *ChoiceStream*: This is a personalization and recommendation software. Their advertising CRUNCH platform creates custom audiences for every campaign

and dynamically adjusts the audience throughout the campaign based on real-time response rates.

■ *Lotame*: Behavioral ad services, twitter, blogs, and social media. They offer over 100 prepackaged audience segments such as Sports, Travel, or Movies, as well as refined sub-segments such as Golf, Vacation, or Comedy, in addition to segments by age and a host of consumer groups.

Q. What social networking marketing provider to use?

■ *Pandemic Labs*: They provide viral marketing and social media blog services including strategy, design, implementation, management, and metrics. They also can create, execute, and track ad campaigns where brands and consumers actively engage in two-way communication.

■ *LivingSocial*: Social advertising network for monetizing device traffic. LivingSocial offers daily deals with discounts of up to 90% at local restaurants, bars, spas, theaters, etc.

■ *33Across*: 33Across is focusing on where people sit in their social graph. It has built a platform called SocialDNA Targeting. This technology enables clients to discover and reach the social networks that surround their brands. At its core, 33Across technology helps marketers identify high-potential prospects who are socially connected to existing customers and brand loyalists.

■ *Jivox*: M3 marketers can create, deploy, and monitor their own video ads. They offer a technology driven interactive video advertising delivery platform. Jivox enables brand advertisers to use the powerful medium of the web and mobile to reach audiences via interactive video ads.

■ *Cubics*: Their advertising network targets users of Facebook and other social networks. Their Super Rewards ad network allows marketers to target users of social networks serving billions of impressions per month across 2500 top games and A5s.

■ *Powered*: It builds programs that combine social networking, recently acquired by The Dachis Group. Their technology and approach is to construct within a social business ecosystem a mixture of devices, services, and A5s that mix proprietary and open offerings.

■ *ContextOptional*: It enables the construction of A5s on Facebook, mobile devices, and other social platforms. Their Social Marketing Suite ties together publishing, advertising, app-building, and analytics into one single, integrated solution for social marketing on Facebook.

■ *KickApps*: It provides social networking, message boards, video sharing, and viral widgets. Their KickApps Platform makes it easy to build and manage a virtually unlimited set of integrated social experiences for websites and connected devices including custom forums, social sites, widgets, contests, Facebook pages, and video players.

Q. What mobile marketing advertising network provider to use?

- *Jumptap*: Mobile search engine and advertising network. It can be used to find and engage the most receptive customers on any mobile device to achieve the highest possible ROI. The network is made up of over 10,000 sites and apps. It handles all carriers and digital devices, reaching more than 83 million mobile users. It can deliver targeted audiences to dozens of verticals including entertainment, finance, news, sports, and social networking.
- *Amethon*: It offers outsourced WAP hosting and SMS gateway. Mobile operators and mobile marketers use their technology to understand how people use their devices to interact with mobile websites and devices—to enable them to leverage the value of mobile content—through managing, monitoring, measuring, and monetizing traffic.
- *AdMob*: It targets mobile users to monetize traffic, recently acquired by Google. Mobile advertising provides M3 marketers with targeted access to mobile users. Research shows that mobile campaigns outperform online campaigns across key metrics.

Q. What real-time analytical streaming service and software to use?

- *RiverGlass*: Streaming search software that can gather content from multiple data sources and consolidate disparate content types. The software can automate categorizations of content by topics. The software allows interacting with live visualizations to get a clearer overall picture of the data, to discover new information and insights to drive relevant content to the forefront using context-aware search.
- *Sybase*: It provides a real-time streaming analytic platform. Their Sybase Aleri Streaming Platform enables rapid application development and deployment of robust applications that derive insight from streaming event data, empowering instant responses to changing conditions.
- *InferX*: It offers real-time behavioral inductive analytical software. Their technology provides with a unique platform to deal with distributed structured and unstructured data. The information may reside in different systems and even in different locations offering an opportunity to achieve high ROI.
- *Streambase*: CEP streaming software. Their platform enables the rapid development, deployment, and modification of applications that analyze and act on large amounts of real-time streaming data.
- *AudienceScience*: Flexible targeting platform for digital media, with 270 billion data insights daily to over 386 million people worldwide; they make it simple to find, reach, and achieve one-to-one marketing at scale.

Q. What IP Geolocation provider for triangulation of digital devices to use?

■ *Quova*: Geolocation of IP Addresses down to 20 miles. They research the Internet on an ongoing basis to determine geographic and network connection information about all assigned and allocated IP addresses on the web.

■ *Digital Envoy*: It identifies the IP addresses location, domain name, and connection of devices. It delivers the de facto standard in IP Intelligence and geolocation technologies, which are leveraged by ad networks, publishers, emerging technology companies, social networks, and analytical platforms.

■ *MaxMind*: It determines the country, region, city, and ISP of Internet devices. They provide the ability to customize their websites to better serve client devices. There are currently more than 2000 clients using their GeoIP technology.

■ *Akami*: Performance management, streaming media services, and content delivery platform that is made up of nearly 100,000 servers, deployed in 72 countries, and spanning most of the networks within the Internet. These servers are all controlled by Akamai software that is constantly monitoring Internet conditions.

■ *DNSStuff*: It offers DNS and network tools, DNS reporting, and IP information gathering. They provide on-demand troubleshooting tools to solve problems with e-mail, DNS, and connectivity.

Q. What behavioral ad marketing network to use?

■ *AdWords*: Google's platform offers both CPC and cost per impression pricing. Select keywords; when devices search on Google, the ad appears next to the search results.

■ *FetchBack*: It specializes in a form of behavioral targeting called retargeting, which means putting messages in front of lost prospects that have left a website in order to attract them back and convert them to finish their purchase.

■ *DoubleClick*: This is a Google's ad network for agencies, marketers, and publishers. Their DoubleClick for Advertisers (DFA) is an ad management and ad serving solution that helps M3 marketers manage the entire scope of digital advertising programs. DFA streamlines workflow for planning, trafficking, targeting, serving, optimization, and reporting.

■ *Valtira*: On-demand landing pages and personalized content via widgets. It integrates with Google Adwords, Google Website Optimizer, and Google Analytics. Landing pages will improve cost-effectiveness by driving visitors to the right offers.

■ *eLoyalty*: Consulting services focused on optimizing customer interactions.

Q. What engagement marketing providers to use?

■ *Satmetrix*: Software and services focused on customer experience management. Their Satmetrix Xperience™ is a SaaS application for acting on the voice of the customer and managing the end-to-end customer experience.

■ *MotiveQuest*: Brand advocacy service for understanding customer motivations. They assist marketers to understand devices via their online anthropology to discover what motivates groups of consumers and how to convert them into advocates.

Q. What voice and text recognition provider to use?

■ *Yapme*: Their service allows digital devices to send text messages by talking to them. They provide a platform for "long-duration" dialogues, which are conversations and audio content ranging from seconds to several hours.

■ *PhoneTag*: It converts voicemail to text and delivers it via e-mail. PhoneTag is integrated into every major U.S. carrier network, enabling devices to read voicemail.

Q. What profiling psychographic targeting providers to use?

■ *aCerno*: This is a clearinghouse for anonymous cookies. It was recently acquired by Akami to create an online cooperative of shopping and purchase data to enhance their Advertising Decision Solutions (ADS) platform.

■ *Mindset-Media*: It provides psychographic metrics and targeting. Their research and ad technology help M3 marketers define, understand, and reach their psychographic targets.

Q. What real-time demographics provider to use?

■ *Acxiom*: ConnectionPoint-X for interactive marketing. ConnectionPoint-X combines device data with InfoBase-X®, Acxiom's demographic and lifestyle data, and AbiliTec® linking technology, for the most complete customer view possible.

■ *Experian*: It can be used with their VeriScore to measure consumer device loyalty. Their Audience IQ^{SM} enables M3 marketers to increase the ROI of their digital advertising by improving effectiveness, customer experiences, and lead conversion abilities across all channels.

Q. What digital fingerprinting company to use?

■ *BlueCava*: It has already captured 1 billion digital device signatures. Their device-locked software can identify uniquely the 10 billion Internet-connected devices on the planet for targeted advertising.

- *41st Parameter*: Already testing with mobile devices. Their DeviceInsight for Marketing is fast, scalable, and robust. It is available as both SaaS and in-memory API, with response times as low as sub-milliseconds.
- *iovation*: It can identify the exact location of any device in the planet. They can identify the device being used for a transaction and then, checking against a dynamic, device history database of 650 million deep, to deliver a device reputation, exposing their behaviors and connections.

Some of these vendor offer services and software which companies may want to consider as part of their overall M3 marketing strategy. Marketers may want to use an RFP to evaluate and document expectations and parameters of performance by these solution providers. M3 marketers will want to test and compare the results of these firms to evaluate them prior to employing them. The marketer must plan and test what technology, network, behavioral, social, transactional, privacy, and contextual data to consider.

The targeting of devices via M3 ensures consumers' privacy is preserved in this new marketing landscape, which caters to machine behaviors rather than that of individuals. M3 marketing via device behavioral analytics means focusing on consumer choices leading to actionable insight and action. Advanced technologies and techniques enable M3 marketers to calibrate how devices behave and to predict and respond in real time. The key objective of M3 is to offer devices the content, product, and services most aligned with their desires, values, wants, and needs. In the following chapter, several case studies will be discussed, which hopefully will assist marketers in aligning their solution to their client's needs.

Chapter 4

Case Studies

Examples of M3 and A5 in Action

In this last chapter, we provide examples of how the technologies, tools, techniques, and solution providers have been used for M3. As previously mentioned, the modeling of wired and wireless device behaviors can be accomplished by use of inductive and deductive analytical software, such as WizRule, CART, and RapidMiner; the following is a case study of such software.

WizRule Case Study

WizRule is an intuitive and easy-to-use database cleansing and auditing program that performs a complex analysis of databases quickly and easily and then reveals inconsistencies in the data. Almost anyone who works with databases—from simple end users to sophisticated database managers and auditors—are well aware of the great number of errors that occur in data sets. These errors are the result of a range of different factors. In many cases, they are caused by faulty data entry, whereby the user types in one value instead of another. In other cases, errors are made intentionally, such as in cases of fraud. Errors are also sometimes the result of software or hardware malfunctions, resulting in corrupted data.

Obviously, such errors can cause considerable damage, which cannot be easily measured, but is undoubtedly of serious proportions and can result in direct loss of both income and reputation. A number of complementary methods are commonly applied to eliminate data errors. These methods approach the problem by either attempting to reduce the incidence of inaccurate data entry during keyboarding or by analyzing the entered data to reveal potential errors.

While these methods are in wide use, the abundance of errors—and the damage they cause—is evidence that a more thorough and reliable database cleansing and auditing method is required. Furthermore, these methods are rarely capable of distinguishing between actual errors and cases that are simply exceptions. The WizRule program implements an innovative approach to automatic database cleansing and auditing. It is based on the assumptions that, in many cases, errors are exceptions to the norm. For example, if, in all sale transactions to a certain customer, the salesperson is Mr. Greene, a single transaction in which the salesperson is Ms. Violet—whose name is usually connected with other customers—can be considered a "deviating transaction" or a suspected error.

To create a software application that discovers exceptions to the norm requires the program to first discover all the rules in a given database. This is just the point of strength of WizRule. WizRule is based on a mathematical algorithm that is capable of revealing all the rules of a database within a very short span of time, usually within a few minutes. The main output of the WizRule analysis is a list of cases (fields in records) found in the data that are unlikely to be true in reference to the discovered rules. These cases are suspected errors or at least cases to be examined. Prior to using WizRule, you should prepare the database that you wish to analyze. You simply select the file and the software does all the rest. Within a short time, the analysis report is either displayed on screen or printed on a connected printer. When analyzing a database, WizRule performs the following operations:

1. It first reads the database. You are given the opportunity to "fine-tune" the analysis by defining parameters such as "minimum probability of if-then rules" and "minimum number of cases of a rule." You can also define exactly which types of rules WizRule should search for.
2. Within a short time, WizRule reveals the rules of the database and also indicates the reliability of each rule.
3. WizRule then analyzes each field in each record relative to the revealed rules and calculates its degree of likelihood.
4. WizRule then lists—per rule—those record cases with the highest degree of unlikelihood, that is, the suspected errors. For each file it analyzes, WizRule issues a *rule report*, a *spelling report*, and a *deviation report*.

WizRule does not reveal all data errors that may occur in the file. Its sophisticated algorithm enables the software to determine that certain exceptions to rules are actually acceptable deviations rather than errors. This reduces the number of "false alarms" that other data cleansing and auditing methods might reveal. WizRule analyzes databases by revealing three general types of rules: mathematical formula rules, if-then rules, and spelling-based rules.

An example of a mathematical formula rule is

$$A = B * C$$

where
    A = total
    B = quantity
    C = unit price

Rule's accuracy level: 0.99
The rule exists in 1890 records

"Accuracy level" in formula rules indicates the ratio between the number of cases in which the formula holds and the total number of relevant cases. The cases in which the formula holds are those cases in which the formula matches the data exactly except for a deviation that may have resulted from rounding out a number. WizRule reveals all the arithmetic formulas with up to five variables that hold in the database.

    An example of an if-then rule is

If *Customer* is *Summit*
and *Item is Computer Type A*
Then
Salesperson is Dan Wilson
Rule's probability: 0.98
The rule exists in 102 records.
Significance Level: Error probability < 0.1

    "Probability" in if-then rules designates the ratio between the number of records in which the condition(s) and the result hold and the corresponding number of records in which the condition(s) hold with or without the result.

    "Accuracy level" in formula rules indicates the ratio between the number of cases in which the formula holds and the total number of cases of the rule itself. (In if-then formula rules, the accuracy level relates to the number of cases in which the rule's condition holds.)

    "Significance level" indicates the degree to which the rule can be relied upon as a basis for predictions of rule validity. It is equal to 1 minus the "error probability," which quantifies the chances that the rule does not hold in the entire population and rather exists incidentally in the file under analysis. In the if-then example given here, the significant level would be $1 - 0.1 = 0.9$, indicating that there is a fairly solid basis for assuming that the rule holds true for the entire file.

WizRule reveals all the if-then rules with no limit as to their number of clauses. An example of a spelling rule is

The value Edinburgh appears 52 times in the Customer field.
There are 2 case(s) containing similar value(s).

These rules are mainly presented in order to reveal cases of misspelled names. A name is considered misspelled if it is similar to another name in this field; at the same time, the frequency of the first name is very low, while the frequency of the second name is very high. Following the discovery of the rules that govern the database, WizRule checks the deviations from these rules. However, not every deviation from a rule is a suspected error. For example, suppose that WizRule reveals the following rule:

If Customer is Summit
Then
Salesperson is Dan
Rule's probability: 0.95
The rule exists in 1003 records
significance level: error probability < 0.001

Since the rule's probability is 0.95 and the rule exists in 1003 records, there are approximately 50 records in which the name of the salesperson deviates from this rule. Reviewing each of these 50 records is quite tedious, and usually many of these deviations are not errors. To avoid such false alarms, WizRule calculates the level of unlikelihood of each deviation. This parameter indicates how much the deviation is unlikely in reference to all of the discovered rules. In general, the level of unlikelihood is calculated according to the following steps:

1. WizRule checks whether the deviation is explainable by another rule that holds in the database. If the deviation is explainable, then the specific case is not a suspected error. For example, there may be a number of cases of "If the item is computer, then the salesperson is John," and this rule may explain some of the previous deviations. Since these deviations are explainable, they are not considered to be suspected errors.
2. WizRule also checks whether the value of the deviating case is infrequent relative to the overall frequency in the database. If it is not, then once again, the case is not considered a suspected error. For example, if the salesperson in two of the deviating records is Frank, and these are the only cases in the entire database in which Frank is the salesperson, then these cases are not considered to be suspected errors.
3. WizRule then calculates the level of unlikelihood of each deviation that meets the prerequisites in the first two steps. The calculation is based on

the number and the significance level of the rules implying that the case is a deviation. The higher the level of unlikelihood, the higher is the probability that the deviation is indeed an error.

WizRule is an ideal tool for auditors of accounting and banking records because it enables them to perform fault detection easily and reliably. Database managers can use WizRule to perform reverse engineering on legacy databases to find which rules exist in the file and which, if any, deviations occur in the data.

Although WizRule is based on sophisticated mathematical algorithms, the software has been designed for users with little or no knowledge of mathematics. WizRule performs its calculations in the background and then displays the results of the analysis in clear, easy-to-understand formats.

The WizRule algorithm itself is far too complicated to be presented in a software user manual. However, it is important to note that the algorithm is not heuristic but deterministic, meaning that it can be proven that the algorithm reveals all the rules under investigation. In any case, you will see for yourself that although WizRule is based on highly sophisticated mathematics, it is actually very simple to use. You need only to select the file to be analyzed, and the software does the rest of the work.

Both the WizWhy and WizRule applications discover underlying rules in databases. WizWhy is a data mining program that uses the rules and patterns it discovers in the database to predict the values of future cases. WizRule uses the discovered rules to reveal errors in the databases themselves.

Groupon Case Study

Here are the metrics from a real Groupon coupon ad campaign. It is expected that the results will vary from business to business and especially between different industries. Following are the numbers of the coupon campaign:

- *Business Type*: Very casual dining.
- *Business Age*: Fairly new business.
- *Groupon Offer*: $20 certificate for $10.
- *Groupon's Commission*: 50%.
- *Total Sold*: 1225.
- *Redemption Rate*: 68% (32% were never cashed in).
- *Average Ticket Amount (with certificate use)*: $20 (people spent pretty close to the face value amount).
- *Estimated Number of New, Recurring Customers*: 75%. This is expressed as a % of the total number of certificates sold. These are people that will come back even without a certificate.
- *Estimated Long Term, Recurring Customer Income*: $20. Without a certificate, the average ticket is about $10. This means that it is assumed the

new, recurring customers mentioned are expected to come in about four times over the "long term."

▪ *Normal Margin on Sales*: 230% margin or cost of goods sold (COGS) is about 30% ticket price.
▪ *Brand Value*: $0. This is such a fuzzy number that was left at zero.

The real world result is that this business owner was paid $6000 with costs around $5000. Using the numbers as mentioned previously, the analysis shows

▪ *Campaign Profit*: $1,076.52
▪ *Total Long Term Profit*: $13,883.33
▪ *ROI over the "Long Term"*: 130.77%

Not too shabby. There are some notes worth mentioning:

▪ The business was paid by Groupon in three equal payments over 1–2 months. They were happy with this.
▪ Purchases with certificates with tickets less than $20 do not get change. Typically, they would order something else to get over the $20 level.
▪ Redemption volume was heavy in the first and last months, and the numbers were
  Month 1–225
  Month 2–150
  Month 3–100
  Month 4–50
  Month 5–50
  Month 6–250
▪ The number of new, recurring customers is very difficult to determine and is basically a gut check. It is assumed "Long Term" meant over the course of a year when determining some of the more "magical" numbers.

Living Social Case Study

In Fairfax, Studio BE is the only Pilates studio that is an actual commercial studio. Just because Pilates is an expensive form of exercise, the people who come regularly are usually in their early 30s and up and fairly well off. With the Living Social deal, I was targeting a little different group. Our mat classes are the most inexpensive classes we offer, so that was my target with the Living Social campaign. It worked out perfectly, as far as who responded and who bought the packages. More of the younger people went for the mat classes, I had a pretty good range of clientele that purchased the private classes, and then I had a mixture of clients that bought the combo classes. It worked out just like I thought it would (Figure 4.1).

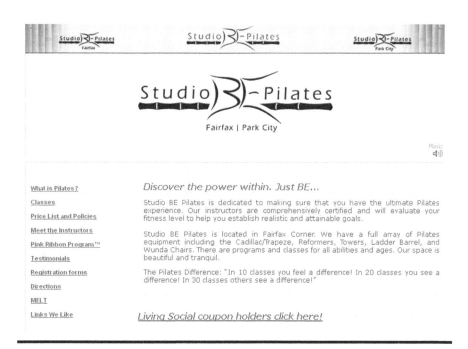

Figure 4.1   Pilates studio coupon from Living Social campaign.

With Living Social, the first ad they came up with had nothing to do with my studio. I said, "You know what, I don't like this. I want to see this and this," and they came up with a great ad. I had something a little different in mind, and the Living Social people were pushing me more toward offering group classes. However, you cannot have somebody that has never done Pilates before come in and do group equipment classes with people who have been doing Pilates for years.

At first I was a little bit put off, feeling like, "You know what, you guys don't really understand this." Living Social had worked with different Pilates studios before, but some other Pilates studios have total beginners classes where everyone is a beginner, and our studio does not run that way. We require clients to do five private sessions before they start taking any group equipment classes. But, we also teach a mat and tower combination class, because the tower is a little easier and a little safer than the reformer. So, I structured the offer so that new clients could do the combo classes and I added new classes onto the schedule to accommodate these clients.

What ended up happening was the Living Social people started taking the new classes, and then some of my existing clients started feeding into them as well. I actually had very few Living Social people feed into my current combo classes. I think it was because of the demographics. The younger people need to get in either early in the morning or late in the evening. My current classes are usually 9 o'clock classes, so those are usually your stay-at-home moms, people that are retired, or just are not working anymore and are more flexible with their time.

Well, I wanted to go with Groupon first and I called them three times and they never returned my call. I know a couple of other people in the area that have yoga studios and they went through Living Social, so I asked them about their experience, and they were happy. So then I called Living Social and they called me back. To be honest, not returning calls was the only thing I found. It was the same with Living Social. I understand it completely—they are swamped. They are busy and they can only help so many people. I am assuming they are helping people in the order of when their deal is going to run.

With Living Social, I sent them the copy and the pictures, and the first ad they came up with had nothing to do with my studio. It was nothing I sent them. I said, "You know what, I don't like this. I want to see this and this," and they changed it and came up with a great ad. So, they were easy to work with and were fairly responsive.

The one thing I will say, and this is an after-the-fact, is that it stated right in the copy of the ad that you were only allowed to buy one deal per customer, and you could purchase up to two more as gifts. Even though it said that, people were still allowed to buy more than one package. Some people get excited and they just hit the button. So, I had a lot of people who bought more than one package and they were upset with me because I would not honor it. I hated to send them back to Living Social for a refund, but Living Social totally understood and I guess their software did not allow them to do that. Whereas, I am pretty sure Groupon's software does. I buy stuff from Groupon, and when I buy the second, it only allows me to buy it as a gift.

Living Social wanted me to honor it anyway, but I was like, "I really can't because I have people that would've bought more," and that was my biggest concern. I did not want to upset my current clientele or put them off. You want to take care of your current customers first and not have them say, "Oh, I can't take a class because all these new people took my spot."

Overall, it actually worked out really well. I was afraid it would not, because I have a friend who has a day spa, and she ran a hair laser removal coupon. Groupon sold a thousand of them, and I got an e-mail from the spa saying, "We understand people are having problems getting through to us," because everyone was calling to book their appointments.

That is the other thing. I have Mindbody Online, which is an online scheduling system. We were able to feed people right from the Living Social voucher to our website, which gave them instructions on how to register and sign up for classes. They could do everything online, so I did not have to worry about having my desk manned all day. That is another thing that people do not always take into consideration. Your phone is going to be ringing off the hook for a while, and your regular customers might get a little ticked off.

I will be honest. I bought my business from somebody who I worked for before, and I remember her telling me that no advertisement she has ever done worked. The only way we got new customers was from word of mouth (WOM) or from the website. Since I have owned the business, I have tried some direct mail stuff. I have had booths at festivals, and I have placed ads in magazines—nothing worked.

I figure even though Living Social may have actually cost me money—because they keep half of it, and I still have to pay my employees—I am paying for people who are already my target audience. And I know they want to do Pilates, as opposed to blindly placing an ad and hoping that somebody gets it. So, I honestly do not know if I would do any other type of advertising besides this in the future. I was happy with it, it worked out well for my situation, and like I said, nothing else in the past has worked.

Zynga Case Study

Zynga is the number one social gaming site on the web, with more than 70 million users playing Zynga games every day. FarmVille, one of Zynga's most popular games, is the single largest application on Facebook® and grew from 0 to 10 million daily active users in the first 6 weeks following its release.

Using the RightScale Cloud Management Platform, just a few Zynga systems administrators easily manage thousands of FarmVille servers in the cloud.

Zynga runs the majority of its production servers in the cloud with RightScale, taking advantage of full automation without sacrificing customization.

The RightScale solution has been so successful that Zynga has launched six games in the cloud and thousands of nodes while continuing to grow extremely fast. RightScale has allowed Zynga to codify best practices for server deployments, which has made the need for training new systems administrators nearly nonexistent.

RightScale's unique approach to managing complete cloud deployments—comprising multiple servers and the connections between them—has been critical to Zynga's success. Zynga's deployments run smoothly, managed by an automation engine that adapts resource allocation as required by system demand, system failures, or other events, all of which are based on active monitoring to ensure real-time response to predefined triggers. In particular, RightScale's dynamic autoscaling and configurability have been key to Zynga's managing large cloud deployments.

With dynamic autoscaling, Zynga can automatically scale its application servers to respond to demand, configuring such factors as the minimum and maximum number of servers in an array, the threshold that needs to be exceeded to start scaling, and the speed at which the array scales. The Zynga team has fully utilized RightScale's autoscaling to bring new nodes online with minimal human interaction. The team creates alerts in RightScale and adds capacity automatically, eliminating the need to manually respond to traffic spikes.

In addition, Zynga systems administrators have taken full advantage of RightScale's prebuilt cloud templates, called ServerTemplates™, to simplify deployments while also customizing them to meet their unique requirements. Zynga has developed internal tools and best practices that combine the use of ServerTemplates and the RightScale API to manage functional groups of servers, facilitate change, and ensure consistency in the production environments.

Tippr Case Study

When Renae Click decided to run a daily deal campaign earlier this year, she knew the publisher she chose would be important. That is why Click, who owns Tomlinson's Feed & Pets with her husband Scott, opted to work with a local hyperlocal publisher in Austin rather than a national company. We have only done the one deal with 365 ThingsAustin. I had a salesperson contact me regarding the possibility of doing the deal. I would only consider deal sites that target people who wish to shop at local Austin businesses like Tomlinson's, so 365 was perfect for us.

We are a local business and lucky to be in Austin, Texas, where consumers are very prolocal. In fact, the popular local slogan "Keep Austin weird" means support local business. 365 is a site for people to whom this concept is important. Buying local is a lifestyle, so it was the only way to go for us. We are not interested in attracting bargain hunters who will come in for their deal and never return. We wanted to convert them into long-term, loyal customers.

It was extremely important to reach new customers. I sent the deal information out to our customers via the newsletter so that they would have the opportunity to participate, but we were really hoping to attract new folks from the 365 site. It is important to reach and win new customers, but perhaps more important to retain current customers—to change them from indifferent shoppers to avid fans. It is our fans who promote our stores by WOM to other pet owners. That is why we sent the deal to customers who had signed up for our newsletter with over 12,000 subscribers. We think that about half of the folks who purchased the 365 ThingsAustin deal were already customers and half were not because out of the 467 unique e-mail addresses we got, about half were already signed up to receive our newsletter.

I wish I had a system in place that could measure whether or not the new folks who bought the deal came back a second time. However, the only concrete way to measure the success of the campaign, I guess, is by the number of people who purchased the deal, how many people actually used their vouchers, and how much they spent on the shopping trip.

As best I can figure, we had 369 of the 594 vouchers redeemed. It is possible that that is not a 100% accurate figure because we have six stores, and we transferred used vouchers from each store to our main office, and it is possible that paperwork could have gotten lost, misplaced, eaten, or whatever. Of the 369, I was only able to track 314 because we failed to copy and retain sales information for the remaining vouchers. Those 314 spent an average of $25.55, that is, after the $20 was deducted, but before taxes. Although some folks were determined to spend exactly $20 to the penny, we had a lot who spent well over the voucher amount. The profit from these sales paid for what Tippr retained from the deal.

A huge worry of mine before we did the deal was that some bozo would try to double, triple, or quadruple dip—make copies of their vouchers and use them at more than one location, since we have six stores in and around Austin. It is difficult with multiple locations and 45 employees to keep up with which vouchers have been used and which have not. I thought that would be a nightmare because we have had some folks get pretty creative with coupons in the past. However, we did not have one person try to reuse their voucher. It was not an issue at all.

Every form of advertising does not reach every type of consumer. Austin is very computer savvy and online, so we were hoping to reach those consumers who get their daily information from their computer rather than from the print media. We also hoped to drive folks to our website and Facebook page who found out about us due to the deal. As I said, with this particular deal site, we were able to target "shop local" friendly folks. Additionally, we added over 200 new e-mail addresses to our newsletter database from the deal.

BuyWithMe Case Study

Houston dentist Dr. Heather Wilmore has plenty of experience with daily deal companies, such as Groupon and LivingSocial having run offers with a handful in just the past year. Her reason for offering group coupons have less to do with turning a profit and more to do with building a strong client base. She has learned to structure her deals in a way that increases the chances that new patients will continue returning for follow-up appointments long after their coupons have been redeemed. Her office manager gets a lot of stuff from Groupon and LivingSocial, and we noticed that dentists were doing deals for bleaching with an exam. So, we contacted Groupon, LivingSocial, and Urban Dealight all at the same time. Urban Dealight happened to be the first one that responded back. So we did a bleaching special with them and had a pretty good turnout.

About 2 or 3 months later, in June, I had a lady from Austin contact me on Facebook saying that she was working for a company called aDealio that does promotions online. I felt like I would give them a try out, and I did. That one was not so hot. I only had two responses compared to the 109 from Urban Dealight. All these new online promotions are popping up, so I might as well try them. Now, I have got BuyWithMe.com. Our representative from BuyWithMe.com used to work with Citysearch, and she knew me from my marketing with Citysearch. So, that helped. My husband found another one when he was looking online last week called Bloomspot and we went live with them on Monday.

I really just work with all of the daily deal companies. When it comes to the deals, we decide the deals together. They come up with what they are suggesting, what they have seen that is sold, and what has been most successful, and then we negotiate exactly what the discount will be and what the cost will be to the customer. It is usually a 50/50 split, but I have to make sure the 50% that I get covers any material. And with the bleaching I have to make sure the 50% portion covers my bleach. With Bloomspot, we are doing a promotion with Invisalign. At first, they wanted to do $2000 for a $5000 case, which is a full case. I told them we could not do that because my lab bill alone is $1600. If we are selling this for $2000, I get a 50/50 split, and my lab bill is $1600, then I am out $600. So, we changed it to $2400 for a $3800 case, which is an express case, and my lab bill is only $899.

The deals are not for making a profit. They need to cover whatever expenses I have, but they are more about having new patients come in and building that clientele. We learned that with Urban Dealight. We did an in-office bleaching, and we learned that a lot people already had other dentists. They did not want to spend the $400, $500, or $600 out of pocket for their dentists' in-office bleaching, so they came here and then they were going back to their own dentists. That is why with the new deals we learned to do an exam with the in-office bleaching. We are going to do an exam, cleaning, and x-rays, so it is really geared more for people looking for a new dentist.

With today's economy, what is important is the price and how much you get for it. I think a lot of it does have to do with the amount, the price, and what the patient is receiving. It is just the way the economy is. A lot of people do not want to go to the dentist because they do not have insurance and they do not have money to spend for an exam and cleaning. They know they need dental work; they just do not have the means for it all. So, with these deals it kind of helps. Now with the BuyWithMe.com special, you get the exam, the cleanings, x-rays, and bleaching for $150. We even have some patients with insurance who are scheduling appointments, and we are not charging their insurance. That gives them more benefits they can use if they need that filling or crown in the future. So, it is just trying to maximize what you have insurance wise.

It is just marketing and getting the name out there. Then learning what marketing works, what marketing does not work, and which one will show some sort of return. Right now what I am doing, too, is I always check online reviews. People write reviews all the time, so I go through the Internet and see if bad reviews were written, and see what people have said. It is really just learning what works. You have to keep up with marketing; knowing what works, what does not, and going from there.

Hyundai Case Study

Online advertising for Hyundai is complex. Its website serves consumers throughout the purchase cycle. Yahoo! Rich Ads in Search made it easy for the car company to engage with consumers at all stages of the process by offering brand awareness via videos to upper-funnel customers and deep links with lower-funnel activities to customers ready to buy a Hyundai.

It is a busy time for Hyundai. With several of its models collecting awards for being best in class and as a major partner of the FIFA World Cup, Academy Awards, and sponsor of the 2011 Super Bowl pregame show, the auto company is increasing its brand reach. These recent marketing initiatives have consumers searching online to learn more about the company. Some want to find information about a specific model while others want to find a dealership, get estimates, customize a vehicle, or simply compare vehicles. Hyundai wanted a better way of serving the wide variety of needs.

That was the challenge that Hyundai brought to search and social media agency Reprise Media. "We automatically put Yahoo! on the media plan because of its reach and audience," says Emil Panzarino, Reprise Media's media director for the Hyundai business. "When Yahoo! launched Rich Ads in Search, we knew that it could address a consumer's needs regardless of where he or she was in the purchase funnel."

"We chose to do Rich Ads because the primary goal is to drive consumer interaction," says Sean McDonald, account director at Reprise Media. "Rich Ads offers a video component to search results, which immediately grabs consumer attention. It also has deep links that provide more opportunities for the consumer to interact directly with the brand."

Reprise Media evaluated Hyundai's needs and established key performance indicators (KPIs), a range of actions consumers could perform on Hyundai's website that help indicate where they fall within the consideration funnel. Reprise Media then took the most engaging KPIs, such as locating a dealer, requesting a quote, calculating payments, and building a custom model, and integrated them as deep links directly within the Rich Ads in Search creative.

The array of choices within the ad unit made it possible to address consumers' interests regardless of where they were in the purchase funnel and encouraged them to interact with the brand. The deep links helped deliver consumers to more relevant pages, which increased their inclination to engage with the desired KPI action.

The Rich Ads in Search campaign was also an ideal venue for repurposing existing television ads, creating another channel to expose consumers to those commercials while extending the life of the creative assets. The video assets were switched out to coordinate with changing Hyundai promotions and to keep the content fresh. They sometimes alternated with static images that matched particular models and keywords.

Using brand and model term keywords, Rich Ads in Search had a cost per acquisition that was 1%–10% lower than traditional branded search. Additionally, volume grew year over year and cost per impression was more efficient.

When Hyundai added Rich Ads in Search to its traditional search campaign, overall conversions increased 227% and cost per acquisition decreased 52%. Clicks increased by a little over 30%, while the click-through rate jumped over 50%.

"The premium top placement for Rich Ads on the search page increases its appeal," says McDonald. "We had that top placement for a relatively average cost per click, in terms of what we saw for the rest of the campaign, and the results were great."

Instapaper Case Study

Instapaper is a leading app that helps users save web pages locally on their digital devices for later offline reading. The company used to operate under the free model—free for a basic version, pay for the premium app—but it recently decided to remove Instapaper Free from the App Store. In a blog post last week, Instapaper founder Marco Arment discussed his rationale for dropping the free version, and his comments provide great insights into the perils of free pricing models.

Ad-supported models will not recoup the paid-subscription price: In Instapaper's case, an ad-supported user needed to use the app everyday for 2 years before it would equate to the revenue of the paid app. While the ad-supported model did increase the total number users, it also drove people away from purchasing the paid version; a trade-off that Instapaper found resulted in lower revenues.

High opportunity costs due to customers settling with the free version: While difficult to quantify the number of users who did not buy the app due to the availability of the free version, Marco did notice that very few users ever upgraded from the free app. Instead, customers were simply settling for the trim downed version or abandoning the app all together.

Increased technology and customer support costs: Not only are development costs higher due to the need to build and maintain a separate app, but Marco found that users of the free app tended to require more customer support and thus cost even more!

Poorer app image due to free version: The free app had stripped down functionality and was ad-supported in order to encourage users to upgrade. But as many customers only used this free version, it was their only reference point. The free app had lower quality ratings versus the paid version, and perhaps more importantly, it catered to an unattractive customer segment less invested in the business idea and more critical when expectations were not met.

While Instapaper is a specific business operating in a specific channel (app downloads), these pain points ring true for many operators of the free model, and a thank you is in order for Marco Arment for providing these real-life lessons so that other companies can better succeed. Instapaper allows for "read later" piles of content for iPhone and iPad.

Kony Solutions Case Study

Kony builds digital device apps for banks, insurers, carmakers, and airlines. A global banking firm has more than 80 million customers worldwide. They realized that to stay competitive and provide the best service to customers their mobile offering had to be a more robust, cross-platform solution that enabled full service banking on practically any mobile device.

Figure 4.2 Kony's banking solution for mobile devices.

In business, time is money. In order to have the desired impact on existing customers and to attract new customers, the bank planned a multicountry rollout of their mobile banking application across BlackBerry, Android, iPhone, and mobile web devices in a number of languages and currencies.

The new solution had to incorporate key features of the existing system without disruption of service and without incurring unreasonable overhead costs. Banking on a global scale means meeting different regulations in each and every country. Language and localization needs require coordinating hundreds of interacting details. Plus, as a global bank, changes to the internal infrastructure require creative solutions for integration and solution testing (Figure 4.2).

Kony Solutions proved it is possible to have a global mobile application up and running quickly without sacrificing performance. Kony's "Write Once, Run Everywhere" technology takes a new approach to application development by using a single code base to define the design elements of the application and then translate those elements to fit the operating system software and unique hardware features of over 9000 individual devices as well as 15 available browsers.

In less time and with fewer resources than serial development of each application version, Kony's platform enables delivery of rich applications to all devices. Kony managed all the interlocking localization details, allowing the banking client to concentrate on the user needs, features, branding, and delivering a unique banking experience. Kony technology kept the development costs down too. Instead of incurring redundant charges for each application and each mobile platform,

"Write Once, Run Everywhere" technology saves significantly over traditional one-by-one application development.

Kony's technology heads off future problems by incorporating OS updates and device improvements as soon as they are available.

So when a new mobile device launches, applications developed with Kony's "future-proofed" technology are ready to go. The new solution achieves crucial integration of web-based services as well as location-based services—ATM and branch locators—and mobilizes core banking services for the bank's customers. Plus, it is targeted to support more mobile platform rollouts and additional services for new lines of businesses in future releases.

Urban Airship Case Study

As the world's largest and most authoritative online dictionary, Dictionary.com provides a destination where users can access a myriad of educational and entertaining vocabulary-building tools. The company's core applications have 22 million installs across iPhone, Android, Blackberry, and iPad, making Dictionary.com the world's most downloaded mobile dictionary. Dictionary.com continually upgrades its application platforms, adding innovative features, such as voice-to-text and dynamic content, that are designed to make their word discovery experience a natural extension of their everyday behavior, style, and personality.

Dictionary.com's Word of the Day was a hugely successful franchise on the website and was included as a main feature of the mobile app. However, demand for Word of the Day was so high that Dictionary.com recognized a need to enable mobile users to access the content without directly visiting the app itself. To help increase the active user rate and engagement for the feature, Dictionary.com considered different mobile-messaging providers to help unobtrusively deliver the Word of the Day to interested users in a manner that would maximize the value of their learning experience.

As Dictionary.com's goal was to offer a word-discovery experience accessible anywhere, anytime, making such popular features as easy to access as possible was top priority. After assessing high usage and positive user comments about the Word of the Day, Dictionary.com decided to offer push notifications to users, enabling them to receive the Word of the Day without any effort on their part.

"We wanted to enhance our users' learning experience by increasing their access to our Word of the Day feature through push notification. Push notification offers our word enthusiasts the added value of accessing one of our most popular features without the need to directly access the app," said Lisa Sullivan-Cross, general manager, Mobile at Dictionary.com.

As Dictionary.com continued to add ancillary features and upgrades to its mobile applications, the company wanted to keep its focus on what was core to its mobile business—the apps—and engage third-party APIs for what was not core—push notifications. Dictionary.com reached out to several players in the marketplace.

After carefully analyzing a number of mobile services platforms, Dictionary.com chose Urban Airship because the mobile services provider was the strongest of the lot. According to Sullivan-Cross, Urban Airship had solid brands on board, offered reasonable pricing, and possessed the technical know-how and experience that fit into Dictionary.com's vision for its mobile applications. Following a quick and seamless implementation, Urban Airship began delivering Dictionary.com's Word of the Day via push notifications to millions of iPhone devices on a daily basis.

"Dictionary.com's mission is to provide a total destination for word discovery, that enables our users to effortlessly expand their knowledge and mastery of language," said Sullivan-Cross. "Urban Airship has helped us accomplish this by making one of our most popular features more easily available, which has undoubtedly contributed to Dictionary.com's success as the world's most downloaded dictionary app across all mobile platforms."

As a result of leveraging Urban Airship, Dictionary.com has seen an uptick in active user rates and visits per month to their mobile application. For example, on the iPhone application alone, Dictionary.com has seen a 6% increase in visits to their mobile app through the daily notification. Along with positive user feedback from customers, Urban Airship's push notifications have kept Dictionary.com application users engaged with the apps, reminding them of the useful and informative content that is available within the application.

The success of the push notification program has also been a key component to Dictionary.com's overall brand strategy. "Urban Airship has played a key role in helping us increase active user rates and engagement while holding true to our vision of delivering an immersive word discovery experience to our customers," said Sullivan-Cross. With Urban Airship, Dictionary.com has achieved its goals around increased active user rates and engagement while holding true to its vision of delivering valuable information on word learning to their customers.

Foursquare Case Studies

This popular anonymous advertising apps anywhere anytime (A5) rewards devices for "checking in" at shops, airports, and retailers, the following are some case studies:

Starbucks Offers Nationwide Mayor Special: Starbucks extends local store mayor specials to all its stores with a single $1 frappuchino coupon for any Starbucks mayor at any Starbucks.

BART San Francisco Transportation: BART, the Bay Area Rapid Transit, offered "a BART-themed badge that can be unlocked by regular riders of BART, which provides train service in the San Francisco Bay Area. BART awarded $25 promotional tickets each month for the next 3 months to riders chosen at random from all the riders who have logged Foursquare check-ins at BART stations, starting in

November, 2009." The goal of the promotion was to embrace Foursquare use on BART already and to further encourage use of public transit.

Bravo TV Markets Shows and Personalities: Bravo offered Foursquare user "badges and special prizes when viewers visit more than 500 Bravo locations. The locations will be picked by Bravo to correspond with select Bravo shows including The Real Housewives, The Millionaire Matchmaker, Top Chef, Kell on Earth, Top Chef Masters and Shear Genius."

Metro News Canada: Metro, Canada's number one free daily, added "their location-specific editorial content to the Foursquare service. People who choose to follow Metro on Foursquare will then receive alerts when they're close to one of those locations. For example, someone close to a restaurant that Metro has reviewed would receive a 'tip' about that restaurant and they have ability to link through to the full Metro review on metronews.ca."

The History Channel Sprinkles Historical Facts All Over: The History Channel created tips on Foursquare that share historically significant facts with users when they check into a location of note, for instance, the first building that bought an Otis elevator.

Eat Free at Golden Coral: The Foursquare mayor can eat free once per day. Check-ins on other location services give you a chance to eat free as well as a chance to win an iPad as part of a larger contest than the daily eat free special.

Hubspot's Virtual Check In at SXSW: At SXSW 2010, Hubspot did not have an exhibitor booth, but they did set up a check-in spot at the SXSW convention center and added tips for folks to check out their Foursquare Grader and Speaker Grader tools.

College Basketball T-shirt Giveaway: UNC Charlotte, the first college/university to implement location-based social network special on campus, offered free t-shirts to students that checked in at certain basketball games and other events.

Harvard Fully Embraces Location: Harvard encouraged students to rate campus venues, share tips, and work to earn the Harvard Yard badge by checking in to a certain numbers of locations. They also left tips at locations on and off campus for students and visitors alike to explore.

The Pit BBQ's Community Growing: This Raleigh, NC, local restaurant used Foursquare early on to grow a community with its patrons and invest in WOM. They reached out via Twitter and Foursquare to their most social users and used these opportunities to reward these users.

Coach Men's Store Cologne Giveaway: For opening weekend of their Men's Store in NYC, Coach gave away free cologne ($85 value) to the first 200 customers who checked into the store on Foursquare. Ten percent of the traffic to the store that weekend came with Foursquare check-ins. Causation or correlation is tough to say, but it looks like the promotion helped drive awareness and buzz for Coach's first Men's store launch.

The Today Show: "Foursquare users who head to 30 Rock this summer for the Toyota Concert Series on *Today* will be able to check in, earn badges and compete for mayorships via this service." *The Today Show* also has three custom Foursquare badges that visitors can earn: (1) They are the Newbie badge for first check-ins, (2) a "Roker" badge for three check-ins, and (3) a "10 to 10" badge for those that check in at the Plaza concert series 10 times or more.

Gowalla Case Studies

Airport Rides with Chevy and Gowalla: Chevy and Gowalla partnered up at SXSW 2010 in Austin, TX, to give users that checked in when they arrived at the airport, free Chevy car service downtown to their hotels.

The Nets Leave Free Tickets at Sports Locations: The New York Nets hid free pairs of virtual game tickets throughout New York City sports related check-in spots, like sports bars, parks, and gyms. The virtual tickets could be exchanged for real tickets to a specific game, which 15% of people did. Attendees won t-shirts and the chance for other prizes.

Kentucky Derby Louisville City Tour and Bar Crawl: Gowalla and the *Courier Journal*, Kentucky's largest newspaper, partnered to create a city tour and city bar crawl. Users could follow suggested Gowalla check-ins and get special badges by visiting eight sites on a "Louisville Tour" that included Louisville Slugger Field and the Kentucky Derby Museum. They could also get a badge for the "completion of the 'Louisville Bar Crawl', composed of different restaurant, bar and club venues that should prove useful to both visitors and residents—not to mention the owners of those businesses."

National Geographic and Washington Post Expand Trips Feature: Gowalla expanded their trip's feature and launched the new beefed up feature with some big partners.

> The National Geographic branded Gowalla Trips includes fifteen walking tours to explore destinations like the Seine in Paris, the Avenue of the Arts in Philadelphia and San Diego's Balboa Park.

> The Washington Post has curetted its own adventures. The Washington Post trips are designed to help travelers discover attractions and explore Washington, D.C. and all the museums, the Mall and other national treasures with maps of the Metro.

Hipstamatic Case Study

To build awareness for The Dali Museum's fantastical new building, we developed a customized picture-editing app that creates dreamy surrealist overlays over photos.

With a zero dollar budget, we turned to the style-makers at Hipstamatic to help bring it to life. They liked the idea so much that they waived their fees and pledged to donate any product sales income to the museum. Plus, their 1.2 million loyal followers provided the critical mass we needed to reach the general public.

In the first couple of days after the release, the Hipstamatic site crashed due to extremely high traffic. And a "Tap Your Inner Salvador Contest," curated by John Waters, has helped momentum grow. After only 4 weeks, the application had been downloaded 30,000 times.

In the end, we are proud to have built a modern-day tribute to the brilliance of Mr. Dali that not only is not costing the Museum money but also is actually bringing in much-needed funds. Hipstamatic uses the iPhone camera to sell analog prints.

PointAbout Case Study

The automotive listing giant Cars.com was quick to embrace mobile, and with over 1 million visits per month to its iPhone app, it has clearly paid off.
Cars.com has taken a three tier approach to mobile:

1. A mobile website
2. A native application
3. Expanding that native application into multiple mobile platforms

Cars.com's mobile product manager, Nick Fotis, discusses the business decisions behind his company's mobile strategy with PointAbout. "In our space, we were a mobile player very early," says Nick Fotis on launching a mobile website in April 2007. As the first company to dive into mobile among its key competitors, Cars.com has seen a steady increase of traffic since its mobile web launch.

The mobile web strategy was twofold; "It's offering our product to consumers in the context of when it's most valuable to them—when they're actually on the lot, and then it's capturing new consumers who might not be aware of Cars.com, by being a credible mobile product when they happen to do a search from their digital device."

Even though the mobile website strategy garnered the company 800,000 visits a month as of January 2010, Nick Fotis and the executives at Cars.com made the weighty decision to move into the mobile app space. "As we see mobile devices becoming more of a replacement than a complement to desktops and laptops, we knew we had to grow our content through our mobile platforms," Fotis explained.

"How we do that is a fundamental challenge, a critical challenge to growing our business."

First we decided whether to build an app—"We had always taken a very device-agnostic approach to mobile," Nick said. "It was a huge departure for our group to pick a device and start developing around that"—and then, which platform to utilize.

A third consideration was deciding hybrid app versus native app. A hybrid app is a shell that gets downloaded to a user's phone, which then calls in a website to open within the shell, allowing Cars.com to repurpose its existing mobile web page. A native app is fully unique software that gets downloaded to a user's phone, generally leading to more usage due to quicker response times and the ability to save online data to the device.

"The hybrid approach is really tempting, and was very tempting to our senior management," Fotis said, mainly to ensure a consistent brand experience and save on the initial investment on native software development. In the end, the decision to go native on the iPhone consisted of three compelling reasons: (1) Testing the Apple App Store as a distribution channel—Cars.com wanted to evaluate the market size of consumers who look to the app store when performing information tasks. (2) Device adoption and usage pattern—"There is no such thing as people who possess iPhones and use them a low amount," Fotis said. "That category doesn't exist. People who have iPhones by definition are heavy users of them." (3) User experience—which is the key to a successful launch, whether it's for an app or a website.

Cars.com launched its iPhone app in the first week of February 2010. The Apple App Store featured the app prominently in February, leading to 200,000 downloads in its first month. The initial wave has led to more than 1 million visits per month to the app.

"Today, people who at first were dubious of the native approach will say without hesitation that they are very thankful we went the native way," Nick said. "The benefit in user experience far outweighs the incremental cost of developing a native platform," says Fotis. "While it was more expensive to invest in building a native app, it was worth the cost," Fotis adds.

Even the Blackberry using upper management and executive members were convinced after the performance metrics started to flow in: Users of the Cars.com iPhone app average double or triple the number of page views per visit as users of the mobile website. "The app is just much quicker," Nick said. "Our mobile site and our online website average of 12 to 15 page views per visit. Our app averages between 25 and 35 page views per visit."

Going native has also paid off in user retention as the Cars.com app has consistently received ratings of three stars or more in the App store. "There is consensus at Cars.com that we would not have achieved such consistently high ratings and number of downloads if it were a hybrid app," Nick said. The Cars.com iPhone app also had unanticipated uses. Instead of users consisting solely of consumers searching for cars, the company heard from dealers who reported that they marked competitors as favorites on the app, which enabled them to easily check out how the competition was pricing their inventory and then price their cars competitively.

Cars.com maximized the benefits of choosing the iPhone as the native device by giving the app a smart, flexible architecture and built-in ad positions that can be easily changed.

"A guiding principle for us—not just with advertising but with all data in our app—is we want to be able to change information, data, and advertising without updating the app, so we tried to stay as far away as we could from hard coding the elements which may change," Nick said. Once the app was out, it quickly became a topic of conversation. "The iPhone app process was a huge morale boost internally. It is hard to release products that people are excited about and proud of but this mobile app was a resounding success."

MLB Case Study

For fans around the globe, MLB.com is the home of Major League Baseball (MLB). The site offers a wealth of information and services, including Game Day, a flash-based audio application that enables fans to follow every pitch as it happens. MLB.com wanted to make its website as "sticky" as possible so that fans would want to come to the site, get involved, and stay for a long period of time. It therefore decided to develop a new instant messaging facility to enhance the features of Game Day.

At first, the organization had some concerns about the project. A previous attempt to develop instant messaging had been unsuccessful because the solution implemented had been neither sufficiently scalable to meet demand nor visually exciting enough. MLB.com therefore knew that the success of the new venture would depend heavily on its choice of platform. The organization had to find an instant messaging server that would give it both the flexibility to innovate and the confidence to grow.

In the previous year, MLB.com's Game Day application had attracted over 85 million users. MLB.com knew how many concurrent visitors it attracted to its site on game days and it knew what its average year-on-year growth was. It also knew how many fans had used its earlier instant messaging service. Using these figures as the basis for some solid statistical analysis, it anticipated that demand for its new chat facility would not only be huge but would also grow steadily over time.

MLB.com interviewed a lot of potential partners for the project and carried out practical product evaluations. However, the solutions that it initially tested failed to provide the flexibility and scalability that it needed. Then, MLB.com met ProcessOne at a conference in California. "We were immediately impressed by ProcessOne's offering," says Joe Choti, CTO of MLB.com. "ProcessOne was head and shoulders above everyone else."

ProcessOne provides high performance instant messaging servers that are based on ejabberd, an open source technology that is mainly written in the Erlang programming language. As it runs in a cluster mode, ejabberd is highly robust and can be easily expanded in size, making it ideal for large-scale deployments. MLB. com was familiar with ejabberd and quickly identified that the ProcessOne Instant Messaging Server could meet all of its requirements.

"ejabberd is a full featured jabber server compared to the other products that are in the market," explains Christian Gough, system administrator at MLB.com. "The ProcessOne Instant Messaging Server offered every feature that we desired. By leveraging the scalability of Erlang, the solution allows us to easily expand and adapt the server whenever we want to in the future."

The CEO of ProcessOne travelled to New York to work directly with MLB. com's internal team and specify the precise requirements of the solution. "His help was extremely timely and useful," says Gough. "The quality of support that we have received from ProcessOne has been very, very good."

For MLB.com, the visual concept of the solution was just as important as the underlying technology. The organization wanted to create a Game Day chat facility that would give fans the look and feel of experiencing a live game with other fans. It therefore based its new instant messaging service on a virtual ballpark. Fans can visit different sections of the online ballpark during a game to join different chat sessions on different topics with different groups of people.

In one part of the virtual ballpark, fans of the home team can be discussing the state of the pitch or the decisions of the coach. In other parts of the ballpark, fans from opposing teams can get together to argue the merits of different players. "This is by-appointment chat," explains Choti. "The ballpark opens when the game begins and closes when the game ends. An automated session manager feature manages the chat rooms and ushers users out at the end of a game, just as they would be ushered out of a real ballpark."

As part of the project, ProcessOne developed a customized module for MLB. com to allow its ejabberd-based instant messaging server to interact with the company's existing web services and authenticate users against its user database. "Users can now log in once to MLB.com and use a range of different services, including the chat facility, without having to log in again to a separate system," explains Gough.

The entire instant messaging solution, including the customized module, was deployed in a very short time frame. "ProcessOne took us from conception to deployment in just three weeks," recalls Choti. MLB.com is delighted with its new chat service. Over the course of each season, it now facilitates different instant messaging sessions at as many as 25,000 venues. This Game Day chat facility is helping to attract more users to the site and is encouraging visitors to stay on the site longer.

This gives the company more opportunities to cross-sell and up-sell from its range of merchandise and services. In addition, MLB.com anticipates that the chat service will also help it to attract higher value advertisers to its site.

The feedback from users has been very positive. "Users absolutely love it," says Choti. "We believe that we now offer one of the most exciting chat facilities available today."

The ProcessOne Instant Messaging Server is performing very strongly. "The use of Erlang and clustering in the solution architecture not only ensures scalability, but also adds to the solution's stability and flexibility," says Gough. "The ProcessOne Instant Messaging Server offers a plethora of features and we have been able to easily extend it to meet our unique requirements." "The ProcessOne Instant Messaging Server has met our requirements 110 per cent," adds Choti. "From the very first day that we brought the server online, we have not had a single problem with it. It's a champ!"

Now that its Game Day chat facility is up and running, MLB.com does not plan to stand still. Every year it tweaks and enhances its website with new features. "We are very confident that the ProcessOne platform is scalable and robust enough to support us in whatever direction we go," says Choti. He concludes: "Our success has been based, not only on the technical solution provided by ProcessOne, but also on the personal support provided by ProcessOne. ProcessOne is not a vendor; it's a partner and that's a very important distinction."

Dunkin' Donuts Case Study

The stimulative effects of coffee have long been celebrated in the popular culture, as evidenced by tunes like "The Coffee Song" and "Coffee Break" from the musical "How to Succeed in Business Without Really Trying." But how much can coffee energize people in a virtual world? Dunkin' Donuts coffee, as well as its pastries, will be integrated into the Sims Social game for Facebook being introduced by Electronic Arts.

Dunkin' Donuts, part of Dunkin' Brands, is about to find out as it agrees, for the first time, to be integrated into an online game.

For the next 6 months, the coffee and pastries sold by Dunkin' Donuts will be featured in the Sims Social Facebook game to be introduced on facebook.com by Electronic Arts. Financial terms of the deal are not being disclosed. Dunkin' Donuts will be one of a small number of brands and products to be integrated into the game; the total is likely to be three. Electronic Arts is shying from disclosing the identities of the others just yet.

The placement in the Sims Social game on Facebook is part of larger efforts by Dunkin' Donuts to raise its profile as the brand's restaurants are expanding their geographic presence beyond their longtime stronghold in the Northeast. Other examples of efforts to raise the Dunkin' Donuts brand profile include its first integration into a movie, with "Captain America: The First Avenger," and its first sponsorship of a concert tour, with the country singer, Joe Nichols.

The goal is to "make the brand more relevant to a broadening audience," said Dan Saia, vice president for consumer engagement at Dunkin' Brands in Canton, MA. In this instance, the idea is to "continue to reach out to young adults," he added, who are spending an increasing amount of time "in the digital world."

As part of the integration of Dunkin' Donuts into the Sims Social game, players will be able to give each month a cup of coffee and a food item to their Facebook friends. For instance, a cup of Dunkin' Donuts coffee will be described as a "Dunkin' Donuts coffee boost."

"Our products will provide value" to players during the game, Mr. Saia said. "Maybe gifting a doughnut to a friend will put them in a better mood." Also, players who visit the Dunkin' Donuts page on facebook.com (facebook.com/DunkinDonuts) and click "like" will receive two bonus Dunkin' Donuts product items to display in their virtual Sims home.

Dunkin' Donuts joins a short list of brands and products that have previously been integrated by Electronic Arts into versions of the Sims games. For example, Ikea was part of the Sims 2 and the Toyota Prius was part of the Sims 3.

The Sims Social will mark the first time that a Sims game will have more than one product or brand incorporated into the game at the same time, said Denny Chiu, a spokesman for Electronic Arts in Redwood Shores, Calif. More information on the Sims Social game can be obtained on facebook.com or at thesimssocial.com.

The Dunkin' Donuts agency, Hill, Holliday, Connors, Cosmopulos in Boston, was the creative steward of the Sims Social in-game integration as well as handling the media buying. Hill, Holliday is part of the Interpublic Group of Companies.

Skyhook Case Study

The Skyhook Location Engine in its A5 Android version was used to augment the native location system for Priceline in all its mobile devices. The Hotel Negotiator app for Android lets travelers use their Android devices to quickly find and book last-minute hotel rooms at up-to-the-minute current published prices. Or, for deeper discounts of up to 60%, they can bid on hotel rooms using priceline.com's Name Your Own Price® hotel service. Hotel rooms can be booked up until 11:00 p.m. ET on the night the room is needed.

"Hotel Negotiator is designed for on-the-go travelers who need last-minute hotel rooms," said John Caine, senior vice president of marketing at Priceline. "In fact, early data showed that 35% of our mobile customers were within a mile of the hotel they eventually booked. Consequently, it's very important that travelers can trust the app to identify their current location quickly and accurately, and provide them with the best local lodging options. Skyhook provides that needed level of location accuracy and will allow us to build further enhancements into our Android app."

Hotel Negotiator makes booking especially easy and convenient for travelers. Imagine being stuck on an overnight flight layover in a strange city. You are exhausted, the last thing you want to worry about is where to spend the night. Hotel Negotiator can help you locate and book a local top-rated hotel quickly and easily at the best price.

"Reliability and speed of a location result is critical for an app like Hotel Negotiator," said Ted Morgan, founder and CEO of Skyhook. "Skyhook technology enables Priceline's app users to know precisely where they are in a town and where their best hotel options are located. We believe the highly accurate location information provided by Skyhook will significantly enhance the overall experience and satisfaction among Hotel Negotiator app users."

eBay Mobile Case Study

Over the last 10 years, eBay has grown to become the world's single largest online auction website. The company realized that its next major area of growth is in mobile shopping and made significant strategic investments in m-commerce. Mobile Breakthru was brought on board to design, develop, and deliver on eBay's mobile strategy. Six months later, eBay launched its first iPhone application and a major revamp of their mobile websites in 13 countries. eBay Mobile now accounts for $650 M annual revenue with over 200% increase in revenue since 2009.

eBay had a strong global online brand, but few users knew eBay also had a mobile presence. As mobile data usage skyrocketed in 2008, subscribers increasingly looked for well-known brands on their phones. With only a limited functionality U.S. mobile website, the challenge for eBay was to reintroduce all of their users to a mobile experience that delivered a balance of mobile-specific functionality and feature parity with the traditional website.

Mobile Breakthru led the redesign and deployment of eBay's mobile websites for 23 carrier partners, 13 countries, and 7 languages. We managed remote development and design teams and developed product requirements that defined key features such as commerce-grade encryption, SMS integration, custom device detection, and a new buyer/seller dashboard with notifications.

Functionality from the mobile site redesign carried over to the v1 iPhone app project that debuted with the launch of Apple's App Store and the iPhone 3G. Mobile Breakthru was also instrumental in negotiating distribution deals with software, hardware, and carrier companies. Finally, to ramp up eBay's internal teams, Mobile Breakthru produced training content and project planning templates to enable a seamless transition of project ownership.

The measures of success for the eBay Mobile engagement exceeded all expectations. In 6 months, we improved operational efficiencies with eBay's vendors and helped to reduce the development and maintenance costs while increasing business volume 2.6 times to a run-rate of $234 M. In 2009, mobile generated over $650 M in annual revenue, with $400 M coming from the iPhone application alone. Altogether, eBay Mobile has seen 200% year-over-year growth and is set to grow even more with the launch of the first Android application for an increasing number of Google mobile devices from multiple carriers.

TheFind Case Study

TheFind is the world's largest online shopping center where more than 500,000 online and local stores can be found selling over 400 million products. Opened to shoppers in 2007 and profitable since late 2008, TheFind is growing quickly and already hosts more than 17 million unique monthly shoppers. TheFind, headquartered in Mountain View, CA, has received multiple patents for its innovative shopping aggregation and search technology that combines an unsurpassed array of stores, products, coupons, reviews, and other information relevant to all shoppers. Investors include Bain Capital Ventures, Lightspeed Venture Partners, and Redpoint Ventures.

One of the most important issues to users about an online retailer is its procedure for safeguarding personal data such as credit card numbers that travel over the Internet when customers make purchases. With the rampant growth of phishing and identity theft, consumers are increasingly wary about providing this information, especially to companies they do not know. Therefore, one of the pieces of information TheFind publishes about retailers is the protection they employ for transmitting private data. In many cases, a generic "SSL Encryption" logo appears. When the retailer uses VeriSign® SSL Certificates, however, users see the VeriSign seal.

"When a retailer uses VeriSign® SSL certificates to enable encryption, we explicitly call that out because like a select number of other trust marks, the VeriSign seal is a well-recognized symbol that means something to consumers," explains Dave Cook, Senior Director of Marketing for TheFind.

TheFind knew that the presence of the VeriSign seal matters a lot to users and recently decided to measure how much of a difference it makes. The company began by segmenting its retailers into two groups: large, household-name companies and smaller, lesser known firms. Then, for each group, it measured click-through rates for those who displayed the VeriSign seal and those who did not. The results: Companies that display the VeriSign seal received 18.5% more click-throughs than their peers who did not display the VeriSign seal.

"Our study confirmed that there is a lot of value to merchants in displaying the VeriSign seal," says Cook. "At the point where shoppers are ready to choose a store and likely ready to buy, the VeriSign seal helps merchants stand out."

Vivaki Case Studies

Razorfish

In celebration of its 125th anniversary, Mercedes-Benz debuted a new commercial focusing on its long history of making amazing vehicles. To generate excitement leading up to game, the brand asked Razorfish to create marketing effort worthy of such a milestone. The solution? The world's first Twitter-fueled race.

During the week prior to the big game, four teams each took possession of a specially configured Mercedes and made their way to Dallas. This race, however, was not about how fast each team could get there; instead, the goal was to rally support through social media.

The competition comprised two basic components: driving and challenges. In order to drive, the teams required tweets as "fuel." Each tweet in support of the team was worth a quarter-mile. And for the special challenges, the teams had to recruit their followers and networks to support them. Through this process, the teams generated a total of 323 million earned media impressions.

In developing this program, Razorfish and sister agency Denuo crafted the game mechanics and solved for the technical requirements, and because this was the first initiative of its kind, these elements were all created from scratch.

Digitas

Snickers is a popular brand with footballers across the Middle East. But in the spring of 2010, everyone would be advertising football (soccer) campaigns. Snickers asked their agencies, including VivaKi-agency Digitas, to figure out how to speak to their fans in a way that stood out.

The solution? Effective targeting and a smart insight. Market research showed Digitas UK that the majority of Middle East football fans were young men who watched football together in "majlis" (man dens). A significant tradition was also uncovered—these men loved to brag and show off when their teams and players won.

Digitas set out to give them the ultimate brag, inviting them to "step up" and participate in the World's Longest Football match. A total of 36 men were selected from over 13,000 hopefuls. They came together to play their hearts out and became something much bigger than a football match—part of football history.

It was a record breaking, interactive online experience. www.makefootballhistory.com live streamed the game while photos and player information were posted on the site and the official Facebook page. Video messages and fan comments of support flooded in from across the world. The campaign reaching over 9.7 million people, helping Snickers not only reach their current fans but gain a significant number of new brand champions. In fact, people are already demanding the next big brag!

360i Case Studies

Coca-Cola partnered with 360i to execute a long-term strategy for the brand's Facebook Page that would continue to promote the core values established by its fan founders: community, openness and a pure, uninhibited passion for the brand. The objective was to expand the community and maintain Coca-Cola's position as one of the most engaging brand pages on Facebook.

Figure 4.3   Interactive 360i marketing campaign.

The fan's first approach has helped Coca-Cola become one of the top brand presences on Facebook and one of the most engaged brands in social. The 18 million, strong community is less about big brand advertising and more about enabling consumers to celebrate their love of their brand on their own terms. One of the ways established brand can leverage is via the use of action-packed web apps, such as the "Create Your Own Comic," that enables users to customize their own custom comic strip (Figure 4.3).

Every element from layout and design to backgrounds and settings can be personalized to the user's liking, and the comic strip can feature their choice of Marvel characters. For both its design and usability, Create Your Own Comic has garnered industry accolades and praise from publications such as Wired Magazine and Mashable.

Coca-Cola also partnered with 360i to execute a long-term strategy for the brand's Facebook Page that would continue to promote the core values established by its fan founders: community, openness, and a pure, uninhibited passion for the brand. The objective was to expand the community and maintain Coca-Cola's position as one of the most engaging brand pages on Facebook.

The fans' first approach has helped Coca-Cola become one of the top brand presences on Facebook and one of the most engaged brands in social. The 18 million, strong community is less about big brand advertising and more about enabling consumers to celebrate their love of their brand on their own terms.

Nearly 21% of U.S. households do not know when they will get their next meal. In 2010, Kraft Foods teamed up with Feeding America to help families in need and raise awareness of America's hunger problem. We worked with Kraft to bolster the cause by getting consumers involved in online spaces.

The 360i solution was to garner meal donations through everyday actions in social media: liking the Kraft Foods page, tweeting a special hashtag, playing a Facebook game, and more. The entire program was aggregated within a vibrant microsite, which presented the call to participate through a fun, user-friendly digital experience. By empowering consumers to become personally involved and providing a centralized platform through which they could track progress, Kraft created a social echo chamber that triggered the donation of more than 20 million meals.

Red Roof Inn asked 360i to help to improve the creativity, usability, and functionality of its website. The result was a digital refresh of the Red Roof Inn brand—a cleaner design that maintained the core brand identity—with the addition of new features that make the site experience more interactive and user friendly.

In addition to the site refresh, 360i helped Red Roof Inn raise its natural search visibility through a smart local search strategy that increased the brand's footprint among geo-modified keywords, Maps, and Universal Results. As a result, the brand experienced an enormous lift in local search results for RedRoof.com.

360i helped Alamo move the needle on key brand metrics in the weeks leading up to the busiest family travel time of the year. From the media placements to the creative concept, 360i wove Alamo's "Drive Happy" motto throughout the entire paid + earned media program.

All media sponsorships and advertising offered consumers a chance to engage with the brand and experience their dream vacation. Paid investment was enhanced by Digital Word of Mouth® outreach and a social marketing strategy that engaged millions of people. The campaign outperformed Dynamic Logic benchmarks for purchase intent and brand favorability by approximately 2000%.

Guided by consumer insights that showed how moms enjoy Oreo and milk moments with their children during the summertime (while playing at the beach or pool), 360i worked with the brand to translate a memorable print advertisement into a fully interactive digital experience.

To bring the summer fun online, 360i developed a display and social campaign where moms could play a fun Marco Polo game with Oreo cookies in a pool of milk. The banners synchronized with the print campaign and also connected to a Facebook tab hosting the game that could be shared with other moms.

360i worked with Panasonic to create the Groom U iPhone App, which invites men to "paint" a beard or mustache on their face in a way that is reminiscent of the popular magnetic beard kids' toy. App users can also color the facial hair and then shave it off with the Panasonic shaver.

The concept for the app was based on consumer insights, which revealed that men care more about their own appearance when thinking about the quality of a shaver and less about technology or cost. Through targeted display and mobile media, combined with Digital Word of Mouth, the 360i app generated tens of thousands of app downloads in the first month, driving strong brand awareness and engagement (Figure 4.4).

Figure 4.4 360i A5 created for Panasonic.

Skype Case Studies

Skype is assisting *HTC Columbia* in connecting 85 employees across four continents with friends and family. Athletes are away 200 days a year; Skype video calls let them stay connected with home for this number one cycling team in the world, with over 39 riders from 17 nations.

For *Maxim*, a Fortune 1000 company and leading manufacturer of high-performance microchips with 70 offices across the world, everyone with a desk phone can make Skype calls through their SIP-enabled PBX; with Skype, Maxim can work as one big team across the world.

For *Rip Curl*, a designer of sports equipment and leisure wear with 3000 people worldwide, they can cut straight to the issue using Skype with works where they work (office and beach); they can talk instantly in real time.

Clearwire Case Study

Clearwire is using microwave links and an all-IP network to enable high-capacity backhaul for its award winning 4G mobile network spanning the United States. Clearwire's multiyear build-out is enabling advanced fixed digital voice and high-speed mobile Internet service at speeds several times faster than 3G.

Clearwire recognized early on that WiMAX would be the first wireless technology to enable a true ubiquitous broadband experience, allowing connectivity for a multitude of new high-bandwidth online services and applications that users rely on more and more in their daily life. The need for people to stay connected at high speed, regardless of location, was clear. In order to meet this demand, Clearwire set out to pioneer the United State's first nationwide 4G network, and it planned to do so at a much lower cost yet with much greater capacity than traditional cellular networks.

A key enabler of their strategy was the use of a cost-effective backhaul solution that was simple to install and manage. Deploying fiber would have resulted in immense capital costs, while leased lines would have meant large monthly expenses and, in many cases, would fail to deliver the capacity that Clearwire needed. It became apparent that microwave was the backhaul solution of choice, offering an optimal combination of capacity, reliability, and cost efficiency.

Building a greenfield microwave backhaul network afforded Clearwire the flexibility to select microwave radios that met the following key requirements: packet-based, all-IP solution to ensure greater efficiency and compatibility with next-generation applications and services and high capacity and scalability with low latency supporting real-time applications including voice and video over IP. An extensive assessment of microwave vendors led Clearwire to select DragonWave as one of its microwave radio suppliers.

Clearwire is currently deploying Horizon® Duo microwave radios and modems in its high-capacity backhaul network ring architecture. Clearwire is also currently evaluating DragonWave's next-generation microwave radio and modem products—the Horizon Quantum—for potential deployment in its network.

Greystripe Case Studies

Greystripe, a division of ValueClick (NASDAQ: VCLK), is one of the largest brand-focused mobile advertising network in the United States by reach. Greystripe delivers engagement and sophisticated targeting for brand marketers and revenue for publishers and app developers. Greystripe's proprietary advertising platform serves billions of rich media impressions to over 30 million users of touch-driven devices through more than 3500 application titles and mobile websites across all major mobile platforms. App developers create a thriving ad-supported business in partnership with Greystripe, the network with one of the best CPMs in the industry. Following are just a few examples of the revenue A5 developers have earned:

Sudoku Master Free

> Highest monthly U.S. eCPM: $1.06
> Highest global monthly revenue: $1,663
> Highest average monthly CTR: 0.24%
> Highest monthly global impressions to date: 1,681,049
> Ad Format: iPhone Banner

Jungle Party Lite

Highest monthly U.S. eCPM: $0.71
Highest global monthly revenue: $713
Highest average monthly CTR: 0.88%
Highest monthly global impressions to date: 1,986,757
Ad Format: iPhone Banner

Tap 'n' Pop Lite

Highest monthly U.S. eCPM: $0.98
Highest global monthly revenue: $3,585
Highest average monthly CTR: 1.59%
Highest monthly global impressions to date: 5,167,086
Ad Format: iPhone Banner

Simulation Game

Reached number 6 on iTunes Free App list
Average U.S. eCPM: $2.56
Highest monthly eCPM: $3.95
Average global monthly revenue: $8,217
Highest monthly revenue: $31,705
Ad Format: Full Screen

MobilityWare Apps

Platform: iPhone, iPad
Highest monthly U.S. eCPM: $3.13
Highest monthly revenue for All Apps: $298,309
Average daily revenue (June 2010): $10,287
Ad Format: Full Screen

Board Game

Reached top 10 on iTunes Free App list
Average U.S. eCPM: $1.02
Highest monthly eCPM: $3.11
Average global monthly revenue: $8,679
Highest monthly revenue: $12,656
Ad Format: Full Screen

Beer Pong Challenge

> Publisher: Super Experiment
> Reached top 10 on iTunes Free App list
> Average U.S. eCPM: $3.83
> Highest monthly eCPM: $7.03
> Average global monthly revenue: $5,320
> Highest monthly revenue: $9,707
> Ad Format: Full Screen

iLlumination US—Universal Flashlight

> Developer: Erik Storli
> Highest monthly eCPM: $2.67
> Highest global monthly revenue: $2,498
> Highest average monthly CTR: 5.4%
> Ad Format: iPhone Banner

Univision Case Study

Univision Online, Inc. is the interactive division of Univision Communications, Inc. (NYSE:UVN), the premier Spanish-language media company in the United States. Univision Online owns and operates the most visited Spanish-language Internet destination in the United States, located at www.univision.com. Each day, users visit Univision.com nearly 850,000 times, accessing everything from the latest entertainment and sports news to classified ads and reader forums. Univision Online, Inc. is a wholly owned subsidiary of Univision Communications, Inc. Univision Communications, Inc's portfolio includes television, radio, music, and Internet offerings that entertain and inform more Hispanics each day than any other media company in the country. Television operations include the Univision Network, TeleFutura Network, Galavisión, and Univision and TeleFutura Television Groups. Other operations include Univision Radio and Univision Music Group.

Maximizing revenue from its popular online property is one of Univision's chief goals. Univision Online discovered early on that contextual ads are a meaningful way to do just that. As a result, Univision.com began delivering contextual ads in January 2004. Although the ads immediately generated income, Univision Online sought to increase revenue even further, as well as improve click-through rates and ad quality. "We were doing relatively well with contextual advertising," recalls Charles Walter, Director of Product Development for Univision Online. "But we also had a suspicion that we could improve our metrics manifold, including click-through rates, revenue per thousand impressions and overall income."

In addition to boosting revenues, Univision Online sought to ensure that they delivered ads that were relevant, tasteful, and useful to visitors—ads that meshed well with the content and site design of Univision.com. Among the biggest considerations was the ability to deliver a mix of ads in both English and Spanish. This is especially important because of the prominence of the Spanish language among the more than 40 million U.S. Hispanics. The U.S. Hispanic population makes up approximately 14% of the total U.S. population and is driving the nation's population growth. Analysts predict advertisers will spend more than $3.4 billion this year to get their attention.

With these goals in mind, Univision began investigating contextual advertising more fully and changed ad vendors, implementing Google AdSense for Search and AdSense for Content in June 2005.

Walter reports that it was easy to get up and running with AdSense, and that AdSense "runs itself." According to Walter, Google ads are highly appropriate. He notes that he was immediately impressed with Google's content matching and ability to crawl the Univision website with unmatched accuracy.

In terms of revenue, the Univision team immediately saw positive results. Gauging the success of AdSense a year later, Univision has seen AdSense for Search revenues grow by 160%. Revenue from both Google AdSense for Search and AdSense for Content increased by 103%—Univision has subsequently expanded its use of Google tools by implementing site targeting with the goal of attracting advertisers who want to promote their brand specifically to Univision's highly sought after user base.

"We've had significantly better results since switching to Google," said Javier Saralegui, president of Univision Online. "Google helps us monetize our site better."

For Univision, AdSense has become an exceptional complement to traditional advertising. It produces revenue without requiring an internal sales staff, providing a way to fill ad space at lower fixed costs and letting smaller advertisers benefit from the broad reach of Univision Online. "Google is an important strategic partner," says Saralegui. "Not only are we pleased with the relationship, but we believe both users and marketers on our site are benefiting as well."

LTech Case Studies

LTech was founded to provide enterprises with best-of-breed technology solutions. Since then, they have evolved into a leading cloud technology integrator. As an early Google Enterprise Partner, they have helped dozens of customers benefit from Google Apps and the Google Search Appliance (GSA). Their experience of working with a diverse set of clients—from startups to Fortune 500 companies—has made them a trusted name in enterprise class technology services. The following are several LTech case studies:

Advent International

Advent International is one of the largest private equity organizations in the world. With over 20 years of experience and offices in 15 countries, Advent has become a leader in international private equity investing. Advent required a full web presence in 1999. At the time, Advent's technology footprint did not allow them to install databases in a production environment. Since then, Advent needed a trusted technology partner to help manage its web operations, implement content management solutions, and improve its on-site search functionality.

LTech worked with Advent's creative team to design information architecture, site templates, and a content management system that met their needs. In 2007, LTech rebuilt the entire site using a SQL database to provide for more advanced content management. LTech's migration of the website to SQL Server increased the speed of the site, and provided Advent with an expandable framework for their public communications platform. LTech's continued management of Advent's web presence has allowed them to communicate effectively via the web to prospective investors and customers.

New York Life

New York Life is the largest life insurance company in America and one of the largest in the world. They provide a variety of securities products and mutual funds.

Challenges

New York Life's existing intranet search was fragmented and unable to return relevant results. They decided to go with a GSA solution from Google to greatly improve their user experience. Their content was spread out across a diverse array of systems, including Vignette V6 and V7, IBM WebSphere Portal, and Oracle databases, all run by different development groups. In addition, they had unique security requirements that required viability testing for delivering secure content. They needed help in configuring the GSA to answer all of their problems, by crawling all their content, delivering secure search, and providing search to their enterprise applications. In order to ensure the success of the project, a short-term proof-of-concept was executed, and LTech was chosen to participate.

LTech worked closely with New York Life's development team and provided guidance and solutions on a wide array of GSA topics. First, LTech was able to deliver a proof-of-concept that resulted in a functioning secure search implementation for New York Life. And then a plan for full-scale deployment was delivered, allowing New York Life to staff and execute the project.

PC Magazine

First released in 1982, PC Magazine is a biweekly magazine published for technology professionals with previews and reviews of new hardware and software.

The magazine, which spawned an online edition in 1994, contains articles written by experts in the field of information technology.

PC Magazine wanted to improve the search feature on their website. With thousands of products and reviews available to search on the site, they needed a way to provide more organized and relevant search results. LTech set up PC Magazine with a custom GSA implementation, which allowed users to search products grouped by category, price, brand, and more.

PayPal

PayPal is an e-commerce business and subsidiary of eBay that allows consumers to make secure payments over the Internet without using traditional paper methods. PayPal processes transactions for online vendors and other sites. The PayPal website offers a link with a "comment card" for users to rate and comment on their PayPal experience. At the time, all data were sent to OpinionLab with no simple way for PayPal employees to access it. PayPal required an easier means of searching the responses they received from users.

LTech configured and implemented a Google Mini, working with PayPal and OpinionLab to create a search interface for PayPal employees. With the Google Mini, other servers and code were eliminated, making it much easier for PayPal to access user suggestions and ratings.

The new search interface enabled PayPal employees to browse users' comments themselves. This provided a much more efficient way for PayPal to evaluate suggestions in order to determine possible improvements for the site. LTech was able to customize the GSA in order to reflect the company's needs and the requirements of the site. The GSA helped PC Magazine give their users faster and more relevant search results, as well as various filtering options.

Discovery Communications Case Study

In its epic new television series LIFE, Discovery Channel showcases never before seen creatures and the behaviors they adopt to survive and thrive. Because LIFE is like no other show on TV, Yahoo! created a digital advertising campaign unlike any other. Discovery Channel needed to drive viewers to tune in with an awareness campaign of unprecedented scope and creativity for its LIFE television event. A ground-breaking 11 part series narrated by Oprah Winfrey, LIFE featured never-before-used filming techniques to capture animals, habitats, and behaviors never previously witnessed by humans. Discovery began building buzz for LIFE with key influencers through VIP screenings in Los Angeles, New York, and Washington, DC, as well as blogger events in smaller theaters all over the country.

"LIFE was the biggest show Discovery had done since Planet Earth so we wanted the promotion to be big and forward, because it truly represented an epic moment for the channel," says Donna Murphy, vice president of marketing for Discovery.

"With LIFE, we needed to creatively ignite passion—for the show, for the creatures, for the natural history—with the broadest audience possible."

The cable channel and its media agency PHD wanted to translate the "metamorphosis" idea at the heart of the show into its promotional media. By conveying the sensation that the advertising was constantly adapting to whatever the user was doing, Discovery felt the user would be drawn in by the true essence of the show.

"We felt from a media standpoint that digital—since it's ever changing, ever evolving and extremely dynamic—was the best medium to deliver the kind of interactivity, iconic imagery and feeling of curiosity that Discovery wanted," says Jeffrey Liang, group digital director at PHD. "Yahoo! was selected as one of our digital partners for its extensive reach, its rich media capabilities in search and its creative ability to build first-of-its-kind ad concepts."

Yahoo! fundamentally redefined its digital canvas to create a customized solution for Discovery. The LIFE campaign included a number of creative "firsts" on Yahoo!, starting with nonuser-initiated ad elements that floated from the edge of the page across the Yahoo! home page toward the 300 × 250 ad. Throughout the day of the LIFE premiere, everyone who visited the Yahoo! home page could select a LIFE-themed "wallpaper" design that stayed visible each time the user returned to that page, which on average is four to six times a day. This marked one of the first times Yahoo! created a custom home page with floating ad elements, delivering a revolutionary user experience to drive engagement and curiosity.

One of Discovery's top priorities was to make sure that the beautiful photographs and videos were pushed out across all of its online advertising. "It was very difficult to do that with the traditional ad specs of most sites, especially search where ads are text-based," Liang says. "But Yahoo!'s Rich Ads in Search allowed us to showcase our videos in search results."

When users searched for LIFE on Yahoo! Search, Rich Ads in Search returned results with top placement on the page along with deep links and a video to draw the user in. When a user clicked on the video, the ad expanded to display hi-def content from the show. This placement not only allowed Discovery to showcase its video footage but it also required no additional expense since it simply featured repurposed assets.

In a first ever for an entertainment advertiser, Discovery featured LIFE in tandem video ad units on the Yahoo! Mail welcome page. Tandem ad units draw the user in by framing the top right corner of the screen and creating a cohesive visual message. The vibrant imagery of the LIFE creatures evoked the precise sense of the dynamic, interactive natural world captured on the television show.

Discovery also strategically leveraged Yahoo!'s reach in mobile to connect with natural history lovers wherever and whenever. On March 20–21, LIFE was featured on the Yahoo! Mobile home page in an expandable ad placement. Once again the arresting imagery from the show took center stage. Best of all, the placement helped Discovery target the highly desirable 25–54 age demographic.

Discovery used two unique placements to drive both targeting and scale goals. First, LIFE was featured on the Yahoo! Sports home page, building awareness with men, a core demographic for the channel. LIFE also sponsored the NCAA Scoreboard on Yahoo! Sports on March 21—the day of the show's premiere and right in the thick of March Madness. Additional placements on Yahoo! news and Yahoo! TV further extended the reach and drove intent to tune in.

Touch Press Case Studies

Major League Entertainment Experience

What is better than enjoying a sports event from the luxurious setting of an executive skybox? When a regional hockey team began searching for some new ideas to improve their luxury skyboxes, they turned to Touch Revolution. Using the beautiful, multi-touch 21.5″ TRu™ Touch Monitor, a skybox multimedia platform was created specifically for them—taking their fan experience to a new level.

Touch Revolution, with a trusted software partner, created an exceptional skybox opportunity for hockey fans. Using three 21.5″ TRu Touch Monitors, fans are now able to enjoy instant replays, research player bios and game stats, send out Tweets, post to Facebook, and interact with other fans in the stadium. This innovative solution delivers an unprecedented level of excitement to the serious hockey fan within the comfort of a skybox.

Wrapped up in an elegant *projected capacitive touch* experience, Touch Revolution's custom solution combines the best of video coverage, multimedia resources, Internet connectivity, and social media. Of course, this interactive experience adds to the general excitement of any hockey game. The end result is a leap forward for the total hockey fan experience and a new way to market the sports team and increase skybox sales. Now that is cool.

Executive-Class Travel Experience

When a major mass-transit provider wanted to add multimedia entertainment to their newest fleet of long-range executive buses, they turned to a custom Touch Revolution integrated NIMble™ solution.

The customer needed a turnkey computing solution. NIMble offered just such an answer. Touch Revolution's application engineering team, with customer input, established a complete list of specifications for the design of the NIMble solution—exactly meeting the customer's needs.

The solution included a 10.1″ Fusion™ touch display, allowing the customer to take full advantage of the Touch Revolution Experience. Each seat on the bus is equipped with a personal pendant containing a complete multimedia entertainment system powered by Touch Revolution technology. The result is an optimized Android-controlled system, designed with an engaging touch experience, to entertain each passenger as they travel.

Twitter Case Studies

Best Buy

Best Buy wanted to be a resource for customers beyond their experience in the stores. The company developed a unique way to connect with customers through their @twelpforce account to provide real-time customer service.

Best Buy empowered the "blue shirt" members of its Geek Squad tech support service and corporate employees to staff their @twelpforce account on Twitter. People use their own Twitter account to ask questions directly to @twelpforce, and any Best Buy employee, working on company time, can provide answers using an @ reply to the customer. By tagging their tweets with #twelpforce, the answer is sent through the @twelpforce account, allowing anyone to search the feed for topics they are researching.

As of December 15, 2010, @twelpforce has provided over 38,000 answers to customer inquiries. They have had a tremendous response from employees as well, with over 2900 signed up to answer questions.

Best Buy's thought at the beginning was simple: be relevant. Give customers something of value so they find themselves invited into conversations and welcomed into the purchase/support cycle. They wanted to leverage Twitter and let the real people behind @twelpforce set them apart from competitors by sharing knowledge on demand.

Through conversational employee/customer interactions via Twitter, they hoped to humanize their entire organization. Twitter let the employees be authentic, transparent, and bring more of "themselves" to the table. They felt the @twelpforce initiative in particular was a game changer since it was the first time a company used Twitter to create real-time customer service.

Etsy

Etsy is an online marketplace for buying and selling handmade goods and hosts shops for over 400,000 sellers. Through their @etsy account, they share tips and tricks and highlight interesting products from sellers in their marketplace. Etsy joined Twitter in December 2007 in the early days of the service and, at the time, were unsure how to make best use of their account. Soon the Etsy team saw the powerful ways many Etsy sellers were using Twitter to promote their handmade items in their Etsy shops. By observing the tweets of followers of @Etsy, the Etsy team found insights from their followers about how to best utilize Twitter. The person that manages the Twitter account for Etsy, Anda Corrie, points out, "Our community always comes up with great ideas."

Etsy began using their Twitter account as a way to share new posts from Etsy's blog, a technique looked at now as a "newbie mistake." After realizing Twitter could be more than just a RSS feed of their blog, Etsy decided to experiment with using Twitter in a variety of ways.

@Etsy now uses Twitter to alert followers to creative products from Etsy sellers, share tips & tricks, and provide information about upcoming events and promotions on the site. They also retweet individual Etsy sellers and monitor feedback and ideas in real time. This essentially allows the Etsy team to create focus groups from their @etsy followers. In Etsy's experience, as a company that constantly seeks to build community and "voraciously" learns from its users, they have found that Twitter is an "amazing way of harnessing the collective brains of so many people."

JetBlue

JetBlue was one of the first major brands to join Twitter, which it did in Spring 2007. Today, the company has over a million followers, and its account is often cited as an example of smart corporate Tweeting. But the company started out on Twitter with modest goals. It wanted to help customers.

"Some people were asking for help, and others were saying things that weren't correct," recalls Morgan Johnston, JetBlue's manager of corporate communications. He had been spending time on Twitter search and he had realized that JetBlue customers, often on the move, were tweeting about travel problems. "You can only see that a few times before you want to jump in and do something."

He proposed the idea of setting up a JetBlue account on Twitter and cleared it with communications executives at his company. They were very supportive—in part because they could start by just dipping a toe in the water. "It helps that as a business, you're not immediately exposed to hundreds of thousands of people," says Johnston, who's based in New York. "It's a slow scaling process."

Gradual growth turned out to be just what JetBlue needed on Twitter, as it learned what worked and what did not. Chatty posts and customer service assistance tended to generate a lot of replies and new followers. Press releases and announcements were met with silence.

From this experience, Johnston hit on what he calls the Twitter "kernel of truth": be receptive to what your followers want. How do you know what that is? You can gauge their responses to your tweets, and—as it turns out—you can also ask them.

When JetBlue faced dead air after pushing out new route announcements, Johnston started wondering what people wanted from the account. So he asked. The responses surprised him. "People said simply, 'This is what we want. We want to see you asking.'" He adds that people even went as far as to say that they wanted the company to see them as a resource for helping JetBlue deliver a better product.

Moxsie

Twitter's platform has enabled Moxsie to amass a loyal following of indie fashion-philes while still being a small company. Moxsie started using Twitter as a voice of expertise for fashion trends but have grown to use their @moxsie account as a place to converse with their followers about a variety of topics: products they sell, cutting-edge trends in fashion, and peeks in to unique parts of the industry, all while getting to hear what their customers want.

Moxsie has used its @moxsie Twitter account to redefine fashion trend discovery by allowing everyday people direct access to cutting-edge apparel in real time. A concept previously reserved exclusively for fashion designers and industry insiders, Moxsie has used Twitter to provide its followers with premier access to a multitude of indie fashion labels.

The @moxsie account uses media to engage its followers as well. By tweeting photos of new merchandise, designer's latest product lines, recent shipments, and fashion photo shoots, the Moxsie team shares a back-stage peek with the Twitter community in real time.

Via Twitter, Moxsie also gauges people's reactions to new styles via @replies. Their followers are rewarded with exclusive access to a side of the fashion industry not usually seen. In addition to sharing links to the Moxsie online retail store, Twitter has enabled the company to create a unique presence as a fashion industry insider with valuable backstage access.

Salesforce Case Study

AOL Advertising—the industry's largest domestic digital advertising network, based on reach—needed to effectively manage sales, increase pipeline visibility, and integrate with systems. AOL Advertising, which includes AOL's leading media properties and more, wanted to consolidate multiple existing instances of Salesforce CRM globally. The ability to provide a unified view while supporting different processes for multiple business units was a key objective for Salesforce and AOL—the solution also had to integrate with the company's order management systems.

AOL Advertising upgraded to Salesforce CRM Unlimited Edition, consolidating over 1000 users across several business groups on one instance of Salesforce CRM in just 3 months. The company integrated salesforce.com with its order management systems, which in turn feed the company's ad servers. Using Force.com workflow management, the company can efficiently support pre- and post-sales functions. Salesforce.com Premier Support helps to customize Salesforce CRM beyond a mere transactional tool.

Dashboards and reports are easily created to track sales activities.

AOL Advertising's sales team now shares information more efficiently and works more cooperatively, reducing duplicated effort and wasted time. Armed with a tool that better manages opportunities, sellers now focus on those with the highest probability to close, driving revenue. Salesforce CRM provides better visibility into the sales pipeline.

The company also benefits from better reporting for management. Managers use dashboards to track the activity levels of their teams—from how many calls are made to how many meetings take place. The cloud computing model means AOL Advertising can quickly make customizations to meet its unique business needs.

Shopkick Case Study

This A5 is a product of Palo Alto, California-based app developer that enables retailers and mall owners to reward device carrying customers for entering stores or malls. Further functionality allows customers to get additional rewards for scanning products and trying on clothes. It is a way to incentivize activities that retailers know increase on-site purchases.

What's most significant about the application's rollout is the all-star roster of firms that have already endorsed it. Macy's, Best Buy, American Eagle Outfitters and Sports Authority are rolling out Shopkick at its stores, as is Simon Property Group, the largest regional mall owner in the United States.

"We've wanted to be in the mobile space for a while and started a process of evaluating players in that space about a year ago," says Les Morris, a spokesman for Simon. "We feel like we have an obligation to our retailers to present things that are very cool and that will help them get traffic into their stores and make shopping fun. One of the reasons that we like Shopkick in particular is that their app is very much retail-focused, as opposed to being social media-focused with a retail component added on."

Shopkick is currently active at about 25 Simon malls in New York, Los Angeles, San Francisco, and Chicago. By the holiday shopping season, Simon plans to roll out the application at more than 100 of its properties. The application, which has been about a year in the making, is meant to encourage more store visits, says Cyriac Roeding, Shopkick CEO.

Stores that want to use Shopkick install a location device on-site that emits a silent audio signal when a customer with the app on his or her smart phone steps inside the store. At Simon properties, the devices have been installed at the entrances to the malls, as well as in food courts and common areas. Shopkick's audio transmitter is several degrees more precise than standard GPS technology and costs less than $100 to install, Roeding notes.

"With GPS, you have no idea whether you are inside the store or just close to it," Roeding says. "We can reward you for being present in the store. The signal stops at the entrance." For the customer, Shopkick works by adding so-called kickbucks points to the customer's account for engaging in activities retailers want to encourage. Walking into an American Eagle store, for example, automatically gives you 35 kickbucks.

Scanning the barcode on a shirt or a pair of jeans adds additional kickbucks to the account. In a deal that is so far exclusive to American Eagle Outfitters, customers also get rewarded for trying on clothes; the retailer has installed special Shopkick panels in its dressing rooms that allow shoppers to alert the app that they have been inside.

The kickbucks points the customer collects can then be applied toward a number of online and offline purchases. The customer can get a gift card that can be redeemed on-site, download songs or online games, or donate money to charity. There is a cap on how many kickbucks a shopper can get per day, so you can not simply walk in and out of a store repeatedly and redeem the rewards. And it also takes quite a few kickbucks to earn a tangible reward. For example, a $5 gift card at American Eagle requires 1250 kickbucks.

As payment, Shopkick gets a fee from the mall owner/retailer for every kickbuck earned and a percentage of the sales that can be directly attributed to the app.

"For us, Shopkick is really the first solution for bringing mobility, loyalty and precision" to our marketing approach, says Mike Dupuis, vice president of marketing and operations with American Eagle Outfitters Direct. "It's about how we can leverage the capabilities within the app to make more targeted offers to our customers." As of now, 52 American Eagle stores in New York, Los Angeles, San Francisco, and Chicago are participating in the Shopkick program. The retailer plans to increase the number to 200 by November and expects to have the app available chain-wide within a 15 month period.

Customers can download the app for free from the iTunes store. It is currently available exclusively to iPhone users, but an Android version will be unveiled within a few months, Roeding says. He notes that Shopkick initially approached Best Buy, Macy's, American Eagle, Sports Authority, and Simon about rolling out the app because it saw the companies as market leaders in their respective fields and felt they would be more open to adapting an innovative approach to marketing. But the company is already talking to more potential clients. "This is largely a non-exclusive arrangement," Roeding says. "The more retailers participate, the more value you get."

IKEA Case Study

IKEA stores are designed to offer shoppers not just with products and prices but also with knowledge, inspiration, and the joy of discovery. The IKEA brand is about improving consumer lives at home with prices everyone can afford. Our mandate was to live up to this powerful standard in defining the IKEA online experience.

IKEA asked HUGE to develop a long-term strategic blueprint for its retail websites. HUGE was involved in the project from its inception, which allowed us to deploy our full research and design methodology. This included strategic planning, competitive usability testing, persona and user scenario development, interaction design, visual design, prototyping, production, and tracking analytics.

Over the years, consumers have developed their own personal ways of negotiating the range of IKEA products and the way products are organized in the catalogue and store. So before we could develop a system for successfully navigating such a large number of products through a digital interface, our first task was to understand the customer's mental model of the information space. A customized card sorting exercise was conducted in New York and Munich to discover patterns inherent in how customers dealt with IKEA's massive product range and carried out tasks such as configuring their choices. This ultimately led to the creation of a brand-new Internet-specific product categorization and tagging system within IKEA—a significant undertaking considering that the IKEA product range contains over 15,000 articles.

IKEA was not quite ready to roll out full-scale e-commerce in all markets around the world. In cases where capabilities were limited, our job as designers was to inform the customer in a direct and usable way about the level of e-commerce they could expect. The design solution had to be configurable locally to support a substantial number of permutations.

Our overall creative approach centered on "Goal Directed Inspiration." How do you design a page that stops a rushed web user in their tracks and tells them about inspiring new products, design ideas, services, and solutions? How do you do this without compromising on usability or perceived convenience? HUGE developed an exacting methodology for testing the placement of new messages, knowledge, content, and other forms of data into the core product browsing experience.

How do you maintain a focus on the approved strategy throughout a long project lifecycle? With focused, highly specific Measures of Success that are often more effective than strategic briefs and other planning artifacts that can be open to interpretation.

The Measures of Success HUGE developed for IKEA were effective because they were clear, specific, and concise. Our deep experience with major tracking and analytics packages means we can tease out reliable metrics based not just on page views and conversions but on meaningful customer click streams and scenarios.

From a maintenance perspective, the vision was to build a single solution that could support IKEA's aggressive international expansion plans. HUGE helped IKEA define a single system of flexible templates that could be produced and localized annually in several alphabets, catering to the specialized needs of local IKEA markets from Beijing to Seattle.

For a project of this scale rolling out in so many markets and languages, it was essential to create tight interdisciplinary teams including designers, engineers, and many other stakeholders. Everyone needed to have a close understanding of the strengths and weaknesses of the various technical platforms. To control quality and communicate the evolving design solutions, particularly in the tricky areas of product configuration and sorting, HUGE developed functional prototypes to allow quick user testing and improvements. By the end of the project, the entire team (both client and agency) developed an aggressive,

Figure 4.5 IKEA's Anna digital store assistant.

results-driven approach to assessing the value of proposed features and enhancements—both to the IKEA business and to its customer.

IKEA has a proud history of ignoring trends and fearlessly presenting customers with unconventional approaches to retail that works. We began working with IKEA on an idea for allowing customers to ask questions with natural language queries. After a few months of experimentation and user research, *"Ask Anna"* was born (Figure 4.5).

"Anna," the IKEA Help Center assistant, is an animated character that engages IKEA customers in conversation and answers their support and furnishings questions. Anna has enabled a more convenient shopping experience and led to significant reductions in customer service costs for each market in which she has been deployed. In a review of automated support tools, the *Wall Street Journal* called her "the closest to speaking to an actual human."

Over the years, we've partnered to create a singular site experience where a large percentage of site visitors actively interact with inspirational rich content modules that showcase the products and with planning tools that allow visitors to customize IKEA solutions. It is no secret. The biggest opportunity for IKEA, by far, is to better prepare customers for their store visits. Since HUGE's partnership with IKEA, time spent preparing online is strongly correlated with higher checkout tickets at IKEA stores.

We know that visitors that interact with the rich content modules have significantly higher conversion and engagement rates than visitors that do not; they have longer site visits, view more products, and prepare longer shopping lists for in-store visits. In addition to an overhauled product presentation system centered on all the rooms of the house, our work included a way to check stock, a shopping list, and the integration of local store pricing and promotions into the product browsing path.

To engage with IKEA's high-value lifetime customers, HUGE developed a suite of downloadable room planning tools prior to scheduling an appointment with a room expert in the store. The planning tools not only increased the number of fixtures sold, but they also reduced the average length of in-store consultations with IKEA experts.

As IKEA's ongoing digital partner, we have significantly driven IKEA's business to the point where IKEA.com is now the #1 customer touchpoint in the world for the company, and digital efforts significantly drive in-store sales. Engagement with IKEA.com and other digital platforms has more than tripled since our 2007 redesign, and in-store sales are over 50% higher for individuals who have visited the website prior to going to the store.

HUGE has subsequently had the privilege of handling several other IKEA projects, including the retailer's Corporate and Franchisor websites. And, we continue to work with IKEA on an ongoing basis to continually improve the IKEA online experience.

Urban Outfitters Case Study

Urban Outfitters, Inc. is an innovative specialty retailer and wholesaler offering a variety of lifestyle merchandise through three brands—Urban Outfitters, Anthropologie, and Free People. In addition to its retail stores, the company promotes its products and brands directly to the consumer through its e-commerce websites and catalogs. Urban Outfitters has achieved compounded annual sales growth of approximately 29% over the past 5 years, with sales of approximately $1.2 billion in fiscal 2007.

As a leading multichannel retailer in a highly competitive market, Urban Outfitters understands how website aesthetics and features play a critical role in ensuring a satisfactory shopper experience that encourages store visits and purchases. Constantly incorporating new technologies that help keep its websites fresh and engaging, the company planned to launch redesigned websites for its three brands on a new web platform. Knowing that high performance and availability would be critical to the success of its relaunch, Urban Outfitters turned to a trusted partner—Akamai. Urban Outfitters needed to meet four key requirements to support its brand and objectives:

1. *Seamlessly handle traffic surges*: As a retailer earning the majority of revenues during the back-to-school and holiday seasons, Urban Outfitters needs its sites to scale to handle any amount of traffic.
2. *Ensure optimal customer experience*: The company wants to make sure that its customers enjoy a superior online shopping experience, regardless of their location.

3. *Protect brand image*: Well aware that its websites are an extension of its brands, Urban Outfitters wants to deliver rich, engaging websites without fail.
4. *Sub 1s response time on home and gateway pages*: To satisfy its target demographic of consumers, it needs to keep web page response times as fast as possible.

Urban Outfitters' brand sites are heavily trafficked by consumers from all around the globe. While the company serves an average of 120–130 million page views monthly across all brands, that number spikes to 200 million per month during the back-to-school and holiday seasons. "With Akamai, we supported a 40% increase in monthly page views while decreasing front-end bandwidth utilization by over 30%," explains Keary McNew, manager of IT Engineering for Urban Outfitters, Inc.

As Urban Outfitters planned the relaunch of its sites, it knew that optimal performance was a must, especially for interactive features such as checking inventory and adding merchandise to a shopping cart. "Today's consumers expect Web sites to perform quickly and without fail. This is especially true of our Urban Outfitters' site, where we are catering to the younger generation who expect a seamless online experience," says McNew.

Prior to implementing Dynamic Site Accelerator, highly trafficked pages—such as the home page and gateway pages that serve as the landing page for products—were not being delivered as quickly as the company wanted. "Our goal is to deliver those key pages in less than one second but we weren't able to do that. As soon as we put Dynamic Site Accelerator in place, we achieved our goal," continues McNew. Urban Outfitters views its websites as a logical extension of its businesses and brands. Putting Akamai in place enables the company to ensure the performance needed to support the rich and interactive applications that promote that concept.

Tumblr Case Study

Moving Pictures is a distinctive, socially aware movie magazine striving to bridge the gap between audience and filmmaker by "telling the stories behind the movies." Articles often focus on how specific films or film trends affect society and individuals within society.

With Moving Pictures, there were two primary goals. The first was basic: to visually articulate what Moving Pictures stands for. The second: to build a brand that would accomplish the magazine's stated mission (to "tell the stories behind the movies") and appeal to both industry insiders and outsiders by offering a fresh take on the entertainment business. It was important that this fresh approach be evident both in the content and the design.

Since the magazine's unique content demanded an uncommon design outlook, we explored different ways in which the magazine could "flow," balancing longer articles with shorter, easily digestible bits of info and art. The overall strategy was to construct a dynamic, artfully produced publication that could sit with distinction on the coffee table of any Hollywood bigwig or amateur enthusiast.

Magazines are locked into a horizontal format because that is the way the English language works: left to right. This being a movie magazine, we tried to utilize space the way movies do—not only horizontally but also vertically. We approached the pages of the magazine as movie screens, allowing for elegant, classic forms and more modern ones, a timeless format that could accommodate the latest sci-fi blockbuster or a Chaplin silent film (Figure 4.6).

Moving Pictures reached a 75,000 earned print run in its first year, averaging a 30% sell-through rate on newsstands. As industry insiders know, this is no small feat for a new magazine in the highly competitive entertainment market. Moving Pictures also received the 2006 and 2007 Maggie Award for Best Overall Magazine in Communication, Advertising, and the Arts. Tumblr lets devices effortlessly share anything. Post text, photos, quotes, links, music,

Figure 4.6 **Tumblr case study—Moving Pictures.**

and videos, from any browser, tablet, phone, desktop, e-mail, or wherever; the user can customize everything, from colors to a theme's HTML.

Crimson Hexagon Case Study

How do you figure out all the ways that people are using online services like yours? That was the question Microsoft's Bing marketing team wanted to answer after launching a service—Bing—meant to capture mindshare from a major Internet search competitor. With a goal of targeting specific interest groups, the company needed a clear understanding of each group's needs and habits. While the company actively harnesses social-media channels in its marketing efforts, it needed a way to better manage the flow of online conversation.

Microsoft Bing had positioned its service as a way for the online audience to find answers to their questions. Though it had developed a sophisticated way to analyze the online conversation—and had plenty of resources at its disposal—Bing was unable to quickly sort through and make sense of the information it had collected. "We were drowning in data and struggling to reconcile conflicting information," explains Lise Brende, director of marketing analytics, Bing™ and MSN® at Microsoft.

Once it became aware of the Crimson Hexagon ForSight™ platform, Microsoft Bing engaged with Crimson Hexagon to overcome its challenges. Crimson Hexagon experts configured the ForSight platform to track and analyze the key segments the company's solution team had identified. "We felt confident that the ForSight platform could help us analyze the online conversation and understand when and how our target audiences engage online," says Brende. After analyzing 1 month of online conversations, Crimson Hexagon was able to provide Microsoft Bing with answers to the following:

- Who influences the online conversation?
- Where do online conversations take place?
- How can the company make use of this information?
- What drivers and behaviors do online conversations reveal for key segments?

"The insights revealed to our team by Crimson Hexagon's ForSight platform have become an integral part of developing and executing our marketing strategies and tactics," says Brende. "The analysis allows us to see and understand the nuances of online conversation from our widely varying customer segments and we've been able to learn what's working and what isn't in real time, adjusting along the way. Our team has crafted more effective marketing campaigns and responded to customers' expressed opinions in a way that has definitely enhanced our service delivery and overall business."

While Crimson Hexagon analyzed conversations on both blogs and forums, it found that the bulk of conversations were taking place in forums. It also identified the top 20 forums for each of the two key audience segments. "Now we know where to spend time to learn more about—and interact with—our target audiences," says Brende.

The analysis yielded a surprising result. The target segments viewed the online channel as more of a way to share their thoughts and experience rather than to find answers to their questions. For instance, feedback dominated the conversations of those interested in creative projects, such as cooking, painting, or making videos. On the other hand, those with health concerns seemed most interested in sharing personal stories.

Crimson Hexagon was also able to identify those personalities who influence the online conversations in these two segments. While Crimson Hexagon's analysis had shown that the masses trade information via forums, it also revealed that influencers spend their time on blogs. By understanding who is considered an influential blogger, the company can consider outreach efforts and marketing campaigns that tap into these resources. "We now know where to focus our efforts when it comes to expanding our community involvement," says Brende.

Overall, the analysis helped the company identify ways that it can connect with its target audiences in more interpersonal ways. Just as important, it enables the company to adopt a finely honed strategy, rather than one more akin to throwing spaghetti at the wall to see what sticks. "Crimson Hexagon helped spark ideas for viral-marketing campaigns and identified ways we can connect more deeply with our target audiences," concludes Brende.

Crimson Hexagon, founded in 2007, is a provider of real-time social media monitoring and analysis to brands, agencies, media firms, and their partners. Powered by patent-pending technology developed at Harvard University's Institute for Quantitative Social Science, the Crimson Hexagon ForSight platform overcomes the limits of traditional market research by delivering a real-time view of how engaged online consumers truly think and feel about a brand or issue.

Usablenet Case Studies

Usablenet offers the leading technological platform for transforming and optimizing web content, a platform that helped us become one of Fast Company magazine's 10 most innovative companies in mobile. But we are more than our technology: we are a diverse team of experienced professionals who are completely dedicated to our clients' success.

ASOS

ASOS is a leading U.K.-based fashion retailer that attracted millions of people to its Facebook page. The company wanted to capture more business on Facebook, so they hired Usablenet to build their Facebook store. The integrated shopping app enables customers to securely shop the entire ASOS product range without leaving Facebook. Usablenet also built an m-commerce site for ASOS, attracting more than £1 million sales in its first quarter after the launch of the first Facebook store in Europe.

Fairmont Hotels

When your customers are by definition travelers, being able to reach them on mobile devices is critical to building closer relationships with them and bridging the gap between inquiry and reservation. Fairmont Hotels contracted with Usablenet to create an iPhone app that would enable frequent travelers and preferred customers to view photo slideshows of Fairmont properties, search for hotel packages by theme, book or change reservations, and learn of nearby attractions and activities. Fairmont concierges may have reason to worry.

Garnet Hill

Garnet Hill began as an importer of English flannel sheets and has grown into a distinguished brand and multichannel marketer. Before launching its mobile site, 80% of users surveyed were unable to complete a product purchase and 45% of them abandoned the transaction due to the site's inability to load. At the end of 2010, Garnet Hill rolled out its m-commerce site, built by Usablenet. Within 2 months, the company saw a 300% increase in mobile sales.

JC Penney

Founded in 1902, JC Penney is both a venerable and intrepid retailer that can boast it was the first department store to sell its goods online. With an assist from Usablenet, in December 2010, JC Penney also became the first major U.S. retailer to offer its entire inventory via Facebook. Elevating the social networking site from a place where people transact in opinions to one where people use real money to purchase real products, JC Penney has more than 1.5 million "Likes" to support its innovative venture.

Marks & Spencer

With a 125 year history, Marks & Spencer is one of the world's great retail brands. In 2010, the company launched its first m-commerce site. Created by Usablenet, the site provides extensive functionality, including product search, store finder, and access to 24,000 products in a range of categories. Since its launch, it has had more than 1.2 million unique visitors, over 10 million page views, and has processed more than 13,000 transactions for products from televisions to sofas to clothing.

PacSun

PacSun, a leading supplier of clothing and accessories for fun in the sun, is pressing ahead aggressively on a number of fronts to make it the first choice of hip, active men and women. The company has been selling its products through an optimized m-commerce site since 2009 and engaged with Usablenet to create a full-featured iPhone app that enables customers to buy any product within the app. Usablenet also created a solution for fixed computer terminals in more than 800 PacSun stores that run an optimized, touch screen version of its website.

Bazaarvoice Case Studies

When devices tell enterprises exactly what they think about their products and services, their insights have a huge impact on their business. Bazaarvoice enables clients to become truly customer-focused by integrating social data across their entire organization.

Benefit Cosmetics

Benefit Cosmetics has long understood their customers' natural desire to share cosmetics advice and product recommendations with each other. The beauty brand aimed to further engage this natural conversation on Facebook. They partnered with Bazaarvoice to capture these conversations and create a loyalty loop that keeps customers returning to Benefit Cosmetics.

Sears Canada

Sears Canada launched Bazaarvoice Ratings & Reviews™ and Ask & Answer™ in May 2009, followed by Stories™ in June 2010. In May 2010, they launched Social Alerts™, which automatically sends follow-up e-mails to site visitors who opt in after submitting reviews, questions, or stories. These e-mails inform contributors when their content has been approved or rejected, based on the company's unique moderation rules. In the case of questions, Social Alerts lets contributors know when their question has been answered. Because these e-mails reach customers as a direct result of their actions, the message is highly relevant to recipients.

DRL

DRL Ltd. is the leading white goods retailer in the United Kingdom, operating the e-commerce site AppliancesOnline.co.uk, as well as the appliance websites for nearly a dozen other major U.K. brands. The company launched Bazaarvoice Ratings & Reviews in April 2009 and Ask & Answer in August 2010, aggregating all of their user-generated content (UGC) at Appliance-Reviews.co.uk.

Evans Cycles

Evans Cycles is the United Kingdom's largest independent bicycle and cycling gear retailer. Recognizing their customers' intense passion for cycling, Evans Cycles launched Bazaarvoice Ratings & Reviews in November 2009 and Ask & Answer in July 2010. UGC has proven search benefits, so to maximize those, Evans Cycles launched SearchVoice Inline (SVI) for their reviews in July 2010. SVI embeds the text of the first few reviews on a product into the product page's code, effectively updating the content to feed the freshness search engines crave.

Epson

Epson is a globally recognized brand in consumer and enterprise electronics manufacturing. Recognizing the use of high-scrutiny devices when researching and buying electronics, Epson launched Bazaarvoice Ratings & Reviews in April 2009. The brand found that shoppers who interact with reviews showed higher intent to purchase, conversion, and revenue per visitor than shoppers who did not interact with UGC.

Quova Case Studies

Quova's customer was one of the largest commercial airlines in the world serving approximately 67 million people annually with more than 2800 daily departures to both U.S. cities and 56 different countries.

With the airline's international customer base growing rapidly and it is domestic flights in key metro areas continuing to prosper, the marketing team launched an initiative to improve the performance of its 56 international web properties. In addition, the company wanted to begin promoting regional offers in specific U.S. metro areas.

Prior to implementing geolocation, each visitor to the airline's website, regardless of where they were logging in from, was taken to a landing page dictated by the language setting of the web browser. Although, at the time, this technique was advanced in relation to how most global companies today handle international website traffic, many visitors who failed to localize default browser settings were redirected to the wrong site. Visitors would then have to choose their country from the lengthy list of 56 countries and navigate to the correct site. Besides the high page abandonment rate this procedure caused, it also added additional steps to the sales cycle.

The airline's marketing team realized that improving the match between customers and countries would enable them to better serve new users, enhance the overall web experience for existing customers, and, hopefully, improve overall sales conversion rates. After much research, they opted to integrate IP geolocation data into their web applications to enable more accurate automatic redirects at the country level.

Besides identifying the country of a visitor, the airline's marketing team also wanted to be able to segment their web traffic down to a granular metro level. These identifications needed to be made the instant a visitor hit their web server. However, the team was concerned that serving multiple versions of pages might disrupt service or even slow down their web performance.

The airline tested data from several geolocation service providers and based their vendor selection on four criteria: the granularity of the data, the data's accuracy, the frequency of data updates, and the ease of integration. Quova scored the highest on all four accounts.

Quova was able to provide IP address location data down to a metro area (25–50 miles) and was the only geolocation provider to submit its network collection and accuracy methodology to an independent audit firm—PricewaterhouseCoopers. Their audit attested that Quova's data were 99.99% accurate at a country level. In addition, Quova updated its database of information on more than 1.8 billion IP addresses on a weekly basis, seeing a change rate of nearly 7% a month. The airline knew that vendors who provided only monthly or even less frequent updates would have stale data and cause them to perhaps make the wrong redirect.

Implementing Quova's data was a simple process of setting up an API from Quova's GeoPoint database to query the airline's web server, returning real-time information on the country and city of each IP address. For the airline, creating the inventory of localized content to support the geolocation capability took much longer.

When a query to Quova's GeoPoint database was made by a visitor to the airline's website, the location of that IP address was returned instantly. Based on the answer, the visitor was automatically redirected to the geographically relevant web page. The airline's website was localized for 56 countries and territories and was offered in six languages. With this capability, the airline began to see a significant increase in conversions leading to ticket sales from its international properties. Even a slight increase in conversions represented a major increase in revenue for the company.

The airline also began deploying geotargeted homepage banner ads with geographic offers in three metro areas in the United States—Cleveland, Houston, and New York. Based on location, a visitor saw either a generic landing page for the United States or a page with a localized promotional message. In just 6 months, the company saw a 200% increase in click-throughs of its localized banner ads. As a result, the company planned to roll out geographic offers to several additional cities and also initiated e-mail campaigns, with links leading readers to landing pages with geographically relevant offers.

BBC

BBC Worldwide is the United Kingdom's leading international TV channel operator and exporter of TV programs. Managing a total of seven operating businesses focused on publishing and selling content, the organization's aim is to deliver profits back to the BBC, supplementing the Corporation's license fee from U.K. citizens. During 2008, BBC Worldwide achieved sales of £916 million.

BBC Worldwide gained BBC Trust approval to introduce advertising to the international traffic to bbc.co.uk. The service, known as bbc.com, was launched and is visible only from outside the United Kingdom. The revenues allow BBC Worldwide to invest in the website and make bbc.com the showcase of the BBC's key brands and genres.

Developed by BBC Worldwide in conjunction with BBC Global News, the proposition taps into the vast audience that bbc.co.uk already attracts from outside the United Kingdom, reported by comScore stats at 29 million unique users. This equates to a total of 1.4 billion page impressions from outside the United Kingdom per month.

BBC.com faced two key challenges: fulfill contractual obligations to advertisers by ensuring that adverts are served to all non-U.K. visitors to the website and ensure license paying, U.K.-based users are shielded from all advertising. BBC Worldwide chose to implement IP (Internet Protocol) geolocation data from Quova to properly identify the location of its users.

"BBC.com is a popular site for news and related content, so as part of BBC Worldwide's drive to monetize non-UK traffic, we realised that we needed a solution to identify where visitors were coming from before we could reach out to advertisers," commented Jean-Louis Acafrao, Head of Technology, BBC.com, BBC Worldwide. "Quova technology has provided that solution." Quova delivers a detailed analysis including geographic and network characteristics for each IP address. BBC.com wanted to use these data to identify which country a user was accessing the website from and then act on this information accordingly.

Today when a user visits BBC.com, BBC's system instantly assesses their geographic location using the IP lookup data from Quova. If that user is deemed to be based outside the United Kingdom, access is granted and the agreed advertising is served. If that user is deemed to be within the United Kingdom, they will be automatically redirected to bbc.co.uk without being served any advertising. In this way, BBC.com delivers content only to customers within the predefined, contractually restricted geographic territories, monetizing all non-U.K. traffic and ultimately helping to drive advertising revenues through a CPM (cost per million) impressions model.

Importantly, license-paying U.K. citizens already contributing to BBC revenues via the license fee are shielded from advertising, benefiting from the familiar service previously enjoyed at bbc.co.uk.

Receiving over 1.4 billion page impressions per month, BBC.com reported a 99.96% country accuracy rate for visitors to the site. In addition, the organization initially logged a number of e-mail queries in relation to the advertising, with a high percentage of e-mails actually being received from British citizens abroad, unaware of the technology underlying the process of directing traffic and enquiring as to why they were being served adverts. In just over a month, these enquiries have already dropped to less than 10 per week, equivalent to under 0.001% of traffic.

Three advertisers launched with the BBC.com site. Luxury watch maker Hublot advertised on the news home page, British Airways within the news and sports pages targeting European users, while aircraft manufacturer Airbus chose the BBC.com landing page to target its international audience.

24/7 Real Media

24/7 Real Media, Inc. is the global leader in providing innovative digital marketing, powered by the industry's most advanced technology, to online agencies and publishers. 24/7 Real Media enables ad delivery across multiple mediums, including the web, wireless, and interactive television. Using its award winning ad serving, targeting, tracking and analytics platform, Open AdStream®, powerful search marketing technology, and global network of websites, the company has turned the art of reaching audiences across virtually any digital medium into a measurable science.

IP geolocation is one of many critical elements in 24/7 Real Media's business model. Geotargeting is built into the functionality of the Open AdStream ad management platform for publishers. The company also uses geotargeting to package media across its own network of websites and allows advertiser and agency clients to create custom geotargeting segments—packaging advertising for users in a specific geographic location, from an entire country down to a particular zip code, also powered by Open AdStream. All of these applications require highly accurate geolocation data.

24/7 Real Media was already providing geotargeted advertising to its customers using another geolocation vendor's data but was unconvinced of the accuracy and quality of the data provided. In the interest of maximizing the accuracy of its data while preserving the privacy of its users, 24/7 Real Media returned to the market in search of a new provider.

After an extensive vendor analysis and data testing process, 24/7 Real Media selected Quova. Quova's IP geolocation data provides the geographic location of any web visitor in real time—down to the metro-area level, if required—while protecting the privacy of the individual user. 24/7 Real Media partnered with Quova to integrate their data directly into its Open AdStream ad servers—Quova's IP geolocation data has enabled 24/7 Real Media to provide its customers with unsurpassed data quality, giving them a precise targeting tool that helps their advertisers reach their marketing and advertising goals. Customer feedback has been very positive and 24/7 Real Media has been delighted with the quality of Quova's data and its commitment to user privacy.

Procera Case Study

The Virginia Commonwealth University Rams are the surprising Cinderella team at this year's men's NCAA Basketball Tournament. From "play-in" win over USC, they have muscled through six-seeded Georgetown and three-seeded Purdue to the

Sweet Sixteen round. With all the buzz on campus, you can bet Internet traffic is through the roof. Is the extra streaming video and social media sapping the bandwidth from teaching and university business?

Before this school term, the VCU Technology Services department installed an appliance that has them as confident as the school's round ball team. They upgraded from a maxed-out traffic shaper to the PacketLogic Smart Campus solution from Procera. They are operating at 2 Gbps on their way to 10 Gbps. They can zoom down to know what a single user is doing, where they accessed the network and what device they are using. They also know in real time what load is crossing the link and have plenty of tools to make adjustments before congestion causes performance problems. And they will have 2 years of accurate history to recognize trends, report to other departments, and strategize infrastructure build-out.

Clickstream Technologies Case Studies

ClickSight was recently used in a study to determine how users interact with Adobe products. ClickSight was downloaded onto the PCs of opt-in Adobe customers, and data were collected for about a month. The data were compiled into metrics that showed Adobe the most and least used features, application switching behaviors, and possible problem areas within their applications. ClickStream showed Adobe which features were used widely, which features were used very little, as well as which applications were used together. ClickStream gave Adobe insight into which products should be marketed together, which features they needed to invest more resources in, and which features they needed to prioritize development on, based on Clickstream's feature usage data. ClickStream allowed Adobe to focus development on the right areas.

A leading player in the increasingly competitive search market asked ClickStream Technologies to improve its brand of search. ClickStream customized its ClickSight technology to collect data about the searches of the participants as well as other application activities they engaged in while searching.

ClickSight revealed participants were 15% less likely to remain in our client's application after performing a search, as compared with competing search applications. Combining these data with our research on concurrent application use, ClickStream Technologies advised the client how to design a more engaging product that integrated search with other application features. Follow-up research shows a 9% increase in participant usage plus customer reports of increased productivity and product satisfaction.

A large media delivery company kept losing business to its competitors. They approached Clickstream Technologies to discover why. We recruited hundreds of their users through an anonymous survey and conducted analysis of the usage results. Our study showed that although our client still retained a leading market share, it was losing ground to two specific competitors. Applying ClickSight technology, we identified and analyzed features in competing applications for comparative analysis and recommendations. We also integrated the usage data with demographic segmentation to better target new users.

Applying ClickStream's recommendations, a follow-up study showed that participants spent 32% more time using the new version of the application. On top of this boost in usage, by identifying the demographics of the target market, ClickStream helped our client increase sales by 21% within specific markets. The information and analysis provided by ClickStream Technologies catapulted a floundering technology into a competitive market position.

When the profits of one of the largest graphic software companies began to level off, ClickStream Technologies was asked to find strategies to make its software more compelling based on actual user interaction. After developing a custom pilot version of ClickSight that recorded all user activity and deep user interface actions, ClickStream launched a full-scale study revealing that two programs within our client's product bundle overlapped features by 35%. The data also revealed the extent of concurrent application use of our client's products and competing products. We also helped to identify the program's most and least used features.

As a result, the development time of the new version of our client's software decreased by 18% through test matrix efficiencies and new feature optimization, all based on actual customer use.

RapLeaf Case Study

An e-mail service provider (ESP) with a strong focus on marketing segmentation tools for small businesses, easily integrated Rapleaf's API into their software platform to provide real-time segmentation data to its users. Their users are typically small businesses that use e-mail marketing software to stay in touch with their own e-mail list on an ongoing basis.

One of the most frequently posed questions to ESP's from a potential client is, "I understand e-mail marketing, but I need more value than just an e-mail delivery from my marketing software. Can you help?" This company turned to Rapleaf to help build e-mail segmentation and insight tools and, consequently, add even more value to their product.

1. *ESP used Rapleaf to provide basic demographic data free*: Company offered age, gender, and location data for free on its customers' entire e-mail list via Rapleaf's API.
2. *ESP offered on demand premium data*: When querying Rapleaf for the free data, they were able to provide hit rates for premium data available on the customers' e-mail list, such as income, interests, etc.

3. *ESP's customers can access data instantly*: After seeing the value of segmentation, their customers can instantly upgrade to "Get Premium Data" for further insight on their list, unlocking the Premium values from Rapleaf.

4. *ESP's customers see success with e-mail segmentation*: Customers now have a rich data set including age, gender, location, and household demographics that can be used to segment lists and personalize their e-mail messaging.

The ESP grew 8.3% in new customer sign ups after 1 month by offering free segmentation data as an incentive. The ESP increased revenue per customer by 12% with the up sell of premium data. They also added a new, unique product feature that continued to service the marketers' needs.

TARGUSinfo Case Study

Charming Shoppes, Inc., a leading multichannel apparel retailer specializing in women's plus-size apparel, operates 2269 retail stores in 48 states under the names Lane Bryant, Fashion Bug, Fashion Bug Plus, and Catherine Plus Sizes. The chain captures contact information in its retail stores for remarketing and modeling, so the accuracy of its customer data has a deep impact on its bottom line. Charming Shoppes' Crosstown Traders also operates catalogs for apparel, accessories, footwear, and gifts, including the following titles: Old Pueblo Traders, Bedford Fair, Willow Ridge, Lew Magram, Brownstone Studio, Regalia, Intimate Appeal, Monterey Bay Clothing Company, Coward Shoe, and Figi's.

When match rates on mail-deliverable addresses gradually plunged 50% from previous totals, Charming Shoppes became alarmed. The company was unable to obtain 12,000–15,000 customer addresses each week because of incomplete data coverage. The cost in lost sales was multiplied exponentially. Charming Shoppes uses its customer addresses for a weekly direct mail list and sends out several hundred million pieces of direct mail per year.

Charming Shoppes sought a new data capture solution and was impressed by TARGUSinfo's client base, including prominent chain stores such as Domino's, Carter's, and Meineke. The solution had to reliably serve Charming Shoppes with the most accurate and current consumer data available. So Charming Shoppes chose the solution with the flexibility to fit its needs for data capture: TARGUSinfo On-Demand Identification for CRM & marketing.

"One of the things that we liked about TARGUSinfo over the other providers was that TARGUSinfo has a much more tailored process for picking up phone numbers," said Robert O'Connell, manager, CRM for Charming Shoppes. "We were able to choose the criteria for matching a customer's phone number to her address." With the potential for future sales tied to each customer's address,

Charming Shoppes needed data that were not only easy to implement but also comprehensively up to date. TARGUSinfo uses 90-plus sources that provide over 600 million records every month to verify its On-Demand Insight®. Charming Shoppes noticed the difference in currency from other solutions that relied too heavily upon White Page listings.

Charming Shoppes put just as much importance upon the precision and relevance of TARGUSinfo's On-Demand Insight. The solution provided information that was immediately actionable. "When TARGUSinfo did a review of what we sent to them, they gave us more insight into the type of phone numbers that we were collecting," O'Connell said. "They provided back to us what percent of the phone numbers were cell phone numbers, what percent of them were home land lines, what percent were businesses and so on."

Charming Shoppes chose TARGUSinfo over its incumbent consumer data provider as well as two other competitors. And with On-Demand Identification, Charming Shoppes found that part of its problem stemmed from a rising tendency of customers to give cell phone numbers, which currently have lower match rates than land lines. Charming Shoppes now has its salespeople ask, specifically, for home phone numbers. Charming Shoppes takes the phone numbers that it collects at the point of sale and matches them against its existing customer phone number database. New phone numbers get sent to TARGUSinfo, which appends names and addresses and returns the On-Demand Insight.

After it learned of the need to increase the percentage of home phones that it collected, Charming Shoppes saw its point-of-sale matches rebound past 40,000 customer addresses a week. The weekly decline of addresses was erased. "It's a pretty significant increase and it doesn't take a lot of math to figure out what impact that could have on the company," O'Connell said. Now direct mail campaigns can target an estimated 250,000 customers that Charming Shoppes was previously unable to identify each year. The chain can factor in a conservative estimate for its response rate and still expect to see a huge benefit.

"It's not unreasonable to say that we ought to be able to earn nearly $1 million in gross margin from those customers during the next year," O'Connell said.

Beyond that immediate payoff, TARGUSinfo will help with Charming Shoppes' planning as well as customer modeling. "We get a better profile of our customer," O'Connell said, "because the more transactions that we can match up to an individual customer, the better we can find out what she is buying, how often she visits us and what different departments she shops in. If we can match that transaction up to a customer, well then, we can aggregate everything for that customer."

Given Charming Shoppes' recent acquisition of Crosstown Traders, Inc. and its 11 catalog brands, the chain is poised to reap great benefits for the new accuracy in its customer database.

Quantcast Case Studies

Case Study One

At Virgin America, we have our sights set on reinventing air travel in the United States by offering innovative in-flight features such as on-demand meals, movies, and broadband. To do so, we need to go beyond typical analytic results from our digital advertising activities, such as click-through rates and conversions. We want deeper demographic and behavioral insight into the specific users who actively engage with our marketing messages and book online travel as a result, so that we make smarter digital marketing investments.

We placed Quantcast tags directly within the creative of our display campaigns, as well as our landing pages and conversion events, which gave us an in-depth demographic breakdown of the unique users who were both exposed to and clicking on our ads. Monitoring our online campaigns in near real time, Quantcast provided us with click-through metrics broken down by multiple demographic attributes such as age, income, education, and geography.

The Quantcast tags placed on our website revealed invaluable insights. We now understand our audience better than ever. Among other fascinating things, we learned a +500% difference in conversion rate by head-of-household education, a +200% difference in conversion rate by household income, and a +71% conversion rate by age.

Case Study Two

As one of the world's most recognizable luxury automotive brands, we are always looking for new ways to reach large numbers of in-market car buyers efficiently, something that is tough to do outside of search, retargeting, and endemic content. Typically, we purchase display advertising in relevant content areas or by utilizing a specific publisher's "behavioral targeting." While effective, these tactics do not always deliver the specific audiences we are trying to reach, and they do not scale across the web. What we needed was to drive prospective customers in a more efficient and scalable way.

Quantcast enabled us to understand our audience at each stage of consumer engagement. These data were used to analyze the various differences in consumers from vehicle to vehicle and at different points in the marketing funnel: visitors to the home page versus consumers configuring a specific vehicle. Quantcast Marketer insights were also broken out on a geographic level, allowing us to better plan for local and regional dealer initiatives. By leveraging Quantcast Lookalike targeting, we succeeded in driving a high volume of leads, while at the same time our cost-per declined—a win-win!

We strategically placed Quantcast's tags across all events we deemed KPIs: conversion areas, specific vehicle landing pages, and more. Once tags were live,

Quantcast allowed us to anonymously determine thousands of unique attributes about who our most valuable customers were and were not. We were then able to deliver our message to just those matching our audience profile across the media partners of our choice.

Case Study Three

With dozens of advertisers and billions of ads seen by consumers each month, the beauty category is one of the largest and most competitive in the online advertising world. As one of the segment's most sophisticated players, we wanted to enhance our proprietary ad and landing page. To grow our business, we need to expand our inventory presence beyond the portals, where our display campaigns have historically run. But performance on other destinations consistently disappoints. We needed Quantcast to give our extended display strategy a makeover.

We placed a Quantcast tag on a skin care product purchase confirmation page. From just a few thousand conversions, a Quantcast Lookalike model was generated to find millions more customers like the ones already converting on our site. To test performance, we started two campaigns targeting the same inventory via a premium ad network. One campaign used the network's standard optimization technology; the other was powered by a Quantcast Lookalike. Both campaigns used identical creative execution and the same set of ad units. Quantcast's Lookalike campaign delivered head-turning results with a click-to-conversion rate a stunning 300% above the control campaign.

Case Study Four

A leading national after-market auto parts retailer relies on digital advertising to attract new customers and drive online sales. Working with a variety of portals, ad networks, and behavioral targeting vendors, this marketer was disappointed with its online advertising initiatives. They had plenty of campaign clicks, but not enough conversions, and while retargeting was delivering great return on investment (ROI), it simply could not deliver the scale required to grow the business. Following a successful test, this marketer challenged Quantcast to power campaigns that would deliver high conversion rates, high conversion volumes, and media efficiency that could top its incumbent suppliers.

These Quantcast Lookalikes were based on converting customers who had completed an online purchase. The full conversion funnel was modeled so that the distinction between passersby and converting customers could be incorporated into the models—the aim being to find an audience that looks most like the people who actually purchase and only get clicks when they are likely to convert. Selecting the right objective for your campaign is critical. Select the wrong target, and you will find the wrong audience!

Case Study Five

As a major wireless phone company, we know there is no more aggressive environment than the online advertising, lead generation, and acquisition business. We compete with carriers and an extensive network of marketing companies for consumers' attention. On top of this, margins are tight, so we wanted to see if Quantcast could produce higher conversion rates versus our existing tactics. Our lead generation partner has a deep arsenal of ads that do a great job of getting users to click, but we need a conversion boost to make our purchase inventory translate into improved ROI and enhanced scale.

In a matter of days, we were able to build a Quantcast Lookalike model of our audience by using converting mobile customers. How? By piggybacking Quantcast on our existing ad serving code. Next we ran campaigns with two existing inventory partners, comparing the resulting conversion rates (lookalike vs. non-lookalike). Quantcast delivered a 76% increase in conversion rates above the marketer's optimized content-targeted campaign. Our lookalike data allowed our lead generation to achieve significantly higher conversion rates over content-targeted inventory purchased from the same inventory sources.

Case Study Six

The hotel travel space is highly competitive, and with profitable customer acquisition through paid search increasingly tapped out, travel marketers are exploring alternative tactics to expand their online bookings. This leading hotelier had experimented with both contextual and behavioral display advertising only to find that its cost per acquisition (CPA) goals resulted in limited ability to drive scale. The question: Could Quantcast Lookalikes drive an increase in profitable bookings at a scale that was meaningful to its business?

Online travel companies aggressively market to consumers, driving up costs for paid search and contextually targeted display ads—especially during peak travel seasons. High costs and limited media opportunities restrict the volume of profitable bookings that travel marketers can attain. In addition, these tactics tend to limit the opportunity to influence a broader set of consumers who may not utilize typical online travel media within their consideration process.

The marketer chose to Get Quantified™ and tagged its site with Quantcast tags. Within a few days, it gained deep insights into the demographic, interests, behaviors, and affinities of its customers. A Quantcast Lookalike audience was built by modeling consumers who had booked travel on the marketer's site. Quantcast then used this profile to deliver an expanded group of consumers who looked just like the marketer's converting audience—millions of potential new customers.

The marketer deployed Quantcast Lookalikes directly with premium publishers and across the real-time exchange inventory they secured. The portability of the Quantcast Lookalike audience segments ensured that delivery goals could be achieved within the desired short time frame, reaching the maximum number of consumers with a high affinity to the marketer's converting customers during the critical booking season.

Case Study Seven

We are one of the world's most recognizable consumer food brands. In our industry, marketers have traditionally had two choices: cast a wide net and accept the inefficiency of a broad target, or narrow the target for efficiency's sake, limit scale and miss large numbers of potentially interested consumers. In the very noisy online environment, measuring awareness for food products is tricky. Our challenge to Quantcast was to outperform other digital campaigns using a Quantcast Lookalike-powered campaign across a broader selection of content than simply endemic epicurean sites.

We placed Quantcast tags directly on the special recipe page we created to give consumers advice on different ways to prepare our products. Activities such as printing a recipe or downloading an in-store coupon indicated audience segments that were highly engaged. From these data, we were able to create a very successful Quantcast Lookalike model that turned 50,000 consumers into an audience of 25 million with the highest affinity for our campaign. The Quantcast Lookalike audience delivered click-through rates across all creative that were on average 97% higher than the content-targeted custom cooking channel.

Case Study Eight

As one of the world's largest credit card companies, we are constantly looking for new ways to identify qualified applicants who can make it through our rigorous approval process. We are not interested in simply attracting bulk applicants for our credit card products. What we need is to send qualified applicants information on the appropriate credit card for them. Can Quantcast help us scale our efforts and find us high-quality potential customers?

Credit card marketing is a multibillion-dollar annual business that is brutally competitive. Single percentage point changes in conversion rates represent huge gains or losses for each card product. Because of the high volume of traffic driven to our site, we use retargeting extensively, but retargeting offers limited scale needed to continually feed expansion of our qualified consumers.

Using Quantcast, we ran campaigns across multiple inventory sources, including VivaKi's Audience on Demand (AOD) networks and publishers. The creative was aligned for each card product, with a broad mix of retargeting, behavioral, content, and Quantcast Lookalike targeting utilized with AOD. All campaigns were run within the same flight dates, utilizing the same creative, geographic, and frequency cap controls. Quantcast helped us learn what makes our best customers unique across all of the cards we offer, and the Quantcast Lookalike model enabled us to find and reach just that audience at scale. We gained the insight, precision, and scale we were not able to achieve in the past.

A single point increase in approval rates represents millions of dollars in lifetime customer value. The across-the-board 45% increase delivered by the agency trading desk and Quantcast is transformational for us. We let Quantcast place secure tags throughout our application pages and enabled it to model the consumer groups who completed applications. Using an anonymous matching technique, we were able to subsequently notify Quantcast of approvals for each card product. Quantcast Lookalike audience segments were then created for each individual product based on approvals, not applications, which meant we had a very clear picture of our ideal customer.

BrightCove Case Study

With the rise of digital television, Channel 4 has introduced a range of additional TV channels including E4, More4, and Film4 and is continually growing its online activities and services such as channel4.com. In recent years Channel 4 has witnessed the tremendous growth of online video as a new means for viewers to consume content. As a result, Internet TV is providing a range of new methods for content providers to attract new audiences and ultimately build out new revenue streams. Channel 4 was quick to recognize the need to deliver a range of innovative new media services to engage with consumers and differentiate itself from its competitors, by promoting its lineup of linear TV channels and encourage adoption of the 4oD service.

Jen Topping, business manager, Online Video, Channel 4 New Media, was tasked with the roll out of Channel 4's new Internet TV platform and to deliver an online portal for channel4.com users to view, interact, and discuss short-form video for a richer visual experience. The decision to steer away from creating an in-house solution was due to cost, time constraints, and maintenance fees, which opened the door for a dedicated Internet TV platform provider to deliver its service.

Based on a formal RFP, Channel 4 selected Brightcove as its provider of choice to provide a short form video platform for all clips and online exclusive material on channel4.com, allowing the broadcaster to incorporate video content across most of its online properties (such as sister site e4.com). "Brightcove was selected for the key reason that its Internet TV platform came out absolutely and clearly on top of the competition," said Topping. "Brightcove had a clear idea of a broadcaster's needs, and also could demonstrate a proven track record with an impressive list of media clients including other broadcasters doing what we were trying to do."

According to Topping, Brightcove offered Channel 4 some essential features that tipped the balance with Brightcove continually investing in and upgrading its delivery technology. C4 could be confident that it could grow its Internet TV offerings organically to meet future online audience demands. Brightcove has a clear understanding of how media providers need to run their online businesses and as a result has built-in flexibility to its platform solution. Channel 4 could align its product roadmap for clips and online exclusive video material with Brightcove's to maximize ROI and introduce new efficiencies through technology integrations.

Channel 4 was looking to rollout its short form online video content as quickly as possible. Brightcove had the infrastructure, expertise, and knowledge to provide the platform much more quickly than an in-house effort could deliver and eliminated the need for a dedicated Channel 4 web development team. The platform solution allows insertion and tracking of advertising, as well as geoblocking on a case-by-case basis.

"In the last six months, our digital properties have seen a 21% increase in video views, compared with the same six months a year ago when we didn't have Brightcove," said Topping. "Deploying the Brightcove player platform has greatly improved the turnaround times needed to publish media to the internet and as such Channel 4 has seen a much faster throughput of its content. Brightcove's encoding tools are extremely reliable and the insertion of metadata is a simple and accurate process."

Rocket Fuel Case Studies

Belvedere Vodka

Determine the cost to generate a Facebook "Like" via display media run outside Facebook. Rocket Fuel built a custom model that predicted the baseline daily "Like" growth based on current "Like" level, trend, and seasonality information. The difference between predicted and actual "Like" count identified the effect of external display media impressions and clicks on "Like" growth. Successfully isolated the impact of display media on the growth of Facebook "Likes" and determined the cost to acquire a Facebook "Like" for Belvedere Vodka via display media.

Brooks®

Not just a shoe or apparel company, Brooks® Sports is a running company. The company conveys its spirit with the motto "Run Happy," a celebration of the essence that makes running the most addictive sport the world has ever known. Their objective was to drive top of mind awareness and engagement with target audience of "core runners"—leverage top-of-the-funnel metrics to increase online purchases through the Brooks website—and reach runners cost-effectively and at scale beyond the usual suspect digital media buys and remarketing tactics.

Brooks leveraged real-time surveys for in-flight Progressive Optimization to drive top of mind awareness and engagement among runners; along with Rocket Fuel Connect and their Real-Time Brand Optimization modules. The brand campaign hit every key audience metric and even drove enough direct sales to pay for it. They reached over 16 MM runners cost-effectively and at scale—drove over 93,000 unique website visits—sold more than 1000+ shoes from the Brooks Sports website and gained unique audience insights to leverage for future marketing efforts. Terms like "kids" and "PGA" had positive content association for this campaign's objectives. Terms such as "China" and "games" proved to have negative content association.

Ace Hardware

Ace Hardware is the largest retailer-owned cooperative and leader in the convenience segment of the hardware industry in terms of wholesale and retail sales and strength of the brand. Ace has 4600 stores in all 50 states and more than 60 countries. Horizon Media is their media services company. Their mission was to create the most meaningful brand connections within the lives of people everywhere. They wanted to find a media partner who could reach "New Movers" with high audience volume and drive top of mind awareness and engagement with a target audience that are adults of age 25–54, who will move in the next 90 days or who have moved in the past 90 days. Rocket leveraged real-time surveys for in-flight progressive optimization to maximize audience volume and delivered "New Mover" audience with a 13.7× over index (Figure 4.7).

Figure 4.7   List of Rocket Fuel clients.

Lord & Taylor

Since 1826, Lord & Taylor has built a reputation for service, for quality, and, most of all, for style. By creating a unique mix of the latest trends and the timeless classics, they have become the favorite store of generations of shoppers. Their agency Morpheus Media, NY, is a full-service provider of interactive marketing solutions to Fortune 500 companies and those aspiring to land on that list. They wanted to find technology-driven media partner to help boost women's fashion sales by building a custom fashion segment tailored to specific campaign objectives. Rocket delivered ROI that was 3.6 times greater than the client's goal while reducing effective CPA by 73%. The agency and client wanted to boost online sales for fashion apparel and accessories by driving traffic to their branded online store, with an aggressive ROI goal to boost online sales among their target demographic, which is women 30+ in the Northeast region, via display media with suggested targeting criteria.

Admeld Case Studies

Pandora

Pandora, the popular online music discovery service, leveraged Admeld's capabilities to generate a 95% increase in the publisher's yield from unsold inventory in one quarter. Pandora approached Admeld seeking to maximize the value of their online and mobile ad inventories and looking to decrease the operational drain's they were experiencing due to the lack of an automated solution.

After consulting with Pandora about their business rules and block lists, Admeld configured Pandora to start using real-time bidding (RTB), which efficiently selects the most lucrative mix of ads across a variety of demand sources. Admeld's client service team closely monitored the ad quality, worked with Pandora to create custom performance reports, and handled all related billing and reconciliation. Pandora experienced a 95% increase in yield from their discretionary ad inventory. The company has since seen significant reduction in operational costs, as they have been able to focus on their core business, the direct sales channel.

IDG's TechNetwork

IDG's TechNetwork partnered with Admeld to create a private exchange in which they could aggregate their high-end inventory in an exclusive, biddable marketplace called The Tech Media Exchange (TMX). With publishing brands such as Macworld and PC World, International Data Group (IDG) is one of the world's leaders in technology content. IDG's TechNetwork aggregates premium audiences across more than 460 high-quality, independent sites spanning business technology, consumer technology, and digital entertainment worldwide. In order to drive higher revenues and attract additional sites to its network, IDG sought to create a private ad exchange over which they had complete control.

Launched in January 2011, IDG's TMX was the industry's first private exchange for the technology content vertical. Based on technology from Admeld's core platform, TMX gives IDG the ability to demand highest possible rates and, in turn, provides marketers access to a premium tech-focused audience through an RTB environment. The exchange was launched with more than 500 select websites and is currently accessible to a select group of demand-side platforms (DSPs) and agency trading desks on an invitation-only basis. TMX had proven to be a win-win situation for both buyer and seller. IDG commands a significantly higher dollar amount for their properties, and the buy side only accesses to top-quality, highly targeted inventory.

Forward Health

Forward Health, a premium provider of original content and health information, implemented RTB through Admeld, generating a revenue increase of 700%. Forward Health approached Admeld in July 2010 looking to increase revenues by further monetizing their unsold inventory for each of their five properties:

1. womenshealthbase.com
2. menshealthbase.com
3. pregnancygirl.com
4. all-allergies.com
5. goodcholesterolcount.com

Previously, the publisher had focused on direct sales and they realized there was an opportunity to make additional revenue by optimizing their secondary channel. Brand protection and quality control were critical requirements for Forward Health as their clients consist of top-tier pharmaceutical and medical companies whose corporate integrity is at stake.

Admeld recommended running RTB to reach Forward Health's eCPM goals. RTB provided increased visibility into advertisers coming through their unsold inventory and gave them control over the rates paid by those advertisers. Forward Health also included traditional ad network tags to compete for additional impressions. Forward Health immediately saw a spike revenue from their unsold inventory. Revenue from this channel increased 700% for Forward Health over a 6 month period.

adBrite Case Study

Pogo wanted to drive qualified registrations to their free online game service. They also wanted to learn which games delivered the best response rates to engage users in a seamless way. adBrite's reach of 70,000 sites, completely transparent network, and variety of ad formats led Pogo to choose adBrite. Pogo wanted to create brand awareness in the gaming industry and to better identify their ideal target demographic for their flash-based online games by targeting Cost-Per-SignUp in their promotional landing page.

adBrite's conversion rates consistently outperformed target CPA by nearly 50%. Within 1 month of using adBrite Ad Optimizer, Pogo's average CPA improved by 35% and was implemented to automatically scale on the best-performing site ad bids on social networking and gaming sites.

Datran Media Case Studies

ChaCha

ChaCha the online publisher leveraged Aperture measurement to provide a key advertising partner with greater, more effective target audience reach. The result? Greater sales for ChaCha and a 400% ROI for its advertising partner!

PGA

Looking to liven up the inbox for millions of avid golf fans, PGATOUR.com leveraged Datran Media to deliver e-mails with live streaming e-mail embedded within the message. This video not only helped increase click-through rates by 20%, but it was also awarded DPAC's best e-mail marketing campaign of 2009.

Sony

Datran Media's strategic and analytic services team engaged with Sony to analyze their messaging programs and develop strategies to drive program growth and increased customer lifetime value. Awarded the MarektingSherpa Gold award for best automated e-mail series, this campaign drove significant incremental engagement with their web properties for the audience segments who received it when compared to a control population.

eHarmony

Datran Media and eHarmony decided to put their campaigns to the test and measure them against Dynamic Logic's brand favorability methodology. The study measured the effectiveness of an e-mail acquisition campaign at increasing brand metrics and attributes. An AdIndex control-exposed methodology conducted via e-mail was employed. The study details these findings with results highlighting how many percentage points e-mail lifted key branding metrics including awareness and brand favorability.

NASCAR

NASCAR.com launched an e-mail campaign using Datran Media's StormPost e-mail automation solution to promote its new subscription-based audio service. Through the power of e-mail and the expertise of Datran Media's hardworking pit crew, NASCAR.com finished the campaign in first place, seeing a 72% increase in subscriptions.

BabytoBee

BabytoBee, a one stop shop for expectant parents to fulfill all their baby needs, primarily used off-line direct marketing and telemarketing to drive revenue. Understanding that the addition of e-mail direct marketing to the infant-care brand's direct strategy could greatly increase sales, BabytoBee partnered with Datran Media to provide a comprehensive customer management solution to meet its e-mail marketing needs. Ultimately, Datran Media helped BabytoBee increase subscriptions, clicks, and conversions.

NetMining Case Studies

Case Study One

A top auto insurance provider wanted to increase online policy sales by engaging prospective customers who may have initiated the registration process but failed to complete it. The provider utilized Netmining's ad network alongside several competitors for a broad remarketing campaign. Our proprietary audience targeting engine developed sophisticated audience profiles that included data such as product interest, propensity to buy, and monetary value for each site visitor. This allowed us to deliver a highly efficient ad campaign that reached only the most qualified customers with ad messaging targeted to their specific needs. By reengaging these lost customers, Netmining's ad network performed 24% better than competing ad networks and the customers targeted were 45% more qualified than those of the closest competitor, based on the percentage of users who purchased a policy after requesting a quote.

Case Study Two

A world-famous American apparel brand wanted to boost sales by engaging prospective customers who demonstrated high interest in specific product categories but failed to convert after visiting the retailer's website. The retailer launched a remarketing campaign across the Netmining ad network to recapture lost conversions. Netmining's proprietary audience profiling engine was used to create a sophisticated visitor database for the brand, enabling us to deliver ads that were dynamically tailored to each of their website visitors' current product interests. These ads were both highly relevant and timely, and were served across the Netmining ad network to visitors at the moment when they had the highest propensity to convert. In targeting those customers with the highest interest in the retailer's products at the best moment, Netmining's ad network outperformed competing ad networks by 83% on average and performed 70% more effectively than the next closest ad network, based on pure conversion to impression ratio.

interclick Case Studies

Case Study One

A leading car manufacturer wanted to target auto intenders to promote its new models and summer sales events. It put interclick in the driver's seat with a mission: design an efficient campaign that would drive traffic to its website and generate buyer leads.

Using our audience targeting platform, Open Segment Manager (OSM), interclick developed a 2 month strategy to help the manufacturer reach its target audience and drive leads. We implemented third-party behavioral data for the client's brand and car models to target their most likely customers. Competitors' make and level data were also applied to entice ambivalent consumers and gain market share. We placed a retargeting pixel on the client's website to reconnect the auto brand with its most responsive audiences.

interclick's innovative data-driven strategy delivered remarkable results for the leading car manufacturer. Our operations team constantly optimized the campaign to ensure the best-performing data were used. As a result, interclick dipped the client's overall KPI of $3.36 by 67%. We surpassed their CTR goal by 120% as well. Our proven ability to flawlessly execute campaigns earned interclick the incremental budget to connect the car brand with its most responsive audiences.

Case Study Two

America's leading fruit juice brand had been experiencing a decline in consumption due to consumer concerns about nutritional value and price point. To reverse this trend, the brand teamed with interclick to design a campaign connecting them with consumers at all stages of the purchase funnel. Goals included raising awareness, driving traffic to the juice producer's website, and promoting a rewards program aimed at enticing people to purchase their juice.

Leveraging our audience targeting platform, OSM, interclick crafted a 1 month campaign combining DataLogix frequent-buyer data to target consumers by lifestyle, including soccer moms, suburban families, affluent baby boomers, and healthy living enthusiasts. We also used demographic for data targeting adults 25–54 and mature adults 55+ to reach nonbuyers and gain market share. We used a channel site list to connect with targeted consumers at their passion points—a retargeting pixel on the juice brand's website to reconnect with hand raisers (consumers who showed interest).

By combining sophisticated statistical treatments with media execution, interclick proved to be a valuable partner for the fruit juice producer. Our combination of custom audience targeting and channel site lists yielded a skyrocketing visitation rate, driving an 820% increase in unique visitors to the client's website among the core target audience (comScore Media Metrix, July 2010).

Case Study Three

With fantasy baseball growing tremendously in recent years, America's leading fantasy sports platform wanted to reach existing users and gain share from competitors for the upcoming MLB season. It teamed with interclick to design a premium advertising experience that would generate new registrations and reengage current users.

interclick developed a comprehensive 1 month campaign leading up to baseball season, using our audience targeting platform, OSM. We leveraged a combination of behavioral targeting and custom channels to help the fantasy sports platform reach its most likely customers. We implemented custom channels focused on both news and sports to connect with the client's target audience of men 18!49. We utilized behavioral targeting data to connect with baseball fans across the web. Our operations teams applied proprietary optimization algorithms to ensure the client's goals were met and exceeded.

Our innovative, data-driven advertising solutions delivered remarkable results for the client. interclick dipped the target CPA of $6 to an overall CPA of $5.88. We also produced a high rate of visitation, driving a 142% increase in unique visitors to the client's website among men 18!49, month over month (comScore Media Metrix, August 2010). Our performance and consistency led the fantasy sports platform to continue to rely on interclick to boost their fan base recruitment.

Case Study Four

With the World Cup kicking off, a leading fast food restaurant chain teamed with interclick to raise awareness among both World Cup fans and consumers interested in the quadrennial event. The chain required an efficient campaign that would align the event with in-store promotions, leveraging excitement around the matches. As an incentive, consumers were given game pieces after each purchase to use in a web-based online shootout game to win prizes.

interclick implemented a 1 month strategy during the World Cup, using our audience targeting platform, OSM. We applied two data segments to target World Cup Fanatics, comprised of users who visited niche sites and checked World Cup stats daily. World Cup Discoverers comprised of users who searched World Cup sites to learn about the event's history, teams, players, rules, and regulations.

interclick's ability to combine limitless amounts of data and inventory delivered remarkable results for this restaurant chain. As a result of proper advance planning and building the right audience, we exceeded the client's CTR goal by 80%. interclick was considered the top performer for the client's World Cup campaign.

Case Study Five

With the launch of a brand-new smartphone in the crowded mobile category, a leading technology company teamed with interclick to raise awareness, increase consideration, and drive sales skyward. interclick designed a campaign to promote the capabilities of the new device, targeting early adopters looking for a smartphone that was ideal for both work and play.

interclick implemented a 7 month strategy to connect with techy consumers in-market for a new smartphone. Utilizing our audience targeting platform, OSM, we found the tech company's ideal audience by implementing search retargeting data to connect with in-market smartphone shoppers, from coast to coast and beyond by placing a retargeting pixel on the client's website, targeting users visiting the site.

interclick's ability to combine sophisticated statistical treatments with media execution delivered astounding results for the client. We proved to be one of the top performers for this campaign by producing an $8.75 eCPA, surpassing the extremely aggressive $9 eCPA goal. As a result, interclick will be part of the media plan for the product launch later this year.

Case Study Six

A leading consumer appliance manufacturer wanted to raise awareness and drive sales of its Energy Star® products during the month of April. The month-long national campaign strived to connect with the most elusive consumer: moms 25!54 looking for high-quality products they can trust at good value. To entice moms to seek out more information about energy-saving products, the manufacturer partnered with interclick, hoping to reach these consumers at every stage of the purchase cycle.

Leveraging our audience targeting platform, OSM, interclick modeled the manufacturer's target consumer at various stages of the purchase cycle, utilizing a combination of demographic, psychographic, brand affinity, in-market, and behavioral data. To raise awareness among modeled consumers, interclick created a custom channel aligning the manufacturer's brand with content related to Home & Garden, Home Improvement, Green, and DIY. interclick implemented targeted data to connect with moms actively researching new home appliances. To continue the conversation with the most valuable prospects and encourage them to return to the manufacturer's website, interclick implemented a remessaging solution merged with targeted data.

The home appliance manufacturer's strategic partnership with interclick was a major success in connecting with moms and driving user engagement. interclick exceeded the client's expectations, surpassing CTR goals by 61% and outperforming all other partners on the media plan. In addition, the campaign drove almost 300,000 unique visitors (comScore Media Metrix, June 2010) to the client's site, a 29% increase compared to March. Crucial to the success was the employment of targeted data, which doubled performance. This campaign is a great example of how proper modeling of data and inventory can reach the most valuable audiences.

Case Study Seven

With holiday shopping starting earlier each year, a leading sportswear manufacturer wanted to connect with outdoor enthusiasts at each stage of the purchase cycle. It teamed with interclick to drive traffic to its new website, increase sales, and position its brand as the best way to experience the great outdoors.

interclick developed a 4 month strategy to build momentum in preparation for holiday shopping, utilizing our audience targeting platform, OSM. We implemented a custom site list to align the sportswear brand with outdoor, active lifestyle, sports, and travel content. We designed custom behavioral targeting segments for outdoor enthusiasts and outdoor products to follow consumers' passion points. Finally, we placed a retargeting pixel on the client's landing page to reconnect the sportswear brand with its most responsive audiences across the web.

The campaign enabled the sportswear brand to engage with outdoor enthusiasts, driving up its site visitation rate by 150% among unique visitors quarter over quarter (comScore Media Metrix, July 2010). In addition, interclick delivered clear results and maximized the ROI for the brand, which dropped other media partners and continues to work with interclick.

Case Study Eight

To reach consumers planning their summer vacation, a leading national transportation company wanted to promote its travel and vacation packages among West Coast residents. As an incentive to drive trial, it implemented a sweepstakes geared toward budget conscious travelers 35+. interclick teamed up with the company to generate leads and contest entries.

interclick developed a 2 month geo-targeted strategy to reach the company's most responsive audiences, utilizing our audience targeting platform, OSM. We implemented a custom site list targeting West Coast travelers to raise awareness about the new offerings. Demographic and lifestyle data were overlaid to reach the transportation company's likeliest potential customers.

interclick's ability to combine limitless amounts of data sources allowed the client to efficiently connect with its target audience. To ensure top performance, we optimized the campaign against hand raisers, dipping the $10 overall eCPA goal by 70%. In addition, interclick surpassed all of our competitors in sweepstakes entries and opt-ins. This campaign's great results motivated the transportation company to increase its media budget with interclick by 50%.

Case Study Nine

A leading luxury car manufacturer wanted to target wealthy adults consumer looking for a stylish convertible. Given the fragmented media environment, the company needed a data strategy to identify and target the most responsive audiences. It selected interclick based on our capability to understand and interpret the intricacy of very complex data sets. interclick designed a 2 month, high-impact campaign to drive lead requests for style-seeking convertible shoppers.

Leveraging our audience targeting platform, OSM, interclick developed a comprehensive data targeting strategy to drive conversions by helping the company reach audiences across all levels of the purchase funnel. interclick implemented the client's model-level data from its own historical database and purchased additional third-party data sets to target loyal consumers. We developed a data strategy targeting ambivalent consumers considering competitors' convertibles. Simultaneously, we applied class-level data targeting additional consumers in the market for convertibles. Lastly, interclick did site retargeting of hand raisers.

interclick's ability to combine limitless amounts of data types and sources connected the car manufacturer with the most receptive audiences across all levels of brand commitment. Within each audience segment, interclick optimized the campaign to ensure top performance, dipping the overall $600 KPD goal by 45% and saving the car manufacturer $332.69 per lead. In addition, interclick plunged the retargeting KPD goal of $100–$81.39. Based on the campaign's great results, the luxury car manufacturer now partners solely with interclick to connect efficiently with audiences for greatest marketing impact.

AudienceScience Case Studies

Automotive

A national automotive company's primary objective was to increase conversions, improve campaign performance and decrease their eCPA. Utilizing AudienceScience® Gateway for Advertisers, the automotive company was able to reduce eCPA from an average rate of $291 in May 2010 to $0.66 in September 2010.

A leading northwest high-end auto franchise wanted to drive traffic to their site to increase online leads. AudienceScience delivered banner ads to prospects that previously visited the website and then surfed to another site on the AudienceScience Targeting Marketplace™. Users were 20 times more likely to click on the targeted ads.

Consumer Products

The client's goals were to drive demand for the new pen, improve brand awareness, and gain maximum exposure during the new product launch. The campaign not only drove traffic to the website but also increased sales. In fact, over just a 2 month period, the client received an ROI of over 264%. Additionally, in 3 months AudienceScience delivered 22% of all click-through traffic, which accounted for 70% of all online sales from display advertising, proving that behavioral targeting helps drive audiences who not only have an interest but also intent to purchase.

Entertainment

MediaForce, the media representation business specializing in local and regional news and community media, was keen to identify new opportunities to grow revenue from existing advertisers as well as attract new prospects. Audience Syndication allowed them immediately to extend and enhance their current offering to advertisers by delivering more precise audience segments alongside the broader high-reach segments they already had available.

Finance

Financial Times' FT.com employed audience targeting in an online campaign for NTT DoCoMo, with positive results. The audience targeting portion of the campaign generated significantly better results than run-of-site ads. Awareness increased as much as 193% in behaviorally targeted audiences compared to run-of-site audiences and positive brand perceptions as much as 83%.

Manufacturing

An international oil manufacturer used audience targeting on Guardian.co.uk to help educate consumers about how to reduce CO_2 emissions. Not only was audience targeting advertising found to be more effective than run of site at reaching citizens who are "very concerned" about the impact of vehicle CO_2 transmissions on the environment, but conversions were much higher as well.

Pharmaceutical

The client wanted to drive traffic and increase registration for their $20 rebate coupon and their "find a doctor" website function. AudienceScience drove significant improvements in impression volume and increased actions taken by targeted users. The campaign delivered a cost per sign up that was 83% lower than the previous campaign average.

Retail

SKECHERS, a global retailer of award-winning lifestyle footwear for men, women, and children, sought to maximize return on its advertising spend for its retail website by specifically targeting lost conversions. SKECHERS saw compelling results from its audience targeting campaign with AudienceScience. Their return on ad spend was 827% over the course of the campaign.

An industry leading home furnishing retailer gains new audience intelligence leveraging AudienceScience Gateway and receives exceptional ROI benefits. Throughout the 16 week campaign, total ROI, in terms of total media cost over total revenue generated, improved by 160%! Also, the custom audience segments created with Audience Gateway for Advertisers outperformed standard site retargeting for the life of the campaign by 185%.

A leading interactive advertising agency looked to implement an advertising program that would increase a nationwide bridal retailer's conversion rate and drive visitors back to the site, creating a second chance for sales. In the month of February 2007, retargeting delivered more than 40,000 people back to the retailer's site and achieved an astounding conversion rate of 15% with a 1 day conversion rate high of 33%.

Discovery Communications, the world's number one nonfiction media company, sought to drive consumers to the product landing page to learn more about the appliances and build brand affinity. According to a brand study conducted by Vizu, the overall campaign performance experienced an 11.1% brand lift by working with AudienceScience to develop a comprehensive media campaign focusing on content placements across key Discovery home-related media, as well as audience targeted segments such as Home and Garden Enthusiasts, Shoppers, and Home Owners.

PubMatic Case Studies

In order for large publishers to truly maximize their ad revenue made from ad networks and exchanges, optimization is needed. PubMatic has real-time algorithms that decide, on the fly, which ad network or ad exchange can best monetize each impression. Publishers using Real Time Optimization consistently see higher ad pricing as compared to manual ad operations solutions, whether in house or outsourced (Figure 4.8).

Turn Case Studies

Automotive

To raise awareness for various vehicle lines, a major automotive brand tapped the Turn Media Platform for a series of incremental branding campaigns that focused on specific types of vehicles and promotions. To drive awareness for specific vehicles and promotions, the automotive brand leveraged real-time strategies using a mix of remarketing, behavioral targeting, and run of network (RON).

Figure 4.8 PubMatic increases eCPM for publishers.

Turn drove the campaign strategies through its Turn Media Platform to identify KPI to remarket to consumers, retargeted to individuals that clicked on an ad served through behavioral targeting and/or visited brand homepages or landing pages, and leveraged third-party data sources. With Turn's breakthrough technology, the automotive brand successfully achieved their eCPA performance goal and successfully achieved top performing tactics, including remarketing and KPI conversions.

Retail

A major women's fashion retailer was on a mission to increase new customer acquisitions and reach beyond its remarketing audience. Using the Turn Platform's algorithmic intelligence, the fashion advertiser expanded its target group of relevant audiences and reached new customers across the web. The challenge was to identifying new audiences with like behavior and produce effectively driving awareness.

The Turn strategy was to find new customers and the optimal audience for the fashion retailer through Turn's predictive algorithms and data partnerships. Turn identified two high-performance segments: corporate women with high net worth and retail focus on women's fashion and accessories. Turn used look-alike modeling to scale segment and tested multiple audience segments; it utilized predictive targeting to increase reach. Turn was able to exceed CPA goal by 100% and increase client spending by 113%.

Telecommunications

RTB and audience targeting provides new opportunities for advertisers and publishers but is still a relatively new method for media buying and targeting. To show the capabilities afforded by RTB, Turn launched head-to-head test that compared RTB versus non-RTB performance for a major telecommunication advertiser.

Turn's customer, a prominent telecommunications provider whose campaign employs geotargeting across 14 Western states including Arizona, Colorado, Idaho, Iowa, Minnesota, Montana, Nebraska, New Mexico, North Dakota, Oregon, South Dakota, Utah, Washington, and Wyoming, demonstrated significant lift in RTB inventory and audience targeting. The campaign goal is the successful launch and rebranding of the brand's flagship high-speed Internet service with a focus of driving efficient transactions. The emphasis was on new customer acquisition for high-speed Internet but also included a strong up-sell incentive to existing subscribers to bundle existing packages. The campaign goal is based on cost per transaction.

Red Aril Case Study

Red Aril, a leading Data Management and Audience Optimization Platform (DMP), and Catalyst S+F, a leading strategic marketing firm, today announce the results of a pivotal study on the affects of using DMP-enhanced media solutions. In the first phase of a broader performance-validation study, Catalyst S+F and Red Aril worked together to deliver three times the ad campaign performance of non-DMP-enhanced media solutions. The study's first phase comprised a month-long, 6 million-impression campaign designed to validate the advantage of using Red Aril's DMP against non-DMP-enhanced media solutions. Catalyst ran the campaign on behalf of its client, the University of San Francisco (USF), to engage applicants for three master's degree programs.

The challenge was to target ads to an audience with the right qualities: ambitious people under 35 who are interested in continuing education to boost their careers. The ability to match ads with the right audience improves campaign's relevance and response rates. It also lowers the cost of buying media to drive a desired action, which, in this case, was engagement with the master's degree program content on USFCA.edu.

To help the ads reach the right audience, Red Aril's DMP employed a unique method of leveraging USFCA.edu visitor data (first-party data) and combining data from outside vendors (third-party data). The DMP then used predictive modeling to build target profiles derived from the first- and third-party data. For instance, information technology professionals who recently shopped for high-end cars were identified as one good audience profile.

Red Aril's DMP distributed the profiles to standard media buying solutions, also known as DSP, which automated the process of buying media on ad exchanges and ad networks. When visitors clicked on the ads and visited the USF website, their onsite activity looped back into the Red Aril DMP, enabling Red Aril to optimize the audience targeting in real time.

The results from January 10, 2011, to February 10, 2011, were as follows:

	Geotargeting	*Social Site*	*Mobile/Geo*	*Red Aril*
Cost per action[a]	$22.46	$19.53	$11.49	$6.43

[a] In this phase, a single action included all of the following steps: clicking the ad, loading the landing page, and clicking through to additional content.

The Red Aril DMP not only provided the lowest cost per action, but its predictive modeling enabled the campaign to scale and reach campaign goals.

DataXu Case Studies

Education

Leader in education space wanted to generate online leads while driving scale in media spend. DataXu used a combination of audience targeting and dynamic decision making to find the most responsive audience for the best price. DataXu platform beat CPA goal by over 100%. Agency said DataXu was "by far the best performing partner on the plan."

Travel

Direct response client, with highly competitive campaign, seeks more cost-effective leads. DataXu was run under a standard setup. Platform found performance that align with business people trip planning. DataXu delivered campaign, with scale in lead volume, while beating average CPA by 214%.

Financial

A major regional bank looking to acquire new checking accounts online and expand its customer base turned to DataXu to run an optimization campaign on its DMA-targeted geographic area. After a test, DataXu delivered the best performance among other DSPs and ad networks.

Triggit Case Study

Triggit was selected by Amazon.com to serve as a DSP for Amazon's digital display advertising. Triggit will provide Amazon with its sophisticated RTB software to enable Amazon to show the right ads to the right users across nine ad exchanges and more than 4 million websites. The company's other clients include Kodak, Mazda, and Orbitz.

BlueKai Case Studies

Automotive

The goal was to increase the scale and targeting precision of a major auto manufacturer online campaign. As a data buyer, interCLICK supplemented its own vertical market data with BlueKai in-market auto data to identify an audience of auto prospects who displayed intent to purchase a specific type of car from its client's and competitors' brands. The BlueKai data returned a response rate 200%–300% greater than ordinarily achieved with traditional contextual or demographic targeting. BlueKai data were the most effective data source interCLICK tested for this campaign. With BlueKai data, interCLICK assembled a qualified in-market auto audience of more than 3.1 million impressions in less than 1 month.

Travel

BlueKai and AdReady created campaigns for travel clients to identify and target true in-market travel prospects who have shown purchase intent by searching on top Over-the-Airs (OTAs) or travel meta search sites. Using the data from these searches, users were qualified to be deep in the purchase funnel for a particular type of travel and are targeted with timely and relevant marketing creative across ad inventory secured by AdReady on behalf of its clients. On average, these campaigns hit their booking goals while reducing overall CPA costs by an average of more than 40%. Performance exceeded straight geo-targeted buys as well as other behavioral targeting segments without compromising campaign scale. For one campaign, the top three segments generated over 4 million impressions across multiple ad networks.

Appliances

In order to raise brand awareness and drive sales for a leading consumer appliance manufacturer of Energy Star products turned to BlueKai. Using its Segment Manager, interCLICK modeled the marketer's target consumers at the various stages of the purchase cycle. They utilized a combination of demographic, psychographic, and brand affinity (only in-market and behavioral data), all acquired through the BlueKai platform. interCLICK surpassed the client's CTR goals by 61% and outperformed all other partners on the media plan. In addition, the campaign drove almost 300,000 unique visitors to the client's site, a 29% increase compared to the prior month. Crucial to this success was BlueKai's targeted data, which doubled performance.

Xplusone Case Study

CCP Games, developer and publisher of EVE Online, a science fiction-based multiplayer online game (MMOG). CCP sought to attract hardcore MMOG gamers, which it knew from experience were typically 20-somethings with higher income and education levels than the average online player.

CCP turned to [x + 1], the leader in predictive marketing with patented technology that utilizes real-time decision making to improve the scale and efficiency of online marketing. CCP began with a 1 month trial of [x + 1]'s *Media+1*, which creates dynamic custom ad networks by aggregating targeted web pages. *Media+1* is supported by [x + 1]'s patented Predictive Optimization Engine, POE™, which leverages sophisticated mathematical models to make optimal segmentation and targeting in external media campaigns.

The results from the trial were impressive, with *Media+1* delivering great CPA performance at scale. CCP decided to go a step further, using [x + 1]'s *Site+1* to optimize eveonline.com. *Site+1* analyzed hundreds of variables to dynamically generate web pages with the most relevant offers for each visitor.

Placecast Case Studies

Some of the brands that have been using Placecast's ShopAlerts to connect with customers to increase traffic and sales via their mobile devices are as follows:

The North Face

Summit Signals, The North Face's location-based messaging program, enables fans of the brand to stay connected about the latest gear, local events, sponsored sports events, and tips for outdoor activities.

White House Black Market

Fashion Alerts, the location-based mobile program from White House Black Market, offers the brand's customers exclusive offers and promotions as well as the insider scoop on new product arrivals and VIP store events.

SONIC

SONIC Drive-In customers participated in the restaurant's Sonic Signals programs and received special promotions and offers when they were in geo-fences created around SONIC restaurants in the Atlanta area.

O_2

Placecast's collaboration with O_2, the second-largest mobile operator in the United Kingdom, enables ShopAlerts to be utilized directly by the carrier for more than 20 brands and advertisers and more than 1 million opted-in subscribers.

TellMe Case Studies

Financial

A global financial services company needed to improve phone channel quality to achieve a business goal: providing extraordinary customer service. Legacy touch-tone systems created an undifferentiated caller experience on hundreds of millions of calls per year, forcing callers to make multiple calls to the system in order to access different applications. The company set a goal to increase utilization of self-service functionality and simultaneously reduce call durations in phone self-service.

Tellme proposed an application solution that optimized the balance between cost containment (automation) and caller satisfaction. The resulting solution created one-stop access to all accounts and applications. The implementation consolidated more than 15 DTMF applications to Tellme's on-demand platform. In doing so, they achieved carrier-grade reliability while reducing capital and maintenance expenditures. Working together with the client, Tellme built a roadmap for future enhancements to drive personalization, integration of brand assets, and cross-channel convergence with the web.

First and foremost, callers have reported a dramatic increase in the quality of their self-service. With the Tellme solution, a single call provides access to all the financial service's applications, enabled by a streamlined authentication procedure providing faster, secure access to their data. This solution resulted in significant automation rate improvements of 4% points and a parallel decrease in IVR and agent talk time, especially for the highest volume applications. Through the improved caller experience, the elimination of legacy infrastructure, more accurate routing, and a unified, more stable platform, this top services brand has realized over $10 million in savings annually to the business.

Banking

A well-known bank needed to align its IVR with the business strategy to maximize "share of wallet" (checking, credit card, mortgage, etc.). The legacy IVR had a different customer service phone number for each type of account, with varying caller experiences for each phone number. These were powered by multiple legacy touch-tone systems. With hundreds of millions of calls per year, the bank was missing out on a huge cross-selling opportunity.

Tellme's voice portal solution promised to transform the caller experience into a voice-driven, single-phone-call view of a customer's entire relationship with the bank. Tellme performed significant restructuring of the applications, creating a cross-account framework with task completion modules.

The solution leveraged dynamic personalization features on the Tellme platform to make the application more proactive. For example, the application delivers frequently requested account information immediately after authentication, without requiring the caller to navigate menus. The entire call showcases superior audio through patented concatenated speech algorithms. To encourage cross-selling for the bank's business goals, the Tellme Marketing Suite delivers relevant offers in the call flow based on the context of the task being performed and the content from the Personalization Data Store.

The solution led to a 10% point IVR containment rate increase plus a dramatic reduction in average IVR call duration, driving a cost savings of millions per year. Cross-sell response rate jumped, driving millions in new revenue in the first year. The seamless caller experience across the customer–bank relationship increased the number of accounts accessed and tasks per call, reducing callbacks by 25%.

Shipping

Sure, a lot of companies staff-up for the holidays: One global shipping carrier, for example, hires over 60,000 seasonal employees to help them "play Santa" in December. The 40% single-day spike they see in deliveries ripples through the phone system as customers call wondering if their packages made it out of the North Pole, and managing the deluge of calls is a critical need.

To stem the tide, they teamed up with Tellme to power their automated tracking system—an interactive voice service that uses advanced speech recognition technology to provide fast package-tracking over the phone. Tellme's world-class, network-based infrastructure allows them to scale their capacity on demand, no matter how large or concentrated the spike.

For the holidays, and all year round, shipping customers can get a spoken response to package tracking requests in less than 2 s, reducing a complete call to just about a minute, which is less than half the length of an average call to an agent. This rock-solid performance creates consumer trust in Santa's shipping helpers, and the logistics experts trust Tellme's world-class platform to never drop a customer call.

Mobile Posse Case Study

Ford recently deployed idle-screen advertising via mobile digital devices to help drive interest in its Taurus. The idle-screen ad racked up an enviable 20% average click-through rate. Working with Mobile Posse, Inc., a provider of mobile marketing services, Ford increased purchase consideration and referred consumers to the

Taurus mobile website, where they could view product videos, find a dealer, and receive more information.

Medialets Case Studies

HBO

This innovative iPhone ad utilizes a dramatic approach to promote HBO's *True Blood* series, employing tactile features that leave bloody fingerprints as the user interacts with the screen, followed by a transparent overlay that shows blood dripping down and a link to the trailer video. The creative generated extraordinary buzz among True Blood fans and the advertising community and was broadly recognized for mobile rich media.

JP Morgan Chase

As an exclusive sponsor of *The New York Times*' Editor's Choice iPad application, Chase wanted to deliver an engaging creative that took advantage of the iPad's size and features. Medialets concepted and built an ad featuring a Chase Sapphire card that, when tilted, "spilled" out reward elements and links to a mobile site where users can learn more about rewards and the card.

MicroStrategy

This MicroStrategy creative was part of a broader campaign that ran within various premium news apps. The campaign, which included a range of ad formats from interstitial to banner, promoted MicroStrategy's iPad app. The creative showcased screens from the iPad app and, upon tap, led users to the App Store (Figure 4.9).

AdMob Case Studies

Flixster

Movies by Flixster is a comprehensive movie app for the iPhone or iPod touch with over 6 million downloads since release, making it consistently the highest ranked movie application in the App Store. Within the app, users can watch movie trailers, get show times, read reviews, view photos, and connect with Facebook friends.

Flixster worked with AdMob to reinvigorate the Movies ranking by driving downloads to push the app back into the Top 50 overall free app list. This ranking allows users to discover the app from their mobile device, as well as in the App Store on a PC. Since most users discover apps while browsing on their device, top 50 ranking is critical for new user acquisition. After this campaign, Flixster sustained

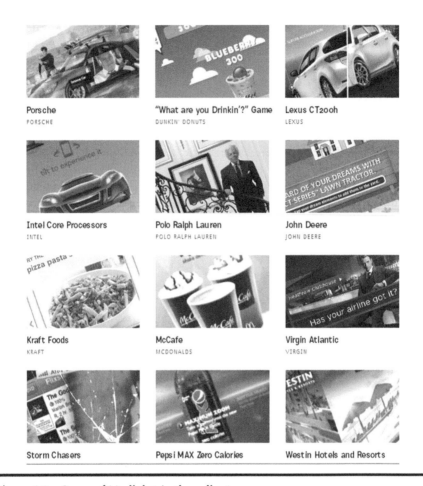

Figure 4.9 Some of Medialets' other clients.

ranking with ongoing advertising investment to take advantage of the organic download boost and easy discoverability of being in the Top 50 free app list.

Flixster focused advertising efforts on a Wednesday through Friday run to maximize their App Store ranking before the weekend, when use of a movie app is the highest. The text ads ran across AdMob's network of more than 2500 iPhone and iPod touch apps. Each ad led directly to the App Store download page, where users could download and use the app immediately.

They ran a variety of ad variations focused on specific movie titles, actors, and actresses, as well as more general ad text around finding show times, trailers, and other movie information. By trying different ad copy, they were able to see what type of message attracted the most user attention.

The campaign utilized AdMob's Download Tracking to measure downloads generated as a result of each ad. This allowed them to optimize their campaign investment in flight, based on actual app downloads not just impressions or clicks. AdMob drove over 18,000 downloads during the 48 h the campaign ran. At the start of the campaign, Movies was in position 51 in the Top overall free app list. Within 48 h, Movies moved up 14 positions to number 37. By the following Monday, Movies ranked number 31.

Flixster continued to see the effects of the campaign after it ended with 25% more organic downloads daily. The overall cost per download exceeded targets and they were able to set a new daily traffic record in their new position. With minimal continued daily investment, Movies held its position in the Top 20s–30s overall and number 5 in the Entertainment category following the ranking push.

Volkswagen

Volkswagen (VW) AG is a leading producer of vehicles in Europe with production sites worldwide. Recognizing the potential of advertising on mobile, VW partnered with their agency Beyond Interactive and AdMob to drive increased brand awareness of the new Volkswagen Golf. The objectives of VW's campaign were to engage with a high value, tech-savvy German audience in order to drive traffic to their mobile site where users can download a video, screensaver, or other information about the new Golf.

VW leveraged AdMob's significant reach and geo-targeting capabilities in order to focus this campaign specifically to consumers in Germany across a range of premium mobile sites and applications. With the objective of accessing a high net worth demographic and tech-savvy audience, VW ran ads across AdMob's network focused on Blackberry and iPhone users.

AdMob's rich media and highly engaging ads enabled VW to connect users directly to their mobile site. Once on the site, they could learn more about the new Volkswagen Golf or even download-related content such as screensavers. AdMob's team of mobile experts helped VW every step of the way, from setting up the campaign, optimizing to ensure objectives were met, and reporting throughout.

VW and their agency Beyond Interactive achieved their goal of reaching tech-savvy consumers in Germany to drive interest in the Volkswagen Golf. They found AdMob to be both a cost-effective and high-performance channel in which to engage with their key audience of consumers. AdMob delivered click-through rates of 1.7% on average and more than 25,000 visits to their mobile site. Overall VW was very pleased with the brand visibility and performance achieved through advertising on mobile with AdMob.

Adidas

Adidas worked with the agency Isobar and AdMob to reach their target audience of young urban influencers. Adidas' overall goal for the campaign was to build brand awareness and develop the brand associations of originality and self-expression with the Adidas Superstar brand.

Adidas has worked with AdMob on other campaigns such as Basketball is a Brotherhood, and they have seen high engagement rates both with their ads and the action users took on the landing page. In addition to their goal of driving traffic to their mobile site, Adidas also had goals for activity on their mobile site: to drive video views and ringtone and wallpaper downloads.

AdMob ran graphical banner ads and text link ads targeted toward college students as well as toward users in our Downloads and Communities Channels across select sites in our network. AdMob's graphical banner ads and text link ads drove traffic to the Adidas Originals mobile website.

This sophisticated mobile website lets users select their favorite type of music and listen to sample tracks from up-and-coming artists of each genre. Users could then download ringtones from the musicians they liked best, view videos of their performances, opt-in to receive more ringtones in the future, send their friends ringtones, and even enter their zip code to find the nearest location where they could purchase Adidas Superstars. Additionally, AdMob worked with Insight Express to conduct a brand study for Adidas, in order to measure the impact of this highly engaging campaign's key brand metrics.

The Adidas mobile site engagement drove over 290,000 visitors who downloaded over 100,000 ringtones. The buzz campaign went viral with over 10,000 Sends to Friends. Adidas has continued to work with AdMob based on the strong performance of this and other campaigns.

PhoneTag Case Study

PhoneTag invented the voicemail-to-text industry. For the past 5 years, the company has delivered high-quality transcripts of voicemails to busy business people in America, Australia, and the United Kingdom. Unlike Google Voice and other automated solutions, PhoneTag prides itself on the accuracy of the transcripts it provides. Each voicemail is immediately understandable.

After signing a contract with a new large client, PhoneTag needed to rapidly add 100 transcriptionists to their global transcription pool. Unlike previous ramp ups, these people needed to be online in 45 days to meet the client's demands. The normal process of recruiting, hiring, and training a transcriptionist took 3–4 months.

PhoneTag turned to TaskUs because of the company's stellar record of being able to rapidly scale campaigns that deliver results. A team from TaskUs' offices in Los Angeles met with managers from PhoneTag and agreed on a course of action. Members from the TaskUs team were on the ground for the entire 6 week process of recruiting and training transcriptionists. Over 100 transcriptionists were successfully on-boarded during this period.

The new client came online without a hitch. Internal data showed that TaskUs produced equal or better results to all of the services of other production centers. Since then PhoneTag has added more transcriptionists at TaskUs' Manila offices, making TaskUs the second largest provider of transcription services to the company.

Xtract Case Study

Our client was faced with a significant challenge to reduce high rate of churning customers. Xtract knows that a subscriber's immediate neighbors in their social network and their actions have a real impact on churn. To prove the positive effect of Xtract's Social Links, we tested it in two separate campaigns for the same service. The product in focus was a fixed line service where the subscribers can call for free among the network and at a reasonable price outside the network, against a monthly fee.

A "traditional" churn management campaign is a form of campaign where targeting is typically based on the analysis of the subscriber's individual behavior. It is a campaign where the churn propensity scoring was also influenced by the social network, that is, by appropriate targeting of highly influential, high-propensity churners in the social network-based campaign, one could reduce churn not only among those targets but also in their communities.

Two control groups were used—first the traditional ad campaign and the second one for a social network-based campaign—metrics were captured for these target groups, respectively and their churn was measured over a 3 month period. The results were clearly in favor of Xtract's social-network-based campaigns: the churn was reduced by 26% compared to control group, versus reduction of 19% in the conventionally targeted group—a 37% relative improvement!

Reducing churn has a major effect on the operator's bottom line results, so the impact of a successful churn campaign can be huge. Using CDR and network analysis in addition to demographic data produces, in this case, a 21% better accuracy in predicting churn than a corresponding regression model based on demographic information only.

BayesiaLab Case Study

The databases relative to the customers can be used to elaborate profiles by using data mining methods. These profiles can then bring objective information to the marketing department; they can also be used to reduce the cost of the campaigns by selecting only the prospects that have a high probability to reply positively. We describe here the use of BayesiaLab for the profiling of customers with respect to a bank product that has various modalities. The database used contains variables describing the customer, such as age, socioprofession, gender, etc.; their bank account, such as facilities, rate of consumption, etc.; and the modality of their bank products.

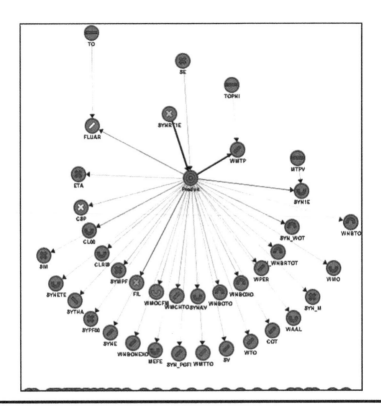

Figure 4.10 BayesiaLab network of consumer profiles.

This last variable allows using supervised learning methods. Instead of learning a Bayesian network representing all the probabilistic relations that hold in the database, it is possible to use the supervised learning algorithms of BayesiaLab. For example, the Markov Blanket Learning algorithm allows focusing the search only toward the variables that really characterize the target variable. Figure 4.10 represents the Bayesian network that has been automatically learned.

This bayesian network, which represents the Markov Blanket of the bank product, makes the analysis easier by reducing the number of variables to take into account. The complete analysis toolbox of BayesiaLab is also very helpful: arc length relative to the strength of the probabilistic relations, automatic positioning of the nodes that takes into account its strength, and analysis of the probabilistic relations between the variables and the target variable or one of its modality (Figure 4.11).

The quality evaluation of the learned Bayesian network on a data set that has not been used for learning has allowed measuring *a gain of 20%* in precision with respect to the profile used then. Figure 4.11 represents the evaluation tools of BayesiaLab Total precision of the Bayesian network, Confusion matrix to measure more precisely the quality of the model—displayed with occurrences, reliability,

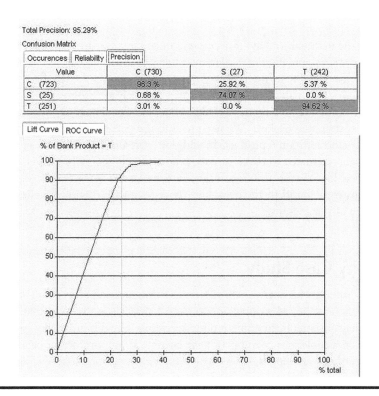

Figure 4.11   Bayesian network is extremely accurate.

or precision—and Lift or ROC curves that constitute useful tools for choosing the probability thresholds that will be used in the decision rules.

BayesiaLab can then exploit the Bayesian network to build adaptive question-naires for sorting the monitor variables (i.e., the questions) based both on the information brought to the knowing of the target variable and on the cost associated to the knowing of the question variable. The Bayesian network can also be used to predict the bank product for new customers. As BayesiaLab returns the probability associated to that prediction, it is possible to use this probability to reduce the cost of the campaigns by using this probability to select the prospects.

PolyAnalyst Case Study

A national communication services provider was introducing new services. The client was seeking a solution that could learn from the input of marketing, sales and engineering activities—in order to predict geographical areas of high demand—and identify the best individual target customers. The client needed a tool to determine the best metropolitan areas to offer their services and the number of customers likely to select various services within each market. Later, the same tool was to be capable of driving, tracking, and learning from the marketing effort and changing the national strategy if necessary. Since there was no available history on a new product, a population with demonstrated pent-up demand was identified and then modeled with the help of PolyAnalyst to generate customer profiles.

The goal of the analysis was to determine how likely a customer would purchase a specific product, given the knowledge of what other items are already in this customer's "shopping basket." We need to find the percentage chance of purchasing this specific additional product. In addition, measures of statistical significance needed to be calculated to make sure that these percentages were greater than random chance. Finally, the most significant rules needed to be extracted. Meaningful conclusions were found in the data, and these were shared with the client after a description of the analysis.

Attensity Case Study

Las Vegas accounts for nearly 70% of Nevada's revenues and tourism is the primary industry of the state. Most operators on the Las Vegas strip now garner half or more of their revenue from nongambling spending. Hotel rooms, once given away to encourage people to stay and play, have become an important source of income, especially at high-end hotels.

Las Vegas Sands Corp. owns and operates two major properties in Las Vegas: The Venetian Resort Hotel & Casino and the new Palazzo Resort Hotel & Casino. Combined with the adjacent Sands Expo Convention Center, these hotels are part of the largest resort complex in the world, featuring 7128 hotel rooms and suites. The Venetian and Palazzo compete with other luxury resorts including Bellagio and The Wynn.

As cost of travel and airline tickets increases due to recent fuel costs and incoming flight frequency declines, these properties are facing an increasing competition to fill their rooms. Analysts predict the same number of visitors, but with shortened visits or reduced spending during their stays—situations compelling hotels to work harder to capture their share of consumer spending.

Travelers to Las Vegas in search of an exclusive getaway experience have more luxury rooms, entertainment choices, shopping options, and gourmet restaurants to choose from than ever before. As the economy tightens, resort operators need to differentiate themselves to stay ahead of their competitors.

Information on the Internet has empowered consumers to make more informed purchase decisions than ever before. Guests are savvier and increasingly more vocal, sharing opinions online from their check-in experience to the quality of a hotel's spa. These opinions have a significant impact on future travelers' booking decisions.

The challenge for executives at Las Vegas Sands Corp. was to understand online consumer feedback at a detailed level, measure the impact of that feedback, and make adjustments to increase customer satisfaction and loyalty.

"The Las Vegas strip is a highly competitive market," says Rom Hendler, vice president of Strategic Marketing for the Venetian and Palazzo properties. "To stay ahead of the game, we need better customer intelligence tools."

Attensity Opinion Insights was used to collect and analyze actual customer opinions from a broad universe of websites including TripAdvisor, Travelocity, and Expedia. An initial analysis was delivered to the client based on tens of thousands of individual posts online for the Venetian and Palazzo, as well as 10 other Las Vegas properties identified as prime competitors.

Attensity analysts then used Opinion Insights to produce and deliver a benchmark study that identified how the Venetian and Palazzo resorts stacked up against their top competitors overall and on an individual property attribute level. The report identified customer feedback, highlighting strengths as well as areas where improvements could be made to increase the company's leadership in the Las Vegas luxury hotel, resort, and casino market.

"The level of insight Attensity delivered to us is truly amazing. We were able to pinpoint exactly what aspects of each property received significant positive customer feedback as well as what needed improvement. We were also able to compare our results against individual competitors and determine where the gaps were," says Hendler.

Based on the results delivered, Las Vegas Sands Corp. has undertaken several follow-up initiatives to improve customer experience. Among the findings from the initial report, it was clear that customers loved the pool at the new Palazzo; however, some customers brought up the lack of shade as an area of concern. Another finding indicated that guests wanted to avoid long lines at check-in. Both of these findings generated interest and action at the highest levels of the organization. With the Palazzo, the company was also able to set benchmarks from which to monitor the hotel's performance during its inaugural year of operation.

"Census-based, real time, plus competitive monitoring—and at a granular level that allows us to target our resources to address specific areas we can change," says Rom Hendler. "This platform is revolutionary. I feel like we have discovered an amazing new source of customer intelligence that delivers detailed insights about our property and competition that we've never seen before."

Clarabridge Case Study

A national quick service restaurant chain known for burgers and freshness expands its menu in response to consumers asking for greater choice in healthy options. A variety of new wraps are introduced across the nation, generating customer responses through several traditional channels—call centers, e-mails, online chats, and paper and website surveys.

As expected, volumes of comments spiked, but helping to provide more metrics and context was Clarabridge's addition of unstructured data to the mix.

Sentiment analysis showed that when people discussed one of the new wraps it was usually in a negative manner. The cause? The wrap—advertised as a low-carb option—was mistakenly being prepared with the standard tortilla.

With Clarabridge's processing speed and power, not only were results available quickly but they were delivered in actionable reports that quickly and graphically illustrated the locations experiencing this issue, helping the franchise to respond with training reinforcement and inventory controls. Rather than hide significant issues in rolled-up reports, this restaurant's customers get the whole story and the whole wheat, right away.

dtSearch Case Studies

Simon Delivers

Simon Delivers is delivering on its promise to be the web grocer of choice for its core Minneapolis market, thanks in part to new search features the online retailer has been phasing in over the last several months. Simon Delivers carries more than 8000 online stock-keeping units (SKUs). With a full range of supermarket inventory, it makes fresher produce a centerpiece of its value proposition by shortening the typical supply chain and investing heavily in what CEO Christopher Brown calls "chill chain management"–refrigeration storage technology in its warehouses and trucks to support that.

In the past few months, Simon Delivers has been on a new product expansion binge, offering a wide array of new items such as DVDs and magazines as well as more deli items and liquors. To compete more effectively with traditional chain grocers and give more choice to its more than 70,000 customers, Simon Delivers sees expanded inventory as critical to its business plan. For instance, the web grocer now stocks more than 300 brand-name beer, wine, and hard liquor items on its liquor product pages.

But too much choice can be overwhelming to online grocery shoppers, who are typically pressed for time and do not mind paying extra for the convenience of doing their grocery buying over the web. To make it easier, Simon Delivers has expanded site search to give busy shoppers more ways to find and purchase the items—particularly fresh produce and meats—that they are looking for. For instance, Simon Delivers now has a page with tips on simple or advance search techniques that help shoppers reduce the time it takes to find, click, and purchase groceries.

The online grocer's internal design team and search engine management vendor, DT Search, have refined the site's databases and search software to recognize different spellings and abbreviations. If a shopper types in "Huggy" instead of "Huggies" or "Welchs" rather than "Welch's," the search will still take them to the same products. To locate items faster, shoppers can also search by interactive grocery aisles, much as they can in a real store, and by new items and weekly specials.

Simon Delivers is growing. Annual web sales now total more than $70 million, and the average order value is almost $125. But Brown says better site search is key to helping customers find precisely what they need in under a few seconds. "If a customer wants a particular brand of chip and we carry it, our search functions will get them there quickly," he says. "Customers shouldn't have to worry about spacing, abbreviations or misspellings when they are shopping and pressed for time. A good search function will take care of that situation, and that is what ours does."

Cybergroup

Conceived in the mid-1990s to change the way residents find local information, this major metropolitan directory utilizes one of the most unique and powerful local databases available today. The database includes local businesses, schools, and attractions, including listings by payment types accepted, hours of operation, and a variety of other qualifiers.

In an effort to take their database searching to the next level, the client contacted Cybergroup, Inc. to add several significant enhancements. Greg Bean, president of Cybergroup, quickly turned to dtSearch. "Our client needed to retrieve and present information from local business web sites, as well as from their SQL databases. And they needed to present relevant information to their searchers. Those requirements were 'a natural' for dtSearch," said Bean.

Cybergroup used dtSearch's custom field capability and a Cybergroup-developed indexing module to marry documents with the SQL databases. The end result provides a much more powerful and relevant tool for those searching for local information. The customer stated: "Our clients have always been impressed by the quality of information we provide. With the enhancements we've added through dtSearch, our directory offers an unparalleled search solution for local searchers as well as our client businesses."

Cybergroup is a leading provider of Internet/Intranet technology solutions that enhance communications and commerce between organizations and their customers, suppliers, and other constituencies. Cybergroup provides a comprehensive range of Internet, Intranet, Extranet, and website solutions and services, with a primary focus on web to database integration.

Reditus

Reditus Web Strategy Consulting, an online web strategy and development company, and dtSearch Corp., a leading developer of text search software for enterprise and developer customers, announce a highly successful implementation by Reditus embedding the dtSearch® Text Retrieval Engine for Reditus' client BestBuyEyeGlasses.com (BBE).

BBE tasked Reditus with enhancing the high-end eyewear retailer's online shopping site to attract more visitors and convert a higher percentage of sales. As a result of Reditus' comprehensive web analysis, shopping cart overhaul and implementation of the dtSearch Engine, BBE boosted its conversion rate and total online sales by 50%. Said Daniel Kandler, president, BBE: "For any business to boost sales by 50% is a dream come true."

After analyzing BBE's online business, Reditus concluded its client would benefit from a more powerful and efficient shopping cart solution. The new shopping cart alone significantly increased BBE's total sales. While BBE was elated, Reditus continued its analysis.

"By studying how customers interacted with the e-commerce site, we recognized there were some process barriers that were translating into lost sales," said Yuval Karjevski, principal web consultant at Reditus. "When clients use your e-commerce solutions to showcase upwards of 40,000 products and cater to millions of visitors monthly, even the slightest improvement can significantly impact the bottom line."

One area that went under the microscope was the eyewear retailer's onsite search engine, which left a percentage of visitors unable to locate products that were, in fact, available on the site. Reditus upgraded BBE's online search component to the dtSearch Text Retrieval Engine. "Of all of the search engines we evaluated, we found dtSearch's advanced technology to be the fastest and most flexible," said Karjevski.

The developer component of the dtSearch product line, the dtSearch Engine provides.NET, C++, and Java APIs for custom programming by developers such as Reditus. The dtSearch Engine can index over a terabyte of text in a single index as well as create and simultaneously search an unlimited number of indexes. Indexed search time is typically less than a second, even across terabytes of data.

The dtSearch Engine offers more than two dozen search options. After a search, the dtSearch Engine can highlight hits in popular web-based formats, while displaying links, formatting, and images. The built-in dtSearch Spider supports static and dynamic web content, with WYSWYG hit-highlighting. The dtSearch Engine can also convert non-web-ready file types to HTML for display with highlighted hits.

"The dtSearch component alone is invaluable to our business," said Mr. Kandler. "It helps us ensure customers are finding our products. And, in the event we don't have what they're looking for, we can act on it and add desired products to our catalogues. It benefits our bottom line, promotes customer satisfaction, and helps keep our customers coming back."

"We welcome Reditus as an experienced dtSearch Engine developer," said Elizabeth Thede, vice president of sales, dtSearch Corp. "I checked out their search engine installation at BestBuyEyeGlasses.com, and promptly ordered two pairs of sunglasses."

As a final piece, Reditus integrated cutting-edge tools to allow BBE to monitor search trends and manage custom content displays. "The eyewear industry is incredibly competitive, which made it especially important to let analysis and hard data tell the story rather than speculation," noted Mr. Karjevski. "Even the smallest miscalculation could put our client several steps behind their competitors."

"We're absolutely thrilled with the results, which far exceeded our expectations," said Mr. Kandler. "Best of all, thanks to the systems we now have in place; we're able to enjoy sustainable revenue and growth."

Lexalytics Case Studies

DataSift

DataSift is a real-time content curation system empowering developers, businesses and individuals to filter real-time data in a variety of different ways. DataSift brings together live-streamed content alongside a variety of data analytics services, including the Lexalytics Salience Engine, to provide the ultimate in filtering for real-time streams. Lexalytics teamed up with DataSift to provide accurate and accessible "sentiment analysis."

DataSift gives developers the ability to leverage cloud computing to build very precise streams of data from the millions and millions of tweets sent everyday. They can tune these tweets through a graphical interface or a bespoke programming language—with data streams consumable through Lexalytics API and real-time HTTP—to construct comment and rank sentiment streams that can be created by the twitter community.

"An important part of the metrics we provide through DataSift is the sentiment (tonality) of the tweets. We needed an engine that could integrate quickly into our environment and start immediately providing accurate sentiment analysis across all of Twitter," says Nick Halstead, CEO & Founder, Favorit LTD. "Lexalytics Salience Engine provides us with a great combination of flexible integration, high performance, and accurate sentiment analysis." Lexalytics Salience Engine is processing over 9 TB of tweet content a day in a single 8-core server for DataSift.

Northern Light

Northern Light provides strategic research portals for market research, competitive intelligence, business analysis, product development, and technology research. Their client companies are the Fortune 50 leaders in telecommunications, computing, pharmaceuticals, agricultural equipment, banking and financial services, logistics, software, and more. Every company is a household name.

A typical strategic research portal from Northern Light might contain one or more repositories of internal primary research, dozens of licensed external secondary research subscription sources, business news, financial analyst reports, government databases, and content acquired from custom web crawls. Over 200,000 business analysts are using Northern Light's research portals to make product and business decisions that touch all of us.

Northern Light's SinglePoint product aggregates all external research for a given customer. SinglePoint is integrated with 104 research providers: companies like Gartner, IDC, and their equivalents in other market spaces. When these analysts publish research, they simultaneously publish into the SinglePoint system. This research is combined with news from 8000 news sources and any internal research, competitive or market intelligence, to provide a singularly powerful research tool.

Northern Lights' MI Analyst product mines the SinglePoint database using Lexalytics Salience text analytics functionality in combination with extremely strong technical and business-issues taxonomies. MI Analyst can then expose concepts like "change in market share," "cost cutting," and "competing with generic drugs" in combination with entities more traditionally defined in taxonomies (companies, technical terms, people, etc.).

To get a sense of the scale of this problem, consider this example from pharmaceuticals: MI Analyst can extract a company name that is "near" a clinical trial, that is, in turn, "near" a notable disease. This combination defines a significant business event, which are then exposed by the MI Analyst user interface as various scenarios to the user. In order to pull that off, MI Analyst leverages Lexalytics Salience Engine to look for *over 1.9 Trillion relationships on each and every document* for their pharmaceutical customers. And that is for just one market space.

"In order to provide the MI Analyst service, we need extremely precise customization of entities and relationships along with the ability to deeply embed text analytics into our production processes" says David Seuss, CEO, Northern Light, Inc. "Lexalytics Salience Engine is completely shapeable in just the way we need."

Leximancer Case Study

When Nigel Martin and his colleagues at Australia National University (ANU) needed a way to perform advanced text analytics on their social sciences research, they turned to Leximancer. When they had to take thousands of documents and translate these into actionable insight and usable information, they turned to Leximancer. When they needed a way to save employee time and department money, they turned to Leximancer.

Leximancer became the only viable solution to their complex text analytics problems.

Some of the team's recent work has been funded under an ANU College Research Grant project that has looked into the community reactions to the proposal to establish systems based on smart card technologies for delivery of health and social services. Another project that is just starting to take off is work with the Department of the Prime Minister and cabinet looking into industry and community views of the proposed Emissions Trading Scheme and Greenhouse Reporting regime for businesses.

Suffice it to say, they have many applications for Leximancer software in the social sciences area. ANU needed a tool that could translate all of this information—quickly, easily, and accurately—into visually grouped concepts that they could understand and use in many different practice areas, including accounting, information systems, and business analysis. For this research, they were gathering thousands of pages of information on subject's behaviors, attitudes, beliefs, comments, etc. To extract this information and be able to analyze it properly, ANU was spending hundreds and hundreds of hours. And even so, there still was room for incorrect analysis or lost concepts.

This is where Leximancer came in. Martin and his team used Leximancer as a concept analysis and data mining software tool for exploratory research of subject behaviors, viewpoints, attitudes, beliefs, and comments. Martin's team could download all the available information into Leximancer and send out readable and usable concept maps that could tell ANU not just WHAT their subjects were thinking and feeling, but WHY they were feeling this way—insight that no other software had been able to provide.

One example was the connection between information security and personal privacy beliefs in the smart card technology domain. Even with more than 400,000 words in a single data entry, using Leximancer the team was able to analyze and interpret the data in a quick amount of time. Further, Leximancer analysis helped the researchers visually uncover relationships and insight that may never have been exposed using manual methods. It is this type of research velocity and precision improvement where Leximancer makes such a large contribution.

"Leximancer has assisted with processing the vast data blocks that confront our social sciences practice. It means that we can process hundreds of thousands of words and texts in compressed timeframes without the need for employing more and greater skilled staff members. It also allows us to undertake several projects simultaneously, so that our overall research productivity is greater than if we were tied to a single project for an extended time period due to the manual data processing," Martin said.

Martin tried to do the same type of work using another system at his previous company but found the costs were prohibitive and having to program the tools before using them was both time consuming and tedious. Leximancer takes this part of the work out of your hands and allows you to do the more valuable analytical and interpretive work.

According to Martin, Leximancer "is probably the most cost-effective and efficient concept analysis and data mining software tool available in the current market."

So this cost- and time-effective software helps ANU collect the information they need behind-the-scenes that can be presented to government and community figures, industry experts, and top-line journals in order for the research to be published. Leximancer has worked for the ANU time and time again, telling researchers WHY their subjects think and feel the way they do and giving researchers usable information to present their findings. This information is invaluable to their research and without Leximancer, simply would not be possible.

Nstein Case Studies

ProQuest

ProQuest, a division of the Cambridge Information Group, creates specialized information resources and technologies for libraries and researchers worldwide. For the past 5 years, the company has used Nstein's TME (Text Mining Engine) to assist in organizing, categorizing, and writing abstracts for a growing body of news, dissertations, and academic papers. Nstein allows the automation and standardization of these tasks so reducing Editorial involvement.

Prior to Nstein, the company had 70–80 people manually indexing 700 journals a day (a ratio of 1:10). With Nstein, the company was able to automate processes and triple the number of journals indexed, while redeploying resources. The number of articles indexed daily, after automatically eliminating duplicate content (de-duping), is around 75,000. At a time when so many publishers are experiencing subscribers shrinkage, ProQuest's subscriptions are up. The company is not certain whether the more granular classification is the cause or not, but it does know that users are finding information more quickly and with greater precision!

"In addition to improving the quality of our tagging, automating these processes resulted in significant cost savings, which were channeled into adding value to our product offerings," explained John Taylor, vice president of Product Development and Technology for ProQuest. "We increased the amount of content aggregated from 700 journals to now nearly triple that. Further, we created a stronger taxonomy to increase the depth of classification, allowing end users to find the exact content they're looking for with greater precision and speed."

evolve24

evolve24 analyzes traditional and social media to determine a businesses' overall information landscape and provides quantitative metrics around perception, reputation, and risk that let clients understand the key areas of impact in their marketing, communications, and management efforts. Because of their ability to correlate perception to KPIs, evolve's services are highly sought by Fortune 500 companies.

"Reputations are built over time and are the response to actions taken by a corporation," explained Scot Wheeler, vice president of Strategy & Client Services for evolve24. "For example, reputation can be hurt by unaddressed negative responses to products and services, including poor customer support, regulatory or legislative issues, insensitive ad campaigns, or any perceived affront to an audience, while a new product announcement, a viral campaign or launch of user groups may create highly positive coverage in influential publications and blogs which will help build reputation."

This sentiment analysis reputation risk management firm gauges public reactions. Nstein TME's sentiment analysis module allows evolve24 to quickly determine the tone of an article, which offers a key insight into the firm's representation through media. "We have estimated that a person at peak performance can 'tone' 200 articles a day—or 25 an hour," Wheeler said. "With Nstein, we can literally score tens of thousands of pieces of content a day for each of our clients—all of them broken down by brand or topic—using a single person to manually test and verify results."

Gesca

Gesca is a Canadian publisher of French-speaking dailies. Cyberpresse was in search of tools that would allow it not only to showcase the quality of its content— aggregated large newspapers in the Gesca publishing family—but also to provide the online news agency the ability to generate up-to-the-minute, in-depth content on the fly. With seven properties, and an arthritic publishing system, Gesca wanted a content management solution that would allow it to aggressively innovate and meet audience's—and advertisers'—needs. All that was missing was the robust, flexible, and cost-efficient CMS solution to allow the news portal to deliver a product that added timeliness to its value proposition. Its CMS product was adequate for its implementation at the time, but the ongoing cost of hardware, software development, and bandwidth was quickly making it less than optimal for Cyberpresse's expanding needs. Further, the system was not agile enough to allow updates to breaking news, and creating specialty sites required a tremendous amount of IT input.

In his role as Gesca CTO, Matthieu Delorme approached the task of sourcing a new content management system by building a list of negotiable and nonnegotiable features. Tops on his list were speed to go online and skill sets required. Past solutions required knowledge of an arcane language; Delorme wanted to make sure mainstream programming skills would suffice. Having worked with Nstein's text mining in the past, he built that functionality into the requirements doc.

Delorme implemented the system and tested the system with a new product Mon Volant—an automotive site. The challenge was all that much greater because sales had found a sponsor who wanted the site live for an automotive show that was a mere 6 weeks away. The challenge was met, and the test passed. When the whole portal went onto the system, Cyberpresse saw a 20% increase in traffic, but, more importantly, it saw a meteoric rise in audience engagement, for which Delorme credits the text mining.

The real success story may be how pleased the editorial team is. What used to take 20 min to publish a breaking story—now only takes a minute.

Recommind Case Studies

Law

The business services law firm of Davies Ward Phillips & Vineberg LLP (Davies) has an integrated team of more than 245 lawyers located in Toronto, Montreal, and New York. Its clients consist of commercial companies, financial institutions, governments, regulatory bodies, charitable organizations, international agencies, educational institutions, individuals, trusts, and estates.

Like every law firm in the digital age, Davies has struggled with managing burgeoning amounts of e-mail data. In the last decade, as the volume of e-mail quickly dwarfed the volume of nondigital documents, the need for an efficient solution became critical. At the very least, the firm required a sure-fire way to assign a client matter number to e-mail correspondence. Available e-mail systems and e-mail archives had no classification provision or feature for assigning such a number. Law firms found neither the ease nor reliability they needed from the search capabilities built into these systems; vital, and often privileged, material is now commonly embedded within the body of an e-mail that requires the same careful treatment as the same information that once could predominantly be found in a document. Recommind provides control over e-mail-based information at the time of its creation or receipt.

Energy

Recommind's customer has tens of thousands of laptops, desktops and e-mail accounts, numerous file shares, and an OpenText Livelink™ enterprise document management system. The volume of electronically stored information (ESI) within these systems alone poses a great challenge to effectively manage the risks associated with litigation, regulatory compliance, and, generally, conducting business in this digital age. After mining the market for the best eDiscovery solution, the company turned to Recommind to help it effectively manage its ESI and provide a powerful yet cost-effective Early Case Assessment (ECA) tool. The company's needs included managing the unsustainable risks and costs posed by litigation and regulation, thereby reducing processing.

The energy firm required document filtering, legal hold management, manageable risks, costs, and extended waiting periods involved when outsourcing ESI collection and processing in a scalable solution for connecting seamlessly to not only its current but also future, enterprise data sources such as laptops, desktops, OpenText Livelink, file shares, MS Exchange, and structured databases. Recommind was able to provide numerous customer references due to its focus on customer service and extensive domain experience within the corporate and legal markets.

Search and Social

Today's knowledge workers are no longer a select group of highly trained information seekers; they include everyone from the chairman to the receptionist. Everyone in the organization is looking for information throughout their day: relevant documents to answer questions, experienced people to consult with, and matters or projects with reusable value.

The goal of an enterprise search engine is to provide everyone with answers, giving them actionable information that is accessible, relevant, timely, and in context. While most search projects focus on finding a document, if the document is returned out of context, true knowledge is lost. It is not enough to just find content (what) if you do not know its author and contributors (who) and for what purpose it was written (why).

In an enterprise search environment, "what" is any content—documents, websites, data, and e-mails—that can be indexed and searched. "Who" are the people and contacts that were involved in creating the document. "Why" are matters or projects that are associated with documents and identify the reason the documents were created. By maintaining all these dimensions in the enterprise search system, the user is presented with actionable information.

Early search engines addressed the first dimension of search (what) by uncovering valuable documents previously locked in disparate information repositories—document management systems, file shares, corporate intranets, and the like. These first-generation search systems made progress in the quest to provide the right document to the right person at the right time.

As users become more accustomed to the social aspects of the Internet, they are also looking for information of interest to them because it is of interest to others in their network. Social networking sites affect everyone and have an impact on the expectations of information workers. If it is easier to find people and information on Facebook or LinkedIn than within a firm's own intranet, the second dimension people (who) they may start using those sites for business unless their firms have a better and more engaging tool.

Adding social aspects helps, but many of the answers that people are seeking still remain unanswered, unless you add a third dimension (why)—associating information with matters or projects. Why was a document written, and what purpose did it serve? Once users have this third dimension in place, they can understand "how" to use the information. Without the reason behind the creation of the content, the true purpose of the information remains unknown; with this final dimension in place, a user gains an "understanding" dimension.

However, information sources are everywhere and are growing exponentially. Most search engines try to manage information on a document level and therefore require the author to profile the document for future retrieval, such as to assign the document type. Since not everyone profiles documents in the same way, when searching for documents, users are often overwhelmed by over inclusive and vague results. Thus, a results list presented with no additional context becomes meaningless.

Faceted navigation, or smart filtering, has helped address this problem but is often limited in scope. Most searches can produce an author name and the date the document was created or last saved. But what about the valuable context related to that author: what group does he work for, what region or country is he located in, and what level of seniority does he have?

Search has now expanded beyond flat documents to a second dimension (who), where information seekers can find content based on their social network. Rich enterprise search taps into the metadata behind the information. The metadata level is, for example, that John Smith wrote this document on this date. The meta-metadata is that John Smith was in the Brussels office working in the tax group as a senior associate.

Now users can sort information based on multidimensional criteria, not just flat data. This additional information, compared to knowing only that the author was John Smith, allows users to take more decisive action. When searching for content, the business context in which the people who created that content were working is an important piece of information and meaningful when it comes to making informed decisions. In this second dimension of search, users can find the right information by locating documents a knowledgeable person has created.

By revealing these links between people and the content they create, users can find not only documents but also the right person based on what that person has written and whom they know.

With this final dimension in place, when users see a document in a result set, they know whether it was used for a project similar to theirs and can instantly judge whether it is more relevant than a document with the same keywords but for a nonrelated project. By adding this critical third dimension, users are empowered to choose the best information for their needs based on full context.

By keeping the linkage between the three dimensions—content, people, and matters—users can also find relevant matters and discover, for example, the people involved in the project, the documents related to that project, the time and billing notes that tell what work was done for that project, and additional valuable context.

However, many firms that have realized this third dimension of enterprise search may still be providing only a sliver of available knowledge to their information seekers. The vast majority of today's valuable information—more than 90%—is hidden in firm members' e-mail silos, so it is crucial for e-mail to be added into the enterprise search mix.

Without a central organized repository, how is e-mail brought into the mix? E-mail by default already contains two of the three dimensions needed: it has the "what" (text) and the "who" (author and recipients) already embedded in the file, but what is often missing is the "why" (what project was this e-mail related to?). Some e-mail eventually gets filed among documents in the document management system, but the vast majority of e-mail is locked up in individual e-mail boxes.

Even within these disparate e-mail silos, most information is not correctly tagged or filed to a project. Even when provided with the seemingly user-friendly option to "drag and drop" e-mail to a file, however, the majority of people do not file their e-mail with any consistency, and key knowledge about the project remains hidden. Given the amount of data that people are dealing with daily, for most, the e-mail management barrier is still set too high.

However, there are systems available that help to automatically file an e-mail to a project folder, providing a simple way to get information out of the inbox. One of the unique characteristics of e-mail is that it is duplicative—there are many copies of e-mail sitting in the e-mail boxes of everyone who is copied on it, which they have to each manage and file that same e-mail. By automating the filing of e-mail across users, thereby removing this step of having each individual file the same e-mail, amazing efficiencies can be realized, easing the path to better sharing of information.

Due to the semi-private nature of e-mail, security is a difficult—but vital—subject to address when working on enterprise search. A system that handles e-mail management must be able to meet a precise and complex set of security rules yet not keep all that valuable information locked down in individual e-mail silos.

As anyone who has worked on an enterprise search implementation knows, a percentage of sensitive documents within all firms are unsecured, that is, until enterprise search uncovers this failure in the system and enables (or forces) staff to fix it. But users' expectations around e-mail privacy are completely different and at a higher level compared to document security (whether this is valid or not is debatable), and so e-mail security and permissions need to address a firm's policy.

All of this can be done with an automated system. By adding this enormously valuable e-mail resource into the search mix, firms can truly provide significant content in context and increase the value of enterprise search tenfold. When content, people, and matters are all connected and e-mail is part of the sea of searchable information, users can find everything they have access to in the organization.

C5.0 Case Study

The objective—ID high income devices—the C5 software was used to segment nearly 200,000 individuals described by seven numeric and 33 nominal attributes. The task was to predict whether an individual's income was above or below $50,000.

The cases were split into equal-sized training and test sets. From the 99,762 cases in the former, See5/C5.0 required only 4.3 s to produce a classifier consisting of 84 rules, 33 for low-income individuals and 51 for those with high income. Here are some machines business rules:

```
Rule 1: (19425/1, lift 1.1)
    family members under 18 = Both parents present
    -> class - 50000 [1.000]

Rule 6: (1603/8, lift 1.1)
    education = 5th or 6th grade
    capital losses <= 1876
    -> class - 50000 [0.994]

Rule 34: (32, lift 15.7)
    dividends from stocks > 33000
    weeks worked in year > 47
    -> class 50000+ [0.971]

Rule 42: (132/12, lift 14.6)
    education = Prof school degree (MD DDS DVM LLB JD)
    dividends from stocks > 991
    weeks worked in year > 47
    -> class 50000+ [0.903]
```

The 83-rule machine-learning classifiers constructed by See5/C5.0 correctly categorize 95% of the 99,761 unseen test cases. (This is an example of the type of business rules that can be generated in microseconds for machine-to-machine marketing.)

CART Case Study

Fleet Financial Group, a Boston-based financial services company with assets of more than $97 billion, is currently redesigning its customer service infrastructure, including a $38 million investment in a data warehouse and marketing automation software. To profit from this repository of valuable information on more than 15 million customers, Fleet's analysts are using data mining software, including Salford Systems' (San Diego, CA) CART®, to learn about their customers and to better target product promotions, such as home equity lines of credit.

"The real key is implementing a disciplined business plan that enables us to sell the right product to the right customer," says Randall Grossman, senior VP and manager of Fleet's Customer Data Management and Analysis (CDMA) group. To do that, Fleet needed to learn about customers' financial characteristics and buying habits so as to target the mailing list for the company's third-quarter home equity product promotion. Victor Lo, a Fleet lead analytic consultant and VP, and his team, were tasked with developing a model to estimate each prospect's probability of responding to the mailing, as well as to estimate the expected profitability of respondents. Based on this expected profitability, the database would be segmented by scores that identify which prospects should receive one of several home equity marketing pieces and which should not receive a mailing at all.

Previous home equity product modeling had been conducted through third-party consultants who used a matrix, or a two-dimensional table, to determine which prospects should be mailed which promotional package. The mailings had been profitable, but Fleet's analysts knew that there was more to be learned about customers and prospects. During the first quarter's (2009) home equity product promotion, Fleet became more involved in the modeling process by assigning prospect response scores and further targeting the mailing. The subsequent third-quarter home equity product mailing list was handled completely in-house by combining CART and other data mining and statistical techniques.

"The goal of the mailing project for our home equity line of credit was to identify characteristics of would-be customers and to create a predictive model that could score new prospects," says Lo. "We chose to employ CART because it is an advanced, non-parametric data analysis technique that can efficiently handle missing data values. By hybridizing CART and logistic regression techniques, we were able to use each methodology's strength to complement the other's. CART, in particular, brings with it the unique advantage of helping analysts understand people's behavioral patterns, and it provides excellent predictive accuracy with a proven methodological track record."

The first step in the modeling process was to gather the historical data on which to create the model. The team selected a sample of approximately 20,000 customers for which Fleet had a record of responses; included were 100% of past profitable respondents as well as 2% of past nonrespondents. The customer records were "massaged" into a data set and output as a text file that could be fed into different modeling tools.

The data set was then transferred into CART to display the interaction of the data. The resulting effects were subsequently incorporated into a logistic regression model that illustrated the overall and local landscape of the data. When the data were fed into CART, the software automatically generated a decision tree whose branches, or nodes, showed the hierarchy of binary data splits and displayed the data set's myriad variables and their interactions. This hierarchy distilled nearly 100 predictor variables into a more manageable amount of approximately 25. In addition, the CART nodes provided probability ratios that were used to understand why one segment would be more responsive than another.

"The CART analysis enables an intuitive understanding about the variables and the interactions among them," says Lo. "In Fleet's marketing of this product promotion, this is an essential piece of the puzzle—CART helps provide a human understanding of why certain segments respond better than others, as well as what their needs are and what types of offers will provoke a response."

The CART model illustrated certain characteristics of "best" respondents by predicting the expected balance they would carry on the credit line, as well as how much they might transfer from another line. In addition, the CART results painted a portrait of the principal characteristics of the least responsive customers. These prospects would either not likely respond to a Fleet product offer because they do not have a need for a large line of credit or, equally of concern, they would respond but their subsequent credit line usage and/or likely losses would not be profitable for the bank. "Within a predictive model, accuracy is very important, but it is also important to obtain a true understanding of one's customers," says Lo. "The more we can learn about why a product does or doesn't suit a certain segment, the better we can manage the business and our profitability in the long term; for this project, CART gave us that understanding."

This home equity product mailing might bring an increase in revenues compared with past product mailings. More importantly, it is expected to have a much higher profitability due to more efficient targeting and lower marketing costs, which would give Fleet a higher ROI. Lo's team is cautiously taking into consideration other factors, such as the mailing's time of year and the number of other financial product offerings customers have received recently.

"Test and control groups are needed to validate the efficiency of our targeting with this predictive model," says Lo. "We are, however, very confident that Fleet will achieve a high response rate with this mailing. Our customers have many more dimensions than the previous mailing model could encapsulate for predictions. Creating a hybrid model using CART and our other data mining and statistical tools was a more sophisticated approach that painted a very descriptive portrait of our prospects, enabling us to increase the probability of their response."

The third-quarter home equity promotion is Fleet's first CART modeling application. The company is currently evaluating and applying many more tools to manage its customer information and data warehouses; in the meantime, future plans for CART include applying it to various neural network algorithms and other projects. Once Fleet has received results from this home equity mailing, for example, the responses will be analyzed again in CART to validate the robustness of the original model and to determine other successes, such as whether or not the probability scores are accurately reflected in the response rate. Then CART will be used to construct a new model for the next home equity product mailing based on this mailing's response rates. Says Lo, "This test and learn approach is on-going, and the demand for better models and sophisticated techniques will continually grow."

Fleet will continue to use CART to gain a deeper understanding of its customers so that the information can be applied to classification and segmentation applications among Fleet's other product lines. "Fleet's product managers are anxious to have us determine customer characteristics, identify cross-selling opportunities for products—such as certificates of deposit, money markets and mutual funds—and build predictive models for their promotions," says Lo. "CART's insight into our customers will help us better support our marketing departments, and it will help Fleet harvest an impressive return on our data warehouse and customer information investments."

XperRule Miner Case Studies

Most organizations can be currently labeled "data rich," since they are collecting increasing volumes of data about business processes and resources. Typically, these Data Mountains are used to provide endless "facts and figures" such as "there are 60 categories of occupation," "2000 mortgage accounts are in arrears," etc. Such "facts and figures" do not represent knowledge but if anything can lead to "information overload." However, patterns in the data represent knowledge and most organizations nowadays can be labeled "knowledge poor." Our definition of data mining is the process of discovering knowledge from data.

Data mining enables complex business processes to be understood and reengineered. This can be achieved through the discovery of patterns in data relating to the past behavior of a business process. Such patterns can be used to improve the performance of a process by exploiting favorable patterns and avoiding problematic patterns.

Examples of business processes where data mining can be useful are customer response to mailing, lapsed insurance policies, and energy consumption. In each of these examples, data mining can reveal what factors affect the outcome of the business event or process and the patterns relating the outcome to these factors. Such patterns increase our understanding of these processes and therefore our ability to predict and affect the outcome.

There is a high degree of confusion among the potential users of data mining as to what data mining technologies are. This confusion has been compounded by vendors, of complimentary technologies, positioning their tools as data mining tools. So we have many vendors of query and reporting tools and OLAP (On-Line Analytical Processing) tools claiming that their products can be used for data mining. While it is true that one can discover useful patterns in the data using these tools, there is a question mark as to who is doing the discovery—the user or the tool!

For example, query and reporting tools will interrogate the data and report on any pattern (query) requested by the user. This is a "manual" and "validation-driven" method of discovery in the sense that unless the user suspects a pattern they will never find it! A marginally better situation is encountered with the OLAP tools, which can be termed "visualization driven" since they assist the user in the process of pattern discovery by displaying multidimensional data graphically. The classes of tools that can genuinely be termed "data mining tools" are those that support the automatic discovery of patterns in data.

We are going to make one more assertion regarding the difference between data *mining* and data *modeling*. Data mining is about discovering *understandable* patterns (e.g., trees, rules, or associations) in data. Data modeling is about discovering a model that fits the data, regardless of whether the model is understandable (e.g., tree or rules) or a black box (e.g., neural network). Based on this assertion, we restrict the main data mining technologies to induction and the discovery of associations and clusters.

Rule or decision tree induction is the most established and effective data mining technologies in use today. It is what can be termed "goal-driven" data mining in that a business goal is defined and rule induction is used to generate patterns that relate to that business goal. The business goal can be the occurrence of an event such as "response to mail shots" or "mortgage arrears" or the magnitude of an event such as "energy use" or "efficiency." Rule induction will generate patterns relating the business goal to other data fields (attributes). The resulting patterns are typically generated as a tree with splits on data fields and terminal points (leafs) showing the propensity or magnitude of the business event of interest.

Sex	Age	Time Addr	ResStat	Occup	Time Emp	Time Bank	House Exp	Decision
M	50	0.5	Owner	unemploye	0	0	00145	Reject
M	19	10	Rent	laborer	0.8	0	00140	Reject
F	52	15	Owner	creative_	5.5	14	00000	Accept
M	22	2.5	Rent	creative_	2.6	0	00000	Accept
M	29	13	Owner	driver	0.5	0	00228	Reject
F	16	0.3	Owner	unemploye	0	01	00160	Reject
M	23	11	Owner	professio	0.5	01	00100	Accept
F	27	3	Owner	manager	2.8	01	00280	Reject
F	19	5.4	Owner	guard_etc.	0.3	0	00080	Reject
F	27	0.3	Owner	manager	0.1	01	00272	Reject
M	34	4	Rent	guard_etc.	8.5	07	00195	Accept
M	20	1.3	Rent	laborer	0.1	0	00140	Reject
M	34	1.3	Owner	guard_etc.	0.1	0	00440	Reject

As an example of tree induction data mining, consider this data table that represents captured data on the process of loan authorization. The table captures a number of data items relating to each loan applicant (sex, age, time at address, residence status, occupation, time in employment, time with the bank, and monthly house expenses) as well as the decision made by the underwriters (accept or reject). The objective of applying rule induction data mining to this table is to discover patterns relating the decisions made by the loan underwriters to the details of the application.

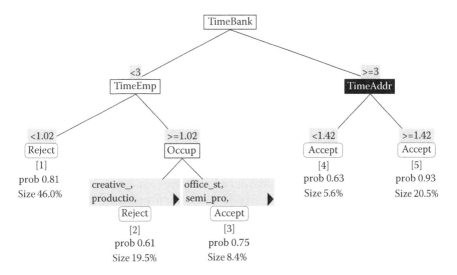

Such patterns can reveal the decision-making process of the underwriters and their consistency, as shown in this tree. It reveals that the time with the bank is the attribute (data field) considered most important with a critical threshold of 3 years. For applicants that have been with the bank over 3 years, the time in employment is considered the next most important factor, and so on. The aforementioned tree reveals five patterns (leafs) each with an outcome (accept or reject) and a probability (0–1). High probability figures represent consistent decision making.

The majority of data miners who use tree induction will most probably use as in automatic algorithm that can generate a tree once the outcome and the attributes are defined. While this is a reasonable first cut for generating patterns from data, the real power of tree induction can be gained using the interactive (incremental) tree induction mode. This mode allows the user to impart his or her knowledge of the business process to the induction algorithm.

In interactive induction, the algorithm stops at every split in the tree (starting at the root) and displays to the user the list of attributes available for activating a split, with these attributes being ranked by the criteria of the induction engine for selecting attributes (significance, entropy, or a combination of both). The user is also presented with the best split of attribute values (threshold or groups of values) according to the algorithm. The user is then free to select the top ranking attribute (and value split) according to the algorithm or select any other attribute in the ranked list. This allows the user to override the automatic selection of attributes based on the user's background knowledge of the process.

For example, the user may feel that the relationship between the outcome and the best attribute is a spurious one or that the best attribute is one that the user has no control over and should be replaced by one that can be controlled. Interactive induction can also be seen as bridging the gap between OLAP-based manual data segmentation/exploration and algorithm-assisted segmentation.

This is the second most common data mining technology and involves the discovery of associations between the various data fields. One popular application of this technology is the discovery of associations between business events or transactions. For example, discovering that 90% of customers that buy product A will also buy product B (basket analysis) or that in 80% of cases when fault 1 is encountered then fault 7 is also encountered. If the sequence of events is important, then another data mining technology for discovering sequences can be used.

A second application of associations discovery data mining is the discovery of associations between the fields of case data. Case data are data that can be structured as a flat table of cases. Records of mortgage applications are an example of case data. In such data, associations can be found between data fields; for example, that 75% of all applicants that are over 45 and in managerial occupations are also earning over £40,000. Such associations can be used as a way of discovering clusters in the data. Note that this differs from rule induction on case data in that no outcome needs to be defined for the discovery process.

A number of case studies are described in the following sections that detail the background to each case study, the data mining approach used, and the benefits gained by the organizations concerned.

Financial

This case study comes from a U.K. Mortgage Lender that had a mortgage portfolio in which 9.8% of all accounts were in arrears (over 3 months in arrears) and 4.1% of all accounts were in severe arrears (over 6 months in arrears). The objectives of the data mining project were to discover patterns relating the propensity of arrears to the mortgage application data.

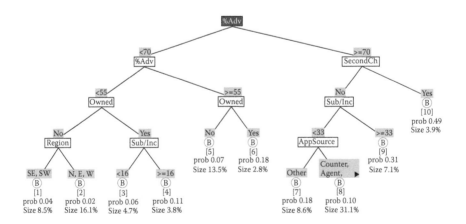

Such patterns can be applied at the front-end applications processing to reduce the level of arrears and can result in better management of accounts that go into arrears.

Rule induction data mining was used with the outcome of the analysis being the arrears status healthy, moderate, or severe. The attributes of the data mining analysis were the mortgage application data such as age, income, occupation, term, loan amount, region, etc. Two separate data mining analysis were carried out; one to discover the patterns of arrears and the second to discover the patterns of severe arrears. Rule induction generated the following tree for arrears with splits on the attributes %Adv (% of loan to property value), SecondCh (second charge on property), Owned (is the property already owned), sub/Inc (subscription to income), AppSource (application source), and Region. The tree reveals 10 profiles with a propensity for arrears ranging from 0.02 to 0.49.

The trees discovered from the arrears data were used in three ways: to generate policy rules that were introduced at the application-processing stage to reduce arrears, to formulate a marketing strategy targeting low-risk profiles, and, finally, to focus arrears management resources on accounts most likely to end up in severe arrears.

This case study is from the Hibernian in Ireland who like other Life Insurer's were facing the challenges of reducing costs, maintaining market share, and meeting market demands. In order to meet these challenges, Hibernian decided to reengineer its Life Underwriting Process in order to speed up the process and reduce its costs.

The first phase of reengineering involved the implementation of a rule-based underwriting system that was used to automate the processing of Life Proposals at the point of application. The system involved capturing underwriting knowledge that resulted in 51% of proposals being underwritten automatically with the remaining cases being referred to head office for manual underwriting.

While the automated underwriting system proved very successful, Hibernian looked for ways of increasing the percentage of cases that can be processed by the system. Attempts were made to capture more advanced underwriting rules; however, this proved to be very difficult. Data mining was then considered as an alternative for generating additional knowledge. The basic premise was that out of the 49% of cases being referred to Head Office, a significant number were underwritten with no or a very small additional premium (less than the cost of the manual underwriting!). It was therefore decided to apply rule induction analysis to cases being referred to Head Office with the amount of additional underwriting premium being used as an outcome. Rule induction analysis generated patterns of low additional premiums of the following format:

If AGE > 30 & AGE < 41 and HEIGHT-WEIGHT = NORMAL Then PREMIUM LOADING = 1%

The generated patterns for low additional premiums were qualified and checked for risk by the actuaries at Hibernian before being added as additional underwriting rules to the automated underwriting system. The result was to increase the rate of automated underwriting to 78%. This case study illustrates how data mining helped Hibernian in Ireland develop new ways of processing life proposals and these methods now underpin a cost-effective new business process.

Energy

This project was carried out for an oil company and was based in a remote U.S. oil field location. The process investigated was a very large gas processing plant that produces two useful products from the gas from the wells, natural gas liquids (NGL), and miscible injectant (MI). NGL is mixed with crude oil and transported for refining, and MI is used to improve the viscosity of oil in the fields to improve crude oil recovery.

The aim of the study was to use data mining techniques to analyze historical process data to find opportunities to increase the production rates, and hence increase the revenue generated by the process. Approximately 2000 data measurements for the process are captured every minute.

Rule induction data mining was used to discover patterns in the data. The business goal for data mining was the revenue from the Gas Process Plant, while the attributes of the analysis fell into two categories: (1) disturbances, such as wind speed and ambient temperature, which have an impact on the way the process is operated and performs, but which have to be accepted by the operators and (2) control set points, these can be altered by the process operators or automatically by the control systems and include temperature and pressure set points, flow ratios, control valve positions, etc.

An important part of the process is where the incoming feed gas is precooled with heat exchangers in two parallel process streams. The oil company has always believed that there is an opportunity to improve process performance by altering the split of flows; however, it was not sure in which way to split the flow and what the impact will be on the revenue. Therefore, flow split was put forward as an attribute for data mining.

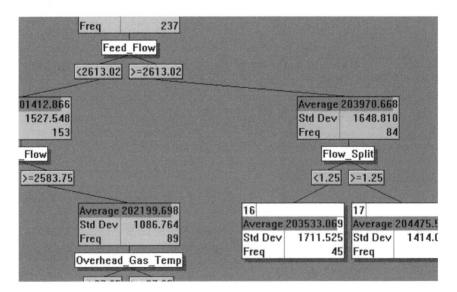

This is the tree generated by rule induction. It reveals patterns relating the revenue from the process to the disturbances and control settings of the process. In particular, the impact of the flow split is revealed with a critical ratio of 1.25:1.

The benefits derived from the generated patterns include the identification of opportunities to improve process revenue considerably (by up to 4%). Mostly, these involve altering control set points, such as altering the flow splits. Some of the discovered knowledge can be implemented without any further work and for no extra cost (e.g., Altering flow splits). In other cases, it is necessary to provide the operators with timely advice about the best combination of settings for a given circumstance. This can be achieved cost-effectively by delivering the rules generated as part of an expert system.

StreamBase Case Study

BlueCrest Capital Management is a leading European hedge fund, based in London, with over $15 billion in assets-under-management and an award-winning reputation for combining "technology, diligence and innovation to produce the most efficient risk-taking possible." BlueCrest has aimed to stay ahead of the curve by anticipating future challenges and investing early in skills and technology. The firm's traders are highly technical with many trained mathematicians.

Complex statistical models form the foundation of some of its trading strategies, and these rely on a rich variety of data feeds to enable them to trade "anything that ticks," as their Head of Trading Strategy Systems, Justo Ruiz-Ferrer describes it, adding, "We trade everything from traditional fixed income, equities, FX and related derivatives, to exotic commodity, energy and alternative asset classes." In such highly competitive markets, BlueCrest soon realized that good data management was as important as their quantitative models. "You may have a Ferrari, but if you fill up your tank at the supermarket, you won't get the performance," observes Ruiz-Ferrer. Scalability and real-time performance were key factors with BlueCrest's data storage demands exploding at 200%–400% per year and exchange-based derivative markets hitting new highs of billions of price ticks per day, not to mention the OTC platforms, as ever more robotraders enter the jittery markets.

Just as the credit crisis was breaking, BlueCrest set up a team under Justo Ruiz-Ferrer to develop a state-of-the-art market data management system. BlueCrest trades 24 h a day, 6 days a week, across multiple markets using a wide range of data feeds. As markets move day to day and week to week, BlueCrest needed to rapidly reconfigure data feed connections and plug the data into real-time models while optimizing management of the necessary data feed licenses. BlueCrest devised a solution that combines the rapid time-to-market event processing capabilities of StreamBase with the instant storage and retrieval functionality of Vertica.

It provides a total market data management solution that is able to meet the needs of low-latency trading and the demanding innovation of their quantitative analysts to achieve greater profitability. As the range of data sources constantly grows with increased cross asset class and exotic derivatives, time to market, low latency, and auditable compliance with complex data licensing rules were essential.

Ad hoc engineering of new data feed adapters had proven to be both expensive and risky due to complex software interfaces, few standards, and low reusability of components. The new system therefore aimed to decouple users from the data sources to create a common interface for accessing, conflating, enriching, and distributing real-time data with minimal latency and assured compliance. Yet, it also had to encourage flexible data sharing across the firm (Figure 4.12).

BlueCrest's new market data system provides both current and historical snapshots and on-demand event processing for both simple requests like last price traded to complex scenarios like volatility surfaces or correlation signals with time windows. It also has to guide the user through the rich jungle of data sources and compliance rules and help resolve queries that may have alternative solutions across the data providers. Each source and derived data-object needs its own access controls, as these cannot always be inferred.

The system was built in three layers: (1) An event layer that includes the data sources and a core event-processing engine from StreamBase to extract, collate, and enrich the source data; (2) the storage layer consists of a real-time, historical tick database from Vertica, backed up on disc, and a last tick store for last known value (LKV) caching; and (3) the control layer includes compliance and management components written in-house in C#. The control layer checks user access

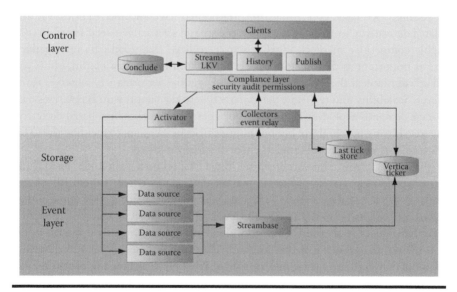

Figure 4.12　StreamBase at the core of real-time event detection and alerts.

permissions, retrieves data from the storage layer, or activates data streams and then dynamically sets up "Collectors" to relay the resulting "event curves," such as volatility, yield, or momentum curves to all subscribed users or their software applications. The whole system is driven by real-time requests from the users or their software models.

Data streams fuel the system. Ticker plant and internal messaging buses feed data to the StreamBase complex event processing engine to clean, normalize, filter, and enrich the event curves. As part of this enrichment, StreamBase can mix real-time events with the historical data in Vertica as needed to evaluate the complex rules, yet still keep pace with the input data rates. StreamBase then forwards the new event curve objects to both Vertica for storage and the Collectors in the control layer, which encrypt them to ensure compliance, cache them in the last tick store, and distribute them to all waiting user processes. Whenever any point changes, StreamBase generates a new event and, therefore, provides a stream of event curves rather than just data points. "It's immensely powerful given the high speed inputs and the complex handling requirements," says Ruiz-Ferrer.

The system works round the clock 6 days a week supporting user services across different geographical locations. Further servers with collectors, local caches, and control software are also located in each office to minimize latencies for last value type queries, which represent the bulk of the workload.

All the core data feeds are now plumbed into the system including the major data aggregators and many direct exchange feeds. However, much of the data actually comes from internal BlueCrest services over the messaging bus. "We can subscribe to everything," says Ruiz-Ferrer, "so we load tested to ten times the whole feed, just to be safe."

Security is tight, hence the encryption, which is the most expensive component in terms of CPU resource, according to Ruiz-Ferrer. Moreover, the system keeps track of who is accessing which service at any time to ensure compliance with the licensing rules. One advantage is that BlueCrest can optimize license fees to maximize sharing when data is not in use. "What a user sees depends on the market data licence. Without the licence, users only see limited price movements, whereas with the license they see everything," explains Ruiz-Ferrer.

In London, all the processes run on a single blade server to eliminate network hops. Each layer of the architecture can be separately scaled across its own set of server blades to meet changing performance and resilience needs. Thus, the whole sequence from real-time source to waiting user servers in London takes under 20 ms on a benchmark test of 2 million updates per second with very low server loadings.

For the middle office and research models, the priority was to leverage the full knowledge base of the firm with great flexibility and rich functionality rather than minimizing microseconds. Indeed the core StreamBase component can typically be completed in well under a millisecond, but complex enrichment and security do add some latency.

The project build started in January and by May it was in production, even allowing for a 1 month delay due to other priorities. The team now is working to port other data feeds and analytics to StreamBase, enriching the visualization tools, as well as making the whole system fail-safe with a high-speed interconnect to the backup site.

Prior to the market data management solution, it could take 2 months or more to add and integrate a new data feed. Now a new service is connected in just 2 weeks because everything is standardized. "This makes the whole business much more responsive and confident," says Ruiz-Ferrer.

Having evaluated many other solutions, the BlueCrest team chose StreamBase because of its real-time performance and flexibility, with many adapters available out of the box for connecting to data feed handlers, messaging and database systems including Vertica, and trading platforms. They found the visual workflow-like design capabilities of StreamBase particularly helpful for rapid development and maintenance.

"StreamBase and Vertica have allowed us to develop our market data environment rapidly with a sound run time behaviour, excellent extensibility and minimum effort," concludes Ruiz-Ferrer. "By investing in a high-speed data storage and an ultra low-latency complex event processing solution, BlueCrest has ensured that its vital market models get the highest octane data mix available to stay ahead of the pack and negotiate the market chicanes at full throttle." BlueCrest has demonstrated once again how innovation can meet the challenges of the rapidly evolving global capital markets.

Google Analytics Case Study

The RE/MAX franchise network is a global real estate system operating in 62 countries with more than 5800 independently owned offices and 114,000 member sales associates who lead the industry in providing real estate services in residential, commercial, referral, relocation, and asset management.

Founded in 1973, RE/MAX provides an entrepreneurial environment that attracts the best agents by providing maximum compensation, advanced support services, and the freedom agents prefer in order to succeed. Since then, the company has continued to provide innovative services to help its members, including relocation and asset management, commercial investment, an international referral network, advanced training courses, state-of-the-art technological tools, Internet and extranet websites, and national television advertising campaigns.

RE/MAX was the first—and is still the only—real estate network to develop and maintain a satellite TV network dedicated to real estate professionals, which is available for viewing in all of the firm's offices and in the homes of individual agents.

As a result of its constant innovation and dedication to supporting its affiliates, RE/MAX has grown every month for more than 32 years.

Increasingly, the real estate market has moved online. A 2004 study by the National Association of Realtors indicated that 74% of consumers begin the home buying process online, and 75% expect their agent to be Internet savvy. In fact, according to industry analysts Borrell Associates, online now accounts for more than one-third of all consumer media time, making it more difficult for advertisers to reach consumers solely through such traditional media as television and print.

As results of this online shift, RE/MAX announced an ambitious new Internet strategy in August 2005. At the heart of this new strategy is the ability for consumers to view all property listings on www.remax.com, whether they are RE/MAX listings or not. This new capability is intended to put more control of listings and lead generation in the hands of RE/MAX agents. As part of the online strategy, RE/MAX turned to Google Analytics for help it in gathering data for its online analysis.

"The goal is to help people find a house and select an agent," says Kristi Graning, senior vice president of IT and e-Business. "In the past, our primary focus was on how many visitors came to our site. But now, consumers are going online so quickly, we want to know more about their behavior in order to serve them better. For instance: Why people are coming to our site? Where they are coming from? And what they do once they get there?"

The insight that Google Analytics provides into online consumer behavior not only confirms many RE/MAX online initiatives; it is also leading to new opportunities. Prior to using Google Analytics, the company relied mostly on focus groups to gauge consumer behavior and interests. But focus groups are time consuming and limited in scope and region. They also lack real-world data.

"With Google Analytics, we will have more true analysis, rather than anecdotal evidence. Plus, Google Analytics offers an international perspective," says Constance Slippy, senior manager of Web Services. "Now we can better understand why people are coming to our site, justify site changes with real data, and make changes that help the consumers."

The RE/MAX site gets more than 2 millions visits a month. With Google Analytics, Kristi Graning and her team were able to see that more than 90% of visitors who came from search engines used search terms that included "remax" in their search query, and about 70% of those visitors subsequently searched for properties on the site.

"We knew that our marketing and TV branding campaigns had worked, since people are so familiar with our name, but now we need to look at other marketing efforts we may be missing that could help drive even more qualified traffic," Graning says. "One obvious example is our ability to expand the keywords we're employing to help searchers find and engage remax.com."

Google Analytics also helped confirm the importance of moving the property search capability directly to the home page. In the past, RE/MAX passed these prospects off to another site. As part of the new Internet initiative, the company will maintain its own property search capabilities and track these leads to agents.

"One of the biggest potentials we see with Google Analytics is the ability to measure our success driving leads to our agents, and the opportunity to eliminate some of the extra fees agents have been paying for lead generation," observes RE/MAX Web Analyst Jeanna Bash. "In the past, we could never track the leads that went to agents from remax.com, because we passed off these searches to Realtor.com. Now, in addition to allowing consumers to search on all listings, we will be able to capture leads, pass them directly to our agents and track and measure our lead to sale conversion rate. This will help increase our value for agents and consumers."

In addition to helping with the new Internet strategy and direction, Google Analytics will also help guide smaller, continual improvements in site design and functionality. For instance, the RE/MAX site offers links to partners that provide complementary services—such as mortgages and moving—as well as informational sections that provide tips and advice. By testing changes in content descriptions and placement of links, the web team can test and track improvements in click through and referrals.

Google Analytics will also provide guidance on appropriate technology for the site. Tracking the type of technology used by visitors—such as computing platforms and speed of Internet connections—will guide RE/MAX as it adds new functionality, such as multimedia files that allow potential buyers to interactively tour properties from their computer.

SAS Case Study

SAS Scandinavian Airlines is the leading airline group in Northern Europe carrying 29 million passengers to over 150 destinations each year. SAS Scandinavian Airlines passengers are able to travel using their mobile phone as their boarding pass. The Mobile Boarding Pass service is available from seven national hub airports: Copenhagen, Gothenburg, Helsinki, London Heathrow, Oslo, Stavanger, and Stockholm as well as 25 regional airports across Scandinavia.

"Currently, approximately 10% of SAS passengers check-in via SMS but our goal for 2011 is that 80% of our customers check-in off-airport, online or via their mobile," says Lars Sandahl Sørensen, senior vice president, Commercial, SAS. "It is very important for us that our customers have the smoothest and simplest travel experience possible with us. We are, therefore, looking forward to rolling out the service later this year, once we have evaluated the trial."

The Mobile Boarding Pass service is available to all passengers with mobile Internet (Wireless Application Protocol [WAP]) enabled mobile phones. Having completed check-in via SMS or the SAS Mobile Portal (www.sas.mobi), passengers click to confirm their flight details and a Mobile Boarding Pass with a 2D barcode is displayed. The Mobile Boarding Pass contains the passenger's flight number, seat number, and departure and arrival time. The 2D barcode contained in the boarding pass can be used when registering luggage at the SAS Self Service Kiosks as well as for Security, Fast Track security, and lounge access.

Unica Case Studies

Citrix

Citrix Systems, Inc. is the global leader and most trusted name in on-demand access to business applications. The only enterprise software company 100% focused on access, Citrix, offers an integrated, end-to-end system that seamlessly connects users, devices, and networks to enterprise resources. More than 200,000 organizations rely on Citrix, including 100% of Fortune 100 companies, 98% of the Fortune Global 500, and thousands of small businesses and individuals. Citrix has approximately 6200 channel and alliance partners in more than 100 countries: its Citrix access PARTNER network is one of the technology industry's largest partner communities. Citrix also supports its offerings with comprehensive, value-added professional services through Citrix Consulting, and training through Citrix Education.

Citrix must manage multifaceted marketing efforts, complex data sets, diverse channels, and multiple offerings, including products, services, and events. Operating in an enterprise environment, with a highly complex sales process, Citrix found it extremely difficult to quantify the value of its marketing investments, both offline and online.

Since the performance of individual marketing programs could not be accurately measured due to the source setup limitations, the organization could not optimize its marketing plans based on experience. When Citrix's agencies would provide reports on campaign performance, Citrix would notice inconsistencies in metrics from third-party sites that could never be adequately explained. Meanwhile, marketing budgets for individual products were set largely based on the revenue those products generated, not on the specific marketing needs and attributes of each individual product or on the results achieved by earlier marketing expenditures.

Years ago, Citrix had implemented a competitive web analytics product. However, that product did not prove effective. After carefully reviewing its options, Citrix implemented Unica NetTracker®, which offers powerful web analytics capabilities for optimizing web programs such as pay-per-click advertising, search engine optimization (SEO), and affiliate marketing. Then, building on what it achieved with Unica NetTracker, Citrix upgraded to Unica NetInsight, Unica's enterprise-class web analytics solution for companies with heavily trafficked websites.

Since NetTracker and NetInsight share similar user interfaces and utilize the same page tagging, the transition between products was seamless. Meanwhile, Citrix chose a new Search Engine Marketing (SEM) agency that utilized NetTracker internally, making coordination even easier and more effective.

Citrix relies heavily on SEM to reach business decision makers. With Unica NetInsight, Citrix can now systematically track the results of its SEM campaigns, work with its agencies to rapidly optimize those campaigns, and reflect current experience in future planning. In its most recent year, Citrix used NetInsight to track 10 campaigns, 42 segments, 91 ad groups, and over 1600 keywords. This generates an enormous amount of information.

To manage all these data points, Citrix makes extensive use of both standard and custom NetInsight reports, such as their Entry Page Breakdown report. Citrix has gained a far better understanding of how customers respond to SEM advertising by engine, campaign, and keyword, and it has learned some valuable lessons. Says Citrix marketing business analyst Susan Zykoski, "Our product managers tended to think in terms of their product names. But those aren't necessarily effective as keywords. In many cases, we've been able to show that generic keywords are much more effective. We also discovered that when analyzing Google and Yahoo!, some specific keyword subcategories performed far better on one engine than on the other. We haven't found any reason why this occurs, but it's real—and we can track and spend money more effectively based on this knowledge."

Citrix holds regular monthly meetings with its agencies to refine its marketing campaigns. "Our NetInsight reports facilitate those discussions and drive better meetings," says Zykoski. "For example, we can look at our results, and quickly say, instead of using A/B creative, maybe we should turn off A." Citrix has also used Unica NetInsight Page and Path Summary reports to help restructure its website, providing more efficient paths for each customer type. "We could see exactly what people were doing, where they were dropping off, who was converting, and how both customers and noncustomers behaved. That has certainly helped us."

With more than 200,000 customers worldwide, Citrix serves an extraordinarily large and diverse user community. Many of Citrix's top customers and prospects come together at the company's flagship annual customer conference event. Citrix has used Unica NetInsight to dramatically improve the way it markets this crucial annual event. Citrix has marketed its customer event through e-mail; SEM and other online advertising; Citrix.com banners; and offline promotions ranging from direct mail to billboards. It set three core objectives for NetInsight: improve tracking of Customer Conference site activity, understand each campaign's effectiveness, and track paid registrations.

Using NetInsight, says Zykoski, "I can now tell you exactly how many event registrations came in from each campaign, which words perform best in SEM, and my ROI on each campaign. The metrics were a huge surprise to us. We discovered which vehicle delivered the most registrations, with the lowest cost-per-registration. But, we also discovered that just four keywords drove 80% of all registrations. And, that there were some campaigns that were not driving any registrations."

"More broadly," continues Zykoski, "we can now ask our managers how many marketing dollars they are willing to spend to get a registrant. Using NetInsight's information, they can think about questions like that, and come up with goals that make sense."

At the highest level, Unica NetInsight has helped Citrix refocus marketing on the customer's needs and thought processes and away from traditional internal imperatives such as specific products and organizational structures. By clarifying what works and what does not, NetInsight has enabled Citrix to link marketing data to decision making.

Says Zykoski, "We can now communicate in 'end-user' language, not 'product manager' language. We can ask the two most important questions: 'what does it all really mean?' and 'what are you going to do about it?' And that has led to some important strategic decisions. For example, we've moved significant dollars from print advertising to SEM."

While driving these high-level benefits, Unica NetInsight has also delivered powerful results "on the ground." For example, Citrix has driven an increase in SEM click-through rates of more than 200%. Even more remarkably, it has driven a 1900% increase in conversions and a reduction of nearly 80% in cost per conversion.

Corel

Corel is one of the world's top software companies, with more than 100 million active users in over 75 countries. Through the years, Corel has built a reputation for delivering innovative, trusted products that are easier to learn and use, helping people achieve new levels of productivity. The industry has responded with hundreds of awards for software innovation, design, and value. Corel's award-winning product portfolio includes some of the world's most widely recognized and popular software brands, including CorelDRAW® Graphics Suite, Corel® Paint Shop Pro® Photo, Corel® Painter™, Corel® VideoStudio®, WinDVD®, Corel® WordPerfect® Office, and WinZip®.

Corel manages a broad product portfolio that spans graphics, photo, video, and office productivity software. With all marketing materials developed in-house (product boxes, flyers, eDMs, and web content) and translated into up to 26 languages, this creates a large volume of work for its internal Marketing Services department. E-mail has increasingly become an inefficient way for Corel to manage content, feedback, workloads, and scheduling because it does not provide a centralized place for multiple people to store files, record feedback, and track progress.

Corel needed a solution that would improve its project organization and scheduling, provide better visibility into content development and feedback, and help to align workloads by easily identifying which staff resources were busy and which were available for extra assignments.

When considering options, Corel ultimately found Unica Marketing Operations OnDemand to be far advanced in terms of reporting functionality. According to

Roisin O'Reilly, Corel's associate project manager, "No other content management/reporting tool measured up; it was like comparing 1980s vintage MS-DOS with modern Windows!"

Marketing Operations OnDemand allows Corel to stay organized and work more efficiently by providing one central location for drafts, feedback, revisions, and scheduling. As drafts are date and time stamped, there is no debating when they are posted for review, or where the delay is if revisions or feedback fall behind schedule. Having the project schedule accessible to all, with tasks assigned to both staff and internal clients, means deadlines are clear and both staff and clients have complete visibility.

"To ease the transition to Unica Marketing Operations OnDemand, we created Quick Reference documents to help project requestors understand how to log a job. Later, we created Best Practices documents to help staff use the product more efficiently and easily. For example, our Best Practices guides tell users which areas of Unica Marketing Operations OnDemand to use for discussion, review and document storage," explains O'Reilly.

With better visibility, more accountability, and higher client satisfaction almost overnight, Corel experienced dramatic gains in efficiency and improvements in client satisfaction. "We've created an environment where both internal clients and resources have complete access to all project information, communications, drafts and schedules," says O' Reilly. "Unica Marketing Operations OnDemand's schedule keeps everyone on track and committed to the deadline. Everyone is automatically notified if their tasks run late. And the review area keeps all drafts in one place, with edits shown—so everyone can track exactly who requested edits, and who made them. Sharing this information has increased everyone's accountability, streamlined communication and dramatically improved our ability to deliver projects on time."

Monster

Monster is the flagship brand of Monster Worldwide, a leading online global careers network. Founded in 1994, Monster now has sites in 23 countries around the world; Monster.com is consistently one of the web's 15 most visited properties. Monster offers a broad array of career-related services for both jobseekers and employers, including job listing search, resume databases, career management tools and advice, networking services, and scholarship search. Monster has generated the bulk of its revenue from employers who pay to advertise jobs and search its resume database; the company is now building a complementary consumer business. In recent years, the Monster site network has grown to encompass sites ranging from Military.com—now the nation's largest military and veterans' membership organization—to Tickle, one of the web's leading social networking sites.

Following several years of breakneck growth, Monster's marketing organization faced a crucial challenge: lead generation revenue growth had hit a ceiling.

Monster recognized that its current media placements would no longer drive the growth it required—new alternatives were essential. In particular, Monster needed to approach e-mail marketing more systematically than ever before, replacing a sporadic, "on demand" approach that was no longer sufficient.

To increase the effectiveness of Monster's e-mail marketing, the company needed to replace its aging, home-grown database marketing system that made it difficult to test, analyze, personalize, segment, and optimize millions of e-mails. After evaluating several solutions, Monster selected Unica Corporation's Enterprise Marketing Management (EMM) suite, for its easy-to-use and highly scalable online and offline capabilities. More specifically, Monster deployed Unica's comprehensive interaction and campaign management solution, Unica Campaign, along with Unica eMessage, a robust e-mail authoring and execution application, as well as Unica PredictiveInsight, for data mining and predictive modeling.

In addition to Unica's EMM suite, Monster decided to implement a new database platform to support its targeted marketing efforts. Together, these applications would enable Monster to design and execute more effective strategies, interact more effectively with customers and prospects, and drive both increases in revenue as well as new cost-efficiencies. By enabling event-based marketing and powerful, network-wide customer profiling, Unica's suite would allow Monster to create highly targeted, value-based communications that maximize each customer interaction, regardless of channel. The next section presents a specific example of how Monster is using Unica's Enterprise Marketing Management suite to drive significant revenue increases.

In order to drive increases in revenue and interact in a timely, effective manner with customers and prospects, Monster has implemented a series of targeted follow-up e-mails based on interest expressed on its website. For example, when an individual visits Monster Learning, an online site that helps individuals find degree programs online in their area, a pop-up advertisement for a specific program may appear. If the individual expresses an interest in the advertisement by clicking "Yes, learn more" or completes a form associated with the advertisement, a confirmation e-mail is sent. This e-mail not only confirms the request for more information, but it is also customized with cross-sell offers, based on the individual's profile, for other relevant degree programs. As a result of these follow-up e-mails, Monster has greatly increased ad value to sponsors.

In the first year since deployment, Monster has already achieved more than $4 million in savings and added revenue as a result of Unica's EMM suite. Monster expected its implementation of Unica's EMM software to deliver multimillion-dollar improvements in resume acquisition and retention. Indeed, in the first year, it generated $3.09 M in value or cost savings. Moreover, this value was achieved with only limited optimization; there are opportunities to achieve even better results going forward.

Previously, setting up a campaign required Monster's marketing and technical professionals to navigate four separate systems: Brio, SAS, web analytics software, and its own proprietary e-mail campaign management tools. With Unica's Enterprise Marketing Suite, this process has been simplified. A campaign that once required 25 h of work now takes only five: an 80% reduction. As a result, Monster increased its throughput from 193 campaigns to over 1000, with only one additional hire. Monster calculates that it is spending $300,000 less to execute the current volume of campaigns than it would have spent without Unica's EMM suite.

In the first year after implementation, Monster anticipated generating $500,000 in revenue from new products made possible by its new marketing and analysis tools. It has, in fact, created two major e-mail-based products: TargetMail for Recruitment, an innovative program of targeted job and career fair opportunities sent to opt-in My Monster members, as well as permission-based e-mail that targets opt-in consumers with relevant product and service offers. These new offerings have generated $1M in new revenue: twice what was anticipated.

"Based on our early successes," says Matt Resteghini, director of consumer relationship marketing, "we've accelerated our marketing plans, setting aggressive revenue goals for this year and beyond. We've committed to achieving 641% growth in the revenue we achieve through database marketing. With the level of quantitative success we're achieving, it's not surprising that we're gaining some real qualitative benefits, too," adds Resteghini. "We've bought ourselves a seat at the table, transforming targeted marketing from an 'afterthought' at Monster to a major, high-profile initiative."

WebTrends Case Studies

Virgin Mobile

Qtel's Virgin Mobile Service (QVMS) leveraged Webtrends Social Consulting Services for their Make it Yours 2011 campaign, a contest in which users submitted their photos for a chance to win a Canon 5D EOS camera package. They were interested in growing their fan base organically, while engaging and connecting with their target market on a personal level.

To achieve this goal, Webtrends developed a custom App that pulled photos from Flickr; displayed them in a gallery; and allowed users to search for, vote for, and share their favorite photos via Facebook and Twitter from a single tab on the QVMS fan page.

Over the course of the campaign, QVMS saw a 57% increase in fan count in just 29 days. Even more impressive was the dramatic growth of engagement among users, evidenced by the sustained 263% increase in daily likes and comments on the QVMS page.

Prior to the Make it Yours campaign, users returned to the QVMS page an average of 1.2 times daily. During the campaign, fans returned to the page an average of 3.6 times daily. This was a dramatic increase indicative of a content, but what is impressive is that the daily comments also increased by 53%, which aligns with the 57% increase in fan count over the course of the contest.

The Make it Yours App not only interested users enough to keep them returning to the page, but it also engaged them to post and comment outside the tab. This is beneficial because users posting and liking content increases Post Quality Score, stream impressions, and EdgeRank. These are all vital ingredients to a powerful Facebook presence that not only attracts new fans but also has the ability to touch fans often and nurture them into conversion, as seen in this campaign with a conversion rate of 60%.

QVMS wanted to tap into Qatar's creative community on Flickr and activate this younger, hip audience to engage with the brand on Facebook. They were particularly interested in the campaign's impact on other channels and the effectiveness of their choice to use Flickr as the contest's point of entry. Webtrends realized their goal and provided post-campaign analysis to illustrate the campaign's significance and success with a 239% increase of average daily inbound traffic from links on Twitter during the Make it Yours campaign.

Flickr.com generated 303% more traffic during the campaign than on Twitter, which was already up 239%, and generated a 262% increase of average daily inbound traffic to the QVMS page from search engines during the Make it Yours campaign. In the week after the App was removed from the page, average daily inbound traffic from Google to the QVMS page was 76% higher than it was before the contest.

The week prior to the Make it Yours campaign, QVMS content received an average of 49 stream impressions daily. In the week after the campaign ended, QVMS content received an average of 113 daily stream impressions. This was a sustainable increase of 131%.

At a $2.00 CPM, the QVMS page generated about $98 of earned media a day prior to the Make it Yours campaign and now generates almost $226 daily. Annualized out, the QVMS page was worth $35,701 in earned media before the contest. It is now worth $82,540.

Rosetta Stone

Eric Ludwig, the senior director of online marketing at Rosetta Stone, shares what his company has learned in Facebook Advertising. He runs social media, SEO, and PPC for Rosetta Stone, the leading provider of language learning software. Rosetta Stone works with Webtrends on their social media strategy.

CPM bidding does not work anymore if you want conversions. Paying per impression is great if you want conversions. Paying per impression is great if you want branding, but if you want clicks, bid CPC. Rosetts Stone had been bidding CPM with minor success until the ad algorithm began to favor placements that had a higher CTR if you mentioned your goal was clicks. While this rewarded CPC bidders, it penalized CPM bidders by shifting their inventory to apps (game traffic).

Use in-line likes: The low CTR on ads resulted in not only a high cost per click but also a high cost per fan. Rosetta Stone was paying over $20 per fan and only 10%–15% of the clicks resulted in an action. An action in this case is becoming a fan but could also be other in-ad actions such as RSVP'ing to an event, voting in a poll, or watching a video. If you send traffic to your site or have a destination URL other than from the drop-down of "I want to advertise something I have on Facebook," the in-line liking disappears.

By enabling in-line likes and by switching to CPC bids, Rosetta Stone was able to cut the cost per fan from over $20 to under $1.50 per fan. His cost per click fell to under a dollar and his fan conversion rate was 60%. That sample tweak did not require new landing pages, programming, or complex campaign changes.

Write short wall posts: Posts that are multiple paragraphs get cut off and are not read. Facebook users have short attention spans. Say it in 10 words or less if you can. By referencing a video or picture, Facebook lets you choose the image, which reinforces the post and increases your engagement rate. Rosetta Stone performed message testing on the wall and saw Post Quality Score fall to low single digits when the wall had lengthy product announcements. When it was short, light-hearted, and not overly promotional, the Post Quality Score would almost reach 10.

Ask questions. Do not just make statements. You want interactions: When your fans hit like or comment, that sends signals into news feeds of their friends. Eric saw the statements on the wall would sometimes get interaction rates less than 1%, while "interesting," short posts that asked questions would consistently get 2%–3%.

Use the contacts Importer for pages: Seems that this feature was recently disabled, though we do not know why; if Facebook brings it back for pages, it allows you to upload your house e-mail list and invite these folks to be friends with your brand. You should expect 5%–10% of your list to convert to fans. If a fan is worth $2.50, you have just created a quarter million dollars of value for zero cost at the press of a button.

Run your acquisition, retention, and organic campaigns at the same time: If you run acquisition campaigns all by themselves, the fans you acquire will be lost, along with the investment you have made there. Therefore, run some campaigns with messages targeting existing fans, such that these are more like messages that happen to be delivered via paid channels than outright advertising. Rosetta Stone runs a different set of ads to existing fans; acquisition campaigns are to create initial connections with folks who want to learn a language. Fan-only campaigns bring users in deeper to try an interactive demo.

Branding is great, but revenue is better: As a publicly traded company, Rosetta Stone does disclose their revenue and is interested in driving shareholder value. What has been a surprise is the revenue that is being driven by social campaigns. Rosetta Stone has a method of assigning a real dollar figure per Facebook fan based on conversion rates, cross-channel marketing overlap, and attribution techniques. Their analytics team slices by last click, first click, and to determine where to spend money profitably.

Gordmans

Founded in 1915, the Omaha-based apparel and home fashions retailer operates 70 stores spread out in over 3.5 million square feet in 16 states, employing more than 4000 associates. When Gordmans went looking for a partner to help them build out their Facebook strategy to increase fan acquisition and engagement as well as drive customers to their brick and mortar stores, they looked to Webtrends. Veronica Stecker, the social media manager at Gordmans, shares what she has learned about marketing on Facebook.

There are two types of Sponsored Stories: a Sponsored Like, which targets friends of your fans, and a Sponsored Post, which shows messages to existing fans. Gordmans ran a highly targeted Sponsored Like ad against the regions where they have 68 retail locations, a female demographic, and interest terms for bargain hunting.

While most Facebook ads are lucky to get a 0.05% CTR, this campaign drove a 0.400% CTR on the first day, which fell by 45% within 48 h to 0.220%. Generally, anything at or above 0.1% is highly optimized! Sponsored likes also decreased the CPC by 70% and CPF by 83% overall. That is like getting a 77% discount off from Facebook!

In 2 days, this ad drove 515 clicks for $76 and gained 418 new fans. That works out to 18 cents per fan and a click-to-conversion rate of 81%. Most brands out there are getting fans at between $2 and $10, the former via self-serve and the latter via premium ads. $0.18 for a new fan, one that is giving your brand permission to talk to them, is a great cost of acquisition.

Gordmans found the key to success with Facebook advertising is leveraging the endorsement of their existing fans. People are far more likely to click on events that are associated with what their friends are doing.

The creative refresh demand of social requires you to be able to iterate much quicker, refresh your content and creative much quicker than what we have seen with the other types of online marketing. Just standing out on a page is not enough; so Gordmans knew they needed to rotate ads to keep them fresh. Facebook Ads are typically served to the same users multiple times, of 10 in the same day, so they quickly tune out repeat ads.

Gordmans also used Webtrends Apps platform to develop fresh and engaging apps rewarding customers for engaging with them through fans-only promotions. While apps have about a 10–14 day shelf life before people start to drop off in interaction, Ads have around 3–5 days before you see a dramatic drop off.

The average human attention span is about 30 s. In fact, successful Facebook advertisers try to relate images to their audience, for example, by serving an image of a local landmark or in Gordmans case including the city name is another way to garner more attention. By injecting the city name in the ad image in conjunction with the geotargeting the ads were more appealing and relevant. Gordmans found that geo-targeted ads with the city name on the ad image performed better than the ads without it. With geo-targeted ads that offered fans the opportunity to check in and claim deals, Gordmans was able to drive customers to their brick and mortar stores.

ClickTale Case Study

Freestyle Accounting is an industry leading firm of contractor accountants providing accountancy and tax planning service to U.K. contractors, freelancers, and consultants. Their comprehensive limited company accountancy service includes everything a contractor needs from initial company formation, business bank account setup, and PAYE/VAT registration, right through to quarterly VAT returns and annual accounts preparation, personal tax return, professional indemnity insurance, plus unlimited IR35 contract reviews and tax advice. The service is offered to contractors and freelancers throughout the United Kingdom, with offices based in Coventry and London.

The main objective of the Freestyle Accounting website is to provide information on the company's services and to persuade visitors to engage by completing their online enquiry form used as leads for its sales team. Freestyle Accounting was using Google Website Optimizer to run split usability testing on its web pages. However, it was still not able to explain why visitors were abandoning its homepage or failing to complete the enquiry form. It needed to understand what visitors were doing inside the web pages.

Freestyle decided to use ClickTale to discover why a large number of visitors were abandoning its homepage and its form conversion funnel. These are the tools Freestyle used and what it discovered using each one. The original homepage contained a lot of text and numerous calls to action. After watching the visitor recordings and actually seeing where visitors were moving, clicking, and scrolling with their mouse, the Freestyle team realized that visitors were confused and not sure where to navigate to next, causing visitor abandonment of the site. Its page content needed to be restructured to create a clearer navigational flow.

The heatmaps revealed what content on the page visitors were paying attention to how they used web page elements and their placement on the page. Freestyle saw which areas of the page were engaging visitors and how far down below the fold visitors were willing to scroll for information. Using ClickTale In-page analytics software for only 2.5 months, the accountancy firm underwent a homepage redesign, incorporating data discovered while using Visitor Recordings and Heatmaps. The homepage now contains significantly less content on the page, clearer separation between content categories, and less, but more prominent, calls to action. Visitors now have an easier time navigating through to additional web pages on the site.

Prior to redesigning the homepage, its conversion rate was only 1.1% from the homepage. Following the redesign based on ClickTale feedback, the firm experienced a dramatic increase to 3.7%, a massive 236% improvement! In addition to the homepage, Freestyle Accounting also needed to work on its enquiry form to increase its overall conversion rate. This ClickTale tool provided some great insight into where the user was either having difficulty or did not want to provide certain pieces of information. It was clear that the amount of fields on the form were either intimidating potential customers or preventing them from submitting the form.

24/7 RealMedia Case Studies

Jamba Juice

Jamba Juice is a specialist vendor of healthy blended beverages, juices, and snacks, with over 600 franchised and company retail outlets in California and over 20 other states. The company wished to carry out a classic promotion: to drive visitors to its stores over the course of a 2 week campaign with a "BOGO" (Buy one get one free) beverage offer.

Guided by digital advertising agency Xylem CCI's media agent, JL 360, Jamba Juice decided to conduct a pure online campaign. This campaign was targeted primarily at women, who predominate among Jamba Juice's customers. 24/7 Real Media was chosen by Xylem CCI and JL 360 to be the digital advertising partner. The resulting campaign included multiple creative variants in different banner formats. All of these creatives invited the viewer to click through to a web page where they could print out a coupon—unique to this campaign—with which to claim their BOGO.

The campaign began with a target of 100,000 coupon redemptions over a 14 day period, with coupons expiring at the end of the campaign. The resulting ads were served on a RON basis across the 24/7 Global Web Alliance network of over 950 websites. They were targeted geographically, aiming mainly toward California as well as the other regional markets where Jamba Juice operates. As women were a main target market, Jamba Juice could reach these potential female customers through 24/7 Real Media's Women's Interest vertical channel. People who visited Jamba Juice's own site at one point and then later browsed the Internet were then also served additional "retargeted" ads when they visited any of the websites on the Web Alliance. As well as regular in-page banners, page load ads were used, in which a full page ad pops up while the user's requested page is loading. The campaign was also supported with a limited outreach of 62,000 branded outbound e-mails to untested subscribers within Jamba Juice's database. These subscribers received the same offer as was extended in the banner campaign.

By the end of campaign day 8, visitors had downloaded all of the coupons that Jamba Juice had allocated to the full 14 days of the campaign, on a spend of approximately 50% of the budget.

Retargeted ads—those delivered to people browsing the Internet who had previously visited Jamba Juice's website—yielded the highest response levels of all ads served. They resulted in a level of success for Jamba Juice's campaign that even the most optimistic projections had not foreseen. Both in this and in a growing number of other campaigns, retargeting over the 24/7 Real Media Global Web Alliance, combined with high-quality creative and other appropriate targeting methods, has proven to be one of the most effective ways of moving campaigns from calls to action to action itself.

Accor Group

The Accor Group is a global leader in the hotel business with over 4000 hotels on five continents. Accor offers stays adapted to each customer. The activities of travel and catering agencies and of casinos complete this unique offer in the universe of tourism and leisure. Accor focuses on employees' needs as well as the productivity objectives of the companies, with objectives to make life easier—for example, lunch tickets as part of salary package—to develop well-being, and to improve overall performance. The Online success of Accor Group speaks for itself with revenue of €431 millions—9.6% of total revenue was generated on the Internet with an increase of 40% for online night bookings—with up to 17,200 nights hotel bookings.

Accor had several goals in mind: to develop animated advertising for their promotions and to be able to frequently renew the communication and subject topics of these advertisements. Additionally, they wanted to increase the sales from their websites by developing promotional offers that would allow them to cross- and up-sell their offerings. And last, they wanted to achieve total autonomy with their functional and marketing publishers. This meant that they wanted to have control over setting campaign parameters, with a clear definition of how the campaign was going to be run, from beginning to end. It also meant that they needed flexibility to update banners at will.

Accor came to 24/7 Real Media because they knew they could achieve several goals.

As stated before, a primary goal was to have a clearly defined set of parameters from beginning to end. Another important goal was to target their internal promotions according to the language and country of the user due to its global status. This coupled with a need to optimize performance through setting capping rules—in order to avoid saturating their targeted audience with the same ads over and over again—created a need for a well-integrated system of ad delivery and analytics.

Accor selected 24/7 Real Media and its ad serving solution, Open AdStream, because of its versatility in handling the issues with which they were concerned. Open AdStream allowed for contextual integration of access links to services and complementary offers from organizations such as Air France and Europcar, which develop both customers' loyalty and Accor's revenue. Additionally, Open AdStream allowed managing promotional campaigns on the booking confirmation screen of Accor's website, which, in turn, allowed for ad targeting according to the destination booked by customers.

Accor chose Open AdStream not only for its ability to deliver targeted ads but also because the availability and the reactivity of 24/7 Real Media's technical teams are second to none. 24/7 Real Media quickly adapted to Accor's style and was able to promptly fix any issues that may have arisen.

Personal Creations

Personal Creations is an online merchant of personalized gifts for seasonal occasions and special events such as weddings, baby showers, and graduations. It offers a wide variety of products, including jewelry, apparel, decorative accents, and furniture, each decorated with the customer's requested customized message or design. In recent years, the popularity of personalized gifts has dramatically increased. This year, approximately 28% of U.S. shoppers will go online to purchase a personalized gift during the holidays and industry insiders expect this market to continue to experience rapid growth.

Personal Creations wanted to establish a cost-effective digital marketing plan that would take full advantage of this growing market. In particular, the company wanted to increase the conversion of nonspending browsers into actual buyers. The company selected 24/7 Real Media to run its campaign on its Global Web Alliance network of websites, as it was best suited to accomplish this objective. 24/7 Real Media has a track record of success—as demonstrated by improved advertiser ROI—both with behavioral targeting in general and with retargeting in particular. Retargeting is a form of behavioral targeting: it involves the identification of users when they visit an advertiser's site, and then at a later time (hours, days, even weeks later) serving them ads from the advertiser on the pages of other sites on a network.

Using the Open AdStream platform that powers the Global Web Alliance, 24/7 Real Media worked with the client to devise and implement a retargeting program. The campaign was executed in order to serve banner and out-of-page ad units to Personal Creations' visitors and whenever they later visited their Global Web Alliance network of more than 950 web properties. The "detonator" for this campaign was a keyword-driven search campaign to increase initial traffic to the Personal Creations site. The campaign went live on November 16 and ran until December 15.

Over the specified period, the campaign raised the overall conversion rate of visitors to the Personal Creations site by 18%, while the conversion rate among those who were responding to a retargeted ad was 9%. The percentage of those who were retargeted with one or more ads who clicked through to the Personal Creations site was 11%. The average value of sales also rose by 10%. The campaign was so successful that Personal Creations ran a follow-up campaign during the Easter/Mother's Day/Father's Day/Graduation time frame from March 1 through May 31.

The use of retargeting demonstrated its prodigious effectiveness as a tool for converting viewers to buyers. When coupled with a network of sufficient size, such as 24/7 Real Media's Global Web Alliance, it not only increases click conversions but also lifts the overall site conversion rate. In fact, this kind of retargeting generates conversion rates close to internal e-mail marketing programs but without their associated headaches and complexities, such as data collection, open rates, transmission costs, and spam. With this retargeting strategy in place, Personal Creations could continue to capture increasing sales and revenues from visitors to its site as well as increase brand awareness and preference.

Forbes

The Forbes websites (Forbes.com, ForbesAutos.com, and ForbesTraveler.com) were using two separate technologies to serve ads on their pages—24/7 Real Media's Open AdStream run on their local servers for traditional banner ads and their own in-house system for rich media video ads. Forbes opted to bring all of their ad serving together in one place using Open AdStream, an integrated ad serving, targeting, and tracking solution with the capacity to handle all kinds of media. Moving their entire ad serving and management to the Open AdStream platform has significantly enhanced the Forbes websites' ability to maximize the value of their inventory while also allowing them to reinforce their competitive market position with more sophisticated and effective services to advertisers.

Forbes.com is the most highly trafficked business and financial news site on the web and operates alongside its sister properties luxury automobile site ForbesAutos.com and luxury travel site ForbesTraveler.com. The Forbes websites have used 24/7 Real Media's Open AdStream technology to serve banner ads on their pages since 2001, while at the same time serving video ads using an in-house solution. The Forbes sites wanted to make their ad serving, campaign management, and analytics more streamlined, efficient, and transparent so that they could maximize the value of their inventory and offer their advertisers the greatest possible effectiveness. Forbes wanted to streamline efforts when setting up campaigns, increase efficiencies in managing them, and integrate reporting capabilities of the two technologies in order to easily reconcile campaign.

The Forbes sites migrated all of their ad serving, including video, to 24/7 Real Media's Open AdStream platform. "It was an easy and seamless process to implement Open AdStream and integrate all of our ad serving and management in one platform," said Forbes.com's Michael Smith, VP and general manager of Operations.

Advertising campaigns involving video are increasingly popular and valuable, and thus it is imperative for Forbes to be well positioned to efficiently and effectively implement and serve video campaigns. The robustness of Open AdStream has made it possible for Forbes.com to set up campaigns in 30 min, whereas previously the process took about 2 h longer. This increase in operational efficiency has allowed Forbes to better serve advertisers while increasing operational productivity and cost savings.

AdPepper Case Studies

BBC

The campaign was successful, enjoying a strong and steady click-through rate. Optimization based upon iSense categories took place throughout the duration of the campaign, with a focus toward the iSense categories of TV Entertainment, TV News, Music, Entertainment and media, Film and cinema, and TV Drama and Soaps. The client was very happy with the results which led to an upsurge in downloads and delivery to relevant content areas. This campaign has resulted in a number of repeat bookings for similar campaigns.

The British Broadcasting Corporation is the United Kingdom's main public television broadcaster. Their iPlayer video on demand service enables Internet users to watch the previous week's programmes on demand. The objective of the campaign was to promote brand awareness, driving traffic to the site, and promoting downloads of the content. iSense was chosen due to reach and content targeting technology. The target audience for this campaign was avid TV followers of BBC soaps, drama, entertainment programmes, and documentaries.

BDO Stoy Hayward

BDO Stoy Hayward is the award-winning U.K. Member Firm of BDO International, the world's fifth largest accountancy network, with more than 1000 offices in over 100 countries. The campaign objective was to create awareness for BDO Stoy Hayward management consultancy services and gain appointments for their consultants within their major target markets. iSense was selected due to the precise content targeting we could offer for their target sectors within the finance, retail, and property industry.

The target audience for the campaign was to be board level company executives and business development managers. The campaign was a major success. iSense was the best-performing campaign, proving to be the most effective in terms of content targeting. The campaign resulted in strong levels of conversions for appointments for the BDO consultants, which, in turn, also led to strong conversions for resulting business. iSense will now perform a major role in future campaigns conducted by BDO.

T-Mobile

The campaign was a resounding success. iSense was the best-performing network and content targeting solution. Click-through rates and especially conversions significantly outperformed the results they achieved through contextual and other methods of content targeting. The campaign exceeded all expectations and has resulted in subsequent rebookings of similar campaigns by T-Mobile.

T-Mobile was granted the exclusive U.K. license for the new Google G1 Android phone. Their aim for this campaign was to create brand awareness and to drive up preorder signups for this groundbreaking product. iSense was chosen because of the ability to accurately target relevant content at page level. The target audience for the campaign was predominantly male, who would be technically aware, early adopters of the latest technology, and were likely to be from an ABC1 socioeconomic group.

Adtegrity Case Study

AccuQuote makes it possible for customers to find the best values in term life insurance. How? By combining instant term life insurance quotes with the personal service of unbiased life insurance professionals that can answer questions, identify important issues, and make meaningful recommendations. AccuQuote generates 500+ qualified leads each month in the United States. A qualified lead consists of a three-page conversion process. All three steps need to be completed for a valid conversion. The CPA rate has varied over the course of the campaign and is currently over $70.

Every field a user has to fill out and each page a user needs to complete can decrease the overall success of the campaign, making it more difficult to generate a high volume of leads. Lead generation in general can suffer at the hands of creative over exposure, resulting in less effective ads over time.

Adtegrity.com's daily hands-on optimization includes day-part targeting, geo-targeting by state and DMA, retargeting, age and gender targeting, creative analysis, publisher site/section optimization, contextual targeting, and data-driven ROI projections. Utilizing these optimization techniques, our highly trained staff easily met and exceeded the clients' expectations for campaign success. We then turned our full focus to helping the client achieve higher ROI's by fine-tuning our conversion delivery to markets and households that achieve the best margins for the client.

BURST! Media Case Studies

Take Care Health Systems

Take Care Health Systems (TCHS) launched Take Care ClinicsSM to bring everyday family health care to nearly 360 Walgreens drugstores throughout the country. TCHS sought to increase brand awareness of recently established Take Care Clinics in nearly three dozen geographical markets. TCHS' agency of record for the campaign came to Burst to drive a clearly defined primary audience of moms with school aged children to the TCHS landing page. Campaign success metrics were based on full delivery, an above-average click-through rate, and optimization efforts as needed.

Burst created a TCHS custom vertical channel that delivered an audience saturated with moms. Comprised of quality health and mom content, the custom channel was built with long-tail websites—sites that draw a loyal audience of consumers ready to act. Burst Media's campaign manager proactively monitored all campaign metrics and gave daily updates to the agency. The manager also provided insight on campaign performance—granularly at the site level—and optimized the campaign by reallocating impressions to the best-performing properties and creative executions.

Fuse

Fuse is a national music television network that brings viewers closer to their favorite artists and bands by featuring video blocks, exclusive interviews, live concerts, series, and specials—all rooted in the music experience. Fuse premiered a new original show, *Redemption Song*, its primary campaign goals were to generate buzz and awareness of *Redemption Song* among nonsubscribers as well as Fuse subscribers, by building an audience and driving users to watch the show during a 10 day media flight. The target audience included reality show junkies, pop culture enthusiasts, music lovers, and cable subscribers, all within the 18–34 age range.

Because of the short campaign flight, Burst recommended a preoptimized custom channel of hand selected sites that appealed to Redemption Song's target audience. Sites in the channel included reality TV, general television, music, pop culture, nightlife, women, and entertainment content. A run of content channels that indexed highest for unique visitors who watch reality television on a weekly basis. Burst's creative solutions team recommended the BurstVideo Cube, powered by Unicast, as the ideal solution to generate high user engagement in the short media window. The BurstVideo Cube encourages user interaction by providing up to six video options for the user to view within a single creative unit.

Kaboose

Kaboose, Inc. is a global media company fully dedicated to meeting the needs of moms and their families. It provides parents with an extensive array of relevant information, resources, tools, and community that support their efforts during the parenting life cycle. Kaboose's websites include its award-winning flagship, Kaboose.com, which gives moms the tools they need to plan an active, healthy, and rewarding family life.

Kaboose approached Burst Media to drive traffic to their website and generate registrations for a sweepstakes promotion to win $10,000 toward baby supplies and expenses. The target audience was moms and "family-minded" women. After examining Kaboose.com's target audience and campaign goals, Burst recommended MomIQ. The channel offers an audience with a high composition index (161) for women aged 25–54 with children, which made MomIQ the smart choice for Kaboose.com.

Working with Kaboose.com, Burst's Campaign Management team tested various creative sizes and placements to identify the best-performing units to use for the campaign. Over a 1 week period, it was determined that a leader board and wide skyscraper demonstrated the highest CTRs and were ideal for Kaboose.com's campaign. Once the media flight began, Burst's Campaign Management team began to actively manage the campaign for optimal performance. Utilizing Burst's proprietary optimization technologies and algorithms, the team quickly identified and removed underperforming placements and reallocated impressions to achieve Kaboose.com's stringent ROI metrics.

Casale Media Case Studies

Industry: Publishing

Prominent U.S. book publisher marries media and creative to achieve wide-scale brand exposure.

Objective: Our publishing client needed to boost awareness for a new book release within an aggressive 7 day period.

Solution: We proposed a Custom Audience Network campaign (our flagship branding solution) combined with our high-impact Videobox ad format that would take advantage of the publisher's existing video assets. Media was selectively focused on the audience segments that indexed highest to the publisher's core consumer base to ensure that only the most qualified users would be exposed to the campaign's creative.

Results: Post-campaign performance analysis revealed that the precision of upfront audience targeting supplemented by the emotional branding power of video resulted in the following:

- CTR 15 times higher than the industry standard for display media campaigns
- No optimization lag time (campaign was outperforming industry standard CTRs by 17 times within hours of launching)

Industry: Telecommunications

Leading telco selects Videobox as a launch pad for new device lineup.

Background: Our telco client ran an interactive product demonstration on MediaNet to generate rapid awareness and adoption of its latest lineup of device offerings. Using the Videobox creative format, Casale Media, in collaboration with the client's creative agency, produced an engaging, multilayered interactive ad to showcase each new product within the Videobox overlay environment.

Solution: The campaign was set up to run nationally, relying on Optimax to fine-tune placement to the most responsive audience segments.

Results: After 1 month in flight, the campaign's CTR was pacing an astounding 26 times higher than the industry average for standard display creative, indicating qualified market penetration at an accelerated rate.

Industry: Automotive

Videobox helps automaker extend TV exposure for social media promotion with higher efficiency than standard display.

Our automotive client ran two concurrent campaigns on MediaNet to promote a social media–driven contest. Each campaign had an identical targeting setup, but one used Videobox and the other a standard in-banner creative.

Setup: The campaign was set up to run on sites skewing to A21+ who owned the client's auto make.

Results: A comparative analysis at the 2 week mark showed that

- CTR for the Videobox campaign was almost five times higher than the in-banner campaign
- eCPC for the Videobox campaign was more than three times lower than the in-banner campaign

Federated Media Case Studies

Client: Milk-Bone

Goal: Increase brand awareness to fuel Milk-Bone purchase intent and heighten customer loyalty.

Solution: Top FM parenting/home partners created custom content about the dogs they love that was distributed through a social-enabled conversational ad unit. The unit also featured Milk-Bone content, a flip book of dog photos from Milk-Bone's Flickr stream, an educational video about Canine Assistants and social sharing tools.

Success: Milk-Bone "It's Good to Give" Facebook Fan Page grew by more than 8000 Fans during the campaign fueling the community dialogue.

Client: My Life Scoop (Intel)

Goal: Create an engaging platform to help consumers understand and adopt technology in order to simplify their lives.

Solution: Intel partnered with Federated Media to develop the MyLifeScoop platform leveraging the social media platforms and the best voices of the Independent Web at FM. MyLifeScoop.com publishes unique *Featured Stories* from A-list bloggers;

practical *Tech Tips and Tricks*; and *Top 10 Lists* with Advice, Conversations, and How-To's and aggregates a featured *Blog of the Week* from around the web. MyLifeScoop actively maintains a strong twitter, Facebook, and YouTube Voice serving all major social media platforms. By providing consumers with original and engaging content via the MyLifeScoop platform, Intel has been able to increase preference for their brand and purchase intent for their partners' computer products. MLS has gained 20,000 Members and 14,116 people "Liked" the LifesScoop Facebook Page, and MLS has 13,500 Followers on Twitter.

Client: Hyundai Tucson Movie Awards Season

Goal: To build Hyundai 2010 Tucson product awareness, promote user interaction with brand by aligning with Movie Award Season and drive traffic and shopping actions to Tucson model page.

Solution: Serious Eats and Bakerella created 14 Movie Awards-themed recipes that were promoted and distributed via shareable widget inspiring readers to cook creatively for their Oscar parties. A social-enabled Conversationalist Ad offered readers quick access to Movie Award recipes and enabled them to share virally with their friends. Generated 200+ comments on the series posts, highly engaged readers shared the widget on Facebook resulting in tens of thousands of external views and clicking directly to HyundaiUSA.com.

Gorilla Nation Media Case Study

Gorilla Nation deploys Cisco ACE modules to consolidate hardware, improve performance, and help with company's green initiative. Gorilla Nation is the world's largest online ad sales representation company. The company exclusively represents the online ad inventory of over 500 leading mid-tail web publishers and sells integrated media and promotional programs to Fortune 500 brand advertisers. As a one-stop shop for online advertisers and agencies, Gorilla Nation assists companies in developing media and creative strategies, executing plans with volume media buys, and delivering campaigns utilizing their advanced ad-serving technology. The company is headquartered in Los Angeles and has offices in New York, Chicago, San Francisco, Toronto, and London.

Gorilla Nation has been the recipient of several business achievement awards, such as Entrepreneur Magazine's Hot 100, the Inc. 500, and Deloitte & Touche's Fast 500 with Rising Star honors. The company also recently placed on the comScore Media Metrix top 15 list for their high number of monthly unique visitors to their website properties, alongside companies such as Google, Yahoo!, and Disney.

"As a company, we have made the strategic decision to raise Gorilla Nation's technology efficiency to the same level as our business vision," says Alex Godelman, vice president of technology. "Our existing solution was aging and approaching end-of-life. We decided to address the areas of highest need, which included high-performing, cost-effective application and highly redundant delivery solutions that were scalable and green."

With high availability and high performance as priorities for Gorilla Nation, Godelman understood pricing might be just as high for the right solution.

"I had recently gone through a similar exercise at another company and had determined that I was going to find a single vendor who was able to put together a unique combination of multiple solutions residing in one box that could also help us support our green efforts." Prior to the evaluation process, Godelman and his technology team had decided that they were going to look for all the necessary functionality through one vendor solution or a maximum of two. The team looked at several vendors including Cisco.

"Unfortunately, a number of the solutions that we looked at were not that great because they could not give us as complete of a solution as we were looking for and those that did meet some of our requirements were still lacking in others," says Godelman. "I had worked with Cisco before and had been one of the early adopters for various Cisco product lines including ACE, and was well versed in its capabilities. The 6500/ACE combo was the only product that had all the functions and capabilities that we were looking for in a single multifunction chassis."

Godelman and his team selected nearly a dozen Cisco® ACE/Catalyst® 6500 Series Switch combinations for use in the company's three data center silos.

"I was literally blown away with the features and performance, and the ability to get a great number of different appliances within the same box," says Godelman. "We immediately decided to roll the ACE out to power three of our silos."

Godelman says the Cisco ACE's virtualization capabilities have allowed the team to load balance in a variety of ways that have been instrumental to Gorilla Nation.

"We're using four different load balancers for each specific tier of our four-tier environment where we have a presentation tier, an application tier or processing tier, a database tier and global or global utility tier," says Godelman. "Each tier has its own designated network that requires the load-balancing features, and through ACE's virtualization capabilities, we are able to provide a virtual load balancer for each environment without having to designate eight different units within two silos, and all with high availability."

Godelman adds that the multifunction and virtualization aspect of Cisco ACE also provides his team with scalability without having to purchase additional hardware.

"We don't have to concern ourselves with how many ports will be dedicated to which load balancer because all of it is virtual and can be repurposed for any of these virtual load balancers at any point," says Godelman. "The ACE gives us flexibility without having to increase our hardware footprint. Our plan is to execute all functions within the 6500 series switch and to not have any other devices outside of the 6500s. This streamlined hardware approach is how we are cutting down on power and helps us fulfill our eco requirements."

Godelman says having multifunctional ability has been the number-one benefit from the upgrade. "The ability to eliminate the need to acquire a number of different technologies from different vendors allowed us to achieve all of the technology goals while not sacrificing or even lowering our performance and scalability standards or our desires to be ecologically friendly," says Godelman. "Moreover, the 6500/ACE solution was able to provide us with what was needed, at the right price point, which allowed us to meet our aggressive TCO [total cost of ownership] objectives."

"The ACE also has incredible richness of features, some of which are simply not available anywhere, even on appliances that are made for a specific stand-alone need that don't have other functionalities that the 6500s have," adds Godelman. "We are extremely pleased with our selection."

Having multifunctionality in single modules also allows Gorilla Nation to meet their internal green goals, according to Godelman. "One of the ways that we are measuring ROI [return on investment] is our eco footprint on equipment. Having the ability to streamline our hardware into single ACE modules has enabled us to reduce the amount of hardware as well as the amount of power consumption that we believe will be reflected on our electric bills in the coming months."

Performance and reduced response time are also results of the upgrade to the Cisco ACE, according to Godelman. "Our sites are very heavy in media-rich content, and Gorilla Nation has very aggressive targets in terms of performance and response time," says Godelman. "The ACE has been so promising, because it lowers our response time to a fraction of what many of our bigger competitors currently offer their users."

Godelman adds that because of Cisco ACE's high-performance capabilities, Gorilla Nation will be able to climb the ranks and continue its success competing with Google, Yahoo, ValueClick, and other top players in the online media space.

"Success on websites is not measured in dollars and cents that way that movies are measured, but are monitored by independent digital measurement sources such as comScore, in different ways such as page views and unique visitors," says Godelman. "We have specific targets for performance and high availability that are very competitive with well-known online players, and we consistently receive high marks with comScore. Cisco ACE is helping us achieve the high availability and low response time necessary to keep visitors coming to our sites while enabling us to effectively play on the field with the top players that we all know. We see Cisco as a strategic technology partner with Gorilla Nation that will help us compete at the highest levels."

InterClick Case Studies

Mobile

With the launch of a brand-new smartphone in the crowded mobile category, a leading technology company teamed with interclick to raise awareness, increase consideration, and drive sales skyward. interclick designed a campaign to promote the capabilities of the new device, targeting early adopters looking for a mobile device that was ideal for both work and play.

Interclick implemented a 7 month strategy to connect with techy consumers in-market for a new smartphone. Utilizing our audience targeting platform, OSM, we found the tech company's ideal audience by implementing search retargeting data to connect with in-market smartphone shoppers, from coast to coast and beyond, and placing a retargeting pixel on the client's website, targeting users visiting the site. interclick's ability to combine sophisticated statistical treatments with media execution delivered astounding results for the client. We proved to be one of the top performers for this campaign by producing an $8.75 eCPA, surpassing the extremely aggressive $9 eCPA goal. As a result, interclick will be part of the media plan for the product launch later this year.

Automotive

A leading car manufacturer wanted to target auto intenders to promote its new models and summer sales events. It put interclick in the driver's seat with a mission: design an efficient campaign that would drive traffic to its website and generate buyer leads.

Using our audience targeting platform, OSM, interclick developed a 2 month strategy to help the manufacturer reach its target audience and drive leads. We implemented third-party behavioral data for the client's brand and car models to target their most likely customers. Competitors' make and level data were also applied to entice ambivalent consumers and gain market share. We placed a retargeting pixel on the client's website to reconnect the auto brand with its most responsive audiences.

interclick's innovative data-driven strategy delivered remarkable results for the leading car manufacturer. Our operations team constantly optimized the campaign to ensure the best-performing data were used. As a result, interclick dipped the client's overall KPI of $3.36 by 67%. We surpassed their CTR goal by 120% as well. Our proven ability to flawlessly execute campaigns earned inter-click the incremental budget to connect the car brand with its most responsive audiences.

Juice

America's leading fruit juice brand had been experiencing a decline in consumption due to consumer concerns about nutritional value and price point. To reverse this trend, the brand teamed with interclick to design a campaign connecting them with consumers at all stages of the purchase funnel. Goals included raising awareness, driving traffic to the juice producer's website, and promoting a rewards program aimed at enticing people to purchase their juice.

Leveraging our audience targeting platform, OSM, interclick crafted a 1 month campaign combining with DataLogix frequent-buyer data to target consumers by lifestyle, including soccer moms, suburban families, affluent baby boomers, and healthy living enthusiasts. Demographic data targeting adults 25–54 and mature adults 55+ to reach nonbuyers and gain market share and channel site list was used to connect with targeted consumers at their passion points, including a retargeting pixel on the juice brand's website to reconnect with hand raisers and brand protection solutions to ensure ads ran only in brand-friendly environments. By combining sophisticated statistical treatments with media execution, interclick proved to be a valuable partner for the fruit juice producer. Our combination of custom audience targeting and channel site lists yielded a skyrocketing visitation rate, driving an 820% increase in unique visitors to the client's website among the core target audience (comScore Media Metrix, July 2010).

Tribal Fusion Case Study

A popular movie company wanted to build awareness and drive in-store rentals for a new movie recently released on DVD, targeting a younger audience who use online movie rental services. Tribal Fusion was selected for the campaign because of the ability to create a unique custom channel to reach the client's target audience and also the ability to provide research measuring the effective reach and attitudinal shift in brand metrics.

The client's objectives were to build awareness, increase in-store rentals among their online users, and measure campaign effectiveness. The course of action for the campaign included the following:

1. Creating a Custom Channel campaign to reach the client's target audience. The channel was comprised of premium Movie, TV, and Entertainment sites in the network and was created using both comScore and proprietary Tribal Fusion data.
2. Tribal Fusion's proprietary Audience Profile Reporting tool was used to measure effective reach, gain insight into the demographics reached by the campaign, and identify future opportunities to help grow the client's target audience.
3. Attitudinal tracking research was conducted using Dynamic Logic. The research provided comprehensive brand analysis measuring awareness, recall, brand preference, behavior intent, and overall lifts against the client's branding objectives for the online campaign.
4. Audience reporting and attitudinal research were combined to reveal key audience characteristics that moved brand metrics.

Thorough analysis of campaign performance, Audience Profile Reporting data, and Dynamic Logic research determined the key drivers of success and opportunities for improving future campaigns:

1. *Audience reporting*: Confirmed that Tribal Fusion's Custom Channel reached the client's target and core audiences. It also identified new segments and the top markets effectively reached by the campaign.
2. *Branding analysis*: Attitudinal research demonstrated that the client's campaign increased awareness among their core audience of females, older respondents, and those with higher household incomes, where baseline awareness was generally lower. It also showed that larger creative sizes and a frequency of 4 or more exposures had a positive effect on all brand metrics.
3. *Additional findings*: Overlaying Audience Reporting with Dynamic Logic data helped uncover a set of actionable insights and creative recommendations on how the client might engage with their target audience for future campaigns.

Value-Ad Case Study

The Professional Provident Society (PPS) offers a comprehensive suite of financial and healthcare products that are specifically tailored to meet the needs of graduate professionals. It exists solely for the benefit of its members who are the "shareholders" and so the better the sales revenues, the greater the returns to their policyholders who share in the net operating income and investment returns; in fact this year, they have given R2,6 billion to their members.

PPS' Member Relations Division (MRD) is responsible for managing and growing their relationships with members through their agents who sell their products. MRD was set up specifically to cultivate relationships with PPS Members who do not have their own brokers, the so-called orphans. These orphans are passed through to agents in the form of leads, which they need to follow up on. PPS' success is therefore predicated on the quality of the leads and the agents' ability to translate them into profitable members.

Value-Ad's Leads Management solution helps organizations to route leads to the correct sales people and monitor and manage their behaviors and test marketing activities for effectiveness in converting quality leads. It is designed to improve the quality of the leads, shorten the sales cycles, and increase the conversion rate of leads into sales.

Value-Ad automated PPS' leads process and these changes made it possible for PPS to improve the process of acquiring and training agents. Using Value-Ad's Leads Management solution, they were also able to increase the quality and value of the leads that they pass on to the agents. The pilot was an immediate success. Value-Ad is now managing the leads to 180 sales agents. PPS has been able to change their recruitment strategy to improve on the quality of the agents that they employ. Within 6 months, the PPS Agency exceeded their targets. Frans Hattingh,

MRD's divisional manager, says "We were astounded at how our numbers immediately began climbing as soon as we implemented Value-Ad's Leads Management system and we quickly exceeded our targets."

In the financial services industry, agent attrition is a problem and PPS has also used Value-Ad's Leads Management solution to reduce the churn. PPS has designed their new sales force around leads management and actually use Value-Ad's Leads Management solution as a viable attraction tool for sales agents to join PPS. Hattingh says "We now have a far more effective and motivated sales force with one of the lowest attrition rates in the industry."

An agent differs from a broker in that agents are employed PPS to sell PPS products, whereas brokers can sell any services including those of competitors. Hattingh says that PPS will be using Value-Ad's leads management solution to entrench relationships with brokers by providing better quality leads. Because PPS can now understand the leads better, they will be able to route specific leads to the most appropriate agents and assist them to build their own portfolios and build solid practices within a professional market. Agents will be able to specialize by the industry in which they have the required relationships and insights. For example, an agent with an architectural background, who is no longer practicing, will be able to serve professionals in this industry better because they understand these people and their industry.

The benefits accrue to the members as well. If an agent leaves PPS for whatever reason, the member could become an orphan again, but the Value-Ad Leads Management solution will allocate another suitable agent who can pick up the relationship and continue supporting the member in the management of his financial profile.

At PPS, Leads Management has proved to be an incredibly powerful tool for managing leads and optimizing the sales force, and their members will be feeling the benefits of this strategic approach to managing revenue.

DRIVEpm Case Studies

AQuantive seems poised for success with its new division, DRIVEpm. The new division buys advertising from only the top 250 publishers and resells it to advertisers with the added value of extremely tight targeting. Increasingly, advertisers are eager to make their ad buys on the basis of different factors for different programs, and they appreciate that DRIVEpm's system can handle as much complexity as they are likely to request.

But Scott Howe, president of Drive Performance Media, will not label his company a behavioral targeter. "Many people," he explains, "believe that behavioral targeting is what TACODA and the others do. But we have a different approach. It doesn't fit the conventional definition. So we call it just plain 'targeting'. Whatever you call it, we work closely with advertisers to offer the right tactics for their various opportunities and situations."

For example, advertisers can use DRIVEpm to selectively serve ads to consumers based on single-publisher surfing profiles. But they can also arrange their advertising programs to take advantage of iterative interactions with consumers, factoring in measures of recency and frequency, as well as conventional demographics, such as the consumer's gender, age, connection speed (broadband or dialup), SIC code, and domain name. Ads can also be selected for serving on the basis of other criteria, including five parts of the day, the day of the week, the surrounding content (gleaned from a real-time page scrape and keyword analysis of what consumers are reading when the ad is being served), and the 62 different PRIZM clusters that marketers traditionally use to divide America into a spectrum of discrete socioeconomic neighborhoods including everything from elite suburbs and landed gentry to urban cores and working towns.

This level of complex decision-making capability gives advertisers a lot more freedom to target their creative materials as precisely as they want. A simple example: manufacturers and retailers are learning to serve more ads between 10:00 a.m. and 3:00 p.m., when people do the bulk of their buying, while entertainment vendors and charities increasingly shift their promotional emphasis to the evenings, when people are in a more receptive frame of mind.

Interestingly, Howe believes today's online targeting capabilities and the traditional segmentation as practiced by direct marketers in the 1970s and 1980s exist along the same continuum. In those early years of computerization, catalogers spent millions developing relatively robust data mining models and began sending catalogs to consumers based on many characteristics. Today, computers are more powerful, the data are more robust, and the decision making is far more complex. But then, as now, the most important variable is whether or not the consumer has already made a purchase. "We're applying those kind of established direct marketing principles," says Howe, "except we're not getting so personal that it becomes 'creepy.' We don't want to be creepy."

One example of DRIVEpm's success is the campaign for a national global coffee company that rolled out a stored-value card to college students. Recognizing that they did not have stores on every campus and that students are a small fraction of all Internet surfers, the company wanted to avoid a broad campaign that would waste a lot of money. Instead, DRIVEpm targeted 80 specific ".edu" domains (such as USC and the University of Washington). This made sure the ads were seen only at universities where the company had a retail presence. "We made a $30,000 spend perform like $30 million," chuckles Howe, with more than a little pride.

Another successful campaign allowed a home mortgage company to sequence its advertising messages over a 30 day period. Assuming that a person visiting its site is considering a mortgage, the company hired DRIVEpm to target people who had been on its site within the past 30 days and to serve them ads in sequence, regardless of where they showed up on the DRIVEpm advertising network. The sequential ads offered follow-on information for people advancing through their consideration cycle.

This kind of targeting can eliminate much of the waste and bring an advertiser's messages to only the most interested and active segment of the general audience.

"Theoretically," says Howe, "we could narrow to a segment of one. But operationally and ethically we think there are limits. We won't serve ads to a segment smaller than 5 K, and generally not smaller than 50 K. The beauty is that, once you understand your segment, you can tell much richer and more interesting stories. And consumers appreciate seeing ads only for things they might actually want to buy, instead of the hundreds of ads they see for things they don't want or already have."

Howe is quick to acknowledge that such tight targeting will never replace general advertising. Everyone in the United States is a potential cola drinker, for example, so Coca Cola will always want to do broadcast, run of site, and RONs advertising just to build a basic desire for the soft drink. But there is room for them to target specific groups—such as 20 year olds and 60 year olds—with different and potentially more appealing messages.

DRIVEpm is careful to partner only with high-quality sites, the top 250 sites, in terms of traffic and name recognition, excluding sites that might be too controversial, offensive, or otherwise questionable. It is also owned by AQuantive, parent to Avenue A, i-Frontier, and Atlas DMT, which serves about 40% of all third-party advertising. This affiliation with Atlas gives DRIVEpm significant scale, as well as access to significant performance information, both of which add power to its ad-serving decisions. The results for advertisers can be ROI increases from 1000% to 10,000%. For example, an airline initially established a CPA of $8 for one part of its online advertising program. DRIVEpm's approach of initial awareness messaging on the airline's site and then remessaging the prospects, when encountered on other sites, with benefits keyed to their most recent ticket search, has driven this down to $1.50.

Linkshare Case Studies

Smartbargains.com

At Smartbargains.com we have leveraged and heavily implemented co-branded landing belts and custom landing pages as key strategies in optimizing and growing our affiliate program. Increased conversion is the ultimate goal of these strategies. Improving this metric allows Smartbargains and our affiliates' efforts to generate more business resulting in a virtuous cycle of success for both parties.

For example, increased conversion increases revenue, which improves Smartbargains desire to grow and invest into affiliate marketing more. Also, partners will send more traffic to Smartbargains as our EPC increases, which results in improved placement on affiliate sites. With more revenue, the partner has more to invest in paid search, tech upgrades, social media, and many more channels that will drive Smartbargains more traffic, thus continuing this growth trend. Following is an explanation of how both strategies have grown our business and helped create success across multiple fronts with limited resources.

Co-branded landing belts have successfully increased conversion. During Q1 of 2010, Smartbargains.com had 31 co-branded landing belts in use. During that same period, 12 out of Smartbargains' top 20 affiliates leveraged a co-branded belt.

This is an example of the quantity in action as well as the strong results these belts help provide as our top partners convert and earn more.

Co-branded landing belts not only increase conversion but also enhance the affiliates brand as the belt provides legitimacy and a smooth transition experience from the affiliate site to Smartbargains. Not all traffic is converted into a sale, but a positive experience has been created that will leave the customer more likely to return to one or both the sites and refer them to friends and family.

From the merchant point of view this also creates a strong recruiting and optimization tool at the same time as affiliates are eager to increase conversion, improve, and establish their brand. Publishers value these efforts and results as they understand the multiple opportunities for success they provide.

One of the challenges of affiliate marketing is that the majority of publishers market extremely diverse product and deal offerings from one another as well as on their own site. Merchants must find a way to gain as many placements, drive, and convert the most amount of traffic possible with limited time and resources internally. Also, with so many partners, it is very difficult to efficiently and effectively communicate with publishers and see something they would then become interested in once they landed. More information and deeper access into the store were crucial improvements we looked to make.

We created landing pages that more than doubled the amount of links on the page; called out two times the amount of promotions; provided links to departmental, categorical, sub-categorical, brand, and product pages; mixed text with text, category, and product images. Smartbargains wanted to create an experience that all types of shoppers could relate to.

We have also created pages that take a promotion and bring to life an experience that matches the aforementioned initiatives and play into the overarching promotional theme.

One good example of this is our "Smart Coupons" promotion. We create 14 coupons on 14 different categories and brands. The landing page—attached in the e-mail—actually has all 14 coupons laid out on the page allowing customers to see our top 14 deals without having to click and be compelled to buy because of the visual experience in concert with the navigational. The true success of this strategy can be seen by looking at a 2 month period, starting on January 1, 2010. Smartbargains, on 58% of the days mentioned previously, sent its affiliate coupon traffic to its regular homepage. On 21 of this 56 day period, the same affiliate traffic was sent to a custom landing page designed to optimize the LinkShare affiliate program.

Toshiba

Whether you are in the market for a customized notebook computer or a portable DVD player, outstanding customer service can help keep you brand loyal. Similarly, if you are a manufacturer of electronics who is not receiving quality service from your affiliate marketing company, you move on.

ToshibaDirect.com migrated to the LinkShare Network. An intensive assessment and focus on Toshiba's needs followed. Without an internal affiliate marketing resource, Toshiba took advantage of LinkShare's one-stop Client Service Ramp, benefiting from the attention of a seasoned account manager and program manager.

When ToshibaDirect joined the LinkShare Network, they had a limited number of affiliates. LinkShare swung into action, and its concerted efforts quickly paid off. In 2 months' time, Toshiba had the same number of affiliates in their program as they had after 2 years with their previous provider. Within 5 months, LinkShare had increased that number by 50%. Now? Toshiba has three times the number of affiliate opportunities.

Quantity was not the only goal. The LinkShare team focused on Toshiba's approach to its affiliates as well, wanting the channel to grow and develop. By following LinkShare's lead, and offering the highest public commission offers of any computer maker, financing promotions, product offers, and free shipping, Toshiba has contributed to its own success.

Toshiba currently takes advantage of the entire suite of LinkShare offerings— dynamic rich media, Merchandiser, data feed, text links, etc. The account team also helps the client coordinate its affiliate marketing program with other online initiatives and media buys in online channels.

To further enhance the program, Toshiba refined its reporting and program analysis to better meet the affiliates' needs. Once an under-tapped resource, affiliate marketing has become a priority for Toshiba and is driving overall online growth at ToshibaDirect.com. To further integrate the LinkShare team and to continue concentrating on recruitment and growing the number of order-generating affiliates, Toshiba will soon hire an internal resource. With insight from the back-to-school and holiday season under their belt, Toshiba is committed to listening to affiliate feedback and working to improve its overall program.

North Face

When exploring new terrain, you want an experienced and trusted partner by your side. A well-known brand and 40 year strong, The North Face wanted a fresh way to increase its visibility in new markets and drive sales on its newly created e-commerce site. The supplier of advanced, high-performance apparel, equipment, and footwear for avid climbers, explorers, endurance athletes, and outdoor enthusiasts partnered with LinkShare to build an affiliate program.

Cautious about protecting its valuable brand name, The North Face needed a partner known for quality and collaboration. The breadth and depth of LinkShare's affiliate network helped extend The North Face brand beyond its usual target market that resulted in above-average returns within the first 3–5 months of the program and has remained a steady percentage of The North Face's overall revenue each month since.

Embodying its Never Stop Exploring™ mantra, The North Face is committed to expanding its affiliate network to reach new consumers through new partners and to continuously create new experiences with its brand. By incorporating more of LinkShare's tools such as Storefronts and Near Real-Time Reporting, The North Face is making its program more robust, while making it easier for their affiliate partners to earn money while out exploring.

The success of the program is a testament to the teams' collaboration. LinkShare's commitment to relationship building has introduced The North Face to publishers beyond the beaten path. Through regular meetings, personalized training, and, particularly, the LinkShare Symposiums, all parties get to know each other better, build up a level of trust, collaborate on their marketing plans, and are better equipped after every encounter to reach a new altitude in e-commerce.

Epic Direct Case Study

Nikon has turned its marketing energies toward the iPad with an ad program meant to complement the brand's existing television campaign. The camera manufacturer tapped Epic Media Group's Traffic Marketplace division for the Flash-alternative rich-media ad campaign that leverages the capabilities of the iPad platform. "Nikon was able to garner click-through rates more than 10 times higher than average mobile or Web click-through rates on standard ad units," said Charlie Black, general manager of Epic Media Group's Integrated Traffic Management platform, New York.

Nikon is a multinational corporation headquartered in Tokyo, Japan, specializing in optics and imaging. Traffic Marketplace is Epic Media's digital marketing services arm.

In addition to running standard static ad units, Nikon also used an in-banner, 300 × 250 video ad unit. The unit was user initiated and opened to full screen upon clicking. The ads promoted Nikon's CoolPix Zoom cameras (Figure 4.13).

Consumers that click on the ad are able to view a video. Once the video is finished, the consumer is served another banner ad. When this ad is clicked on, consumers are routed to a page that has information on various Nikon CoolPix Zoom products. The campaign underscores Nikon's ability to be cutting edge. The strategy was to build off Nikon's successful TV commercials through driving video views, brand awareness, and user engagement on the iPad. The advertisements ran within the Bigoven.com application for the iPad. Other brands advertising within the application are Lending Tree, The Los Angeles Times, 24-Hour Fitness, and Travelocity. "Nikon was able to move quickly to leverage the burgeoning iPad market," Mr. Black said. "This campaign was one of the first campaigns on the iPad device—in fact, within about a month after the device was introduced."

Figure 4.13   Nikon banner ad.

ShareASale Case Study

After only a few short months the ShareASale pay-per-call platform, powered by RingRevenue, is exceeding expectations, delivering strong results for merchants, and gaining traction within the network. ShareASale's merchants are signing up to track calls like clicks, empowering their affiliate base to help broaden their reach and boost sales.

"We continue to hear great things about the ShareASale pay-per-call platform from our merchants and our affiliates," said ShareASale founder Brian Littleton. "Quality affiliates are driving calls that convert, providing both our merchants and their affiliate partners with an exciting new way to build their businesses."

ShareASale advertiser Legacy Learning Systems launched pay-per-call services through ShareASale in January 2010. Within the first 30 days, Legacy generated nearly 200 calls. One hundred percent of the calls that qualified for an affiliate commission payout have converted to a sale. Some affiliates have done so well that Legacy increased their commissions by up to 25%.

"The program is exceeding our ROI expectations," said Matt McWilliams, Legacy affiliate manager. According to McWilliams, the pay-per-call reporting, campaign creation and affiliate management tools are easy to use. "It only took about 10 minutes to set up each of my campaigns and it's been easy to analyze the reports, listen to caller recordings and make pricing adjustments to better compensate affiliates for generating quality calls," he said.

Legacy also has seen new activity from previously dormant affiliates, increased sales both online and off-line, and a boost in new registrations as affiliates realize the potential of pay-per-call. ShareASale's pay-per-call platform is responsible for 15%–20% of new signups, said McWilliams. In addition to making pay-per-call campaigns available to affiliates to promote, merchants are also using the platform to track and manage their own direct call-based campaign promotions, where they do not pay affiliate commissions.

"In addition to providing affiliates with tracking phone numbers, our merchants can also instantly activate phone numbers that they can use to better track the performance of their internal online media buys, paid search initiatives, and overall website performance," said Littleton. "It's a very complete solution that's paying off in a big way for our merchants."

AdKnowledge Case Study

A leading health portal with banner inventory coupled with video content turned to AdKnowledge to improve its revenue growth. The strong video content of this site has enabled their sales team to land a number of large advertisers. Organic growth to the portal was not happening fast enough to fulfill their advertisers' needs. They decided to employ an SEM strategy as part of their audience development efforts to supplement the organic growth and acquire new site visitors.

By placing the Adknowledge pixel on the site, the publisher and Adknowledge account manager were able to quickly identify the optimal publishers to deliver their desired performance and volume. Over a 2 month time frame while leveraging Adknowledge's Audience Builder solution, site traffic grew from 50,000 visits a day to over 500,000 visits a day. As a result of the increased traffic, Ad Sales was able to deliver on inventory commitments with consistent, high-quality traffic.

Marchex Case Study

Direct Agents, Inc., a leading interactive advertising agency that provides marketers with the solutions to expand their presence online and increase ROI. Direct Agents partnered with Marchex Pay-Per-Click with one clear goal: Drive highly targeted traffic to their clients' websites, which will lead to an increased number of sales prospects and a higher conversion rate while significantly increasing their client retention rate.

Based on the principle that not all clicks are equal, Marchex Pay-Per-Click's site-specific content targeting solution enables Direct Agents' financial and technology direct marketing clients to place their text listings in front of the highest quality audience on websites like PC World, BusinessWeek, and Computerworld. Clicks that are generated from quality content have proven to deliver more targeted leads and customers for marketers.

Additionally, Direct Agents took advantage of the Marchex Network, a diverse range of vertically focused direct navigation and content destinations offered by Marchex, Marchex Pay-Per-Click's parent company that pertained to the advertising needs of many Direct Agents' clients. According to Webside Story, the average conversion rate for consumers who navigate directly to destination websites like those in the Marchex Network is 4.23% versus just 2.3% for users coming from major search engines. "We are very pleased with Marchex Pay-Per-Click's online campaign and its cost-effective leads. The higher conversion rates and return from advertising have proven invaluable to our success," said Josh Boaz, director of business development, Direct Agents.

"Marchex Pay-Per-Click is able to work across a multitude of premium websites to deliver targeted text ads on the web's most recognized brands such as Computerworld, PCMag, PCWorld, BusinessWeek, and Travel + Leisure, to name a few," said Boaz.

On average, conversions for Direct Agents' advertisers have increased by 10%–15%. "Our campaigns with Marchex Pay-Per-Click have been very successful in terms of conversion rate and return on investment," said Boaz. "With a higher conversion rate compared to what was seen in many other channels, Marchex Pay-Per-Click's marketing solutions have proven to be strongly effective at acquiring customers for our clients and raising product awareness."

On average, client spend has increased by 30%–40% following the implementation of Marchex Pay-Per-Click's site-specific targeting program and the Marchex Network program. "Marchex Pay-Per-Click's site-specific targeting and the Marchex Network solutions reflected in the increase in customer retention rate which have been seen especially by our clients in the Financial Services and Education verticals," said Sanford Harrison, media buyer, Direct Agents.

Vibrant Media Case Studies

Bing™

Vibrant worked with Microsoft/UM/Razorfish to develop a custom program that would introduce Bing to Internet users by conveniently bringing them a dynamic and useful search utility. This custom in-text unit delivered relevant news, images, videos, and web results from bing.com. Search results were delivered from words like "Tiger Woods," "Barack Obama," and "health care reform" inside web content. The campaign continuously optimized toward top trending news keywords and vertical keywords.

Toyota

Toyota endured the largest recall in automotive history this year, and, as a result, they paused all running media in the United States. The very first ads to go live after the recall were our In-Text ads that used a custom filter to target the negative articles and direct users to learn more about the recall and Toyota's plans to address the issue. Toyota was able to speak directly to users within articles about the recall via factual whitepapers, corporate messaging, and contextual video placements on words such as "recall" and "Toyota."

Best Buy

Twelpforce is Best Buy's 24/7 Twitter resource that offers consumers an easy way to get quick answers to basic tech questions. Best Buy sought to leverage Twelpforce to help keep consumers informed while doing their Holiday shopping. This first ever in-text Twitter execution syndicated popular Tweets focusing on questions and answers pertaining to popular Best Buy products, such as "iPhone," "digital camera," and "plasma TV," and delivered real-time tech support inside relevant web content.

Canon

Canon wanted to promote the use of HD Camcorders by introducing a new style of hand held recording called "Freecording" to their target audience of 25–34 year olds. By double-underlining words like "creativity," "film maker," "freestyle," and "high definition," inside relevant web articles, Canon delivered a high impact video that showcased people "Freecording." The campaign surpassed Canon's CTR success metrics, increased micro-site traffic, and enabled them to perfectly illustrate the core brand messaging (fun, creative, and exciting).

BlogAds Case Studies

Norml

Goal: Entice new advertisers to purchase.

Approach: The blogger placed an ad in their blogads adstrip for their site, promoting the strong readership and offering a 20% off coupon to first time purchasers.

Success: The blogger doubled his typical monthly income.

Gala Darling

Goal: Entice small businesses to advertise.

Approach: The blogger published a post introducing her 125 × 125 ad units and offering an enticing rate for small businesses.

Success: It tripled her typical monthly income and exposed her site to 57 new advertisers and potential repeat customers.

Funky Downtown

Goal: Get advertisers to repeat their purchase.

Approach: The blogger published an adverpost with a link to the advertiser's site at no cost, and passed the link along to the advertiser in a personalized e-mail.

Success: The advertiser renewed for February and achieved a higher than 36% CTR for both months.

Drudge Retort

Goal: Get advertisers to repeat their purchase.

Approach: To call more attention to an advertiser's currently running ad, Drudge Retort places a link to the landing page at the top of his homepage.

Success: These links receive between 300 and 700 clicks for the advertiser and often generate active discussion.

Pheedo Case Study

Socialtext, Inc. is a leading provider of Enterprise 2.0 solutions. Socialtext captures the best features of web-native tools called "wikis" and "weblogs" and brings them inside their clients' enterprise to create a collaboration and knowledge tool that works the way people do, their 3000+ clients rely on Socialtext's social software to help foster collaboration and productivity within their organizations.

Pheedo's FeedPowered™ad platform helps advertisers to leverage their existing content assets as a tool to engage their target audience. The Pheedo Ad Network, comprised of hundreds of top tier sites and niche blogs, allows advertisers to reach an early adopter audience of RSS users.

RSS users rely on their RSS readers (Google Reader, NetVibes, NewsGator, etc.) to manage the information that they wish to receive. An RSS reader allows a user to reclaim their inbox for the types of relevant and permission-based communications it was designed for. RSS users are now able to unsubscribe from e-mail newsletters and instead receive the same information by subscribing to the site's RSS feed. The user has complete control over the content that they receive. They only receive content that they subscribe to and have the ability to unsubscribe at the click of a button. The user's information is never "shared" among publishers. Unlike e-mail, deliverability challenges and spam issues do not exist and feeds are lighter than e-mail messages and take-up less space.

Socialtext, like many young companies in an emerging space, are challenged with educating their prospect and customers about their niche vertical as well as the specific enterprise level solutions that they provide. Specific campaign goals included, creating brand awareness, driving impressions and page views to the Socialtext blog.

Pheedo leveraged Socialtext's existing content assets, repurposed it within a series of FeedPoweredads, and distributed these ads to relevant, targeted segments of the Pheedo RSS network. Said Jeff Brainard, director of product marketing at Socialtext, "The Pheedo results were impressive, on a small budget, we were able to drive nearly 500,000 new impressions for our Socialtext blog content and generate over 1,000 unique clicks. Compared to alternate approaches like banner ads or e-mail newsletter sponsorships, the campaign yielded click-thru rates more than double the industry average."

Sedo Case Study

The right domain name can make all the difference when it comes to targeting potential customers for your business through the web. Shorter domain names that are five characters or less are highly valued properties since they are easy to remember and help position your business as a leader in your industry. These shorter domains also offer reduced risk of typo errors, strong brand recognition, and increased flexibility in promoting the domain, your business, and the services your company offers.

However, often times the ideal short, pithy, and memorable domain for your business, particularly if it is a premium.com address, is already taken. So, what do companies do when someone else owns the domain name they want? Just ask Manchester, New Hampshire-based Dynamic Network Services, Inc. (Dyn, Inc.), a leading managed DNS service provider.

As part of a strategic move to streamline its brand, the company wanted to acquire the domain name, dyn.com to integrate all of its business units under one short and easy to remember web address. These units include Dyn, Inc.'s consumer brand, DynDNS.com, which has served over 12 million home/SMB users, and the company's corporate/enterprise brand, the Dynect Platform, which has several hundred customers on its globally deployed DNS network.

Prior to acquiring the dyn.com domain through Sedo.com in August of 2009, the company had been using dynamicnetworkservices.com, which was too long and difficult to remember and had a high risk of typos. Then, Dyn, Inc. started using dyn-inc.com in an effort to make things easier for visitors.

"People thought we were a printer ink company when we used that name, so it was a bit confusing," said Kyle York, vice president of sales and marketing. "Since we're a global company with an international customer base, a hyphenated name didn't always translate correctly across different languages. We're known as Dyn across all business groups, so we wanted to tighten up our branding and try and pull all business units together under one roof."

Similar to traditional real estate, many people try to sell their own homes unsuccessfully and then soon realize that they need a broker to get the job done right. The same is true in the world of virtual real estate. Dyn, Inc. tried to acquire the dyn.com domain name directly from the seller for 6 months.

"We used a lot of man hours to research the seller's contact information, send multiple e-mails and make a bunch of phone calls, and basically got nowhere," York said.

That's when the company knew that it needed a domain brokerage expert to expedite the search on the seller and acquire the domain. Sedo, the leading online domain marketplace and monetization provider, was the natural choice. "Working with Sedo, we were able to acquire the name and finalize the deal in three to four weeks. The process was quick and painless, so we were glad we finally decided to turn to the experts, as this domain was of strategic importance to us," said York.

Obtaining a domain name directly from the owner is not as simple as it sounds. Relying on WHOIS alone for domain owner information is not ideal, as Dyn, Inc. discovered, since you cannot tell if the domain owner information is current or even correct. With secret registration now becoming more prevalent, that task will only get more difficult.

"On the other hand, a well established domain brokerage firm such as Sedo does all the vetting on their clients' behalf to ensure that both the seller and buyer are legitimate," said York.

Working with seasoned domain brokers also ensures that the buyer and seller are not exploited or cheated and that each party ends up buying and selling the domain for the right price.

"We acquired the domain name for $15 K through Sedo, but people often assume we paid ten times the price. For us, it was a steal of a deal. If only we had done it six months sooner," said York.

Cymfony Case Study

A global financial services corporation launched a new investment brand and needed to understand the competitive environment in real time. Their main goal was to increase and maintain market leadership in a challenging economy permeated with consumer distrust.

Cymfony developed a Maestro listening platform and reporting structure to evaluate consumer sentiment and behaviors related to banking, savings client's and investment activity to assist the clients design of their social media engagement strategy. Cymfony also developed listening methodologies to compliment other market research measurements.

The financial services client uses the insights gleaned from Cymfony's Maestro platform and reporting structure to guide their digital marketing and social media engagement strategy in this crucial stage of brand infancy. Listening and observational data are used to ensure the evaluated rapidly changing consumer mindset is effectively evaluated.

Jivox Case Study

Interactive Video Ads are helping thousands of technology companies to promote their new software and hardware solutions online. Google is one of the world's top technology companies offering online search and advertising services, web-based tools including its popular Google Docs and Google Chrome web browser. Google used Interactive Online Video ads, powered by the Jivox technology, to promote its new version of its Google Chrome browser and allow Internet users to download The Chrome browser to their PCs directly through their video ad. Online Video Ads engage potential customers letting them interact with the ad, drive direct response (clicks, visits, downloads, and more), allow for social interactions, and build brand awareness.

Google was looking for efficient and effective ways to reach online audiences and generate interest for their new Chrome web browser and drive downloads. Through distribution of its 15 s (:15) online video ads, Google achieved spectacular results, far beyond the typical industry averages, thanks to the power of online video ads.

Google used three different video ads highlighting their top three values (speed, simplicity, and security) for Chrome browser and added strong call to actions like a link to their YouTube video channel and interactive widgets to drive direct response. Their online video ads were distributed across the Jivox Video Ad Network of websites ensuring the video ads were delivered to just the right audience online.

Google ran its video ad campaign, and Jivox delivered a staggering 7.8 million video views and maintained a healthy interaction CTR. Google used interactive online video advertising to reach and engage with consumers online resulting in a big adoption of its Chrome browser by Internet users. The video ad campaign performed nearly three times better than typical online display static banner ads. Typical display ads only offer clicks that navigate the online viewers away from the page and disrupt the web experience. Jivox interactive features propelled the specific user engagement with the brand. The results were phenomenal, it drove 39,308 clicks to achieve an interaction CTR of 0.54%, 3,817 users downloaded the Chrome browser and 3,140 YouTube views.

ContextOptional Case Study

Kohl's desired an initiative that would significantly increase brand favorability, publicize the charitable work it has done, engage the community, and build its fan base. The company had multiple successful social marketing programs to date but was looking for an execution that would deliver greater impact (Figure 4.14).

Leveraging Kohl's existing charitable program, Kohl's Cares, Context developed an integrated campaign that solicited UGC and incentivized the distribution of that content throughout a user's social network. With a half-million dollar donation given to the winner, participants were encouraged to nominate and vote for the school they felt was most deserving of the funds and submit their ideas about how the funds could best be used.

The program resulted in a gain of more than 2 million new fans for the Kohl's brand page and drove more than 15 million visitors who cast more than 12 million votes. Viral lift generated more than 500 million additional impressions, spreading brand advocacy across the social graph on a vast scale.

Figure 4.14 Kohl's Care campaign.

KickApps Case Study

Ovation TV, the only multiplatform network devoted to art and contemporary culture, chose KickApps to power its new online community for viewers, with the goal of allowing people who love art to participate with the brand. Members uploaded more than 60,000 works of art within the first 10 months of the OvationTV.com community, a place where members can not only share their creative endeavors but also form interest groups; join discussions; start blogs; vote on programming; chat live; and upload images, videos, and audios. As a result, in less than a year, Ovation TV's online traffic shot up by 145%, page views jumped 311%, and the average time spent by users on the site quadrupled (Figure 4.15).

Ovation TV unveiled its community site and within just three short weeks of signing on with KickApps. The site's features, which include media uploads, blogs, and in-depth discussions, promote the exchange of art and ideas generated by community members.

KickApps functionality enabled Ovation TV's audience to interact with the brand on a daily basis. Ovation TV promoted its new online community via on-air commercials and an online ad campaign. The channel focused on building quality over quantity in its membership, concerning itself less with volume, and more with loyalty and participation. This has also meant staying away from ads,

Figure 4.15   Ovation campaign.

Ovation TV will begin testing ads and video overlays that make sense for the audience's sensibility and demographic.

Ovation TV had a core viewership of art lovers, but their experience with OvationTV.com typically amounted to checking the programming schedule and leaving the site after a minute or two. With a small staff and limited budget, they needed a way to increase his division's value, for viewers and for the channel. It was his first key project in a new job. They turned to KickApps' social media platform to create an online community.

The Ovation TV team built a loyal membership of more than 6000 art lovers in under a year. After launching its KickApps-powered website, online traffic was up 145%, page views jumped 311%, and the average time spent by users on the site quadrupled. That growth has everything to do with the social network. Within Ovation TV, the addition of the KickApps-powered community has boosted ad inventory, expanded the potential for direct sales, and enhanced the channel's affiliate sales proposition. The benefits also extend to advertisers: Geico, for example, is sponsoring an online group inviting community members to create "15 minute masterpieces," a tie-in with the insurer's ad campaign.

ATG Case Study

With its market presence exploding over the last 3 years, American Eagle Outfitters (AE) needed to extend its retail momentum to the online marketplace. But its outmoded commerce platform did not scale or integrate customer touch points, making that objective far out of reach.

AE abandoned its antiquated platform for ATG Commerce and now has centralized management of not only its website but also its call center and order management systems. With ATG, AE gained total control of its multichannel business. The new ATG platform enabled AE to manage the entire customer experience, from the retail store to the website to the call center. It also gives them the foundation they needed to grow their existing brand and launch new ones.

Known for designing, marketing, and selling its own brand of laidback, current clothing for teenagers and young adults, AE stands for high-quality merchandise at affordable prices. The retailer's market presence has grown exponentially within just 3 years, with more than 800 stores now in North America. Extending this momentum to the online arena was becoming a difficult, resource-intensive task for AE Direct, the team managing AE's online and call center businesses.

An antiquated commerce platform had multiple, cumbersome integration points with other systems, lacked scalability, and required awkward, manual processes for even small web page adjustments. Growing fast, AE was ready to bring its multichannel commerce initiatives to the next level. But first it needed the right commerce platform. To serve the digital generation, AE needed to replace its outmoded system with a scalable platform that provided central management of not only its website but also its call center and order management systems that had previously been outsourced.

According to Dave Brumback, director of operations at AE Direct, "The new platform had to ensure that the entire customer experience was consistent as customers traverse our physical and virtual stores, and our call center. We wanted to make sure the new platform could support our Web site, call center, and order management systems. Yet we were not looking to mold our business around software. We wanted software that would mold to our existing business."

Moreover, the AE Direct team was not changing its website design. Customer feedback on the existing site was very positive. In moving to the new platform, the goal was to preserve the existing look, yet implement a new back-end that would bring higher efficiency and maximize profitability by integrating with the systems and processes that supported the entire AE business. To accomplish that goal, the new platform needed to use the merchandising, transaction processing, and distribution systems already in place.

And, it had to provide unique online capabilities, such as personalization, dynamic up-selling and cross-selling, robust search, simplified content administration, and e-mail integration. The AE Direct team formed a steering committee that used a formal process to evaluate and compare 10 e-commerce vendors. Their criteria included the overall strength of the platform in terms of scalability and flexibility, the reputation and stability of the vendor, customer references, the ability to run on Java, and ease of content administration.

ATG Commerce won across the board. "The ATG Commerce platform not only met our near-term needs but also demonstrated the ability to easily incorporate new marketing and sales capabilities that would help us build for the future," said Brumback. "While their technical capabilities impressed us, it was the ATG management team's partnership with our business users that really won us over. When they showed us how their software would support our current business and where they believed our multi-channel business could go, it became clear that ATG was the right partner for us."

With their business specifications in place, the new ae.com was launched within the year. What is more, the transition to the new site was seamless, which was critical with the holiday season less than a month away. Commented Lou Pietragallo, manager of Information Technology at AE Direct, "There was no way we would take the site down for even a single day. And given that we were launching the new site in October, we could not risk interrupting our business just before the holiday season. ATG delivered. We had a smooth and controlled migration from our old architecture to the new ATG platform. In fact, AE Direct had a record holiday season."

Aggerateknowledge Case Studies

The clients are not identified; however, they are worldwide brands. Here are a few examples of diverse enterprises using the AK Platform.

A large bank used the AK Platform to identify data bleeding from their data provider when the same cookie was assigned to two different age groups or two different income ranges. By identifying bleeding, the bank was able to count the number of targetable unique users much more accurately than using a count of stamps, which was critical to reveal cross-over with media channels.

A large retailer is using AK to unify all of their data (website, third party, and campaign) around one single notion of the user and better extract the engagement and conversion patterns that materialize across multiple touch points.

An international financial institution used AK to run head-to-head comparisons across two DSPs. Using the ability for AK to distribute exclusive pools of users to two or more DSPs and to audit impression-level activity, AK was able to measure their relative ramp, price performance, conversion performance, and the quality of their audience without ever risking higher CPMs from direct bid competition.

Using the AK Platform, one of the largest automotive companies in the world found that their actual data had proven their internal theory that they were being "gamed" and that real results were in the "upper funnel."

An international financial institution used the AK Platform to reveal that the company's bid-strategy was not maximizing audience reach by reverse engineering the bidders via measurement. In particular, AK showed the difference between the average profile of the audience distributed to the DSP and the average profile of the audience reached by the DSP as a way to measure the ability for the DSP to ID specific audience attributes.

A well-known wireless company used the AK Platform to take control of their data in-house to better enable the customer conversation.

A retail outfit used the AK Platform to tie mobile advertising to their photo application since the platform is a cross media vehicle that can be used to piggy back on their digital strategy.

A CPG company needed to do more, but in a data-driven culture, they could not justify it. Their attribution model did not "apply" to CPG, so they chose AK to build a new model that worked.

The AK Platform showed a large public service organization that their advertising dialog did not respond well with their intended audience; most of their "push" was to "clickers" that did not fit the targeted demographic audience.

InfiniGraph Case Study

Golden Spoon ran a Facebook ad campaign. Golden Spoon owns and operates three stores in Coachella Valley, CA. The ad was designed to drive traffic to the company's Facebook fan page with the call to action being "Like" this page where fans were also asked to complete a registration form to join Golden Spoon's e-mail list (Figure 4.16).

DigitalEye wanted to improve the Facebook ad buy targeting efficiency for Golden Spoon by using InfiniGraph's Social Intelligence analysis to improve social targeting based on what consumers are connected to and most active around the brand and use trending affinities to increase targeting, click-through rates, and "Likes" and improve purchase conversion.

Tasks included running a Social Intelligence analysis on Golden Spoon's Facebook page and Twitter profile to obtain brand affinities, which were applied to the Facebook ad buy.

The prospect list was further refined using InfiniGraph's Social Intelligence Brand Affinities feature, which taps into like-minded groups on Facebook, based on relevancy and activity. DigitalEye used InfiniGraph's control panel to gain

Figure 4.16 InfiniGraph Facebook ad.

additional social intelligence and to determine what brands were trending most. Social Intelligence also aided in increasing click-through rate and reaching the most active consumer base.

Top-line results were as follows: click-through rate, 6%; liked page fan, 51%; conversion to buy, 18%; and coupon redemption rate was reported to be approximately 18% with each e-mail promotion. New Facebook likes were up 162%, while monthly active users rose 105%. Post feedbacks were boosted 612% and post views increased 249%. DigitalEye CEO Gary Brewer adds "We're running promos on slow days Mondays and Tuesdays on Facebook and sales are equivalent to what they are on a weekend."

SocialFlow Case Study

With a flagship location that contains 40 miles of shelves and houses nearly 50 million items, the New York Public Library (NYPL) has a lot to communicate to a growing online audience. The library uses SocialFlow to optimize what they publish and when on Twitter. As a result, the library's digital marketing team has garnered greater engagement, traffic and exposure, as well as creating a more efficient workflow among their staff.

The NYPL is a hive of content creation, including a number of blogs created by "librarians who are passionately writing about things that are important to them and their communities," explains Susan Halligan, Marketing Director at NYPL. But there were no guarantees that their audience was listening. With a comprehensive social media strategy that touches all the major services from Twitter to Facebook, Foursquare, and Tumblr, the NYPL enlisted the help of SocialFlow to build the interest and traffic to their blogs via Twitter.

After signing up for SocialFlow, the NYPL tested the system rigorously, trying to find the optimal number of Tweets to publish in order to maximize engagement measured via clicks per Tweet and clicks per follower on their blog-linked Tweets. The Library uses SocialFlow to Tweet content from 3:30 to 7:30 p.m. At other times of the day, they Tweeted manually or scheduled their Tweets.

The impact of SocialFlow's real-time optimization technology on overall traffic is unmistakable to the Library's Twitter activities. "SocialFlow accounts for 44% of tweets we send out since we started using it, but it garners 84% of the clicks that we get on Twitter in total," says Johannes Neuer, e-communications manager at the Library.

Additionally, unique page views of the blog section have increased by 48% since SocialFlow began optimizing content, and "the number of clicks per tweet are almost double than the one we use for manual tweeting," notes Neuer.

With a large list of Tweets to get out each day covering a number of areas including marketing, customer service, and advocacy, having a tool like SocialFlow has been essential in optimizing their engagement on social media. "We get maximum results for almost minimal effort," Halligan says.

For the staff at NYPL, however, clicks per Tweet and clicks per follower are not just an indication of their success at attracting an audience, but a morale booster, as they inspire passion for social engagement within their staff.

Hyperdrive Interactive Case Studies
Dreamfields Pasta

Owned by Dakota Growers of North Dakota, Dreamfields Pasta offers six shapes of healthy pasta that actually taste good (unlike its competitors, whose pasta often tastes like twigs and shoelaces). As a brand on the rise, Dreamfields great taste and health benefits needed greater recognition and product trial among its various target audiences; as well as a way to bolster its traditional advertising in print and TV.

HyperDrive and Dreamfields decided to completely revamp the brands online presence, beginning with an all-new website and a turnkey interactive campaign featuring highly targeted e-mails to its customer segments, SEO/pay-per-click programs, online grassroots and WOM activities, and flash banner advertising on a variety of demographic-suitable websites.

The ongoing campaign continues to build a base of remarkably loyal consumers, now numbering nearly 90,000, who readily accept and, in most cases, actually look forward to receiving e-mails from the brand! Dreamfields execs enjoys tracking metrics and receiving result reports each month that show campaign progress, something that is difficult if not impossible to achieve with traditional marketing methods.

LaRosa's Pizzerias

LaRosa's Pizzerias, is the country's largest privately owned restaurant chain and a long-time family tradition in the Tri-State area, needed to transition their traditionally newspaper-based "MVP of the Week" high school athletic recognition and Online Hall of Fame programs, whose media costs had become unmanageable, to 100% Internet-based programs.

HyperDrive developed and launched their new website, which continues to be driven by a weekly permission e-mail marketing program. The website and e-mail marketing also contains banner ads, coupons, and pizzeria specials that LaRosa's customers can use to order their favorite foods online.

Today, this consumer involvement program is more cost-effective, honors more student-athletes each week, and has more than 15,000 high school sports fans voting for their favorite MVP each week via e-mail ballot. This program is just one of many that HyperDrive works on with LaRosa's, several of which, due to their ground-breaking success, have been written about in the official magazine of the pizza industry, Pizza Quarterly.

Sharpie

Sharpie, well known as the main provider of colorful fun in the permanent marker category, introduced a new Sharpie Mini brand of markers during Back-to-School buying season. With funds tight due to expenditures in traditional media, the company needed a way to reach a benchmark of 100,000 unique consumers using a viral-based WOM effort that reached out to their key demographics.

HyperDrive developed a customized online game and promotion called Sharpie Mini "BUST OUT" that featured an addictive game in their site and an e-mail marketing opt-in database. The game surpassed its goal of 100,000 registrations by more than 400,000 unique visitors and yielded nearly 4.2 million page views! As a component of the campaign, Sharpie gave away 75,000 samples of its Mini product in less than 4 days. To this day, they consider this online promotion the best in their brand's history.

Sensor Technology Systems

This high-end night vision goggle maker had zero marketing presence when HyperDrive became their agency of record. As part of its parent company The O'Gara Group, a company which HyperDrive also works with on a daily basis, Sensor Technology Systems' (STS) principals knew that it was time to spread the word about their product, which military and defense leaders consider to be revolutionary in its market due to its advanced heads-up-display feature.

We created a full complement of interactive and traditional materials to help STS land military and government contracts around the world, including U.S. Special Operations Command, U.S. Marine Corps, U.K. Ministry of Defense, and the Italian Army. STS has grown dramatically in the time we have worked with them and are now fully operational for trade shows, advertising, website, digital presentations, and sales materials. HyperDrive's assistance contributed to the STS team obtaining revenue growth of over 65% as well as the landing of a the company's first $6.4 million order from the U.S. Marine Corps.

Brains on Fire Case Study

When South Carolina received their tobacco settlement, the Department of Health and Environmental Control was tasked to create an awareness campaign for youth about the dangers of tobacco use. So, they tapped Brains on Fire to tackle a big issue in Big Tobacco's back yard.

When we surveyed the landscape, we saw that other states were pumping their money into huge media campaigns with in-your-face TV ads, which got temporary results. Once the ads quit running, the teen smoking rate went back up. There was no place for them to plug in. There was no culture.

We knew we had to go another route and create a sustainable culture. And we needed to do it using WOM. So we singled out 92 teens to own this thing. They are the ones that played a key role in the development of everything, from the name to the curriculum. We armed them with tools to spread the word and then sent them on their way to find other "ViralMentalists." The teens led weekend retreats: Festi-Viral events across the state. There is a website where they can check in with each other. A RAGE store where you can get SWAG but only if you were out spreading the word.

A recent survey found that South Carolina has had one of the highest smoking rate drops in the nation, 11.5%. That is with no mass media. No tax increase on cigarettes, and for the past 2 years virtually no budget. Anti-tobacco budgets are shrinking across the nation. But since we taught those original 92 members how to use WOM tools and techniques, they passed the 3000-member mark, that is, active members, without needing it.

Likeable Media Case Study

In the 1970s, the New York Department of Health started distributing free male condoms in the city's sexually transmitted diseases (STD) clinics. In the 1980s, the onset of HIV/AIDS led to the expansion of free male condom distribution to HIV/AIDS service organizations and organizations that served injecting drug users. In 2005, the Health Department launched a condom ordering website for easier access and bulk orders. Average monthly condom distribution then rose from 250,000 to 1.5 million. On Valentine's Day in 2007, the agency set a national precedent with its NYC Condom campaign, in which a standard, premium lubricated Lifestyles condom was packaged in a chic, Gotham-inspired, NYC-branded wrapper. The municipally branded NYC Condom provides New Yorkers with a uniquely cosmopolitan condom while increasing condom use and awareness in NYC. In 2009, the NYC Condom Availability Program distributed over 41.5 million condoms, and the NYC Condom can now be found at over 3000 locations around the city. Free female condom distribution began in 1998 and nearly 1 million free female condoms were also distributed in 2009.

The primary goal of the NYC Condom Availability Program is to increase consistent male and female condom use to reduce the transmission of HIV, STDs, and unintended pregnancy in New York City. The program works to accomplish this goal by making condoms more widely available to NYC residents, generating conversation and community buy-in around safer sex through participation in community events, and providing NYC residents with valuable education and training regarding safer sex practices. The program strives to not only increase correct and consistent condom use through out the city, but it also seeks to normalize condom use and accessibility throughout New York City. Recently, the program established a presence on social media platforms, allowing for increased individual engagement and for questions to be directly answered expanding education, visibility, and customer service. The NYC Condom Availability Program became one of the first government agency programs to use the social media platform as a venue to address any programmatic questions, concerns, and/or misinformation.

One recent hurdle that the NYC Condom Availability Program had to overcome was learning how to use social media to appropriately discuss and educate the public regarding the NYC Condom Availability Program. While social media platforms are used to promote products and services, the NYC Health Department was one of the first governmental agencies in New York City to use social media in order to promote a public health campaign. The NYC Health Department had to ensure that all content placed on the page was accurate, engaging, and relevant, while also being educational and respectful of all page participants.

A key goal of the NYC Condom Availability program was that the platforms had to attract fans and keep them engaged with content that piqued their interest and also provided a call to action that would ensure interaction on the page, while also educating people about safer sex and dispelling any misinformation. The development of content for the social media platforms used by the NYC Condom Availability Program is an ongoing process that requires not only research and creativity but also a complex tracking system to ascertain the successfulness of posted content (by using parameters such as how often the content is "liked," commented on, shared, retweeted, etc.).

In an effort to reach out to New Yorkers in media spaces that they increasingly patronized, the NYC Condom Availability Program created a Facebook and a Twitter strategy that included education, calls to action, and interactive polling. All content placed on the page is answered by a staff member of the NYC Condom Availability program and this engagement has allowed for real-time, first person education and communication to occur.

The NYC Condom Availability Program used its Facebook page and Twitter account to announce the NYC Condom Wrapper Design Contest on December 14, 2009. The contest was created to empower NYC residents to take ownership of safer sex by competing to design a limited edition of the NYC Condom wrapper and share in the development of a new NYC Condom media campaign. The objective of the art contest was to creatively engage community members in the NYC Condom Availability program by linking the community's artistic voice with this effective public health tool. The contest ran from December 14, 2009, until January 22, 2010, and was open to any New York City resident 17 or older. A panel of judges evaluated submissions and selected five finalists, which were announced on February 11, 2010. New Yorkers were then able to vote for their favorite design by casting votes online at the NYC Condom Availability Program's official web page, www.nyc.gov/condom. The winning design, which was announced at a press conference on March 9, 2010, was turned into a special, limited edition NYC Condom wrapper that will be unveiled this fall.

Folding content regarding the NYC Condom Wrapper Design Contest into the program's social media strategy was both successful and innovative. Information regarding the contest was placed on Facebook page tabs, fans were invited to participate and were updated on the contest via status updates and images of the five finalists were shared with by linking the Facebook page to the NYC Condom program's official web page. The Twitter strategy was even more proactive. Every Thursday, Friday, and Saturday, night staff would search for NYC-area Twitter users who tweeted that they were going out. Staff would remind them, via Twitter messaging, to take a condom with them. The ground-breaking twist is that staff tweeted *AS THE CONDOM*. The program was looking to make an impact and offer a practical, yet friendly reminder to be safe.

Facebook ads were used to target both voting for the design contest and unveiling of the design contest winner. These location-based, targeted ads reached out to people who were not already connected with the NYC Condom Facebook fan page and/or the NYC Condom Twitter account. Grassroots, WOM marketing regarding the program also occurred by presenting the contest at various HIV Care Network meetings throughout the five boroughs; e-mailing the NYC Condom Wrapper Contest announcement to the entire condom ordering distribution list of over 2500 organizations; and answering individual e-mails and phone calls garnered by earned media regarding the contest, which resulted in over 600 unique entries for the NYC Condom design were submitted from all five boroughs and from around the world, including as far away as St. Petersburg, Russia, and over 12,800 Facebook fans and 2346 tweets.

360 Digital Influences Case Study

In 2005, the California Office of Traffic Safety (OTS) launched the Click It or Ticket seat belt enforcement campaign aimed at increasing compliance with California's occupant protection laws. Since then, the annual effort has contributed to a steady increase in seat belt use rates—up from 92.5% in 2005 to 95.3% in 2009. In order to educate motorists about increased fines for seat belt violations, as well as increased enforcement of the laws, the Click It or Ticket campaign for 2010 was developed.

The 2010 campaign occurred in two waves: the first in May leading up to Memorial Day weekend and the second in November surrounding the Thanksgiving holiday travel period. The campaign strategy combined multiple outreach efforts including media relations, paid advertising, social media, PSAs, and partnership activities.

As the OTS relied heavily upon law enforcement grantees at the local level to promote the Click It or Ticket initiative, the campaign team developed media material templates and coordinated public affairs interviews for OTS staff in an effort to increase media coverage. To augment earned media activities, paid radio advertising coupled with TV, radio, and outdoor billboard PSAs were integrated into the campaign.

Additional components of the 2010 campaign included multifaceted social media outreach and the establishment of partnerships. The California OTS Facebook page provided a unique platform to promote the campaign and generate conversation around the enforcement mobilization and the importance of seat belt use. The OTS Facebook page also included an interactive quiz that allowed users to select how often they comply with seat belt laws.

Through partnerships with multiple state agencies and entertainment venues, including the Department of Motor Vehicles and the Shoreline Amphitheatre, the campaign extended the number of communications channels featuring Click It or Ticket messaging.

The 2010 campaign generated more than 229 million audience impressions and upward of $3.3 million in added value—more than a 300% increase over the 2009 efforts. As a result, California's seat belt use rate increased from 95.3% in 2009 to 96.2% in 2010. The National Highway Traffic Safety Administration estimates that 1365 California lives were saved at the increased seat belt use rate, which was much higher than the national average.

BzzAgent Case Studies

HTC

For those who are fluent in social media HTC's Windows 7 smartphone speaks your language. The phone features people, photo, music, and video hubs that make for easier connections and direct uploads to Facebook while on the go. With smooth transitions, easy upload capability, and cool built in speakers, HTC hopes to change brand perception and generate reach. HTC hoped for consumer engagement and adoption of brand perception while further reaching consumers.

The campaign included 1000 T-Mobile or AT&T customers, ranging from 18 to 49 who were not current i-Phone users. Agents were each given a free HTC phone to try out as well as a BzzGuide with a focused activity on product reviews and Facebook and/or Twitter posts. The campaign generated very high Agent activity levels resulting in hundreds of thousands of detailed product conversations, it reached 234,000+ people via in-person and digital conversations and each Agent influenced 235 conversations. The campaign drove activity among core HTC segment: 25–34 year olds; influenced 499 Facebook posts and 651 Tweets.

Thomas

Thomas' bakers—the English muffin people—recognized that many consumers want the taste and texture of bagels, but do not necessarily want all the calories that go along with them. So in early 2010, they launched Bagel Thins bagels, a breakfast favorite with less guilt.

Consumers were attracted to Bagel Thins bagels because of its 110 calorie count, but research showed they stayed with the product for its taste. But many were hesitant to try. For bagel fans, could a thin bagel really deliver a true bagel experience? For calorie counters, could a bagel be guilt free? Given this dynamic trial and recommendations were key. So, Thomas' included a BzzCampaign as part of their integrated media plan designed to grow brand share.

The campaign was tasked with converting product trial to sales, and Thomas' needed proof of that impact. So, BzzAgent partnered with SymphonyIRI Group to run a Matched Market Test analysis (Test and Control) to measure the sales lift and ROI directly attributable to the BzzCampaign.

The BzzCampaign engaged 10,000 consumers, 18+ who identified themselves as health conscious. Because of the Matched Market Test analysis, the program excluded people who lived in two control markets but opened participation to eligible agents in other markets where the product was available. As with all BzzCampaigns, participants were selected from BzzAgent's network of influential brand advocates and agents needed to opt-in to join the program. Since trial was an essential part of this campaign all participants received one free coupon to spur immediate purchase. The mailing also included, a printed collateral piece, the BzzGuide, with detailed product information and tips for spreading the word.

Agent response to the Thomas' Bagel Thins bagels was overwhelmingly positive. Ninety percent of agents reported a positive opinion at the end of the campaign and they submitted over 1700 reviews with 4+ stars. Agents were aligned with the Bagel Thins value proposition, loving the calorie count and its true bagel taste and texture.

The campaign reached over 1 million people via in-person and online conversations. Facebook, Twitter, and blog posts—coupled with reviews on amazon.com and videos on YouTube—earned Thomas' bakers coveted consumer-generated media that supported their paid and owned channels.

Nielsen BuzzMetrics tracked an increase in online conversations about the Thomas' brand and Bagel Thins bagels, corresponding directly with the campaign timing. The campaign also increased positive sentiment for Bagel Thins by 10%.

All of this activity directly impacted product sales. The Matched Market Test analysis, conduced by SymphonyIRI Group, analyzed in-store sales data to measure the lift in sales volume and units sold in test markets. Based on this sales impact, they calculated the ROI for the campaign. The results from this analysis proved a positive lift in sales volume during a 12 week period, during and immediately following the campaign period; on average, each Agent influenced double-digit purchases, a positive return on Thomas' Bakers BzzCampaign investment.

Black Box Wine

Constellation, a premium wine company, created their Black Box wine; a fine wine that is a great value, convenient, and environmentally friendly. Unlike a corked glass bottle that spoils after a few days after being opened, Black Box wine remains fresh for a minimum of 4 weeks prior to being opened and it is much cheaper than glass resulting in more quality wine for less. Black Box wine hopes to drive Agent trial of their product as well as drive adoption of it.

BzzAgent targeted 1988 agents ranging from 30 to 45 years old with a HHI of $50,000+ living in select U.S. markets and consume wine each week. They were sent a Bzzkit, including mail-in rebates for Black Box wine, Black Box branded

items, including a display case, and carafes and a BzzGuide with product information and activities focused on agent-hosted parties to drive high-volume trial. The
campaign generated tens of thousands of trials through agent-hosted parties that
introduced the wine to friends in a personal social setting. With a reach to over
327,000 people via in-person and digital conversations, each agent influenced 164
conversations.

Keller Fay Group Case Studies

Case Study One

A major beverage company was experiencing a PR crisis with one of their brands.
A custom study was conducted and determined that the problem was not nearly as
big or as fundamental as the client initially thought. A key reason was that while
there had been a surge in negativity in online social media, a representative sample
of offline conversations revealed that the problem was not widespread and unlikely
to persist very long. The brand's future performance was consistent with Keller
Fay's offline WOM research. The client was able to refocus efforts away from the
crisis to long-term brand health. Client asked Keller Fay for monthly monitoring
for all their brands, with WOM reporting up to the C-Suite. Client is providing
data to its media agency to manage planning and buying in order to optimize positive WOM.

Case Study Two

Telecom provider was having a significant sales problem in a major region of
the country. Our TalkTrack® was used for the analysis and custom qualitative
research among their customers and competitors' customers. The research identified new targets to be focusing on in marketing and identified a potential strength
they were not aware of to leverage in their messaging. Client asked Keller Fay to
present the results of the research workshop style to both regional and national
management of the company. Creative briefs were requested to help guide their
agencies. Ideas were employed in sales, marketing, and media strategies. Client
expanded scope of research to support marketing on national basis. Most recently,
Client analyzed TalkTrack data among a hundred different data sources and identified it as one of the most predictive of sales, leading to its continuing use in
market mix models.

Case Study Three

A CPG company wanted to see if WOM research might shed light on how contact points work along the purchase funnel. Data showed so many WOM contact
points that the client was hesitant to believe it. Had a third-party corroborated the

research successfully? Follow-ups were conducted in multiple global markets, also corroborated by a third party. Client gained deep understanding of how WOM worked in their markets as well as an understanding of how to get customers to try the brand following WOM. Currently use it to find which marketing touch points to utilize to generate maximum WOM. Client has incorporated Keller Fay data into its conceptual models for marketing optimization to increase brand adoption. Data are reviewed at the board level.

Case Study Four

Media agency wanted to understand the role of influencers in marketing. Client subscribed to TalkTrack for annual access to all brands, all categories. Client created a WOM opportunity grid to help their clients understand how to target influencers in their marketing. They also built a media model to evaluate media for WOM potential. The client says that ad-generated WOM models behave quite differently from awareness models, and WOM models are a closer predictor of sales than are awareness models.

Case Study Five

Consumer electronics manufacturer won marketer of the year recently and specifically cited their WOM strategy, which Keller Fay had helped inform. They were interested in launching a major new technology platform using a primarily WOM strategy. Wanted to target a nontraditional influencer segment they had identified. Despite being a tech company, they took the view that the most powerful WOM would NOT be online, but rather face to face. Therefore they saw TalkTrack as offering a unique opportunity to define strategy and monitor success. Monthly and quarterly assessments of their position vis-a-vis their competition enabled them to evaluate effectiveness of their different marketing channels from a WOM perspective, and provided a system for the urgent diagnosis of problems or developments in the market that can only be answered with WOM data.

Case Study Six

Automotive company came to Keller Fay with a nontraditional influencer segmentation and wanted us to validate it, while also creating a standardized approach to thinking about influencer targeting. Custom Study and TalkTrack analysis is the process of conducting the research we opened the client's eyes to a new segmentation approach that was more powerful in predicting conversations and recommendations in the auto category and for their brand, in particular.

Case Study Seven

Personal Care and Beauty Products company was launching a significant effort to market to men; they came to Keller Fay looking to understand how WOM works in the male market for grooming products. Custom analyses of TalkTrack data pointed out that females not only give the most advice to men about these products but that their advice is much more valued by males than advice they get from male peers. Study led to new tactics to activate women in giving grooming advice to men.

Case Study Eight

Personal Care and Beauty Products company was experiencing a crisis situation for a diet food brand in which there were rumors of a health problem associated with the brand. Sales were declining. TalkTrack analysis demonstrated that their sales were being undermined by a prolonged period of under-marketing during the crucial pre-New Year's period so vital to the dieting category, and the health rumors bore no effect on the decline in sales. We also identified that the workplace was an extremely important venue in the discussion of diet products, providing new opportunities to the Client who was able to redeploy resources away from the "rumor" crisis and began beefing up marketing to take advantage of New Year's holiday and the workplace opportunities.

Case Study Nine

Investment company wanted to see if WOM research could help them optimize their workplace marketing. TalkTrack analysis provided them a comparison of workplace WOM to WOM that happens in other places and demonstrated that they were performing less well at work versus elsewhere. Analysis further pointed to problems they had with men speaking too negatively about the company and females, though positive, were not talking often enough about the company. Based on research results, the client was able to develop an amplification strategy for women and to work on more positive messaging to men.

Case Study Ten

Quick-service restaurant chain was trying to understand how the teen market, a prime target of theirs, differed from adults from the standpoint of WOM. TalkTrack analysis uncovered a counterintuitive but rapidly growing teen concern about the health issues of their product: teens were talking even more about health than their moms. The research provided an early warning about the countertrend on health and obesity issues among youth. The client, understanding the primary issue, was able to improve their messaging to teens.

Fanscape Case Study

Find and inform the fans of the artists performing at the AT&T blue room live streaming Lollapalooza event. Encourage all fans to watch the event through AT&T blue room. Fanscape tapped into official artist online properties, fan communities, lifestyle sites, e-mails, and grassroots destinations to find the fans online. Fanscape implemented a Partner Integration program with top lifestyle sites on the web as an additional way to reach the Lollapalooza audience. The campaign garnered almost 3 million targeted unique views for the AT&T blue room Lollapalooza webcast as well as over 3 million impressions it secured placements on the official online properties for almost every Lollapalooza artist and reached the core fan communities of all Lollapalooza artists.

BrickFish Case Studies (Figure 4.17)

This social media campaign platform agency has generated over 600 million brand engagements for some of the world's premier brands, including Redbox, Microsoft®, Dell, Blackberry®, QVC, Estée Lauder, Coach and more.

Figure 4.17   Some BrickFish clients.

TREMOR Case Study

Cereal bars are nothing new. Set a dozen brands and varieties in front of the average consumer and their expectation—their schema—is that each looks and tastes pretty much exactly like the other. With the introduction of TLC cereal bars, however, Kashi knew they had something different. The challenge was how, in a busy advertising and media environment, they could generate a disruptive message that would resonate with a Vocalpoint connector, prompt her to try the product, and share it with others in her social network.

To create that disruptive, personal message, TREMOR first conducted qualitative and quantitative research to reveal the core consumer expectations or schemas. What they discovered is that consumers think Kashi TLC cereal bars "look different" and have different ingredients than they had come to expect in the category. These observations led to the disruptive message: *Kashi TLC cereal bars have real fruit you can see. It's not hiding behind unhealthy ingredients like other cereal bars.*

With the message established, 400,000 highly connected women in the TREMOR network received an offline mailer with a sample cereal bar and a coupon for a free box to encourage product sampling. In addition, she was provided with five coupons to share with friends and help trigger conversations. Connectors were also directed to Vocalpoint and Kashi TLC microsites to take a quiz about relevant subjects like artificial ingredients, to vote on new cereal bar flavors and print online coupons for additional purchases.

Porter Novelli Case Study

Porter Novelli was founded in Washington, DC, in the belief that the creative, strategic marketing approaches used in the commercial sector could and should be applied to help nonprofit organizations improve public health and address social issues. Porter Novelli today is one of the world's top 10 public relations firms, helping clients in 50 countries reach out and grow in the commercial, government, and not-for-profit sectors. Porter Novelli manages more than a dozen global programs for clients such as Wyeth, Gillette, Qualcomm, and Dow, coordinating global and regional strategy and execution.

Porter Novelli, a leading public relations firm serving some of the world's most respect and demanding clients, delivers a high-quality service while meeting their clients' needs with ease. An internationally influential energy council recently selected Porter Novelli to assist in a large-scale collaborative effort to enhance communication and interaction among a regionally displaced team of over 100 industry executives. Porter Novelli was able to fulfill their client's very detailed and specific requirements with a single, synergistic solution.

The requested solution had several requirements that were not negotiable. This would prove to make the search for an adequate solution extremely difficult causing them to consider building an in-house solution that would run them far over budget. The primary factor was the delivery of a fully customized navigation and design structure to integrate as a seamless component to their existing site. As the portal would house and cater to many levels of users with varying access rights, a full-scale system to effortlessly manage permissions and monitor activity was essential.

Mitra Falli, senior interactive producer at Porter Novelli, was tasked with finding a solution that not only met the needs of their client but was deliverable within the allotted budget provided. On top of the detailed requirements regarding customization, permissions, and some of the more standard collaborative components such as shared documents and calendar functions, the system was to be administered by a nontechnical division of Porter Novelli; thus, it was a major requirement for the portal to be easily administered, creating new users, structures, and permissions.

Initially, Mitra proposed the development of an in-house solution to accomplish the complex and detailed requirements of their client. After a cost estimate ran them far over budget in this scenario, it became apparent that this solution was not plausible. This brought them to entertain installed solutions such as MS Sharepoint as an option; though it delivered what was needed within budget, it required a hefty investment in hardware and with uncertainty of their client's project duration. Mitra began to take a look at hosted solutions that required no investment or maintenance.

As Porter Novelli began their search for a collaborative solution, it became clear that the hosted collaboration market is a rapidly growing medium for communication and coordination. After reviewing a number of solutions provided by small start-ups and organizations with limited history and untested reputations, it became essential that if they were going to present a hosted product to their client, it must be an application that is confirmed to be reliable with a history of stability and integrity.

This search brought Mitra to HyperOffice, the oldest and most respected player in the hosted collaboration market. With over 10 years in the market, use of the largest hosting facility in North America and a strong international presence, it became clear that the other organizations evaluated were merely opportunists catching the market on the upturn. The availability of training and consultation services and a free support line, served as icing on the cake.

Following a web-based demonstration of the HyperOffice product and its capabilities, it was verified that the complex and detailed requirements requested by their client was able to be successfully accomplished with HyperOffice. With a price point at a fraction of the other relevant solutions and no investment, the choice was clear.

Upon purchase of HyperOffice, a number of hours of training and consultation services were included in the contract. These sessions were positioned to apply directly to their intended application of the product. During these sessions, the focus was to get the system up and running as quickly as possible and to ensure that the portal was to be implemented as a seamless addition to their client's existing site.

Traditionally, the publisher function of HyperOffice is used as a means for a nontechnical user to customize the look and feel of the portal. Since Porter Novelli is a large international organization with a full design and web development team, the design and development would be approached in a separate capacity.

To fully customize the homepage and navigation associated with the portal, Porter Novelli was able to task their design team to mock-up how the portal would look. Following this, the HyperOffice representative assigned to assist in the implementation of the product was able to review the mock-up and make suggestions and point out potential limitations and solutions. The next phase was to send the revised portal mock-up to their internal web design team to translate it to HTML. Once the code was completed, it is dropped into the publisher function of HyperOffice.

Once the design was imported into HyperOffice Porter Novelli was able to link sections, documents or events within HyperOffice to images or text, creating a seamless intranet solution. With the use of modules to populate information from the calendar section directly on the homepage, users are immediately aware of the events applicable to them since the information populates dynamically based on the user that is logged in. In addition, the login to the portal was placed on the client's site and the URL branded, with this application, the client did not know that their portal was a third-party solution.

Once the structure was in place, full implementation was just a matter of adding users, assigning permissions, and populating the content to get the team started. The full implementation has two general levels of users, board members and standard members, and, as one may imagine, the level of permissions would be very different between these levels. In addition to securing certain groups and documents from regular members, the use of profiles allowed the personal section within the portal to be disabled and certain aspects of the group section were removed. This allowed not only for a secure environment where sensitive documents could be held, but it helped ease the usability of the portal and simplify the navigation to improve the implementation's effectiveness.

The program was a major success and implemented below budget. Moving forward, following the upcoming release of the new HyperOffice user interface Porter Novelli plans to utilize HyperOffice within other departments and in additional client applications.

Room 214 Case Studies

Qwest

Qwest approached Room 214 in 2008 with a range of ideas on how to utilize social media to enhance advertising and sponsorship opportunities. Qwest clearly recognized the requirement to first address customer service. This resulted in the "Talk to Qwest" initiative, which successfully leveraged Twitter to positively impact customer retention and brand sentiment. Qwest's goals were twofold: (1) engaging customers online where they were already talking about Qwest and (2) increasing overall positive sentiment to improve Qwest's customer service rating.

Challenge

- Effectively segmenting the volume of online conversation about Qwest
- Educating and enlisting key stakeholder across multiple departments within the company
- Training and integration of customer support personnel to drive timely resolution
- Overcoming the negative customer service perception supported by the MSN/Zogby rating
- Developing a pilot program successful enough to justify additional social media programs

Approach

- Development of over 25 internal stakeholder interviews to identify and educate key groups within Qwest that could participate in impacting the company's online brand perception
- Segmentation and monitoring of online conversations into five main categories: customer service, technical support, billing, pricing, and brand
- Establishment of a baseline to create meaningful metrics for the program's success
- Deployment of a workflow process and guidelines for escalation to in-house subject matter experts to achieve problem resolution and tracking
- Development of the *Talk to Qwest* program, establishing a customer service channel on Twitter to interact with customers
- Creation of a supporting social media page with video introductions of the *Talk To Qwest* team

Results

- Within year 1 (2009), Qwest engaged with nearly 700 customers per month and reached 100% problem resolution.
- Customers engaging with *Talk To Qwest* demonstrated a 9% better retention rate than premier queues and a 15% better retention rate than Qwest's traditional channels for customer service.
- Positive sentiment grew by nine points, and negative postings decreased by five points in 2009.
- Qwest was the first company ever to be removed from MSN/Zogby's negative customer survey list.
- The success of the program garnered support for additional social media programs to support sponsorship and the launch of Qwest on Facebook, leveraging "214 apps."

Travel Channel

Room 214 began working with Travel Channel to customize Facebook pages. As an early adopter, we helped Travel Channel recognize the advantage of segmenting their Facebook strategy to support individual shows. Going outside the standard practice of supporting a single brand presence, Room 214 helped grow Facebook communities to increase web traffic and viewership.

Travel Channel's goals were to leverage social media for increased viewership of network programs, as well as web traffic to support advertising. By actively building its community presence in social media, the network sought to create deeper engagement with its content to drive tune in.

Challenge

- Creating a unified brand approach across multiple social platforms and shows
- Balancing content exclusive to social media and TravelChannel.com
- Integrating talent into the conversation stream
- Avoiding excess promotion in the effort to drive tune in
- Defining metrics to gauge success

Approach

- Influencer identification and outreach focused around the brand, show/host topics, and regional interests
- Creation of brand hubs and "show spokes" in Facebook, YouTube, MySpace, and Twitter
- Game-based Twitter marketing, widget, and custom Facebook applications to extend fan engagement
- Deployment of community managers to monitor, respond, and build a community following
- Marketing dashboard development to support reporting, analysis, and correlation of social activity to show ratings

Results

- Facebook and Twitter—top referring sites to TravelChannel.com
- Proven statistical correlation between Facebook interactions and TravelChannel.com traffic
- Over 1.5 million community members with consistent 30%+ quarter over quarter growth
- Over 175 million impressions per quarter through social media communities
- Ten percent of show-related conversation online now happens while watching an episode
- PRSA Gold Award for social media

Strategic Media

Room 214 has been positioning Strategic Media as one of the top resources for the "Radio Advertising" search term. Based on highly competitive radio advertising terms within Google, Yahoo, and MSN, Strategic Media now typically ranks in the top 1–3 search results for its primary keyword phrase among over 165 million associated search results.

Strategic Media's primary goal was to achieve top search engine rankings for key industry terms in order to increase relevant organic search engine traffic and reinforce brand awareness. Aligning with this goal was the ultimate objective of generating additional qualified leads and new radio advertising clients in.

Challenge

- Identifying the most relevant search phrases considering search volume and competition
- Avoiding the attraction of low-quality traffic due to irrelevant search strategies
- Competing for search visibility in a crowded space
- Dated website with technical limitations to search engine visibility

Approach

- Keyword research, competition, and industry analysis related to SEO
- Focused on optimizing for keywords and meta descriptions that generated the most relevant prequalified traffic
- Performed on-site optimization, off-site optimization, social media optimization, and paid advertising.
- Coordinated editorial calendar, blogging strategies, article distribution, and optimized press release tactics
- Implemented metrics and reporting dashboard to guide on-going strategy and tracking of ROI
- Website redesign, including blog and syndicated article sections

Results

- New page-one Google rankings for 20 of the top 30 industry keywords
- #1 and #2 Google ranking for the most desired terms "radio advertising," "direct response radio," and "radio advertising agency"
- 100% average year over year increase in organic traffic for 3 years
- Over 400% increase in leads within the first year

SmartyPig

SmartyPig approached Room 214 at the beginning of their product launch, recognizing a blog would be one of many primary channels to address product update and customer service requirements. Room 214 provided the direction, design, and technical implementation to make SmartyPig's blog a highly functional aspect of their business.

SmartyPig's primary goal was the successful launch of their company and product on the web without an online advertising budget. Aligning with this goal was the objective of positioning the brand as an innovator and leader in the online savings segment of the financial services industry.

Challenge

- Zero supporting ad dollars
- No brand equity to leverage
- Developing an effective market-entrance and outreach strategy
- Targeting the right audience to generate WOM and online visibility

Approach

- Identification and monitoring of key topics and emerging themes within online conversations about saving money
- Proprietary MavenMap identification of online influencers in blogs, forums, and mainstream media
- Influencer outreach, targeted messaging, and personalized video pitches to incorporate Customer DNA from key, personal finance bloggers
- Custom blog development, customer service strategy, use of optimized press releases, and communications calendar
- Development of Twitter video contests, and deployment of the GetSatisfaction customer support platform
- Social media consulting and reputation management
- Development of Facebook Connect guidelines, documentation, and troubleshooting procedures

Results

- Several hundred blogs covered SmartyPig's story and offering within a 2 week period, including top blogs like TechCrunch.
- Sustained, hockey-stick growth trends on customer acquisition.
- International expansion, applying success model overseas.
- Major TV network and press coverage.
- Garnering of additional financing from a major funding source.
- First implementation of Facebook Connect in online banking.
- Award-winning notoriety for social media innovation within the financial services industry.

Converseon Case Study

The challenge was to establish an authentic and relevant online voice for a beloved 130-year-old crafting company and institute best practices that help build relationships with passionate consumers of online knitting communities. Lion Brand Yarn (LBY) was not sure if its customer demographic would be likely to engage in social media but was willing to experiment with the new technology in an attempt to engage and connect with its passionate consumer base.

They engaged Converseon to help them listen to the online conversation about knitting and crocheting, better understand their customers' social media behavior, identify opportunities for engagement and develop a coherent and measurable social media strategy. The brand's approach to social media hinged on an open approach to conversation and employee-driven content and relationships. The brand focused on "talking" to its customers and prospects and expanded its efforts in social media as the rigorous measurement framework indicated success. LBY has taken a long-term approach to community building and it is now, 18 months after the initial launch of the Yarncraft podcast, that the brand is seeing the most success and measurable ROI.

Lion Brand teamed with Converseon, utilizing our Conversation Mining technology to map the knitting/crocheting online community, identify influential online voices, and identify opportunities for engagement in social media. This listening uncovered a deep, interconnected, and highly engaged community of passionate users spread across blogs, podcasts, and even dedicated knitting/crocheting social networks.

With Converseon's strategic guidance, the "Yarncraft" podcast was launched. Hosted by a pair of LBY employees, the podcast was produced biweekly and focused on knitting and crocheting topics. The podcast was posted to a dedicated blog, distributed via iTunes and also given away as a CD in store for less tech-savvy consumers. The podcast was designed to be a conversation with customers and knitting community figures more so than "Internet radio" in the broadcast model.

The "Lion Brand Notebook" blog was launched, providing content and links to other knitting sources. The blog was also powered by Lion Brand employees with content ranging from customer polls for product development through to "knit alongs" that combine online/offline access allowing customers to knit the same project together. The "knit alongs" alone have proven to be a measurable driver of ROI for the brand as each virtual event drives a direct link to increased sales of the yarn featured.

Lion Brand is one of the 2009 Internet Retailer's "Hot 100" Retail Websites. Their site receives over 2 million visits a month. The podcast regularly has 15–20,000 downloads while the blog attracts tens of thousands of readers each month. A Lion Brand survey of 30,000 of their customers found that those customers who have interacted with the brand through social media are 83% more likely to identify as "very brand loyal" than nonsocial media users and are several times more likely to recommend the brand to others.

Traffic analysis shows that traffic from social media routinely converts at a much higher rate than most sources, outperforming e-mail marketing and banner ads.

LBY initially set out to build relationships with the online knitting community by talking with their customers via a corporate blog and podcast. As a result of an investment in people rather than products, they found themselves with a passionate and brand loyal group of knitters, who not only engage with the brand but also impact the bottom line by buying and using products as a result of social media engagement.

Oddcast Case Studies

McDonald's

For McDonald's promotion of James Cameron's movie, *Avatar*, The Marketing Store and Oddcast teamed up to create Avatarize Yourself, a unique application allowing users to become part of the *Avatar* phenomenon. Utilizing cutting-edge 3D photo-morphing technology, "Avatarize Yourself" invited viewers to upload a head shot—or select one from Facebook—in order to instantly transform it into a believable rendition of a personalized Na'vi. Users could choose their gender and their background and add a message.

Virality was instant and overwhelming with almost every direct visitor generating an earned user by sharing the application. The campaign inspired a number of user-run blogs and Facebook Fan Pages. Social networks were flooded with images of Avatarized users and celebrities. Despite minimal branding, the word "McDonald's" was one of the most commonly used in social media posts about "Avatarize Yourself."

Kellogg

Kellogg's Cheez-It brand and Paramount, the studio behind the new *Star Trek*, launched a major cross-promotion in the months leading up to the film's release. Oddcast worked with Brigandi + Associates to create Trek Yourself, which allows users to upload a photo and transform themselves into a member of the star ship's crew.

Everyone involved in this campaign knew it had the potential to be a huge success, and our foremost concern was making sure it was easy for fans to share their creations. The application was built using widget technology that complemented Oddcast's core sharing engine and incorporated a few new features, including the ability to grab the entire application and post it to blogs, social network pages, and almost anywhere else across the web. This distribution model made promotion a breeze: publisher sites jumped at the chance to present their readers with the full app on their own sites, and within weeks it was live on thousands of sites.

Ford

To promote its new Focus model, Ford tagged Wunderman and Oddcast to create a fun, engaging campaign that would connect with targeted younger audiences and drive brand awareness. The result was "Theme Song-a-Tron," which allows users to upload their photo, dress up in their favorite style, and rock out to their personal theme song.

Many of Oddcast's most successful campaigns utilize voice, whether using record by mic, phone, or by typing using Text-to-Speech. As the Ford Theme Song-a-Tron campaign demonstrates, however, it is possible—and sometimes even preferable—to leave out voice in the interest of a simpler, faster experience. The key is to provide just enough choices to engage the user, but not so many that the user is overwhelmed and abandons the experience before reaching your end goal. The Ford campaign strikes just the right balance.

M&M

Working with IMC2 and World of M&M's, Oddcast created the Candy Lab—a virtual laboratory where users can upload a photo, put their face on an M&M, and make it talk or sing! They were then able to purchase the results of their work as real M&M's at the My M&M's Store.

The majority of Oddcast campaigns are focused on awareness, branding, or generating leads. However, as the success of the M&M's campaign shows, selling products directly from an Oddcast-powered experience can be extremely effective. Because the user is already immersed in your experience and interacting with your brand, it is an easy step to purchasing products. Imagine dressing up characters in clothing that can be purchased or stepping into the role of video game character with the option to purchase. And since users tend to pass on experiences to peers within their demographic, the offer does not just spread virally, but it spreads to the right target audience.

Nokia

Are you an Animal Rocker? A Pink Popper? A Philharmaniac? How about an Electro Blipper? If you are unsure, do not worry: Nokia can help you find your musical style with this site from Wieden+Kennedy London and Oddcast.

Oddcast 3D PhotoFace characters allow users to control every last detail. Sometimes, however, it is better to limit the degree and type of customization. The Nokia campaign is a great example of this: instead of letting users change their eyes, nose, lips, and other features, Nokia used a few simple slider bars to control the overall "attitude" of the character. Slide to the left for a milder look; slide to the right for something totally wild. No fussing with every last detail. It is a great lesson in how to create the feeling of customization while keeping the experience simple, fast, and in tune with your brand.

Mr. Youth Case Study

To get North America geared up for the launch of the 2011 Fiesta, Mr. Youth teamed up with Ford to create an integrated social marketing program to spur consumer engagement with the new car. Event activations in four targeted markets give consumers the opportunity to drive and win one of four Fiestas, while the Ford Fiesta Road Crew keeps fans up to date, sharing photos and video content via YouTube and Facebook. To bring the brand and its tour to life, Mr. Youth created four individual Twitter and Foursquare profiles, each with a persona customized to the region. In the first month, the Road Crew has generated more than 3200 qualified leads with no end in sight.

A social media and social interactive element fosters conversations between the brand and consumers and generates buzz and feedback about the Fiesta. Four personalized Twitter accounts and FourSquare profiles update fans on where the tour is headed and share content. Consumers also are asked to check in on FourSquare or Gowalla and share their experiences via their own Twitter and Facebook accounts.

To individualize the experience, the tour developed a personality for each of the four markets that reflect the target consumer in those areas. Three dedicated vehicles and a road crew of six to eight people travel to each market. Trendy, hipster Tri-State residents who frequent art museums and weekend farmers markets, for example, test drive the Fiesta Lime Squeeze Hatch, Blue Flame Hatch, and Tuxedo Black Sedan, which have been detailed with "tattoos" to reflect the personality of this market. Sporty, spirited, proud Philadelphia folk who jog in the park or escape to the beach on weekends, on the other hand, try out an appropriately decorated Lime Squeeze Hatch, Blue Flame Hatch, and the Red Candy Sedan. New Englanders are casual, fun-loving, and outdoorsy types; Washington, DC, residents are preppy, connected, and in the know.

Throughout the tour, Ford is giving away four new Fiestas, one in each market, to consumers who attend an event, support social media, or sign up on thefordcast.com.

Blue Corona Case Study

The owners of Shower Door Experts (SDE), a custom shower door company located near Frederick, MD, knew that in order to take their business to the next level, they would need to improve their website. Like many small business owners, they were already somewhat familiar with the basics of SEO and had recently revised their website. However, they knew there was more that could (and should) be done to maximize their online marketing performance.

Company president, Tom Huck, is a no nonsense kind of guy. From day one, he fully understood that the first step to get more online leads was accurate measurement and tracking. He engaged Blue Corona's marketing analytics team to accurately track every aspect of his website, including the phone calls generated from various online traffic strategies. Knowing exactly how many visitors their site was getting, where each visitor came from, and which traffic sources generated the most leads was critical information for Tom and his team.

There are three primary ways visitors can find your website: direct (they remember your URL or website address and type it directly into their browser or return to your site via a bookmark), referral (paid or free—a website that has a link to your website—examples include yellow page sites, Facebook, etc.), and search engines. Remember—this traffic growth was almost entirely from organic search as a result of Blue Corona's SEO efforts.

Traffic from organic search increased over 150% from the baseline (pre-SEO) period to the month following the SEO work! Increased traffic is great, but what most small business owners really want when they invest in SEO is more leads—sales, revenue, and profit. The increased traffic to SDE's website resulted in more online leads, but changes to their site derived from Blue Corona's marketing analytics service improved their online conversion rates from 0.78% in April to 3.01% in October.

Mozeo Case Study

The Houston Aeros are an ice hockey team in the American Hockey League, the Aeros play at the Toyota Center in downtown Houston, TX. The Aeros were looking to reach a larger fan base with their marketing strategy in order to promote upcoming games and drive ticket sales. The team was looking for a quick and easy way to reach a great number of their loyal hockey fans at once. Additionally, the Aeros wanted to tie in an attractive in-game promotion as a marketing tool to further reach out to the crowd. Looking toward the future, they wanted to see some immediate results.

Mozeo worked directly with the Houston Aeros to help the hockey team develop a creative marketing strategy. Mozeo's services allowed the Aeros to seamlessly tie together an in-game promotion with their future marketing plans. During a home hockey game, the Aeros and Mozeo had a "text-to-win" contest, with the prize being a hockey stick signed by the entire team. The crowd was instructed to text the word "AEROS" to a special number, and then a winner would be selected at random. By gathering the mobile phone numbers of the respondents, the Aeros automatically built their database of contacts and could then use Mozeo's online portal to easily send text blasts with information about upcoming games, promotions, and other important updates.

This strategy resulted in an overwhelming success. The contest for the signed hockey stick was a huge hit. The Aeros saw a 17% participation rate, which included a crowd with a wide age spread. The Aeros then used Mozeo's text blasting service to reach their newly established mobile customer base. A week after the promotion, the Aeros followed up with their new contacts by sending a text message with a discount code for an upcoming game; the code resulted in 54 additional tickets being sold.

This discount code not only drew fans to the game, but it also served as a measurement tool to see how many of the mobile contacts would act on the discount. With continued promotions and text blasting, the Aeros have seen greater turnout at games and higher ticket sales than they did before teaming up with Mozeo.

After the great success of an attractive in-game promotion coupled with an effective marketing strategy, the Aeros continue to work with Mozeo to expand their database of mobile numbers. By continuing to reach their loyal fans instantaneously, the Aeros will be sure to drive future ticket sales and attendance at their hockey games.

Mobile Web Up Case Study

MSIA is a church and spiritual organization based in Los Angeles, CA. For over a decade, their website at www.msia.org served well both as a powerful fund-raising tool and in providing information and other services to their congregation. In 2009, they decided a full rebuild of the website was in order. Being aware of the rapid growth in Internet mobile devices, web manager Deborah Martinez decided the new website must be mobile friendly.

The new MSIA website features a rich and modern design, integrating social media, audio, and video. By virtue of this richness, the new website as designed would be nearly unusable on even high-end digital mobile devices. Mobile Web Up was engaged to find a solution before the new website's public launch. Mobile Web Up worked to eliminate poor mobile optimization problems such as long loading times, complex navigation menus, unresponsive video boxes, and over-rich designs that rapidly drains mobile phone batteries, driving mobile devices away.

Mobify Case Studies

The New Yorker

Since 1925, *The New Yorker* has imbued the world with is particular brand of humor, renowned fiction, and meticulous articles. Its illustrious publication history is unrivalled; however, with mobile web's rapid adoption, they recognized the need for a web presence beyond a desktop website.

Prior to this, defining features of *The New Yorker* website, like their extensive fiction pieces, broad, in-depth articles, and signature cartoons, would not render well on mobile devices, leading to dissatisfied users who expected the quintessential *The New Yorker* experience, regardless of the platform.

Using the tools provided by Mobify Studio, *The New Yorker* was able to make their site mobile friendly. Mobify Studio allows for full CSS control, mobile analytics, ad server integration, optimized images, text, and navigation style, all while keeping *The New Yorker* experience intact.

Unlike other solutions that use scrapers to periodically crawl new website content and then dump it to a database, Mobify Studio automatically mirrors all the latest updates to the desktop content on mobile. This means that *The New Yorker*'s dedicated reader base now has instant access to all the latest *New Yorker* content on mobile, as soon as it posted on the desktop website.

Since its launch, *The New Yorker*'s unique mobile views have increased over 10 times, with a dedicated mobile user base that keeps returning. More importantly, mobile users are spending more time on the site, with the average iPhone user spending over 6 min browsing the site. When using 3 g, load times were reduced by over 70%, contributing to an all-around better user experience. In combination with their iPad app, *The New Yorker* and Mobify have come together to deliver the flawless experience expected of them, no matter the device.

Threadless

Imbued with a unique, community-centered culture and funky crowd-sourced designs, Threadless is one of the best-known and most popular online clothing retailers in the world. Its desktop site is perfectly designed for their needs, with an online store and core community features, like voting on designs, feedback, and forums. However, with analytics showing more and more users visiting threadless.com on mobile devices, Threadless saw an opportunity to capitalize on market needs.

Threadless was able to use Mobify to take the core Threadless experience from the desktop site and optimize it for mobile. All relevant elements, like community features, galleries, search, and checkout, were optimized for mobile. The Mobify solution seamlessly integrated with the existing desktop site. In fact, the only change necessary on Threadless' backend was to insert a small JavaScript tag into their desktop code. This means that Threadless did not have to invest in any additional IT resources.

For a cutting-edge online retailer like Threadless, SEO and social networking are essential. Fortunately, Mobify Enterprise excels in this by keeping URLs identical across all platforms. While other providers require a redirect to a proxy server that serves a different, mobile-friendly URL, Mobify keeps mobile visitors directly on threadless.com. This means that all search engine results are identical for mobile and desktop sites, which avoids splitting search results between desktop and mobile site URLs and degrading your Google search ranking.

Mobify uses a next-generation HTML5 platform to keep mobile content identical to the desktop site. Where other mobile providers use scrapers to periodically cull updates and dump them to a database accessed by mobile users, Mobify displays content directly from desktop HTML. This means that the instant the desktop site is updated so is the mobile site. This is essential for online retailers like Threadless, who need to display live product availability and price changes.

End users visiting threadless.com from their mobile device are automatically detected by Mobify and receive the correct mobile version of Threadless. Image galleries, font size, and styling are automatically adjusted based on screen size and resolution.

Since being launched, Threadless mobile has seen traffic from iPhone and Android users triple and conversion rates skyrocket. That mobile users still used Threadless' desktop site on mobile is a testament to the strength of the Threadless community. Now that Threadless has a new, mobile-friendly site, users are happier than ever. Mobify clients usually double their mobile sales within 100 days, and Threadless is on track to easily surpass that.

Threadless mobile maintains all of the features of the desktop site. Obvious features like browsing and the checkout flow have been mobified, but so have more subtle parts, essential to Threadless' community. For example, mobile users can still discuss and vote on upcoming designs. This community participation, essential to Threadless' crowd sourced identity, is present on mobile, helping to maintain a consistent brand across all platforms.

Alibris

Alibris is the Internet's largest independently owned and operated marketplace for used books. Since 1998, it has been the premier online marketplace for independent sellers of new and used books, music, and movies, as well as rare and collectible titles. Alibris offers over 120 million items available from thousands of sellers worldwide.

With mobile web use predicted to outstrip desktop browsing within 5 years, having a mobile optimized website is a necessity. Alibris was looking for a way to expand its e-commerce presence beyond the desktop and onto mobile devices. With mobile data users numbering over 205 million in the United States alone, Alibris recognized a huge growth opportunity. At the time, Alibris.com was not optimized for mobile browsers, resulting in high bounce rates and low conversion rates.

Since every mobile user is a potential customer, Alibris was looking for a way to transfer the experience, features, and usability provided by its already established desktop website to mobile. Partnering with Mobify, Alibris was able to optimize its existing look and feel for a broad range of mobile devices. By leveraging the Mobify platform, Alibris also streamlined its key features and content, resulting in greater usability. Content and features are prioritized for mobile operating systems, including Apple's iOS, Android, and Palm's WebOS. This resulted in a reduction of load times by over 75% for those using a 3G data connection.

The Mobify Enterprise solution uses HTML5 to optimize Alibris's checkout on the fly. All mobile content instantly and automatically reflects the newest information on the desktop site. Mobify took the Alibris mobile site from concept to launch in only 3 weeks, allowing Alibris to introduce its mobile site before the all-important Thanksgiving and Cyber Monday sales period.

Mobile traffic has been growing rapidly since launching and more importantly, Alibris's mobile users are now more satisfied. This has translated into lower bounce, improved conversion rates, and a vastly enhanced mobile shopping experience. In fact, due to greatly increased mobile traffic, Alibris is on track to recoup its mobile setup costs in months. Within the same time period, mobile store purchases more than doubled.

There were many benefits to partnering with Mobify. Alibris did not have to invest in any additional IT resources. Shoppers never have to leave the site to a different hosted mobile site, thus avoiding potential security issues with third-party servers. This also allows for efficient SEO, as well as social media compatibility, due to links never breaking, no matter what device they are viewed on.

Usablenet Case Studies

ASOS

ASOS is a leading U.K.-based fashion retailer that attracted millions of people to its Facebook page. The company wanted to capture more business on Facebook, so they hired Usablenet to build their Facebook store. The integrated shopping app enables customers to securely shop the entire ASOS product range without leaving Facebook. Usablenet also built an m-commerce site for ASOS, attracting more than £1 million sales in its first quarter after the launch of the first Facebook store in Europe.

Fairmont Hotels

When your customers are by definition travelers, being able to reach them on mobile devices is critical to building closer relationships with them and bridging the gap between inquiry and reservation. Fairmont Hotels contracted with Usablenet to create an iPhone app that would enable frequent travelers and preferred customers to view photo slideshows of Fairmont properties, search for hotel packages by theme, book or change reservations, and learn of nearby attractions and activities. Fairmont concierges may have reason to worry.

JC Penney

Founded in 1902, JC Penney is both a venerable and intrepid retailer that can boast it was the first department store to sell its goods online. With an assist from Usablenet, JC Penney also became the first major U.S. retailer to offer its entire inventory via Facebook. Elevating the social networking site from a place where people transact in opinions to one where people use real money to purchase real products, JC Penney has more than 1.5 million "Likes" to support its innovative venture.

Digby Case Study

AT&T partnered with location-based mobile marketing platform Placecast to offer consumers ShopAlerts, which consisted of messages, offers, rewards, or coupons sent to their mobile phones when they were near a store or brand. AT&T created a "geo-fence," or perimeter, around a retail location or geographic area to send the location-specific messages.

The location-based mobile messaging service was tested, among AT&T customers in Chicago, Los Angeles, New York, and San Francisco who opted in to receive messages. The pilot included eight major marketers, four of which—Del Monte, Kmart, MilkPEP (the Milk Processor Education Program), and SC Johnson—were Draftfcb clients. The agency conducted a post-test survey among consumers who engaged with ShopAlerts offered by the four marketers to determine consumer preferences and attitudes.

Each of the four ShopAlert participants had different business challenges and goals:

- Del Monte's Kibbles'n Bits pet food brand sought to create awareness for the brand when consumers were in close proximity of Target and pet food stores. The marketer also wanted to generate awareness around its new Nature's Recipe line of dog food.
- Kmart used the service to offer consumers mobile coupons that were scanned directly from the handset at the point of sale.
- MilkPEP leveraged the alerts to generate awareness among consumers that chocolate milk is an ideal post-workout option for replenishing fluids.
- SC Johnson worked with Wal-Mart stores in the geo-fenced locations to drive consumers to store shelves to check out Glade scented household products.

Consumers who opted in for the ShopAlerts received a maximum of three messages per week from three different brands based on their proximity to the brand's geo-fence. The minimum time interval was 2 days between messages received.

Del Monte's Kibbles'n Bits pet food brand delivered text messages like this one: "Dogs are family, & family deserves more than just 1 boring taste. Get NEW Kibbles'n Bits Bistro Meals dog food @ Target Rancho Santa Margarita 2 day."

In the case of Kmart, consumers who opted in to receive the ShopAlerts got a coupon from the retailer if they were within a half-mile radius of a store. They received a text message on their phone that came with the link to the mobile coupon to redeem the offer. For example, the text offered: "Get $5 off any purchase of $50 in the entire store! Shop today and save @375 E Allessandro Blvd." The message was followed by a link to the coupon.

Draftfcb polled consumers who opted in to the ShopAlerts among its four clients after the program ended. With a nearly 100% open rate on the alerts, 50% of consumers who opted in to receive messages from the brands wanted more information. Draftfcb found in some cases there was a 22%–25% purchase conversion on some of the offers.

Moorhead maintains that "overwhelmingly, these kind of geo-triggered offers and alerts programs are preferred by consumers. They trigger immediate action." In addition, he says the program showed that it was not just "deals" that resonated with consumers. MilkPEP, Del Monte, and SC Johnson didn't offer "deals," per se. Consumers want to hear from brands based on the fact that they offer valuable information: "[Brands] may not be able to offer a coupon or a deal, but consumers still want to learn more about products and that supports an awareness goal."

In the next version of the program, Draftfcb is in discussions with AT&T and Placecast about enabling consumers who opt in to indicate their preferences for hearing from certain advertisers or to choose which category of advertiser they would like to receive alerts from. "Allowing consumers to continue to help us refine the relevancy of what we're giving them is a good way to go," Moorhead said.

With respect to geotargeting, "we're now we're at the point with things like ShopAlerts where we're not only connecting an individual user to a specific offer at a specific time, but also at a specific place," Moorhead said. "You're really trying to create almost an impulse purchase."

Bianor Case Study

Today, we are surrounded by a multilevel convergent media world where all modes of communication and information are continuously reforming. Mobile devices manufacturers are constantly competing in offering more and better functions for our cell phones. For a short period of time, the mobile phone turned to be not just a voice communication tool but a complicated device incorporating various media and communication options. The modern cell phone now is a high-resolution digital camera, mp3 player, camcorder and voice recorder, GPS navigator, just to name a few. All these features convert the phone into a mobile multifunctional data carrier.

Still, cell phone's main purpose remains communication. That is why communicating with others, the pictures we have taken with our phone's digital camera is a natural consequence. We can use Bluetooth* or data cable to copy them to the PC or upload them in Facebook, Picasa, or Flickr or just send them via MMS. But can we share the pictures with our friends on the large TV screen at home just with a single click on our handset? The short answer is "Yes."

People are always looking for the fastest and the easiest way. That is how all the innovations came to life. That is why Bianor's team faced the challenging task for developing an application that will allow cell phones to communicate with the TV sets.

We created a simple, user-friendly tool that provides convergence of mobile devices with home entertainment systems, allowing seamless media sharing.

The tool allows multimedia files located on users' mobile phones to be transparently viewed on TVs at home.

Bianor's engineers built a lightweight technology based on UPnP/DLNA protocols to provide Wi-Fi communication channel to share transparently images, video, and audio files between cell phones and DLNA compliant devices, such as the playing consoles PlayStation 3 and Xbox 360. These devices connect the cell phone with the TV set. In the next 2 years, more than 80% of the new TVs are expected to have built in DLNA compliant client, so that no mediating devices will be necessary.

Once having the technology know-how Bianor's team had to apply it in the real life. The best choice was iPhone being a true, next-generation multimedia device with strong users' community and well-developed apps distribution. That is why we chose iPhone's OS for the proof of concept. That is how the name iMediaShare was born.

iMediaShare was listed at Apple's App Store and only in 3 weeks it reached more than 60,000 weekly downloads. The application ranked second to Adobe's Photoshop Mobile on Photography Top Free Apps and was among top apps at New & Noteworthy Chart for more than 2 weeks.

"The first version of iMediaShare for iPhone enables only images sharing. The next major product milestone is enabling audio sharing on the iPhone platform," Kostadin Jordanov, Bianor's CEO said. "We are working towards achieving more and even better functionalities for other mobile operating systems," Jordanov added.

iMediaShare for iPhone proved to be an app with high potential. It provoked Bianor's engineering capacity to make mobile media sharing available for larger audience. On the one hand, we had to further enable more sharing options at iPhone's app and, on the other, to develop the application for other mobile OS.

"Bundling iMediaShare application with mobile devices makes them an even more useful and functional, adding more value to their users. iMediaShare is available for different mobile OS and device manufacturers looking to differentiate their product and respond to customers' demands for more functionality," Jordanov said.

xCubeLabs Case Studies

McIntosh Labs

McIntosh Labs has been synonymous with quality sound reproduction. Its products reflect unmatched level of performance, superlative engineering, and craftsmanship.

McIntosh customers care deeply about the quality of music, reliability, and, of course, the legendary McIntosh style. With the increasing number of users moving onto digital mobile devices for listening to music, McIntosh Labs wanted to bring the McIntosh experience to these millions of music lovers. McIntosh selected [x] cube to reproduce the experience for iPhone, iPod, and iPad users.

McIntosh users are used to nothing but state of the art sound quality and home entertainment experience and McIntosh products have always been iconic not just in terms of performance but also in terms of craftsmanship and aesthetics. [x]cube had the challenge to reproduce the exact McIntosh experience within the limitations of a mobile device. McIntosh wanted the users to have access to the audio library on their mobile devices through the McIntosh interface and also the ability to listen to and playback music from their mobile within the classic McIntosh experience.

At [x]cube, we realized how important and mission critical it is for McIntosh to retain the brand experience as they move on to a new platform (mobile) and ensure that the McIntosh fans are not disappointed. The [x]cube Design Lab studied multiple McIntosh audio device interfaces and eventually recreated the exact Blue Watt meter that has now become a symbol of superior sound quality.

The interface was also carefully crafted for the users to have access to their audio library in the mobile device. Typical to McIntosh, the interface was simple yet elegant. The engineers at [x]cube did a good job of integrating all the features to ensure that the app users cannot just access their audio library through the app but also listen to and playback music from the app interface.

McIntosh AP1 Audio Player has become the perfect app for users to take the McIntosh experience to wherever they go. Complete with the typical McIntosh Blue watt meter and a simple and elegant interface, it became an instant hit among McIntosh fans and attracted thousands of music lovers across the world. McIntosh AP 1 Audio Player crossed 100,000 downloads within 1 month of launch. The app was featured by Apple in New and Noteworthy and was also listed among the Top Free Apps in Music Category for quite some time.

Eat That Frog

Eat That Frog is a lifestyle app based on Brian Tracy's international best-selling book and procrastination killer, *Eat That Frog*! Your "frog" is your biggest, most important task. It's the one you are most likely to procrastinate on, even dread. "Eat That Frog," the iPhone app, has been specifically designed and developed to ensure that your biggest priorities are handled with the urgency and focus required to make you most effective in your business and personal life.

As the successful and highly acclaimed author of many motivational and self-help books, Brian Tracy already had a wide reach and a substantial readership. However, the emergence of mobile platforms such as iPhone meant that the approach had to be refined significantly to appeal to this new demographic. You can not count on people to read a 100+ page book on their mobile phone but you can definitely use the medium to spread your message; undeniably, this was an important demographic to reach out to. Brian Tracy and Equilibrium Enterprises teamed up with [x]cubeLABS to create an innovative solution for this.

Brian Tracy is the renowned writer of numerous self-help books, including titles such as *The Psychology of Selling* and *Get Paid More and Promoted Faster*. Brian Tracy is also popular as a motivational speaker and has reached out to over 4 million people in the course of his career.

Eat that Frog! is a motivational book that focuses on a core concept—managing your time well. In the course of the book, the author presents 21 simple ideas that can help people manage their time better and to stop procrastinating. Along with entertaining anecdotes and valuable tips, the book also offers exercises that readers can undertake, thus ensuring that they can test the benefits of the advice in the book right away.

As an author who had published most of his books in audio format as well as the more conventional print format and as someone who was used to making presentations and conducting webinars based on his content, Brian Tracy was always at least partially neutral to the medium itself and far more focused on the message.

Nevertheless, appealing to the iPhone users' demographic was a very different challenge. While all other mediums were focused on text in some way or the other, it was essential that the iPhone-based approach take advantage of the technology and the computing power and move beyond simple text to get the author's message across. Approaching this problem from the content perspective, it was decided that rather than simply make an ebook or a list of the principles and ideas espoused in the book, the iPhone application would instead make a companion application that would help people implement the valuable advice from the original book.

Your "frog" is your biggest, most important task. Eat That Frog! helps you to quickly establish and track your most important and impactful tasks throughout the each day. You can create as many tasks/Frogs as you like. However, there is a catch: you can only *activate one #Frog at a time*. Each day, you will be impressed with the momentum created from tackling your most difficult tasks, and at the end of each week and month, you will be amazed to see just how much you have completed!

The iPhone application "Eat that Frog," developed by [*x*]cubeLABS for Equilibrium Enterprises as a companion to the original book by Brian Tracy, received over 25,000 downloads, was featured by Apple as a "New and Noteworthy" application in its iTunes App Store and was a remarkable success in respect to brand building, awareness effort that further popularized the author Brian Tracy and led to an increase in sale of the book.

Glympse Case Study

RNA Plant is South Wales' premier road sweeping and road planning contractor. They operate throughout the region utilizing versatile, "state-of-the-art" equipment to provide a service that is second to none. RNA has recently expanded its road planning division and now operates a fleet of four Wirtgen planers. The company's location on the M4, just west of Swansea, makes it ideally placed to service contracts throughout South Wales, from the Severn Crossing to St. Davids.

The introduction of Glimpse™ throughout the fleet has brought major benefits to the organization, especially by removing the stress of day-to-day paperwork battles from the office. Glimpse has thereby significantly reduced the direct cost (time, money, and nerves) of controlling resources in the field, managing the paperwork, providing proof of delivery, and invoicing and credit control. As a result, it has also improved customer satisfaction and cash flow.

The technology on the mobile devices has been accepted very well by the operators and—after a short training session—is being used successfully throughout the company.

In summary, without Glimpse RNA Plant would not now be in a position of strength and able to focus on continued expansion. The introduction of Glimpse has significantly reduced operational inefficiencies and associated costs.

DataXu Case Studies

Social

SIMPLE Mobile, the fastest growing mobile virtual network operator in wireless history, wanted to reach and engage consumers on Facebook for its line of prepaid mobile products. To build awareness and generate new social connections via Facebook Likes and sweepstakes entries, SIMPLE Mobile launched a 7 day sweepstakes contest on their corporate Facebook page, giving their fans the chance to win a new smartphone.

Leverage insights from previous "open Web" display advertising campaigns to discover, reach, and engage with consumers on Facebook, and drive "Likes" and sweepstakes entries on the SIMPLE Mobile Fan page.

In order to reach the most receptive audiences and social affinity groups on Facebook, media plan target tactics included multiple creative assets promoting Smartphone Sweepstakes, run-of-network display, Facebook inventory, social discovery, and media optimization.

DX Social drove more than 5000 new social connections (Likes and sweepstakes entries) and increased Likes by 58.4%. DX Social also increased overall monthly active user traffic to SIMPLE Mobile's Facebook page by 266%, generated a 260% spike in average daily active users, and increased unique daily page views by 12 times, enabling SIMPLE Mobile to outperform its competitors on Facebook by 3× during the campaign.

SIMPLE Mobile initially thought its target audience lived in urban areas and was primarily interested in mobile phones (and related topics). DX Social discovered the following insights: consumers interested in football and located in suburban areas had a much higher level of engagement, and at significantly lower cost,

(CPC) than the "urban mobile phone" audience. Men were more likely to connect with SIMPLE Mobile, click on the ad, and enter the Smartphone Sweepstakes, and consumers aged 25–34 were most likely to "Like" SIMPLE Mobile and click through to the Sweepstakes.

Mobile

Company is looking to increase brand awareness and purchase consideration among software purchase decisions makers and influencers. Primarily C-level executives and software purchase decision makers at companies of all sizes. The mobile media mix included premium content that ran across well-known branded sites; the campaign was optimized on many parameters including creative, device, and time of day. DX Mobile drove 3× the volume actions relative to spend, the CPA for Mobile ad network was 4× the CPA for DX Mobile, and the CPA for Premium content was 8× the CPA for DX Mobile.

Auto

Amid a tough economy and rising gas prices, a well-known North American automaker wanted to reach receptive consumers to build awareness for the new engine available in its flagship truck with best-in-class fuel economy. To positively shift consumer sentiment for the brand, the digital campaign required massive reach across a wide swatch of brand-safe Internet sites.

The objective was to leverage online display advertising to increase consumers' brand awareness and favorability, for a new truck and its special engine features. First ever digital campaign optimized in real time to increase brand sentiment. In order to reach the broadest audience, the media plan targeting tactics included

1. Premium content buys—select blend of exchange-traded media and comScore 250 sites
2. In-ad consumer surveys
3. Proprietary advertiser data
4. Multiple creatives
5. DataXu Brand Optimization

DX Brand achieved a 9.4% lift in brand favorability and 5.8% lift in awareness across 28.8 million consumers, showing an average of just 3.1 ads per unique consumer by

■ Observing sentiment drivers across a range of parameters, including creative, audience demographics, page content, day of the week, time of day, and geography to find consumers at the time and place they were most receptive to the truck brand's messages

- Measuring key awareness, favorability, and intent metrics through in-ad surveys, A/B testing, and multivariate decisioning in real time to automatically optimize the campaign on the fly
- Identifying and buying the impressions most likely to "move the needle" at varying bid values for the optimal ad spend
- Applying insight from each ad served to every subsequent buying opportunity, in run time, so the campaign gets smarter, the longer the campaign runs. Analytical insights, including geotargeting and creative performance, were available to inform subsequent campaigns for improved performance
- Optimizing campaigns in real time to automatically reallocate budget to invest more in what is working and reaching a broad swath of the North American digital population to drive maximum consumer sentiment shift for the truck icon and its latest model

GeniusRocket

Amazon

By providing an affordable and fast way to source high-quality video, GeniusRocket enables brands to create content for specific seasons, demographics, and online properties. Amazon came to GeniusRocket looking for a Christmas focused video that would explain the services of their B2B solution. This video was created to run on Amazon's YouTube and Facebook pages after the holiday season. The goal was to encourage users to turn to Amazon Services to sell unwanted items.

Heinz

Heinz needed viral style videos that would be launched online along with the release of two new products under the Heinz Poppers brand. Heinz looked for two completely different types of videos, one a stop motion animation and the other a mockumentary-style live action spot. Although it was not selected by Heinz, this spot—one of three in a series—was a GeniusRocket favorite, featuring Curt Dunkleman as a "popperazzi" pursuing the "celebrities of the stuffed jalapeño popper cream cheese world."

Aquafina

Pepsi's Aquafina brand was looking for a viral way to generate traffic and buzz around their FlavorSplash product. Pepsi created a strategic creative brief outlining the need for the video to be a edgy and appeal to their demographic of women in their 20s. Pepsi purchased three videos and asked GeniusRocket to seed the "Magic Water" video on multiple platforms. The video was a total success with views exceeding 500,000 in just 3 months. Since then, it has been viewed by almost a million people.

MediaMath Case Studies

Financial Advertiser

Low product awareness in a limited category and the need to reach aggressive efficiency goals: MediaMath used a full-funnel strategy with RTB and premium media sources to progress prospects through the acquisition funnel. TerminalOne drove a 96% increase in awareness and achieved a 450% higher response rate.

Travel Advertiser

Need for higher relevancy and response using travel search data: MediaMath captured O/D data on site and targeted most interested users via personalized dynamic creative and dynamic bidding, resulting in a 75% lift in ROI over a leading dynamic ad solution.

Retail Advertiser

Need to acquire new customers with profitable ROAS: Dynamic prospecting and page-level contextual analysis optimized by MediaMath's algorithm across 15B+ impressions with a 46× return on ad spent.

Profero Case Study

New Look is an international high-street retailer with 613 stores across the United Kingdom and a transactional website selling the full clothing range online. It has over 330 stores in France and Belgium and franchise stores in UAE, Bahrain, Kuwait, Egypt, and Saudi Arabia. With approximately 10.5 million customers in the United Kingdom alone, New Look has an aggressive customer relationship management approach across both its online and offline channels to guarantee it will be the fashion brand of choice for shoppers.

Engaging customers in an interactive dialogue is at the heart of New Look's retail strategy. To enhance its online presence and cater for the increasing popularity of mobile devices among its target audience, New Look recently launched a mobile-optimized site. This includes links to New Look TV, allows users to check out the New Look Fashion Blog on the go, check store locations on Google Maps, and share their favorite links across social media sites through integrated links to Facebook and Twitter.

New Look wanted to run a campaign that boosted brand awareness and drove customers to visit the new m-commerce platform to coincide with the launch of its mobile website. As part of this strategy, New Look wanted to increase the number of click-throughs and conversions that came from e-mail. To achieve this, it meant improving its use of customer data and implementing a cross-channel marketing approach to deliver a personalized and relevant experience to users across e-mail.

Sita Patel, e-commerce CRM manager at New Look explains, "As we launch our new mobile website, it is imperative that we integrate our data sources to produce coordinated campaigns that encourage customers to interact with the brand across all the digital touch points. By providing users with a more targeted experience we can continue to deliver a dynamic and engaging shopping experience. E-mail is the ideal channel to provide a more personalized approach since it enables users to interact with content, click through to the website and discover more about the brand."

New Look had already built holistic data profiles for customers but it wanted to make better use of customer data. To drive mobile users to the new site and increase brand engagement, New Look worked with Responsys to develop a test and learn strategy. This enabled the brand to put in place separate strategies for different types of customers and monitor the responses to understand why certain groups interacted differently with the brand and what could be done to improve communication.

New Look used Responsys Interact Suite to run an e-mail engagement programme that tested the performance of mobile-optimized e-mails. Responsys provided insight into users' web browsing habits, channel preference, and behaviors to identify customers that used mobile devices to view the website. This enabled New Look to automate highly personalized e-mails that were designed to drive traffic to the new m-commerce site, increase sales, and boost customer loyalty.

Responsys enabled New Look to create and measure the performance of two different e-mail types: a mobile optimized version for those users that had engaged with a mobile site and a standard HTML e-mail for those that had not. The mobile version of the e-mail was sent to a list of 1786 subscribers who had browsed the New Look website on a mobile device during the first 3 months of 2011. The mobile version was also sent to a sample 10% of the e-mail audience to test its performance against the standard web version.

The campaign revealed that mobile users are significantly more engaged with the brand compared with nonmobile users. The findings highlight that where a user had a preference for using a mobile device to view the website, the average open rate of the mobile optimized e-mail was three times higher than the standard version. In addition, mobile users were compelled to click more than once on the e-mail, with the total number of clicks per responder being 12% higher than the e-mail version.

Sita Patel comments: "As a new school marketer we wanted to create a campaign that encourages customers to click through to the new mobile site. By working with Responsys we are the first retailer to co-ordinate SMS triggering, automation and fully integrated mobile reporting to test the effectiveness of mobile optimised e-mails. The results showed the effectiveness of developing personalised emails. Overall, we saw a 300% increase in programme performance for mobile-optimised campaigns delivered to the 'mobile' segment, indicating that a combined digital campaign and targeting strategy is more successful in engaging with customers across the interactive channels."

x + 1 Case Study

Every month, 6 million travelers visit the homepage of Delta Air Lines. Delta faces considerable obstacles in delivering personalized, relevant content to each of those visitors. How does the world's largest airline deliver relevant content to travelers from the more than 100 countries it serves? How does it decide whether to present ticketing, partner, or check-in content to customers around the world? How can the team make personalized messaging cost-effective?

Delta's online marketing team faced increased operations and personnel costs from developing and maintaining dozens of landing pages intended for different audiences. Furthermore, Delta did not have a way to drive measurable business results for its web content. Seeking to improve the efficiency and effectiveness of its strategy, Delta turned to [*x* + 1], the leader in predictive marketing.

Delta began a pilot trial of [*x* + 1]'s fully hosted solution to dynamically personalize its website based on visitor profiles and traffic sources. The personalized pages showed a 300% lift in conversion. Bolstered by the success of the trial, Delta expanded the implementation of [*x* + 1] and its patented Predictive Optimization Engine began to build predictive models based on visitor data—geographic location, connection speed, and time of day—and traffic source: search keyword, e-mail campaign, banner ad, etc. Delta's customer data, including SkyMiles membership and home airport preference, will be added to the models, allowing [*x* + 1] to further target Delta's customers. This rich view of each Delta.com visitor enables [*x* + 1] to target the optimal offer to each individual, ensuring that no visit is wasted.

In the first 8 months of full implementation, Delta accrued an additional $25 million in incremental revenue and experienced an average monthly lift rate of 4% in ticket sales.

In addition, Delta has gained valuable insight into the factors driving conversion on the homepage. With a better understanding of which content and offers appeal to which audiences, [*x* + 1] has enabled Delta to better serve its customers online and in the sky.

Victors & Spoils Case Studies

DISH Network

DISH asked us to come up with some national television spots to announce that they were going to begin offering HD service for free. So we came up with this astronauts silliness. People seemed to like it. DISH had never done any work that got so much praise from their customers, and we were happy to do it.

Virgin America

The crazy folks at Virgin America contacted us with an opportunity. They were about to launch service to Toronto, the first destination outside the United States for Virgin America. And they wanted a way to garner excitement for the launch of this service among local Torontonians. Together with Jesse McMillin—creative director at Virgin America—we devised a plan. Let us create a web platform and initiative whereby we search to find one Toronto local to be our brand ambassador in Canada. The perfect person who embodies the sexy and cheeky brand attributes of Virgin America and can work to be a firebrand for the brand itself. So, we decided to create a competition where the best video entry would win this coveted position. We decided we would call it "The Search for Virgin America's Toronto Provocateur." And we were off. We designed the site, wrote the site, and produced the site with the help of Google moderator. And we launched it. The competition worked great. And Virgin America found their Toronto Provocateur.

Harley–Davidson

The first actual work we had the joy of concepting and producing for Harley–Davidson can be seen here. Each of these executions is founded on a completely new brand position (tagline) called "No Cages" that came from the first batch of work we presented unsolicited (see "Reinventing the Pitch Process"). The television spot/web film here as well as the "Cage Free Humans" print both go straight at setting up the brand position of No Cages itself. The other "QR Code" print here uses No Cages as a tagline alone and works to go straight at announcing Harley's first-ever online motorcycle customization platform called "H-D 1." The TV spot ran pretty much everywhere, thanks to a media buy from Starcom, while the print executions ran in publications such as *Maxim* and *Playboy*, also thanks to Starcom.

DoubleClick Case Study

Digitas is a leading relationship management company, combining strategy, creative, and technology to help clients attract and grow the most profitable customer relationships in their industries. The Digitas client roster includes Allstate, American Express, AT&T, Delta Air Lines, and General Motors. Their objective was to improve results for a campaign that had been running on the same sites with the same message for 2 years. The campaign's objective is to increase product usage by driving consumers to print product information for reference or to share it via e-mail.

Out strategy was to utilize a large pool of creative units, with up to 10 different iterations, and monitor campaign results weekly to adjust and optimize creatives aggressively. Digitas implemented DoubleClick's DART® for Advertisers (DFA)

Creative Optimization tool, which automatically optimizes creatives based on specific, user-defined performance criteria, to refine the campaign's results continuously. With DFA Creative Optimization, the best-performing ads were automatically weighted more heavily so they would receive more impressions in the rotation, and the low performing ads were removed. The DFA Creative Optimization tool also provided Digitas with the flexibility to manually adjust the weightings.

ClickTracks Case Study

Mark Seremet is the former cofounder of Take Two Interactive Software, makers of the wildly popular Grand Theft Auto series of video games. He is the current CEO of U.S. Operations for Spreadshirt, Inc., an e-merchandizing company. And he is a happy ClickTracks user who bought the product in order to analyze the SpreadShirt website (www.spreadshirt.com). He had a hunch that visitors were not as excited by the home page as they could be. ClickTracks helped Mark turn his hunch into tangible evidence.

"Before finding ClickTracks, our main method of deciding site changes included relying on our gut feelings and instincts… which are admittedly a fairly unreliable way of doing things," quipped Mark. "We were really unable to get any sort of reliable, actionable data from the site." One of the first things ClickTracks showed Mark and his team was an area that had a lot of room for improvement the site's home page. "ClickTracks' Navigation Report showed us that more than a quarter of all of our site visitors—27% to be exact—left our home page right after they entered," said Mark. "I had believed for some time that our home page graphics just weren't strong enough to convey what we had to offer—that they weren't strong enough to interest the customer. Looking at the site in ClickTracks confirmed that belief as the reality of the situation.

After they installed ClickTracks, Mark and Spreadshirt made a few changes. "We made various tweaks to the home page, changing formats, improving the graphics and tweaking the copy and messaging," noted Mark. "With every change we'd make, we'd fire up ClickTracks to see if the change was having a positive or negative impact on people who visited."

And the result of this create-measure-tweak-measure again formula? "I'm happy to say that, though a combination of all the changes we've made, we've cut those 'dash in and dash out' exits by two-thirds … our homepage abandonment rate is down to 9%. As we continue to make changes to the home page and other pages of the site, we'll continue to turn to ClickTracks to show us how visitors are reacting."

And Did Somebody Mention ROI? How about ROI x27? "In 60 days, ClickTracks paid for itself-more than 27 times what it cost me. Nice ROI, eh?" said Mark. "Spreadshirt's top-notch quality-in our messaging, front and center, to the point that we had a huge button on our home page where visitors could click and learn more," Mark said. "I was convinced that shoppers would click the quality button in droves, in order to find out more … and I couldn't have been more wrong."

A quick look at ClickTracks' site overlay showed that miniscule percentages—something like 0.01% of people—were clicking on my beloved "quality" button. I've since filled in the real estate the quality button had once filled with one of our products called the "Flying Spaghetti Monster." And the Flying Spaghetti Monster is, well, flying off the shelves, thanks mainly to its front-page placement. Mark continued, "ClickTracks showed us that after we put the Flying Spaghetti Monster on the home page, our exits went down by 18%. Conversely, our sales went up, to the tune of $27,000 per month. It's simple math … you just multiply the clickthroughs from the home page to the shirt designer by the designer conversion rate, then the average basket order."

Another area on which ClickTracks provided insight was search—which keyword and search engine combinations brought in people who were just window shopping, which provided serious buyers, and what folks were looking for. "I was incredibly surprised by the exactness—the level of specificity that people would use when searching," noted Mark. "Since we're in the customized apparel business, using ClickTracks' search report to SEE people searching on things like 'a mike Tyson bit my ear shirt' was extremely meaningful. By looking at these sorts of searches, I was able to see patterns and make some educated guesses about our customers. Recurring searches on 'bride-to-be shirts' and 'funny bride shirts', for example, made me very aware of the importance of marketing to women shopping for bachelorette party attire."

SiteSpect Case Study

SiteSpect provided Military.com with an optimization platform that accelerated the testing-to-production process, allowing the company to better tailor its web and mobile content for its members. Military Advantage is the United States' largest online military destination, with more than 10 million members. Its online presence, Military.com, offers free resources that connect service members, military families, and veterans to a host of benefits. Military.com members visit the site approximately 5 million times each month, entering through any of 45 membership gateways that cater to different audience segments. Within these gateways are a large number of web forms used to provide members with information and functionality that ranges from education to insurance benefits to assistance with the GI Bill.

After observing a notable uptick in mobile traffic over the past year, Military.com made it a priority to optimize its web landing pages and forms for strong usability on mobile devices. The objective was to provide an efficient user experience that enabled members to access content through any type of mobile device, from anywhere in the world.

Military.com began their mobile web optimization by defining a very simple hypothesis that could be scientifically tested: for users arriving at the site through a mobile device, would delivering a "lean" page with minimal navigation and form fields be more effective (and convert better) than presenting the equivalent desktop version of the page?

"Our members include active military, their families, and veterans, who access our site from all corners of the earth and from a wide variety of mobile handsets and wireless devices," said Breanna Wigle, online marketing manager at Military Advantage. "Making the site easy to access and the information on services faster to download was our top priority when it came to optimization."

Military.com had previously implemented a tag-based testing solution but "struggled with the challenge of page-tagging, and also in determining where people were abandoning the forms," according to Wigle. After further research and trials, Military.com selected SiteSpect's nonintrusive solution because it required no intervention by IT personnel and provided the organization with the ability to optimize everything on its site without the need to tag pages or change any of the underlying HTML code.

"SiteSpect allows us to easily understand what works and avoid what doesn't. In fact, we've experienced a 70% increase in conversions from our PPC landing pages since implementing site changes based on testing data derived from SiteSpect," said Wigle. "When we decided to expand our mobile web presence, we knew that by leveraging SiteSpect's mobile testing and targeting solution we would likely be just as successful, if not more so."

SiteSpect's mobile targeting solution allows marketers to test and optimize their websites for the rapidly growing segment of mobile web users. SiteSpect's mobile targeting capabilities can be used to test, measure, and deliver the content, layout, and offers that are found to be most effective for each mobile device category. The fact is that globally, more than half of web-enabled mobile devices still do not support full JavaScript, effectively making them invisible to other types of testing solutions. Further, mobile networks are congested and the extra latency introduced by JavaScript tags can significantly slow down the user experience. SiteSpect is the first and only nonintrusive testing and targeting platform that works without any scripting or programming and is the only solution that enables end-to-end optimization with no added latency across the full range of mobile devices.

Military.com set out to test the messaging on landing pages targeting either active military or veterans and found that conversions increased dramatically after this type of content targeting was deployed. Military.com also tested its many forms and conducted a series of tests to determine where the user interface could be best improved. Testing the forms on the mobile website enabled Military.com to redesign and optimize them to produce a 56% increase in conversions and a 130% increase in confirmed leads.

Jumptap Case Studies

Hardee's

Jumptap ran media placements across mobile sites such as The Score Mobile, Boost Mobile, LimeLife, Mocospace, and WeatherBug. Jumptap also targeted males of age 18–34, Hardee's core young, "hungry guy" user group and implemented geo-targeting around Hardee's locations in key markets across the United States. Over the 8 weeks of the campaign, the Hardee's mobile site saw a huge influx of visitors and huge increase in page views. There were 828 product names submitted to the site for the contest, and 407 people opted in for SMS alerts from Hardee's. In addition, 143 mobile greetings were sent from the site.

Swap

Jumptap optimized Swap's campaign and adjusted the daily bids to meet their goals.

Jumptap also created 2 whitelist campaigns that performed very well. The campaign consistently had a CPA under $2 while maintaining over 150 downloads a day and also hitting their cap of $250. This resulted in Swap.com raising their cap to $400 a day.

"Jumptap has been a tremendous asset to our mobile download acquisition strategy. They consistently deliver both quality and quantity of users on a daily basis. The strength of their network and the strength of their people are the two reasons Swap.com only works with Jumptap for mobile user acquisition," said Carl Schwartz, vice president of product & marketing.

Valtira Case Study

Caribou Coffee is the nation's second largest specialty coffee company. With nearly 500 coffeehouses, Caribou Coffee turned to Valtira to deploy their next level website.

"Caribou Coffee needed a scalable, flexible software platform on which to build our new website," said Kathy Hollenhorst, Caribou Coffee's senior vice president of marketing. "We selected Valtira as they had the right combination of content management, personalization and campaign tracking we need today and going forward."

With Valtira, Caribou Coffee can personalize content, imagery, or promotions based on business rules or user preferences. This provides the site visitor with more relevant information on coffee types or coffeehouses. Marketing staff members can also easily update the site to keep content fresh for site visitors. The team can now also track initiatives to better understand the customer. Valtira worked together with web agency Miles Interactive to deliver this new website based on the Valtira

Online Marketing Platform. The results: A site that provides richer options, deeper content, and more interactivity to meet the stated Caribou Coffee goals.

ContextOptional Case Study

Barbie's Facebook page got a makeover for the holidays. In addition to allowing users to sign up for offers and purchase from the store, the brand page also allows users to select a Ken to send to friends as a virtual gift, a hot holi-date (Figure 4.18).

Satmetrix Case Study

Sony has always been a major force in the electronics industry, providing the market with groundbreaking technologies in home and professional entertainment. However, in 2007, with competition on price and technology on the increase, Sony was losing market share. As a result, Sony Europe knew it needed to deliver an excellent customer experience to maintain its market position.

Figure 4.18   Winner of the Outstanding Achievement in Internet Advertising.

Consequently, in addition to measuring sales and profit, Sony decided to add another corporate KPI—the quality of the customer experience.

However, when dealing with 25 countries, measuring the quality of the customer's experience demands a rigorous approach that overcomes logistical issues such as language, culture, cost, time to implement, and buy-in from both senior management and frontline staff across Europe. Furthermore, Sony had to ensure that the loyalty KPI it selected was capable of measuring the customer experience effectively while also enabling a discipline that supported the business-wide cultural shift in putting the customer experience first. Driving actions from the findings was absolutely key.

Sony Europe chose to work with Satmetrix, the Net Promoter® Company, to deploy a customer experience program that would enable all employees, across the EMEA region, to work together with a single focus on what matters most to the customer.

Satmetrix' significant experience in delivering global customer experience programs enabled Sony Europe to deploy their new vision around four strategic components:

1. To implement a simple and consistent measure of customer loyalty across different touch points to understand how well Sony is performing from the customer perspective. They use the Net Promoter Score® as the core metric and verbatim feedback from the customer to identify the impact of the Sony experience at each critical touch point on the customer journey.
2. To take the robust data captured via the Satmetrix customer experience application and to develop diagnostics that drive action, maintain and increase customer loyalty, and create brand ambassadors. These diagnostics included understanding which experiences keep customers loyal and providing fact-based guidance for strategic and tactical initiatives and then critically measuring the success of actions taken.
3. To provide results and analysis that could be viewed by country, by touch point and by product so that improvement initiatives could be tailored to individual market requirements while simultaneously achieving the core objectives.
4. To embed the Net Promoter Score as a management KPI that is integrated into the decision-making process in a structured and systematic way and that can be quantified in financial terms.

To deliver these strategic components, Satmetrix provides an enterprise application that monitors the customer experience in two ways:

1. Continuous monitoring of the experience at specific touch points on the customer journey. This is carried out on a daily basis, with customer feedback distributed in real time to management and frontline staff to allow for immediate improvements and identification of performance gaps.
2. Evaluation of the overall customer experience and how that translates to loyalty and personal recommendations.

This is achieved through two relationship processes where feedback from over 80,000 consumers is collected and distributed to management and frontline staff enabling them to identify loyalty drivers and performance gap by product line, geography, customer segment, etc. Rachel Waite, general manager, Marketing Strategy Office at Sony Europe, comments: "Implementing the Satmetrix program has been critical to our mission of improving the customer experience. It enables us to create a workflow for the customer experience that allows employees to take immediate action on the feedback received."

To assist in the success of Satmetrix, they trained designated Sony Net Promoter champions in each country. These "champions" are responsible for training staff about the benefits of the program and for implementing Net Promoter in their own country. The company has seen significant increases in its NPS: the most notable improvements include a 15-point rise in Poland, an 11-point increase in Denmark, and a 10-point rise in Finland and Norway.

And the latest European Net Promoter Benchmarks show that Sony has the highest NPS in the TV/DVD sector with a score of 38.5%. This is 14% higher than the sector average and a massive 21% higher than the brand placed last in the sector. Commenting on the success of the programme Rachel Waite said: "Until we implemented the Satmetrix Net Promoter, we had a very fragmented view of the customer experience. Now we look at it from the point of view of a complete customer journey. This has allowed employees across functions to understand the impact of their behavior on the customer experience—and ultimately the recommendability of our products and services."

Waite concludes: "I am delighted that this single-minded focus on improving the customer experience has seen us achieve the highest level of consumer personal recommendation in our sector in the latest Net Promoter benchmarks. It is recognition that focusing on the customer does create promoters for the brand."

Nsquared Case Study

Our project brief was to join with the creative team to deliver a robust, technically innovative, interactive software application that would collect target market data for Lexus with regard to their 2009 hybrid concept car (LF-Ch). The interactive software also needed to allow and encourage individuals to contribute to the creation of a worldwide Photosynth project based around their feedback regarding the LF-Ch.

Lexus wanted the means to connect with the individuals of the car's potential target market. It also wanted to create a sense of community involvement with the vehicle's ongoing evolution from concept car through to production vehicle. With hundreds of thousands of visitors expected to visit and explore the interactive piece, the software and hardware needed to be robust.

The vehicle's target market was identified as socially conscious, tech-savvy 18–30 year olds. The exhibition piece, of which the software was an integral factor, needed to appeal to and impress the target market. It also needed to demonstrate the values of the concept vehicle. Unveiled as a concept vehicle at all major car shows across Europe and the United States, the car was planned as a production vehicle for release in 2010 and is now known as the C200-T.

Various options were considered, including Microsoft Surface and Windows 7 PCs. Ultimately, simple touch screens were selected to display the Windows 7 Touch software that would show off the magic of the LF-Ch. The interactive software had to show off the car's features and lines and provide simple rewards for supply of key information. Lexus was specifically looking to capture the e-mail addresses of the LA Car Show attendees and production car color preferences.

For the simple act of providing their e-mail addresses, Lexus exhibit visitors could use the cameras to take photos of their favorite parts of the car to contribute to the LF-Ch Photosynth. Those same photos could be sent to the visitors' e-mail and Facebook accounts, ready for use as "bragging" rights by those same visitors and, of course, valuable marketing tools for Lexus.

Three 32″ touch screen monitors were stationed around the revolving stage of the exhibit. Each 32″ monitor was connected to a local PC and a digital camera. The monitors were mounted on pedestals that housed all required cabling, and each camera was mounted inside tamper-proof housing on a pedestal. The software stood up to our high standards and those of the client: it operated without fault or failure for the entire gamut of shows and required no support during that time frame.

FetchBack Case Studies

Cosmetics

Cosmetics are big business, and this luxury cosmetics company needed to increase its online performance. With a well-known brand available at retail counters worldwide, attracting buyers to the online shop should have been more successful than the results the company was seeing. Enter FetchBack retargeting solutions.

Beginning with a simple static-only campaign, the FetchBack account manager introduced keyword triggering and sequential ad delivery options.

Even before rolling out the strongest ad type (dynamic Flash-based creative), the results have been encouraging. Incremental conversions have yielded more than 2,500 new customers and have driven over $200,000 in sales from retargeted prospects.

Seven Month Campaign Results

Gross conversions: 44,331
Incremental conversions: 2,654
Conversion lift: 6.6%
Average CPA: $14.75
Return per dollar invested: $4.97
Total incremental sales: $201,174
5:1 ROI

Clothing

One of the benefits of targeting an audience of teens and young adults is their comfort with e-commerce. One of the pitfalls is the fickle nature of this age group, so building brand loyalty can be a challenge. However, once your name is established you can command attention. This specialty clothing retailer is developing a name-brand reputation in its market and its styles are popular. Retargeting is a good strategy for both brand-building and incremental conversions.

Interestingly, this client has not yet developed a dynamic ad campaign despite a product line perfectly suited to dynamic. A handful of product categories have yielded an excellent 25:1 ROI from static ad creative, again suggesting the power of the brand name. FetchBack analytics show that this client can profitably expand its advertising into multiple additional categories, which combined with new dynamic Flash creative, and is expected to drive even greater sales in coming months.

Seven Month Campaign Results

Gross conversions: 77,860
Incremental conversions: 2,943
Conversion lift: 4.0%
Average CPA: $3.65
Return per dollar invested: $25.32
Total incremental sales: $281,471
25:1 ROI

Electronics

This e-commerce site is not a household name but is competing with some of the biggest retail brands. By focusing on special daily deals and a wide selection of refurbished and discount-priced items, this retailer holds its own in a competitive niche.

Retargeting has generated a 10% lift in conversions which translates to $700,000 in sales ($100,000 per month) and 30:1 return. With the large inventory to choose from, dynamic Flash ads are a natural choice. The creative has been a great fit for both attracting lost prospects and increasing cart sizes (and overall sales revenue) with complementary products.

Seven Month Campaign Results

> Gross conversions: 42,414
> Incremental conversions: 4,096
> Conversion lift: 10.0%
> Average CPA: $5.64
> Return per dollar invested: $30.43
> Total incremental sales: $703,560
> 30:1 ROI

Future

Mobility

Google projects that 44% of last minute shopping this holiday season will be on phones and tablets. In a new report, market research firm Gartner forecasts that global mobile apps and marketing revenues will triple from $5.2 billion last year to $15 billion in 2011 and keep growing to an astounding $58 billion by 2014.

The premiere market intelligence firm IDC reports that there will likely be more mobile Internet users in 2015 than PC users. And according to a new report from independent telecoms analyst Ovum, global mobile connections will grow by 30% over the next 5 years; the report projects that total mobile marketing service revenues will reach a staggering $1047 billion in 2016.

Because digital devices are moving, the data about their behaviors are everywhere—ubiquitous and intimately detailed—and subject to M3 and A5.

Intelligibility

These days, accessing the same data across multiple devices can be a feat. However, we are moving toward a world in which devices can swipe, flick, and tap to share data from one piece of hardware to another, effortlessly. Devices manufacturers are working to integrate a seamless computing experience between multiple digital machines to make this a reality. Cloud servers service will help make data a nonissue as devices switch from one machine to another. Devices will be able to wirelessly stream video and send it to a larger display that allows for information to be swapped from one to another and back.

Apple is already working on this type of operating system integration, so that one device can be used as a controller for games using its accelerometer and gyroscope and easily swipe what is playing on a tablet to a TV and then back to a phone or laptop. Samsung, which makes a variety of mobile devices, is another manufacturer developing its own seamless computing experience. Sony is another company that is developing a software platform to unify data across its different digital devices.

The Bada operating system also supports information to be easily shared, swiped, and synced between multiple digital devices. There is obvious incentive for these companies to provide a high degree of compatibility and integration between their multiple devices—it means consumers are more likely to buy more of their products, rather than their competitors. By providing this type of digital integration, it ensures consumer retention and brand loyalty, not to mention growth revenue.

$

Follow the money. There have been few breakthroughs in money exchanges: the use of metal coins in Egypt in 700 BC, the move to paper money in China in 960 AD, checks in the twelfth century, and finally the use of credit cards starting in the 1960s, which introduced the concept of buying an item or service and paying for it later. When the world moved from cash to plastic—consumer behavior changed dramatically—it altered people's ideas about what was affordable and their velocity of consumption. And we are about to speed this up.

A new method of consumption is about to begin. Every major bank, credit card company, wireless network carrier, and Silicon Valley players like Google and PayPal are backing a new wave of payment technology—the tap of digital device rather than the swipe of plastic card. For example, the Google Wallet is the culmination of a decade of technology developments and a multiparty, cross-industry battle over a $20 trillion global market for in-store retail transactions.

Other digital payment "wallets" in development include those from Visa, American Express, EBay's PayPal divisions, and Isis, a venture of AT&T Mobility, T-Mobile USA, and Verizon who banded together to create their own wallet in conjunction with Discover Financial Services.

Mobile digital devices will not only become the central repository of bank accounts but also coupons, loyalty points, and membership cards, allowing M3 marketers to route offers and deals at just the right time and place via A5s. Much of the mobile payments activity centers on a technology known as near field communications (NFC). An NFC chip in a mobile device communicates with a credit card terminal over a distance of less than 2″.

Nearly, every mobile digital device manufacturer, including Nokia, Samsung, and Research in Motion, will be packing NFC chipsets in future models. Apple and Google are talking with every NFC startup. All of these companies claim financial transactions will be more secure and faster, but the true golden nuggets are the potential marketing opportunity for mining this mobile purchasing data.

Retailers and M3 marketers will be able to construct comprehensive purchasing profiles, targeting devices with just-in-time offers, discounts, and other incentives. This will be similar to behavioral targeting that takes place on the web. Forecasts are that the number of NFC-equipped mobile devices worldwide will grow from 6 million in 2011 to 172 millions by 2013.

Mining purchasing transactions via digital devices will allow M3 marketers to greatly expand their data collection and modeling abilities via targeted A5s.

Index